THE BIG
CURMUDGEON

COMPILED AND EDITED BY JON WINOKUR

Illustrations by Everett Peck

BLACK DOG
& LEVENTHAL
PUBLISHERS
NEW YORK

ISBN-13: 978-1-57912-697-1

Library of Congress Cataloging-in-Publication Data

The big curmudgeon : 2,500 irreverently outrageous quotations
from world-class grumps and cantankerous commentators /
compiled and edited by Jon Winokur ; illustrated by Everett Peck.
p. cm.
Includes index.
ISBN-13: 978-1-57912-697-1 (pbk.)
1. Quotations, English. 2. American wit and humor. I. Winokur, Jon.

PN6083.B55 2007
082—dc22
2006100875

Cover and interior design: Elizabeth Driesbach
Manufactured in the United States of America

Published by
Black Dog & Leventhal Publishers, Inc.
151 West 19th Street New York, New York 10011

Distributed by
Workman Publishing Company
225 Varick Street New York, NY 10014

g f e d c b a

cur.mud.geon\,k_r-´m_j-_nn [origin unknown] **1** archaic: a crusty, ill-tempered, churlish old man **2** modern: anyone who hates hypocrisy and pretense and has the temerity to say so; anyone with the habit of pointing out unpleasant facts in an engaging and humorous manner

ACKNOWLEDGMENTS

The following well-meaning persons insisted on trying to help: Berton Averre, Norman Corwin, Peter Bell, Tony Bill, Reid Boates, Barry Dougherty, Doug Dutton, Perry Edwards, Norrie Epstein, James Garner, Dewey Gram, Joe Grifasi, Ron Hammes, Nancy Hathaway, Gary Luke, H. Myles Jacob, Margo Kaufman, Lucy Lee, Paul Linke, Raymond Lesser, Judy Muller, Anita Nelson, Susan Nethery, John Paine, Al Rasof, Laura Ross, Tobi Sanders, Nancy Steele, Linda Takahashi, Lawrence Teacher, Dana Trombley, LuAnn Walther, Robert Weide, Bobbie Weiner, Sam Williams, Elinor Winokur, and Mark Wolgin.

JON WINOKUR is the crank behind *The Portable Curmudgeon*, *The Big Book of Irony*, *Zen to Go*, and other collections of wit and wisdom. He lives in Pacific Palisades, California.

TO NOBODY

CONTENTS

Ye shall know the truth, and the truth shall make you mad.
ALDOUS HUXLEY

*It is a fine thing to face machine guns for immortality and a medal,
but isn't it a fine thing, too, to face calumny, injustice and
loneliness for the truth which makes men free?*
H. L. MENCKEN

INTRODUCTION

In the two decades since *The Portable Curmudgeon* was first published, annoyances have multiplied like Starbucks stores. These "fresh Hells," as Dorothy Parker might have called them, defy one's capacity for pessimism. Twenty years ago, there was still a distinction between tabloid and legitimate journalism. Paris Hilton was still in private school, "Dr. Phil" was in private practice, and George W. Bush was in the private sector. Enron, body piercing, $3-a-gallon gasoline, Hummers, the TSA, and deep-fried Twinkies were not yet sickening realities. Mobile phones were the size of bricks and not yet a scourge. "Reality television" was still oxymoronic. Twenty years ago, though naming rights were sold for stadiums, the practice wasn't widespread. Today, municipalities routinely auction naming rights for hospitals, libraries, schools, and public transit stations, and new categories have opened up: In 2005, a newly discovered monkey species was named after an online casino, for a fee of $650,000. Hence, "The GoldenPalace.com Monkey." Today, we have Febreze Noticeables, an electrical warmer that automatically sends fresh scents ("Calypso Breeze," "Hawaiian Paradise") throughout the house. *Noticeables?* The name alone demands a stiff fine and several hundred hours of community service. Today, we have the Hallmark Card with an ostensibly handwritten address on a bright yellow linen envelope with a real postmarked stamp that turns out to be a solicitation from your cable company. Now people bring their "support pets" to restaurants (with doctor's notes). Nowadays, people make marriage proposals on billboards and, worse, in *skywriting*. Nowadays, people wander around like zombies, wearing Bluetooth headsets, muttering into the middle distance. It's a miracle we've survived this long.

Dictionaries define *curmudgeon* as a churlish, irascible fellow; a cantankerous old codger. The origin of the word is unknown, but it might come from an old Scottish word that meant "murmur" or "mumble," or from the French *cœur méchant*, "evil heart." The archaic definition made it a synonym for *miser*, and the word has had recent currency in a somewhat milder connotation, to describe a not entirely unlikable grouch.

Curmudgeons' reputation for malevolence is undeserved. They're neither warped nor evil at heart. They don't hate mankind, just mankind's excesses. They're just as sensitive and soft-hearted as the next guy, but they hide their vulnerability beneath a crust of misanthropy. They ease the pain by turning hurt into humor. They snarl at pretense and bite at hypocrisy out of a healthy sense of outrage. They attack maudlinism because it devalues genuine sentiment. They hurl polemical thunderbolts at middle-class values and pop culture to preserve their sanity. Nature, having failed to equip them with a serviceable denial mechanism, has endowed them with astute perception and sly wit. Offense is their only defense. Their weapons are irony, satire, sarcasm, ridicule. Their targets are pretense, pomposity, conformity, incompetence.

When I was a small boy, my father took me to the Stage Delicatessen in New York, having told me beforehand to keep my eyes open for "celebrities." By the time we were seated at a double table next to a tall, dour man, I had unsuccessfully scanned the place for Uncle Miltie or Captain Video or even Dagmar. Disappointed, I blurted out, "I don't see any *celebrities*!" Our tablemate slowly looked up from his mushroom barley, and with his patented scowl, Fred Allen did a very, very slow burn in my direction. It was the dirtiest look I'd ever received, but I wasn't intimidated. Rather I felt that we'd shared a joke, that I'd been his straight man. He never let on, but I knew he was amused. My father introduced me to Mr. Allen, and as he gently shook my hand without cracking a smile, I felt his unmistakable goodwill behind the curmudgeon's mask.

Curmudgeons are mockers and debunkers whose bitterness is a symptom rather than a disease. They can't compromise their standards and can't manage the suspension of disbelief necessary for feigned cheerfulness. Their awareness is a curse; they're constantly ticked off because they're constantly aware of so much to be ticked off about, and they wish things were better.

Maybe curmudgeons have gotten a bad rap in the same way that the messenger is blamed for the message: They have the temerity to comment on the human condition without apology. They not only refuse to applaud mediocrity, they howl it down with morose glee. Their versions of the truth unsettle us, and we hold it against them, even though they soften it with humor.

H. L. Mencken was the quintessential curmudgeon, the one against whom all others must be measured. He wrote thirty books and countless essays, columns, and critical reviews. He was a lexicographer, reporter, and editor, the literary champion of Sherwood Anderson, Theodore Dreiser, Sinclair Lewis, and Eugene O'Neill.

Mencken was the scourge of the middle class, which he called the "booboisie." In spite of his condescending tone and lack of faith in his fellowman, he was a crusader against bigotry and injustice. He championed libertarianism and derided piety. "Puritanism is the haunting fear that someone, somewhere, may be happy," he wrote.

The other great curmudgeons who have contributed to the general sanity of mankind—from Mark Twain and Ambrose Bierce to G. K. Chesterton and George Bernard Shaw, from Groucho Marx and W. C. Fields to Dave Barry and Lewis Black—have all had the facility for pointing out the absurdities of the human condition.

If there was a Golden Age of curmudgeonry, it was during the 1920s and '30s at New York's Algonquin, an otherwise undistinguished hotel on West Forty-fourth Street. A dazzling array of wits and raconteurs gravitated to the table of Alexander Woollcott, the *New York Times* theater critic and book reviewer, and made it a bastion of urbanity and sparkling repartee. Edmund Wilson dubbed it an "all-star literary vaudeville." According to Groucho Marx, "The admission fee was a viper's tongue and a half-concealed stiletto. It was a sort of intellectual slaughterhouse." Clare Boothe Luce, no doubt because she was a frequent target of some of its members, was not amused: "You couldn't say 'Pass the salt' without somebody turning it into a pun or trying to top it."

The regulars among the artists, celebrities, and intellectuals who frequented the round table included Franklin P. Adams, Marc Connelly, George S. Kaufman, Harold Ross, Heywood Broun, Ring Lardner, Robert E. Sherwood, Robert Benchley, and Dorothy Parker. Other habitués included Oscar Levant, the Marx Brothers, Tallulah Bankhead, Herman Manckiewicz, Herbert Bayard Swope, Edna Ferber, Noel Coward, Charles MacArthur, and S. N. Behrman. As a result, the Algonquin Round Table is the single greatest source for the quotations and anecdotes in this book.

The "featured" curmudgeons in these pages are not necessarily typical. Indeed, curmudgeons are fierce individualists by definition. Nevertheless, an examination of the lives of W. C. Fields, Oscar Wilde, George S. Kaufman, Robert Benchley, Oscar Levant, Dorothy Parker, and Groucho Marx reveals common threads. Many of them had unhappy childhoods and grew into neurotic, reclusive, self-centered adults. Many remained shy and insecure in spite of their celebrity. An inordinate number were prone to alcoholism, drug addiction, insomnia, hypochondria, misogyny, even suicide.

The contemporary curmudgeons I interviewed displayed none of these tendencies. They're all intelligent, articulate, and personable. Many are happily married or mated, and they all appeared healthy and sober when we met. They were unanimous in their reluctance to characterize themselves as curmudgeons without the proviso that anybody who *isn't* a curmudgeon nowadays is just not paying attention. They were invariably forthcoming and responsive to my questions, both pertinent and impertinent. I'm grateful to all of them for their uncurmudgeonly cooperation.

You don't have to be a curmudgeon to make a curmudgeonly statement, so quotes from non- and quasi-curmudgeons are included herein—apparently even the terminally Pollyannish can have flashes of clarity. But the majority of the quotes in these pages are from the world-class curmudgeons listed on pages 25-28.

I think I became a connoisseur of curmudgeons sometime in the early 1960s, when I saw Oscar Levant in a series of television interviews with Jack Paar. Levant had been in and out of psychiatric institutions ("I was once thrown out of a mental hospital for depressing the other patients"), was a mass of tics and twitches, and chain-smoked Newports (although his hands shook so badly, he needed help to light them). I was captivated by the twisted, toothless smile, the lucid mind within the degenerate body. (Paar: "What do you do for exercise?" Levant: "I stumble and then I fall into a coma.") Levant was at once pathetic and brilliant, witty and helpless, the essence of curmudgeonry in one enthralling package, a raw nerve of vulnerability eloquently lashing out at the sources of its torment.

By the early seventies, I began to notice curmudgeonly tendencies in myself. I lost my tolerance for anything cute or trendy. I became increasingly out of step with everyone and everything around me. I developed a permanent sneer. I wrote fan letters to John Simon. I began to cultivate my surliness instead of trying to conceal it. Eventually I gained the courage to come out of the closet, to go from an isolated, would-be iconoclast to an out-in-the-open curmudgeon. (Curmudgeons are like sumo wrestlers: it takes a long time and a lot of abuse to make one; curmudgeons are also like writers: you're a curmudgeon only when someone else says you're a curmudgeon.)

In short order I got an unlisted telephone number, enrolled in law school, divorced my wife, and managed to irreparably insult most of my friends and relatives. And I began collecting this material with the intention of someday compiling it in a book from which other closet curmudgeons might take solace.

This omnibus edition consists of *The Portable Curmudgeon* and *The Portable Curmudgeon Redux*, much of *A Curmudgeon's Garden of Love*, plus additional quotations, sidebars, and interviews. Like its predecessors, it's an attempt to amuse while we wait for the last lug nut to fly off the last wheel of civilization. If it reaches just one other kindred soul and convinces him or her that there's no shame in chronic alienation, that curmudgeonry is a perfectly valid response to an increasingly exasperating world, it will have accomplished its goal.

—J. W.
Pacific Palisades, California
December 2006

WORLD-CLASS CURMUDGEONS

EDWARD ABBEY

GOODMAN ACE

FRED ALLEN

WOODY ALLEN

KINGSLEY AMIS

MARTIN AMIS

JUDD APATOW

MATTHEW ARNOLD

RUSSELL BAKER

TALLULAH BANKHEAD

DAVE BARRY

JOHN BARRYMORE

JOHN BARTH

ORSON BEAN

LUCIUS BEEBE

THOMAS BEECHAM

JOY BEHAR

MAX BEERBOHM

RICHARD BELZER

ROBERT BENCHLEY

AMBROSE BIERCE

STANLEY BING

LEWIS BLACK

ROY BLOUNT, JR.

DANIEL J. BOORSTIN

JIMMY BRESLIN

DAVID BRINKLEY

BROTHER THEODORE

HEYWOOD BROUN

RITA MAE BROWN

LENNY BRUCE

WILLIAM F. BUCKLEY, JR.

HERB CAEN

JACK CAFFERTY

TRUMAN CAPOTE

AL CAPP

ADAM CAROLLA

JACK CARTER

NICOLAS CHAMFORT
E. M. CIORAN
PAT COOPER
G. K. CHESTERTON
NORMAN CHAD
MARGARET CHO
FRANK CHIRKINIAN
JOHN CLEESE
CATHY CRIMMINS
QUENTIN CRISP
EDWARD DAHLBERG
LARRY DAVID
BETTE DAVIS
PETER DE VRIES
MAUREEN DOWD
WILL DURST
JOHN C. DVORAK
LINDA ELLERBEE
CHRIS ELLIOTT
HARLAN ELLISON
JOSEPH EPSTEIN
SUSIE ESSMAN
JULES FEIFFER
W. C. FIELDS
CARRIE FISHER
JOHN FORD
ANATOLE FRANCE

AL FRANKEN
ROBERT FROST
PAUL FUSSELL
LARRY GELBART
GREG GIRALDO
EDWARD GOREY
LEWIS GRIZZARD
MATT GROENING
BEN HECHT
TONY HENDRA
PHIL HENDRIE
BUCK HENRY
BILL HICKS
ALFRED HITCHCOCK
CHRISTOPHER HITCHENS
SAMUEL HOFFENSTEIN
HENRIK IBSEN
HAROLD L. ICKES
MOLLY IVINS
CLIVE JAMES
SAMUEL JOHNSON
ERICA JONG
BEN JONSON
ALICE KAHN
BRUCE ERIC KAPLAN
GEORGE S. KAUFMAN
MARGO KAUFMAN

WENDY KAMINER
GUY KAWASAKI
JIMMY KIMMEL
ANDY KINDLER
ALEXANDER KING
FLORENCE KING
TONY KORNHEISER
KARL KRAUS
PHILIP LARKIN
STEPHEN LEACOCK
DENIS LEARY
FRAN LEBOWITZ
TOM LEHRER
JOHN LEO
DAVID LETTERMAN
OSCAR LEVANT
BEA LILLIE
WILLIAM LOEB
SANDRA TSING LOH
PHILLIP LOPATE
BILL MAHER
HERMAN MANKIEWICZ
SAMUEL MARCHBANKS
DON MARQUIS
GROUCHO MARX
H. L. MENCKEN
MARY MCCARTHY

COLIN MCENROE
DENNIS MILLER
HENRY MILLER
JESSICA MITFORD
NANCY MITFORD
WILSON MIZNER
HENRY MORGAN
ROBERT MORLEY
MALCOLM MUGGERIDGE
MARTIN MULL
VLADIMIR NABOKOV
GEORGE JEAN NATHAN
FRIEDRICH WILHELM NIETZSCHE
RALPH NOVAK
KEITH OLBERMANN
GEORGE ORWELL
CAMILLE PAGLIA
DOROTHY PARKER
WESTBROOK PEGLER
S. J. PERELMAN
J. B. PRIESTLEY
PRINCE PHILIP
PAULA POUNDSTONE
JOE QUEENAN
COLIN QUINN
REX REED
FRANK RICH

ANTOINE DE RIVAROL
ANDY ROONEY
HOWARD ROSENBERG
MIKE ROYKO
HUGHES RUDD
RITA RUDNER
HORACE RUMPOLE
BERTRAND RUSSELL
MORT SAHL
GEORGE SANDERS
GEOFF SHACKELFORD
GEORGE BERNARD SHAW
HARRY SHEARER
WILFRED SHEED
IAN SHOALES
JOHN SILBER
JOHN SIMON
JOEL STEIN
GLORIA STEINEM
JON STEWART
JOHN STOSSEL
AUGUST STRINDBERG
TAKI THEODORACOPULOS

HUNTER S. THOMPSON
JAMES THURBER
CALVIN TRILLIN
MARK TWAIN
GORE VIDAL
NORAH VINCENT
VOLTAIRE
NICHOLAS VON HOFFMAN
ERIC VON STROHEIM
JOHN WATERS
EVELYN WAUGH
CLIFTON WEBB
ORSON WELLES
IAN WHITCOMB
T. H. WHITE
OSCAR WILDE
BILLY WILDER
GEORGE WILL
EDMUND WILSON
ALEXANDER WOOLLCOTT
JONATHAN YARDLEY
FRANK ZAPPA

THE HEART
OF A CURMUDGEON

I think there is only one quality worse than hardness of heart, and that is softness of head.   THEODORE ROOSEVELT

The believer is happy; the doubter is wise.   HUNGARIAN PROVERB

Men become civilized, not in proportion to their willingness to believe, but in proportion to their readiness to doubt.   H. L. MENCKEN

To believe is very dull. To doubt is intensely engrossing. To be on the alert is to live, to be lulled into security is to die.   OSCAR WILDE

Melancholy men, of all others, are the most witty.   ARISTOTLE

Real misanthropes are not found in solitude, but in the world; since it is experience of life, and not philosophy, which produces real hatred of mankind.
                    GIACOMO LEOPARDI

To knock a thing down, especially if it is cocked at an arrogant angle, is a deep delight of the blood.   GEORGE SANTAYANA

Every normal man must be tempted at times to spit on his hands, hoist the black flag, and begin slitting throats.   H. L. MENCKEN

Latent in every man is a venom of amazing bitterness, a black resentment; something that curses and loathes life, a feeling of being trapped, of having trusted and been fooled, of being the helpless prey of impotent rage, blind surrender, the victim of a savage, ruthless power that gives and takes away, enlists a man, drops him, promises and betrays, and—crowning injury— inflicts on him the humiliation of feeling sorry for himself.   PAUL VALÉRY

There is no fate that cannot be surmounted by scorn.   ALBERT CAMUS

Whoever is not a misanthrope at forty can never have loved mankind.
NICOLAS CHAMFORT

A grouch escapes so many little annoyances that it almost pays to be one.
KIN HUBBARD

A man gazing at the stars is proverbially at the mercy of the puddles in the road.   ALEXANDER SMITH

I have been called a curmudgeon, which my obsolescent dictionary defines as a "surly, ill-mannered, bad-tempered fellow." The etymology of the word is obscure; in fact, unknown. But through frequent recent usage, the term is acquiring a broader meaning, which our dictionaries have not yet caught up to. Nowadays, curmudgeon is likely to refer to anyone who hates hypocrisy, cant, sham, dogmatic ideologies, the pretenses and evasions of euphemism, and has the nerve to point out unpleasant facts and takes the trouble to impale these sins on the skewer of humor and roast them over the fires of empiric fact, common sense, and native intelligence. In this nation of bleating sheep and braying jackasses, it then becomes an honor to be labeled curmudgeon.
EDWARD ABBEY

QUOTES ON "A"

ABORTION

If men could get pregnant, abortion would be a sacrament.
FLORYNCE KENNEDY

All my friends are always telling me how hard it is to have kids. "Oh, David, it's so *hard*." That's not hard. You wanna know what hard is? Try talking your girlfriend into her third consecutive abortion.   DAVID CROSS

I want to get an abortion. But my boyfriend and I are having trouble conceiving.   SARAH SILVERMAN

ABSTRACT ART

Abstract art: a product of the untalented sold by the unprincipled to the utterly bewildered.   AL CAPP

ACADEME

Academe, *n.* An ancient school where morality and philosophy were taught.
AMBROSE BIERCE

ACADEMY

Academy, *n.* (from *academe*). A modern school where football is taught.
AMBROSE BIERCE

ACCOUNTING

There's no business like show business, but there are several businesses like accounting.   DAVID LETTERMAN

ACQUAINTANCE

Acquaintance, *n.* A person whom we know well enough to borrow from, but not well enough to lend to.   AMBROSE BIERCE

If a thing is worth doing, it is worth doing badly.   G. K. CHESTERTON

ACTING

It is the most minor of gifts and not a very high-class way to earn a living. After all, Shirley Temple could do it at the age of four.

KATHARINE HEPBURN

Acting is like roller skating. Once you know how to do it, it is neither stimulating nor exciting.   GEORGE SANDERS

I do not regret one professional enemy I have made. Any actor who doesn't dare to make an enemy should get out of the business.   BETTE DAVIS

I love acting. It is so much more real than life.   OSCAR WILDE

ACTION

Actions lie louder than words.   CAROLYN WELLS

The basis of action is lack of imagination. It is the last resource of those who know not how to dream.   OSCAR WILDE

ACTORS

The physical labor actors have to do wouldn't tax an embryo.   NEIL SIMON

If there's anything unsettling to the stomach, it's watching actors on television talk about their personal lives.   MARLON BRANDO

Scratch an actor—and you'll find an actress.   DOROTHY PARKER

I do not want actors and actresses to understand my plays. That is not necessary. If they will only pronounce the correct sounds I can guarantee the results.   GEORGE BERNARD SHAW

Disney, of course, has the best casting. If he doesn't like an actor, he just tears him up.   ALFRED HITCHCOCK

We're actors—we're the opposite of people.   TOM STOPPARD

Some of the greatest love affairs I've known have involved one actor—unassisted.   WILSON MIZNER

You can pick out actors by the glazed look that comes into their eyes when the conversation wanders away from themselves.   MICHAEL WILDING

The scenery in the play was beautiful, but the actors got in front of it.   ALEXANDER WOOLLCOTT

The actor is not quite a human being—but then, who is?   GEORGE SANDERS

Show me a great actor and I'll show you a lousy husband; show me a great actress, and you've seen the devil.   W. C. FIELDS

An actor's success has the life expectancy of a small boy about to look into a gas tank with a lighted match.   FRED ALLEN

Every actor has a natural animosity toward every other actor, present or absent, living or dead.   LOUISE BROOKS

Actors are crap.   JOHN FORD

----------------------- **ADMIRATION** -----------------------
Admiration, *n.* Our polite recognition of another's resemblance to ourselves.
                              AMBROSE BIERCE

----------------------- **ADOLESCENCE** -----------------------
You don't have to suffer to be a poet; adolescence is enough suffering for anyone.   JOHN CIARDI

----------------------- **ADULTERY** -----------------------
The psychology of adultery has been falsified by conventional morals, which assume, in monogamous countries, that attraction to one person cannot coexist with affection for another. Everybody knows that this is untrue.
                              BERTRAND RUSSELL

Adultery is the application of democracy to love.   H. L. MENCKEN

Sara could commit adultery at one end and weep for her sins at the other, and enjoy both operations at once.   JOYCE CARY

When a Roman was returning from a trip, he used to send someone ahead to let his wife know, so as not to surprise her in the act.

MICHEL DE MONTAIGNE

When a woman unhappily yoked talks about the soul with a man not her husband, it isn't the soul they are talking about. DON MARQUIS

When a man steals your wife, there is no better revenge than to let him keep her. SACHA GUITRY

As we all know from witnessing the consuming jealousy of husbands who are never faithful, people do not confine themselves to the emotions to which they are entitled. QUENTIN CRISP

You cannot pluck roses without fear of thorns, nor enjoy a fair wife without danger of horns. BENJAMIN FRANKLIN

You can't tell your friend you've been cuckolded; even if he doesn't laugh at you, he may put the information to personal use. MICHEL DE MONTAIGNE

GEORGE S. KAUFMAN: I like your bald head, Marc. It feels just like my wife's behind.

MARC CONNOLLY (feeling his pate): So it does, George, so it does.

Is oral sex adultery? Yes! There is no discussion! If curling is an Olympic sport, then oral sex is adultery. And oral sex should be an Olympic sport because it's more difficult than curling and if you're any good at it, you deserve a medal!

LEWIS BLACK

I told my wife the truth. I told her I was seeing a psychiatrist. Then she told *me* the truth: that she was seeing a psychiatrist, two plumbers and a bartender.
RODNEY DANGERFIELD

I've been in love with the same woman for forty-one years. If my wife finds out, she'll kill me.
HENNY YOUNGMAN

ADULTHOOD

Adulthood is the ever-shrinking period between childhood and old age. It is the apparent aim of modern industrial societies to reduce this period to a minimum.
THOMAS SZASZ

To be adult is to be alone.
JEAN ROSTAND

ADVERSARIES

In all matters of opinion, our adversaries are insane.
OSCAR WILDE

ADVERTISING

Time spent in the advertising business seems to create a permanent deformity like the Chinese habit of foot-binding.
DEAN ACHESON

Advertising may be described as the science of arresting human intelligence long enough to get money from it.
STEPHEN LEACOCK

Advertising is the rattling of a stick inside a swill bucket.
GEORGE ORWELL

The very first law in advertising is to avoid the concrete promise and cultivate the delightfully vague.
BILL COSBY

Advertising is a valuable economic factor because it is the cheapest way of selling goods, particularly if the goods are worthless.   SINCLAIR LEWIS

Advertising is 85 percent confusion and 15 percent commission. FRED ALLEN

Advertising is the modern substitute for argument; its function is to make the worse appear the better.   GEORGE SANTAYANA

Advertising is legalized lying.   H. G. WELLS

You can tell the ideals of a nation by its advertisements.
NORMAN DOUGLAS

———————————— ADVICE TO WRITERS ————————————
Your life story would not make a good book. Don't even try.
FRAN LEBOWITZ

Unless you think you can do better than Tolstoy, we don't need you.
JAMES MICHENER

If a young writer can refrain from writing, he shouldn't hesitate to do so.
ANDRÉ GIDE

———————————— AFFECTION ————————————
All my life, affection has been showered upon me, and every forward step I have made has been taken in spite of it.   GEORGE BERNARD SHAW

Most affections are habits or duties we lack the courage to end.
HENRI DE MONTHERLANT

AFRICA

Man developed in Africa. He has not continued to do so there.   P. J. O'ROURKE

AGE

The best years are the forties; after fifty a man begins to deteriorate, but in the forties he is at the maximum of his villainy.   H. L. MENCKEN

One of the delights known to age, and beyond the grasp of youth, is that of Not Going.   J. B. PRIESTLEY

AGENT

An agent is a guy who's sore because an actor gets ninety percent of what he makes.   ALVA JOHNSTON

AGING

It is after you have lost your teeth that you can afford to buy steaks.
PIERRE AUGUSTE RENOIR

As you get older, the pickings get slimmer, but the people don't.
CARRIE FISHER

AGREEMENT

The fellow that agrees with everything you say is either a fool or he is getting ready to skin you.   KIN HUBBARD

If you can find something everyone agrees on, it's wrong.   MO UDALL

ALIMONY

Paying alimony is like feeding hay to a dead horse.   GROUCHO MARX

Judges, as a class, display, in the matter of arranging alimony, that reckless generosity which is found only in men who are giving away someone else's cash.
P. G. WODEHOUSE

Even hooligans marry, though they know that marriage is but for a little while. It is alimony that is forever. QUENTIN CRISP

You never realize how short a month is until you pay alimony.
JOHN BARRYMORE

ALLIANCE

Alliance, *n.* In international politics, the union of two thieves who have their hands so deeply in each other's pocket that they cannot separately plunder a third. AMBROSE BIERCE

ALTRUISM

Every major horror of history was committed in the name of an altruistic motive. Has any act of selfishness ever equaled the carnage perpetrated by disciples of altruism? AYN RAND

Men are the only animals that devote themselves, day in and day out, to making one another unhappy. It is an art like any other. Its virtuosi are called altruists. H. L. MENCKEN

AMERICA

America is the only nation in history which miraculously has gone directly from barbarism to degeneration without the usual interval of civilization.
GEORGES CLEMENCEAU

I have never been able to look upon America as young and vital, but rather as prematurely old, as a fruit which rotted before it had a chance to ripen. The word which gives the key to the national vice is waste.   HENRY MILLER

In America, life is one long expectoration.   OSCAR WILDE

An asylum for the sane would be empty in America.
GEORGE BERNARD SHAW

The civilization whose absence drove Henry James to Europe.
GORE VIDAL

In our country we have those three unspeakably precious things: freedom of speech, freedom of conscience, and the prudence never to practice either.
MARK TWAIN

In America sex is an obsession, in other parts of the world it is a fact.
MARLENE DIETRICH

The only country in the world where failing to promote yourself is regarded as being arrogant.   GARRY TRUDEAU

Every time Europe looks across the Atlantic to see the American eagle, it observes only the rear end of an ostrich.   AMBROSE BIERCE

The organization of American society is an interlocking system of semi-monopolies notoriously venal, an electorate notoriously unenlightened, misled by a mass media notoriously phony.   PAUL GOODMAN

America…just a nation of two hundred million used car salesmen with all the money we need to buy guns and no qualms about killing anybody else in the world who tries to make us uncomfortable.

HUNTER S. THOMPSON

America is the greatest of opportunities and the worst of influences.

GEORGE SANTAYANA

In America, through pressure of conformity, there is freedom of choice, but nothing to choose from.　　　　　　PETER USTINOV

If America leads a blessed life, then why did God put all of our oil under people who hate us?　　　　　　JON STEWART

In America you can go on the air and kid the politicians, and the politicians can go on the air and kid the people.　　　　GROUCHO MARX

The discovery of America was the occasion of the greatest outburst of cruelty and reckless greed known in history.　　　　JOSEPH CONRAD

America is still a government of the naive, by the naive, and for the naive. He who does not know this, nor relish it, has no inkling of the nature of this country.　　　　　　CHRISTOPHER MORLEY

America is a mistake, a giant mistake!　　　　SIGMUND FREUD

It was wonderful to find America, but it would have been more wonderful to miss it.　　　　　　MARK TWAIN

The trouble with us in America isn't that the poetry of life has turned to prose, but that it has turned to advertising copy.   LOUIS KRONENBERGER

In America everything goes and nothing matters. While in Europe nothing goes and everything matters.   PHILIP ROTH

Everyone has a right to a university degree in America, even if it's in Hamburger Technology.   CLIVE JAMES

To have a license number of one's automobile as low as possible is a social advantage in America.   ANDRÉ MAUROIS

The trouble with America is that there are far too many wide-open spaces surrounded by teeth.   CHARLES LUCKMAN

Some American delusions:
1. That there is no class-consciousness in the country.
2. That American coffee is good.
3. That Americans are businesslike.
4. That Americans are highly sexed and that redheads are more highly sexed than others.   W. SOMERSET MAUGHAM

The United States is a nation of laws: badly written and randomly enforced.   FRANK ZAPPA

America's one of the finest countries anyone ever stole.   BOBCAT GOLDTHWAITE

It is absurd to say that there are neither ruins nor curiosities in America when they have their mothers and their manners.   OSCAR WILDE

What a pity, when Christopher Columbus discovered America, that he ever mentioned it. MARGOT ASQUITH

Perhaps, after all, America never has been discovered. I myself would say that it had merely been detected. OSCAR WILDE

The thing that impresses me most about America is the way parents obey their children. DUKE OF WINDSOR

In America, health is not regarded as a right, but as a commodity to be bought and sold just like anything else. There are places where an ambulance team will investigate your financial health before it will have any truck with your physical health. WILLIAM GOLDING

In modern-day, new-age America, generally speaking, folks would prefer that your dog vomit on the new Karastan than that you ignite a Don Diego Lonsdale in their presence. In their vicinity. In their lifetime. BRUCE MCCALL

There are three social classes in America: upper middle class, middle class, and lower middle class. MISS MANNERS (JUDITH MARTIN)

Our national flower is the concrete cloverleaf. LEWIS MUMFORD

Oh, and did I mention we owe China a trillion dollars? We owe everybody money. America is a debtor nation to Mexico! We're not on a bridge to the twenty-first century, we're on a bus to Atlantic City with a roll of quarters. BILL MAHER

The trouble with this country is that there are too many people going about saying, "The trouble with this country is—" SINCLAIR LEWIS

AMERICAN CARS

All American cars are basically Chevrolets.   HERB CAEN

AMERICAN FAMILY

The American family today consists most likely of a work-crazed mom trying to raise shopping-mall TV brats in a world gone consumption mad.
ANDREI CODRESCU

AMERICAN MALES

Eternal boyhood is the dream of a depressing percentage of American males, and the locker room is the temple where they worship arrested development.
RUSSELL BAKER

AMERICAN POLITICAL SYSTEM

The American political system is like fast food: mushy, insipid, made out of disgusting parts of things and everybody wants some.   P. J. O'ROURKE

AMERICANS

Americans are the only people in the world known to me whose status anxiety prompts them to advertise their college and university affiliations in the rear window of their automobiles.   PAUL FUSSELL

When you consider how indifferent Americans are to the quality and cooking of the food they put into their insides, it cannot but strike you as peculiar that they should take such pride in the mechanical appliances they use for its excretion.   W. SOMERSET MAUGHAM

Americans are like a rich father who wishes he knew how to give his son the hardships that made him rich.   ROBERT FROST

Americans can eat garbage, provided you sprinkle it liberally with ketchup, mustard, chili sauce, tabasco sauce, cayenne pepper, or any other condiment which destroys the original flavor of the dish.   HENRY MILLER

The three differences between American and British people: We speak English and you don't. When we hold a World Championship for a particular sport, we invite teams from other countries to play, as well. When you meet the head of state in Great Britain, you only have to go down on one knee.
                                                                                                JOHN CLEESE

The genius of you Americans is that you never make clear-cut stupid moves, only complicated stupid moves which make us wonder at the possibility that there may be something to them which we are missing.   GAMAL ABDEL NASSER

The Americans are certainly great hero-worshipers, and always take their heroes from the criminal classes.   OSCAR WILDE

We don't know what we want, but we are ready to bite somebody to get it.
                                                                                                WILL ROGERS

We love violence in this country, we love violence. We all have those little violent tendencies. I know you're like me, when you see someone walking down the street in a Superman tee shirt, you just want to shoot them in the chest. And when they start to bleed go, "I guess not." Don't wear the shirt. Wear a shirt that says, "I bleed if you shoot me in the chest plate" and I will not shoot you in the chest plate, Superbleeder.   DANE COOK

I have defined the one-hundred percent American as ninety-nine percent an idiot. And they just adore me.   GEORGE BERNARD SHAW

Americans are broad-minded people. They'll accept the fact that a person can be an alcoholic, a dope fiend, a wife beater, and even a newspaperman, but if a man doesn't drive there's something wrong with him.

ART BUCHWALD

Americans are childish in many ways and about as subtle as a Wimpy burger; but in the long run it doesn't make any difference. They just turn on the power.

TOM WOLFE

In every American there is an air of incorrigible innocence, which seems to conceal a diabolical cunning.

A. E. HOUSMAN

Americans detest all lies except lies spoken in public or printed lies.

ED HOWE

I worry about my judgment when anything I believe in or do regularly begins to be accepted by the American public.

GEORGE CARLIN

Whatever else an American believes or disbelieves about himself, he is absolutely sure he has a sense of humor.

E. B. WHITE

An Anglo-Saxon relapsed into semibarbarism.

BAYARD TALOR

The IQ and the life expectancy of the average American recently passed each other in opposite directions.

GEORGE CARLIN

Half of the American people have never read a newspaper. Half never voted for President. One hopes it is the same half.

GORE VIDAL

Food, one assumes, provides nourishment; but Americans eat it fully aware that small amounts of poison have been added to improve its appearance and delay its putrefaction. JOHN CAGE

Let's face it, Americans are fat all year round, but the holidays are when we really hit our stride. And you can bet the food we eat will be just as unhealthy as the families we're forced to visit. LEWIS BLACK

The new Airbus plane, the A380, is capable of holding 800 passengers. Or, 400 Americans. JON STEWART

When good Americans die they go to Paris; when bad Americans die they go to America. OSCAR WILDE

You may be sure that the Americans will commit all the stupidities they can think of, plus some that are beyond imagination. CHARLES DE GAULLE

Americans have an abiding belief in their ability to control reality by purely material means…airline insurance replaces the fear of death with the comforting prospect of cash. CECIL BEATON

Finally, Americans have found a political problem that they are willing to come together and do something about. No, not terrorism…close, it's telemarketing! LEWIS BLACK

Americans will put up with anything provided it doesn't block traffic. DAN RATHER

Americans don't want privacy. They want attention! They'll put a camera in their shower and show it on the Internet! To get on television, they'll marry strangers and eat a cow's rectum, and ice dance with Todd Bridges....We are a nation of exhibitionists from "me" to shining "me." And what we really fear isn't that someone's listening; it's that no one's listening. This whole country is one big desperate cry for somebody to listen to "listen to me, photograph me, Google me, read my blog!" "Read my diary; read my memoir. It's not interesting enough? I'll make shit up!" BILL MAHER

Americans adore me and will go on adoring me until I say something nice about them. GEORGE BERNARD SHAW

The people of the United States, perhaps more than any other nation in history, love to abase themselves and proclaim their unworthiness, and seem to find refreshment in doing so...That is a dark frivolity, but still frivolity. ROBERTSON DAVIES

If you surveyed a hundred typical middle-aged Americans, I bet you'd find that only two of them could tell you their blood types, but every last one of them would know the theme song from *The Beverly Hillbillies*. DAVE BARRY

—————————— AMERICAN WAY ——————————
The American way is to seduce a man by bribery and make a prostitute of him. Or else to ignore him, starve him into submission and make a hack out of him. HENRY MILLER

—————————— AMUSEMENT ——————————
Amusement is the happiness of those who cannot think. ALEXANDER POPE

ANIMALS

Animals have these advantages over man: they have no theologians to instruct them, their funerals cost them nothing, and no one starts lawsuits over their wills.   VOLTAIRE

ANTS

Ants are so much like human beings as to be an embarrassment. They farm fungi, raise aphids as livestock, launch armies into war, use chemical sprays to alarm and confuse enemies, capture slaves, engage in child labor, exchange information ceaselessly. They do everything but watch television.

LEWIS THOMAS

APPEAL

An appeal is when you ask one court to show its contempt for another court.
FINLEY PETER DUNNE

APPLAUSE

This strange beating together of hands has no meaning. To me it is very disturbing. We try to make sounds like music, and then in between comes this strange sound.   LEOPOLD STOKOWSKI

APPRECIATION

Appreciation is a wonderful thing: it makes what is excellent in others belong to us as well.   VOLTAIRE

AQUARIUM

There is something about a home aquarium which sets my teeth on edge the moment I see it. Why anyone would want to live with a small container of stagnant water populated by a half-dead guppy is beyond me.

S. J. PERELMAN

ARCHBISHOP

Archbishop: a Christian ecclesiastic of a rank superior to that attained by Christ.
H. L. MENCKEN

ARCHITECTURE

The art of how to waste space.   PHILIP JOHNSON

ARGUMENT

Arguments are to be avoided; they are always vulgar and often convincing.
OSCAR WILDE

It is not necessary to understand things in order to argue about them.
PIERRE AUGUSTIN CARON DE BEAUMARCHAIS

It is only the intellectually lost who ever argue.   OSCAR WILDE

My parents only had one argument in forty-five years. It lasted forty-three years.
CATHY LADMAN

ART

Without art, the crudeness of reality would make the world unbearable.
GEORGE BERNARD SHAW

If more than ten percent of the population likes a painting it should be burned, for it must be bad.   GEORGE BERNARD SHAW

ART CRITICS

[The] tendency to degenerate into a mere mouthing of meaningless words seems to be peculiar to so-called art criticism....Even the most orthodox of the brethren, when he finds himself before a canvas that genuinely moves him, takes refuge in esoteric winks and grimaces and mysterious gurgles and belches. H. L. MENCKEN

No degree of dullness can safeguard a work against the determination of critics to find it fascinating. HAROLD ROSENBERG

—————————— ARTIFICIAL INTELLIGENCE ——————————
The real problem is not whether machines think but whether men do.
B. F. SKINNER

—————————— ASPEN, COLORADO ——————————
Call me crazy, I like a city with oxygen. SUSIE ESSMAN

—————————— ASTROLOGY ——————————
I don't believe in astrology. The only stars I can blame for my failures are those that walk about the stage. NOEL COWARD

—————————— ASTRONAUTS ——————————
Rotarians in outer space. GORE VIDAL

Twenty-two astronauts were born in Ohio. What is it about your state that makes people want to flee the earth? STEPHEN COLBERT

—————————— ATHEISM ——————————
An atheist is a man who has no invisible means of support. JOHN BUCHAN

Nobody talks so constantly about God as those who insist that there is no God.
HEYWOOD BROUN

If there were no God, there would be no Atheists.   G. K. CHESTERTON

I once wanted to become an atheist, but I gave up—they have no holidays.
HENNY YOUNGMAN

No one is more dangerous than someone who thinks he has "The Truth."
To be an atheist is almost as arrogant as to be a fundamentalist.

TOM LEHRER

I'm still an atheist, thank God!   LUIS BUÑUEL

——————————— AUTHOR ———————————
A fool who, not content with having bored those who have lived with him,
insists on tormenting the generations to come.   BARON DE MONTESQUIEU

——————————— AUTHORITY ———————————
I have as much authority as the Pope. I just don't have as many people who
believe it.   GEORGE CARLIN

——————————— AUTOBIOGRAPHY ———————————
Autobiography is an unrivalled vehicle for telling the truth about other people.
PHILIP GUEDALLA

——————————— AUTUMN ———————————
Let's drive up to New England and watch the leaves die.

BRUCE ERIC KAPLAN

——————————— AWARDS ———————————
Awards are merely the badges of mediocrity.   CHARLES IVES

Nothing would disgust me more, morally, than receiving an Oscar.
LUIS BUÑUEL

This medal [the National Book Award], together with my American Express Card, will identify me worldwide—except at Bloomingdale's.
S. J. PERELMAN

It [the Legion of Honor] is taken rather seriously by those who have received it.
ALFRED HITCHCOCK

Awards are like hemorrhoids; in the end, every asshole gets one.
FREDERIC RAPHAEL

H. L. MENCKEN

Stirring Up the Animals

Henry Louis Mencken was born in Baltimore on September 12, 1880, the eldest of four children of a middle-class German-American family. He had a happy, secure, normal childhood: he described himself as "a larva of the comfortable and complacent bourgeoisie" and wrote that "we were encapsulated in affection and kept fat, saucy and contented."

His father owned and managed a cigar factory and imbued his son with a belief in the efficacy of independent action and thought, and instilled in him a love of reading. There was a modest library in the Mencken home, and the young Harry, as he was called, obtained a reader's card at Baltimore's Pratt

Library at the age of nine. It was there that he discovered *Huckleberry Finn,* an event he would later characterize as "the most stupendous of my whole life."

He attended the Baltimore Polytechnic and went into the family business upon graduation, but soon grew dissatisfied with his job and wanted to quit to become a newspaperman. When his father died in 1899, his uncle assumed control of the factory and Mencken was free to pursue a career in journalism. He immediately obtained a series of trial-reporting assignments from the Baltimore *Morning Herald* and within a few months, at the age of eighteen, he became the youngest reporter on the staff. By 1903, he was city editor, and in 1905 he became the editor of the *Evening Herald.* He moved to the famous Baltimore *Sun* papers in 1906, first as a member of the staff of the *Morning Sun* and then of the *Evening Sun.* He became literary critic of *The Smart Set* in 1908. His "Free Lance" column in the Baltimore *Evening Sun,* which first appeared in 1910, influenced journalists all over the country with its vibrant, iconoclastic approach to the issues of the time.

In 1914, he was named coeditor of *The Smart Set,* with George Jean Nathan. In their first issue they published the following credo: "Our policy is to be lively without being nasty. On the one hand, no smut, and on the other, nothing uplifting. A magazine for civilized adults in their lighter moods." In 1924, Mencken became the editor of the *American Mercury,* where he published and supported such young American writers as Sinclair Lewis, James Branch Cabell, and Theodore Dreiser.

H. L. Mencken became one of the most influential and prolific American social critics of the first half of the twentieth century, reaching the peak of his influence and popularity in the twenties. His perennial target was American society, with which he maintained a love-hate relationship all his life. In "Catechism," he anticipated the inevitable question: "Q: If you find so much that is unworthy of reverence in the United States, then why do you live here? A: Why do men go to zoos?"

He considered emotion the enemy of intelligence and tried to hold it at bay whenever possible, a conviction that formed one of the underpinnings of his individualistic, aristocratic worldview. He held pomposity, incompetence, and pedantry in utter contempt. He believed, above all else, in the freedom to speak one's mind about anything at any time.

Mencken abominated Baptists and Methodists and delighted in skewering them in print, a practice that earned him the sobriquet "The Antichrist of Baltimore." But he wasn't anti-Christ, just anti-Christian, though he would have applauded the implementation of the teachings of Christ by Christians. He detested radio and television, abhorred liberals and the "Tory plutocracy," the rabble and the "uplifters" alike. He considered himself a spokesman for the "civilized minority" and attacked anything he deemed inimical to the freedom of the artist. He once described his function as "stirring up the animals."

Mencken had an abiding contempt for economists and economics. When he learned that President Franklin Delano Roosevelt (whom he called "Roosevelt Minor") had devalued the dollar, Mencken erupted in print, calling the measure downright robbery. He even briefly considered bringing legal action against the government. No sooner had he calmed down than the Supreme Court "packing" controversy exploded, sealing his opinion of "Roosevelt Minor" forever and marking the beginning of the decline in Mencken's influence. When Hitler came to power in Germany, Mencken didn't take him seriously and failed to attack him vigorously enough for many of his readers, who denounced Mencken as a Nazi and an anti-Semite.

He was one of our most distinguished and prolific men of letters. Walter Lippmann called him "the most powerful personal influence on this whole generation of educated people." His literary output consisted of thirty books, countless essays and reviews, and voluminous correspondence. It has been estimated that he wrote five thousand words a day for forty years. He was a prodigious reader and probably had one of the largest vocabularies of any American writer. He coined many neologisms, most notably *Bible Belt*, *booboisie*, *smuthound*, and *Boobus americanus*.

The American Language, his monumental study of American English, was first published in 1919 and went through several editions and supplements. It demonstrated conclusively for the first time that American English was a separate entity from its British progenitor. His critical essays were collected in the six-volume *Prejudices*, and his autobiographical essays were collected in *Happy Days*, *Newspaper Days*, and *Heathen Days*.

He led a cheerful, active, gregarious private life. He enjoyed hearty food, good pilsner, and the company of women. He was no stranger to chorus girls, and he was acquainted with many prominent women of his day, among them Anita Loos, Lillian Gish, and Aileen Pringle. He read love poems and would gallantly kiss the hand of a lady when introduced. Contrary to his oft-expressed sentiments on marriage (e.g., "If I ever marry, it will be on a sudden impulse—as a man shoots himself"), in 1930 he surprised his friends and readers by marrying a beautiful Goucher College instructor named Sara Powell Haardt.

They met an Mencken's annual lecture at the college (titled "How to Catch a Husband," it was actually a speech about writing). At twenty-four—eighteen years his junior—she was the youngest member of the English faculty, a frail, self-absorbed native of Montgomery, Alabama, who was active on behalf of women's suffrage. They had much in common: Both were writers, both were of German ancestry; they had many Baltimore friends in common; and they shared the same social and political philosophy, a combination of libertarianism and a Victorian sense of propriety. They both hated sports and flowers, were basically unemotional, and distrusted marriage.

Their courtship lasted seven years, during which his letters to her betray an uncharacteristic tenderness: He admired her courage and cheerfulness in the face of tuberculosis and its complications, consoled her about frequent hospitalizations, recommended specialists, and repeatedly offered to lend her money to pay doctor bills. One hospitalization elicited what must be the closest to a whine that Mencken was capable of: "Tell [the doctor] he is not to hurt you. I can't bear to see you in pain. It must be stopped."

He was, in short, her mentor. He gave her advice and encouragement in her efforts to be a writer, helped her get a contract with Paramount as a screenwriter, steered her freelance essays and short stories to the appropriate publications, and occasionally used his influence with editors on her behalf.

When they married in 1930, the headlines blared:

MIGHTY MENCKEN FALLS
MENCKEN, ARCH CYNIC, CAPITULATES TO CUPID
WEDLOCK SCOFFLA TO MARRY
ET TU, H.L.?

The marriage shattered his image and may even have contributed to his decline in popularity. His explanation to his confused and outraged fans was vintage Mencken: "I formerly was not as wise as I am now."

It was an idyllic marriage. He mailed her postcards with the stamp intentionally upside down, a signal that he loved her; and many of his letters ended with "I kiss your hand." He was devoted, affectionate, attentive. The Antichrist of Baltimore, the hard-bitten, cynical debunker of emotionalism, was a model husband.

With the arrival of the Depression and the election of Franklin Delano Roosevelt, Mencken's popularity began to wane and he withdrew into the marriage. He and Sara spent most of their time at home, together, working on their respective writing. He spent less and less time at the *American Mercury* and finally resigned as its editor in 1933.

The Menckens lived happily together for five years as Sara's health worsened. When she died in 1935, he mourned her loss deeply yet was able to say to a friend, "When I married Sara the doctors said she would not live more than three years. Actually she lived five, so I had two more years of happiness than I had any right to expect." And he later remarked, "I was fifty-five years old before I envied anyone, and then it was not so much for what others had as for what I had lost."

Henry Louis Mencken died on January 29, 1956, eight years after a massive stroke had rendered him virtually aphasic. That he was deprived of his ability to read and write was a grotesque irony that wasn't lost on Mencken himself: shortly before his death, a visitor mentioned the name of a mutual acquaintance who had died in 1948. Mencken thought for a moment and finally said, "Ah, yes, he died the same year I did."

MENCKEN'S AMERICA

The United States, to my eye, is incomparably the greatest show on earth…we have clowns among us who are as far above the clowns of any other great state as Jack Dempsey is above the paralytic—and not a few dozen or score of them, but whole droves and herds.

Nowhere in the world is superiority more easily attained, or more eagerly admitted. The chief business of the nation, as a nation, is the setting up of heroes, mainly bogus.

The American people, taking one with another, constitute the most timorous, sniveling, poltroonish, ignominious mob of serfs and goose-steppers ever gathered under one flag in Christendom since the end of the Middle Ages.

There's no underestimating the intelligence of the American public.

The typical American of today has lost all the love of liberty that his forefathers had, and all their disgust of emotion, and pride in self-reliance. He is led no longer by Davy Crocketts; he is led by cheer leaders, press agents, word-mongers, uplifters.

Perhaps the most revolting character that the United States ever produced was the Christian business man.

I simply can't imagine competence as anything save admirable, for it is very rare in this world, and especially in this great Republic, and those who have it in some measure, in any art or craft from adultery to zoology, are the only human beings I can think of who will be worth the oil it will take to fry them in Hell.

The only way to success in American public life lies in flattering and kow-towing to the mob.

Congress consists of one-third, more or less, scoundrels; two-thirds, more or less, idiots; and three-thirds, more or less, poltroons.

Democracy is the art of running the circus from the monkey cage.

This place [Hollywood] is the true and original arse-hole of creation. The movie dogs, compared with the rest of the population, actually seem like an ancient Italian noblesse.

Democracy is the theory that the common people know what they want, and deserve to get it good and hard.

Democracy is grounded upon so childish a complex of fallacies that they must be protected by a rigid system of taboos, else even halfwits would argue it to pieces. Its first concern must thus be to penalize the free play of ideas.

In this world of sin and sorrow there is always something to be thankful for; as for me, I rejoice that I am not a Republican.

The California climate makes the sick well and the well sick, the old young and the young old.

In southern California the vegetables have no flavor and the flowers have no smell.

Los Angeles seems an inconceivably shoddy place…a pasture foreordained for the cow-town evangelism of a former sideshow wriggler.

[Los Angeles:] Nineteen suburbs in search of a metropolis.

Maine is as dead, intellectually, as Abyssinia. Nothing is ever heard from it.

The New England shopkeepers and theologians never really developed a civilization; all they ever developed was a government. They were, at their best, tawdry and tacky fellows, oafish in manner and devoid of imagination.

New York: A third-rate Babylon.

The trouble with New York is that it has no nationality at all. It is simply a sort of free port—a place where the raw materials of civilization are received, sorted out, and sent further on.

For all its size and all its wealth and all the "progress" it babbles of, it [the South] is almost as sterile, artistically, intellectually, culturally, as the Sahara Desert.

[Texas is] the place where there are the most cows and the least milk and the most rivers and the least water in them, and where you can look the farthest and see the least.

MENCKEN ON MARRIAGE

Marriage is a wonderful institution. But who would want to live in an institution?

The only really happy folk are married women and single men.

[Marriage is] far and away the most sanitary and least harmful of all the impossible forms of the man-woman relationship, though I would sooner jump off the Brooklyn Bridge than be married.

A woman usually respects her father, but her view of her husband is mingled with contempt, for she is of course privy to the transparent devices by which she snared him.

Husbands never become good; they merely become proficient.

No married man is genuinely happy if he has to drink worse whiskey than he used to drink when he was single.

One of the aims of connubial bliss is to punish both parties.

A man may be a fool and not know it—but not if he is married.

That I have escaped [marriage]…is not my fault, nor is it to my credit; it is due to a mere act of God. I am no more responsible for it than I am for my remarkable talent as a pianist, my linguistic skills, or my dark, romantic, somewhat voluptuous beauty.

If I ever marry, it will be on a sudden impulse—as a man shoots himself. Whenever a husband and wife begin to discuss their marriage, they are giving evidence at an inquest.

Getting married, like getting hanged, is a great deal less dreadful than it has been made out.

If I had to live my life over again, I don't think I'd change it in any particular of the slightest consequence. I'd choose the same parents, the same birthplace…the same wife.

It's a grand experience to be able to look a hotel detective in the eye.

QUOTES ON "B"

―――――――――――――――――― **BABIES** ――――――――――――――――――

One cannot love lumps of flesh, and little infants are nothing more.
SAMUEL JOHNSON

A soiled baby, with a neglected nose, cannot be conscientiously regarded as a thing of beauty. MARK TWAIN

I find that the most successful approach to the subject of babies is to discuss them as though they were hams; the firmness of the flesh, the pinkness of the flesh, the even distribution of fat, the sweetness and tenderness of the whole, and the placing of bone are the things to praise. SAMUEL MARCHBANKS

An ugly baby is a very nasty object, and the prettiest is frightful when undressed.
QUEEN VICTORIA

If you were to open up a baby's head—and I am not for a moment suggesting that you should—you would find nothing but an enormous drool gland.
DAVE BARRY

―――――――――――――――――― **BABY BOOMERS** ――――――――――――――――――

I'm trying very hard to understand this generation. They have adjusted the timetable for childbearing so that menopause and teaching a sixteen-year-old how to drive a car will occur in the same week. ERMA BOMBECK

BACHELORS

Rich bachelors should be heavily taxed. It is not fair that some men should be happier than others.
OSCAR WILDE

BAGPIPES

I understand the inventor of the bagpipes was inspired when he saw a man carrying an indignant, asthmatic pig under his arm. Unfortunately, the man-made sound never equalled the purity of the sound achieved by the pig.
ALFRED HITCHCOCK

BALLET

I don't understand anything about the ballet; all I know is that during the intervals the ballerinas stink like horses.
ANTON CHEKHOV

Ballet is the fairies' baseball.
OSCAR LEVANT

BANKS

A bank is a place where they lend you an umbrella in fair weather and ask for it back when it begins to rain.
ROBERT FROST

Except for con men borrowing money they shouldn't get and the widows who have to visit with the handsome young men in the trust department, no sane person ever enjoyed visiting a bank.
MARTIN MAYER

Banking establishments are more dangerous than standing armies.
THOMAS JEFFERSON

I don't have a bank account, because I don't know my mother's maiden name.
PAULA POUNDSTONE

BASEBALL

Baseball has the great advantage over cricket of being sooner ended.

GEORGE BERNARD SHAW

BEAUTY

I'm tired of all this nonsense about beauty being only skin-deep. That's deep enough. What do you want, an adorable pancreas?   JEAN KERR

BEES

Did you know the male bee is nothing but the slave of the queen? And once the male bee has—how should I say—serviced the queen, the male dies. All in all, not a bad system.   CLORIS LEACHMAN, on
The Mary Tyler Moore Show

BEGGARS

Beggars should be abolished. It annoys one to give to them, and it annoys one not to give to them.   FRIEDRICH WILHELM NIETZSCHE

BELIEF

The most costly of all follies is to believe passionately in the palpably not true. It is the chief occupation of mankind.   H. L. MENCKEN

If there were a verb meaning "to believe falsely," it would not have any significant first person, present indicative.   LUDWIG WITTGENSTEIN

BEST-SELLER

A best-seller is the gilded tomb of a mediocre talent.

LOGAN PEARSALL SMITH

BETTING

It may be that the race is not always to the swift, nor the battle to the strong—but that is the way to bet.   DAMON RUNYON

BEVERLY HILLS

If you stay in Beverly Hills too long you become a Mercedes.

ROBERT REDFORD

BIBLE

"The Good Book"—one of the most remarkable euphemisms ever coined.

ASHLEY MONTAGU

It ain't those parts of the Bible that I can't understand that bother me, it's the parts that I do understand.   MARK TWAIN

The Bible tells us to love our neighbors, and also to love our enemies; probably because they are generally the same people.   G. K. CHESTERTON

So far as I can remember, there is not one word in the Gospels in praise of intelligence.   BERTRAND RUSSELL

Scriptures, *n.* The sacred books of our holy religion, as distinguished from the false and profane writings on which all other faiths are based.

AMBROSE BIERCE

The only people who take the Bible literally are atheists and fundamentalists.

ANDY KINDLER

The inspiration of the Bible depends on the ignorance of the gentleman who reads it.   ROBERT G. INGERSOLL

BICYCLISTS

The people I see on bicycles look like organic-gardening zealots who advocate federal regulation of bedtime and want American foreign policy to be dictated by UNICEF. These people should be confined.   P. J. O'ROURKE

BIGAMY

Bigamy is having one wife too many. Monogamy is the same.   OSCAR WILDE

BILLS

It is only by not paying one's bills that one can hope to live in the memory of the commercial classes.   OSCAR WILDE

BIPARTISANSHIP

Bipartisanship: A Republican stands up and says, "I got a really bad idea!" and then a Democrat stands up and says, "And *I* can make it *shittier*!"

LEWIS BLACK

BIRD-WATCHING

I am the kind of man who would never notice an oriole building a nest unless it came and built it in my hat in the hat room of the club.

STEPHEN LEACOCK

BIRTH

Birth, *n*. The first and direst of all disasters.   AMBROSE BIERCE

Being born is like being kidnapped. And then sold into slavery.

ANDY WARHOL

No one recovers from the disease of being born, a deadly wound if there ever was one.   E. M. CIORAN

BLASPHEMY

Blasphemer's Prayer:
All I ask of Thee, Lord
Is to be a drinker and a fornicator
An unbeliever and a sodomite
And then to die.

CLAUDE DE CHAUVIGNY

BLESSINGS

What a blessing it would be if we could open and shut our ears as easily as we open and shut our eyes! G. C. LICHTENBERG

BLONDES

That gentlemen prefer blondes is due to the fact that, apparently, pale hair, delicate skin and an infantile expression represent the very apex of frailty which every man longs to violate. ALEXANDER KING

BLOODSHED

I must apologize for the lack of bloodshed in tonight's program. We shall try to do better next time. ALFRED HITCHCOCK

BOOKS

Books are fatal: they are the curse of the human race. Nine-tenths of existing books are nonsense, and the clever books are the refutation of that nonsense. The greatest misfortune that ever befell man was the invention of printing.

BENJAMIN DISRAELI

Books for general reading always smell badly. The odor of common people hangs about them. FRIEDRICH WILHELM NIETZSCHE

The multitude of books is making us ignorant.   VOLTAIRE

You ever read a book that changed your life? Me neither.   JIM GAFFIGAN

I think it is good that books still exist, but they do make me sleepy.
                                                            FRANK ZAPPA

The age of the book is almost gone.   GEORGE STEINER

I have given up reading books; I find it takes my mind off myself.
                                                            OSCAR LEVANT

BORE

Bore, *n.* A person who talks when you wish him to listen. AMBROSE BIERCE

Bore: a man who is never unintentionally rude.   OSCAR WILDE

He is not only dull himself, he is the cause of dullness in others.
                                                        SAMUEL JOHNSON

Bores bore each other too, but it never seems to teach them anything.
                                                            DON MARQUIS

We often forgive those who bore us, but we cannot forgive those whom
we bore.   FRANÇOIS DE LA ROCHEFOUCAULD

A bore is a fellow talking who can change the subject back to his topic of
conversation faster than you can change it back to yours.
                                                        LAURENCE J. PETER

Every improvement in communication makes the bore more terrible.
FRANK MOORE COLBY

It's so much easier to pray for a bore than to go and see one.   C. S. LEWIS

A healthy male adult bore consumes each year one and a half times his own weight in other people's patience.   JOHN UPDIKE

You must be careful about giving any drink whatsoever to a bore. A lit-up bore is the worst in the world.   DAVID CECIL

—————————— BORN-AGAIN CHRISTIANS ——————————
The trouble with born-again Christians is that they are an even bigger pain the second time around.   HERB CAEN

He's a born-again Christian. The trouble is, he suffered brain damage during rebirth.   ANONYMOUS

—————————————————— BOSTON ——————————————————
When I go abroad I always sail from Boston because it is such a pleasant place to get away from.   OLIVER HERFORD

The last person to get across that town in under three hours was yelling, "The British are coming! The British are coming!"   LEWIS BLACK

I have just returned from Boston. It is the only thing to do if you find yourself up there.   FRED ALLEN

BOTTLED WATER

How did we get to the point where we're paying for bottled water? That must have been some weird marketing meeting over in France. Some French guy's sitting there, like "How dumb do *I* think the Americans are? I bet you we could sell those idiots water." "Look, Pierre, the Americans are pretty dumb, but they're not going to buy water." "Oh yes they are! Let's just tell the Americans the water's from France."   JIM GAFFIGAN

BOURGEOIS

To have a horror of the bourgeois is bourgeois.   JULES RENARD

BOYS

The fact that boys are allowed to exist at all is evidence of a remarkable Christian forbearance among men.   AMBROSE BIERCE

Boys are capital fellows in their own way, among their mates; but they are unwholesome companions for grown people.   CHARLES LAMB

BRAN

You do live longer with bran, but you spend the last fifteen years on the toilet.   ALAN KING

BREAKFAST

Only dull people are brilliant at breakfast.   OSCAR WILDE

My wife and I tried two or three times in the last forty years to have breakfast together, but it was so disagreeable we had to stop.   WINSTON CHURCHILL

BREVITY

Brevity is the soul of lingerie.   DOROTHY PARKER

BRIDE

Brides aren't happy—they are just triumphant.   JOHN BARRYMORE

Hollywood brides keep the bouquets and throw away the grooms.
                                                    GROUCHO MARX

Bride, *n.* A woman with a fine prospect of happiness behind her.
                                                    AMBROSE BIERCE

BROADWAY

What a glorious garden of wonders the lights of Broadway would be to anyone lucky enough to be unable to read.   G. K. CHESTERTON

BROTHERHOOD

The brotherhood of man is not a mere poet's dream: it is a most depressing
and humiliating reality.   OSCAR WILDE

It's silly to go on pretending that under the skin we are all brothers. The
truth is more likely that under the skin we are all cannibals, assassins, trai-
tors, liars, hypocrites, poltroons.   HENRY MILLER

BUG SPRAY

There is no record of one single bug dying from a household bug spray.
Most sprays will cause a bug to lie quietly for about forty-five seconds,
after which the bug will spring up feeling renewed, refreshed, chemically

mutated, and therefore able to fly at supersonic speeds and inject previously unknown poisons into the person who sprayed it.

COLIN MCENROE

——————————— BUREAUCRACY ———————————

Bureaucracy is a giant mechanism operated by pygmies.

HONORÉ DE BALZAC

Bureaucracy defends the status quo long past the time when the quo has lost its status.   LAURENCE J. PETER

In a bureaucratic system, useless work drives out useful work.

MILTON FRIEDMAN

There is no passion like that of a functionary for his function.

GEORGES CLEMENCEAU

If you are going to sin, sin against God, not the bureaucracy. God will forgive you but the bureaucracy won't.   HYMAN RICKOVER

Guidelines for Bureaucrats:
1. When in charge, ponder.
2. When in trouble, delegate.
3. When in doubt, mumble.

JAMES H. BOREN

A bureaucrat is a Democrat who holds some office that a Republican wants.

ALBEN W. BARKLEY

Bureaucrats write memoranda both because they appear to be busy when they are writing and because the memos, once written, immediately become proof that they were busy.   CHARLES PETERS

The perfect bureaucrat everywhere is the man who manages to make no decisions and escape all responsibility.   BROOKS ATKINSON

The only thing that saves us from the bureaucracy is inefficiency. An efficient bureaucracy is the greatest threat to liberty.   EUGENE MCCARTHY

Hell hath no fury like a bureaucrat scorned.   MILTON FRIEDMAN

BUSINESSMEN

I find it rather easy to portray a businessman. Being bland, rather cruel and incompetent comes naturally to me.   JOHN CLEESE

The human being who would not harm you on an individual, face-to-face basis, who is charitable, civic-minded, loving and devout, will wound or kill you from behind the corporate veil.   MORTON MINTZ

JOHN SIMON

The Vicar of Vitriol Loves Animals

John Simon is one of America's foremost critics of the arts. He is the drama critic for *New York* magazine, the film critic for the *National Review,* and the author of numerous books of criticism. He has written extensively on the uses and abuses of the English language, most conspicuously in the best-selling *Paradigms Lost.* He was born in Subotica, Yugoslavia, in 1925. He immigrated to the United States in 1941 and served with the U.S. Army Air Corps during World War II. He was a Fulbright fellow at the University of Paris in 1949 and received a PhD from Harvard in 1959. He taught at MIT and Bard College before joining the *Hudson Review* as its drama critic in

1960. He's been the drama and cultural critic for *The New Leader*, drama critic for *Commonweal*, and drama and language critic for Esquire.

JW: When you walked in, you complained about not receiving any hate mail. Do you really like it?

JS: So much mail that one gets tends to be silly, so one would rather be attacked in it than praised. Which is not to say that it isn't pleasurable to receive a well-written, well-thought-out letter that praises one. But when you get a totally illiterate letter, it might as well be a hate letter so you can at least get a laugh out of it.

JW: Do you consider yourself a curmudgeon?

JS: No, only because it's a funny word. Nobody even knows exactly where it comes from. If you check into its etymology, it may come from an old Scottish word which means something like "murmur," or "mumble," or "grumble." There's a popular etymology which says it comes from *cœur méchant*, but there's no scientific basis for that. Anyway, it's not a word that I would apply to myself because why should I laugh at myself? Let others say it if they wish. If you said misanthrope, I would say—well, yes—but then look at humanity. And what other word might you use? If you were to say *elitist*, it might be accurate, because in this society to be an elitist is almost automatically to be a curmudgeon.

JW: A cynic?

JS: Well, again, a cynic is more like a curmudgeon or a misanthrope—not something that one instinctually is, not something that one wants to be, but something that circumstances force one into. I would distinguish between people who are by temperament that way and people who have been soured into becoming that way, though the end result may be similar.

JW: Where do you place yourself in those terms?

JS: I did not have curmudgeonliness thrust upon me, but if I have it, it evolved gradually as a response to having to see so many bad plays and movies, and review so many bad books. It's not something that I profess with pride or joy; it's just an attitude that becomes less and less resistible under the circumstances.

In my case it is almost always said that I'm a curmudgeon because of my reviews, and to me that is particularly nonsensical because criticism is not meant to be the Red Cross or the Salvation Army. To me, it is proof of the uncultivatedness of this society that it boggles at severe criticism. The trouble is, the society is geared to blandness. Blandness is a curse, as I see it. It's shapeless, it's savorless, it's mindless, it's gutless.

JW: I'd like to run down a list of subjects, things that have bothered curmudgeons. Children, for example.

JS: Babies on airplanes that howl all through the flight, I certainly do not approve of. There should be special baby compartments. I think they should put the cigarette smokers and babies together and see who drives the other crazy quicker.

JW: Do you have anything against hunting?

JS: I don't like it. I love animals. I suppose you can't outlaw it, and I suppose there are certain species that need decimation now and again, but when some very beautiful creatures are killed for their fur or their plumage, or just for the alleged glory of it, I think it's disgusting.

JW: How do you react to religious fundamentalists?

JS: They're good people to debate [with] on television or radio, but that's the only use I have for them. As for born-again Christians, it seems to me that on the whole, one birth per person is enough, and for some even that may be too much.

JW: You've written extensively on the state of the language. I even remember seeing you debate [with] a woman about it on television…

JS: Geneva Smitherman, or "Smitherperson," as I like to call her. Her stock has not only fallen, it has disappeared. That was about ten years ago.

JW: Has the language deteriorated since then?

JS: You don't have to wait ten years—ten seconds is enough. Every day in the *Times*, which is supposed to be our best newspaper, you find more errors, and grosser errors, and that's a telling index to what's going on everywhere. The talk I hear among civilized people, which used to be fairly grammatical until about twelve or fifteen years ago, has now gone completely to pot.

JW: Do you think there's any relationship between this trend and what George Orwell warned about in "Politics and the English Language" or what Karl Kraus railed against: a conspiracy of journalism, government, and industry to erode our linguistic sensibilities in order to control us?

JS (laughs): I must say that the things Karl Kraus was railing against were much better than the things being held up as examples of good usage today. But yes, I imagine, *grosso modo*, that these are all parts of the same ongoing process of deterioration. The worst part of it is that there are all these pseudophilosophical and political justifications for the deterioration. Now if terrible grammar is used, it's justified by liberal or leftist politics: it's everybody's political right to speak as abominably as he or she wishes. There's an organized pull toward undermining the language, whether it's by feminists, homosexuals, or some ethnic minority whose attempts to undermine English are considered their God-given or state-given right. I'm not for conformity for its own sake; I'm for using language imaginatively, but imaginatively does not mean incorrectly. In fact, it's very easy to be imaginative if you are incorrect: If you tie your necktie around your knee instead of around your neck, you are imaginative, but you are imaginative in an imbecile way. It's true anywhere: A director like Peter Sellars takes a play and makes hash out of it. If people are supposed to walk somewhere because it's part of the play, he puts them in a helicopter; if someone is supposed to lie down in a bed, he has him float off in some kind of contraption just to be different. That is not imaginativeness, that is junk.

JW: Is that how we arrive at "dinner theater"?

JS: Dinner theater is reducing art to a commodity in the worst way. It's, by definition, junk. You won't see *Macbeth* at a dinner theater. Dinner theater is anticulture. Start people on the idea that theater is something you can eat at, and next thing you're at a play and someone is shaking the ice in a cup of Coca-Cola all through the performance and you can't hear. Who wants to be surrounded by food containers in a theater?

JW: People seem to be talking more in the theater.

JS: Yes, and it's generally ascribed to the influence of television. You watch it in your living room where you throw beer cans around and make funny remarks and go to the toilet and flush it noisily while the show is on. God knows television has something bad to do with almost everything, so why not that? But I think it's worse than that; I think it's a falling off in manners. Manners are one of the truly lost causes.

JW: What's the cause of this deterioration of manners?

JS: Bad manners are socially inevitable because as the lower orders become more affluent, which God knows no one begrudges them, they come into situations in which they don't know how to behave. Nothing in their training has prepared them for it.

JW: Is it a case of diminishing attention spans?

JS: Yes, yes. More and more ways are being devised to make concentration a thing of the past. Concentration becomes more and more like an appendix or a tail, useless organs we lost long ago. The way painters paint today, you don't have to know anything about painting. Once you admit Jackson Pollock to the ranks of great painters, anybody can paint; once junk can be sculpture, anybody can be a sculptor. The difficulty is being taken out of everything and as a result the riffraff take over.

JW: Would "performance art" be an extreme example of this?

JS: Performance art is nonsense. It's something that anybody without any training, any culture, or any genius can do. If it's bizarre enough, it works. If it's bizarre, it's art. We're back to the necktie around the knee.

JW: What about punk rock?

JS: It's disgusting, it's revolting, it's sheer aggressive sickness, but I don't waste my time fulminating against it because what's the use? What bothers me more than punk rock is supposedly "intellectual rock." When people start telling me that Talking Heads is something very special or when some reputable critic tells me that Dylan is a great poet, that's when my dander is up, because I think it's all junk.

JW: How have you adjusted to your own visibility, your own celebrity? Do you enjoy being recognized?

JS: I'm often recognized but not by the right people. An ex-girlfriend of mine said, "Have you noticed that the people who come up to you in public places and gush about your work are almost always creeps?"

JW: Does Christmas annoy you?

JS: Yes, Christmas is a problem. If it were confined to just a few days, okay, but Christmas keeps moving sinisterly forward, or backward, depending from which angle you're looking at it, so that when they start in July with Christmas shopping, or Christmas planning, or Christmas this and that, it's nauseating.

JW: The family has been a perennial target for curmudgeons.

JS: Yes, one ought to be able to choose those that one is close to. If I like you, I want you as my friend; if I don't like you, I don't want you as my friend—it's that simple. In a family, of course, you don't have that choice, and yet you're forced into closeness with people. It's a curse. If you have an enormous nose, I suppose you can have an operation to make it smaller, but you can't operate away an undesirable family member.

JW: You've talked a lot about your dislike of smoking.

JS: Smoking, I find a disgusting habit. If it were just deleterious for the people who do it, I'd say fine, let them kill themselves, but unfortunately it bothers me and affects my health. And it produces a disgusting smell and creates dirt and burns holes in things, good things; it starts fires in hotels. I find it an absolutely beastly habit.

JW: Are you encouraged by the trend toward banning smoking in public places?
JS: Smoking should be forbidden in all public places, and people should be allowed to say, "I'm giving a small dinner party but I am allergic to smoke, so if you can't live without smoking, don't come."

JW: Do you attend many literary parties?
JS: The problem is, we don't have enough literature to justify all the parties given in its name. Anyway, I don't get invited to many, which may or may not have something to do with my curmudgeonliness. But that's fine because I prefer nonliterary parties as long as they're not illiterate.

JW: Do you really hate actors?
JS: There are good actors and bad actors, and, needless to say, I prefer the good ones; but socially speaking, with the exception of a few Europeans and a very few Americans, actors are basically an uncultured, uncivilized, pretentious lot.

JW: Does that include Ronald Reagan?
JS: Well, you could say that his acting wasn't very serious and that he could just as easily have become a sports announcer; he was not an actor in the sense that Marlon Brando is an actor (or was an actor). Still, acting is not a profession from which I would want my governments to originate.

JW: How do you feel about Teddy Kennedy?
JS: I don't like people who use up good-looking young women in such a way that they end up at the bottom of rivers or lakes. Nor do I particularly care for people who cheat on their exams at Harvard. Nor do I particularly like obesity, and he's gotten very obese. Other than that, I have no special feeling about him one way or the other.

JW: You don't have to be a curmudgeon to dislike lawyers. What's your opinion of them?

JS: There's nothing implicit in being a lawyer that means you have to be boring or repulsive or brash. Certainly, when a man like Alan Dershowitz comes along, it makes you want to go out and stone a few lawyers, preferably him, but there aren't that many Dershowitzes, thank God. I've known some perfectly nice lawyers and some not-so-nice ones. Women lawyers are a separate problem. There's something about the law that makes women unfeminine, and despite what the feminists and homosexuals say, a woman should be feminine and a man should be masculine.

JW: Do you agree with feminists that pornography exploits women?

JS: Pornography serves a perfectly legitimate use: it's trashily enjoyable, essentially harmless, and a safety valve. Of course, there's good pornography and bad pornography—but to go out and militate against it in some passionate, fanatical way I find misguided. It's a legitimate outlet for otherwise frustrated sexuality, and if somebody reads a pornographic magazine or novel or sees a pornographic movie, I don't see any harm in it, generally speaking. Whereas I do see harm in all these self-righteous people crusading for this worthy cause because it supposedly exploits women: They end up being censors. If they're so concerned about it, women should write bigger and better pornography of their own and start exploiting men. Of course, it's another thing when it involves or reaches children; I'm not in favor of exposing any unformed mind to it. And I personally wish, even where consenting adults are involved, that it would not involve bloodletting. Pornography, like anything else, may occasionally have harmful effects. Occasionally a sexual crime may have some connection with pornography, but for all attempts to do so, this has never been conclusively demonstrated. Anything can be harmful if it falls into the wrong hands. A baseball bat is not in itself a bad thing, but it can be used as a weapon in the commission of a crime. Are we then to ban baseball? I think not.

PARAMOURS LOST: JOHN SIMON ON ASSORTED ACTRESSES

LINDA BLAIR, not a very talented or prepossessing youngster then, is even less interesting now, though considerably more bovine; I doubt whether a postpubertal acting style can be made out of mere chubbiness.

DYAN CANNON, as Julie [in *Such Good Friends*], exudes a stupidity that strikes me uncomfortably as the actress's own contribution to the part; her one true talent is for bitchiness, a rather lowly gift.

DORIS DAY: The only…talent Miss Day possesses is that of being absolutely sanitary: her personality untouched by human emotions, her brow unclouded by human thought, her form unsmudged by the slightest evidence of femininity.

SANDY DENNIS: Pauline Kael has aptly observed that Miss Dennis "has made an acting style out of postnasal drip." It should be added that she balanced her postnasal condition with something like prefrontal lobotomy, so that when she is not a walking catarrh she is a blithering imbecile.

SHELLY DUVALL is the worst and homeliest thing to hit the movies since Liza Minnelli.

JUDY GARLAND: Her figure resembles the giant economy-size tube of tooth-paste in girls' bathrooms: squeezed intemperately at all points, it acquires a shape that defies definition by the most resourceful solid geometrician.

KATHARINE HEPBURN: When you think of the great Marguerite Moreno, who created the role [of Aurelia in *The Madwoman of Chaillot*], and then look at this performance, exact replicas of which have already earned Miss Hepburn two ill-deserved Oscars, you may wish to forsake the auditorium for the vomitorium.

CAROL KANE: You have to have a stomach for ugliness to endure Carol Kane—to say nothing of the zombielike expressions she mistakes for acting.

ANGELA LANSBURY: God only knows where the notion that Miss Lans-bury has class originated; perhaps her vestigial lower-middle-class English accent passes for that in our informed show-biz circles. She is, in fact, com-mon; and her mugging, rattling-off or steam-rollering across her lines, and camping around merely make her into that most degraded thing an *outré* actress can decline into: a fag hag.

DIANE KEATON…is yet another of those non-actresses this country pro-duces in such abundance—women who trade on the raw materials of their neuroses, which has nothing to do with acting.

Her work, if that is the word for it, always consists chiefly of a dithering, blithering, neurotic coming apart at the seams—an acting style that is real-ly a nervous breakdown in slow-motion.

ALI MACGRAW: Miss MacGraw cannot act at all. At the screening [of *The Getaway*] I attended, people were laughing out loud at her delivery of lines—rather like a grade-school pupil asking to be excused to go to the bathroom.

MELINA MERCOURI: As for Miss Mercouri, her blackly mascaraed eye-sockets gape like twin craters, unfortunately extinct.

LIZA MINNELLI: That turnipy nose overhanging a forward-gaping mouth and hastily retreating chin, that bulbous cranium with eyes as big (and as inexpressive) as saucers; those are the appurtenances of a clown—a funny clown, not even a sad one…Miss Minnelli has only two things going for her: a father and a mother who got there in the first place, and tasteless reviewers and audiences who keep her there.

CHARLOTTE RAMPLING [is] a poor actress who mistakes creepiness for sensuality.

DIANA RIGG is built like a brick mausoleum with insufficient flying buttresses.

CYBILL SHEPHERD: If it weren't for an asinine superciliousness radiating from her, Miss Shepherd would actually be pitiable, rather like a kid from an orphanage trying to play Noel Coward. In fact, she comes across like one of those inanimate objects, say, a cupboard or a grandfather clock, which is made in certain humorous shorts to act, through trick photography, like people.

BARBRA STREISAND: Miss Streisand looks like a cross between an aardvark and an albino rat surmounted by a platinum-coated horse bun. Though she has good eyes and a nice complexion, the rest of her is a veritable anthology of disaster areas. Her speaking voice seems to have graduated from the Brooklyn Conservatory of Yentaism, and her acting consists entirely of fishily thrusting out her lips, sounding like a cabbie bellyaching at breakneck speed, and throwing her weight around.

ELIZABETH TAYLOR: Miss Taylor…has grown so ample that it has become necessary to dress her almost exclusively in a variety of ambulatory tents. On the few occasions when she does reveal her bosom (or part thereof) [in *The Sandpiper*], one breast (or part thereof) proves sufficient to traverse an entire wide-screen frame—diagonally.

BRENDA VACCARO: With the exception of Sandy Dennis, there is no more irritatingly unfeminine actress around these days than Miss Vaccaro, a cube-shaped creature who comes across as a dykey Kewpie doll.

QUOTES ON "C"

CAB DRIVERS

Cab drivers are living proof that practice does not make perfect.

HOWARD OGDEN

CALAMITIES

Calamities are of two kinds: misfortunes to ourselves, and good fortune to others.

AMBROSE BIERCE

CALENDARS

Most modern calendars mar the sweet simplicity of our lives by reminding us that each day that passes is the anniversary of some perfectly uninteresting event.

OSCAR WILDE

CALIFORNIA

California reminds me of the popular American Protestant concept of Heaven: there is always a reasonable flow of new arrivals; one meets many—not all—of one's friends; people spend a good deal of their time congratulating one another about the fact that they are there; discontent would be unthinkable; and the newcomer is slightly disconcerted to realize that now, the devil having been banished and virtue being triumphant, nothing terribly interesting can ever happen again.

GEORGE F. KENNAN

California is a place in which a boom mentality and a sense of Chekhovian loss meet in uneasy suspension.   JOAN DIDION

In California everyone goes to a therapist, is a therapist, or is a therapist going to a therapist.   TRUMAN CAPOTE

California, the department store state.   RAYMOND CHANDLER

California: The west coast of Iowa.   JOAN DIDION

The Screwy State.   ROBERT GRAVES

Most people in California came from somewhere else. They moved to California so they could name their kids Rainbow or Mailbox, and purchase tubular Swedish furniture without getting laughed at. It's a tenet also in California that the fiber of your clothing is equivalent to your moral fiber. Your "lifestyle" (as they say) is your ethic. This means that in California you don't really have to do anything, except look healthy, think good thoughts and pat yourself on the back about what a good person you are. And waiters in California want to be called by their first name. I don't know why.   IAN SHOALES

It's a scientific fact that if you stay in California you lose one point of your IQ every year.   TRUMAN CAPOTE

Living in California adds ten years to a man's life. And those extra ten years I'd like to spend in New York.   HARRY RUBY

California is like summer or the Christmas holidays. The unhappy children think that they are supposed to be having a good time, and they imagine that everybody else is having a better time. Thus the pervasive mood of envy and the feeling, common especially among celebrities, that somehow they have been excluded from something, that their names have been left off the guest list.   LEWIS H. LAPHAM

It is the land of perpetual pubescence, where cultural lag is mistaken for renaissance.   ASHLEY MONTAGU

California is a tragic country—like Palestine, like every Promised Land.
                                            CHRISTOPHER ISHERWOOD

A wet dream in the mind of New York.   ERICA JONG

Californians invented the concept of lifestyle. This alone warrants their doom.
                                            DON DELILLO

CALMNESS

Nothing is so aggravating as calmness.   OSCAR WILDE

CAMPING

Camping is nature's way of promoting the motel business.   DAVE BARRY

CANADA

Canada is a country whose main exports are hockey players and cold fronts. Our main imports are baseball players and acid rain.
                                            PIERRE TRUDEAU

Canada is a country so square that even the female impersonators are women.
                                            RICHARD BENNER

Very little is known of the Canadian country since it is rarely visited by anyone but the Queen and illiterate sport fishermen.   P. J. O'ROURKE

Canada has never been a melting pot; more like a tossed salad.
                                                    ARNOLD EDINBOROUGH

In any world menu, Canada must be considered the vichyssoise of nations—it's cold, half French, and difficult to stir.   STUART KEATE

Canada is useful only to provide me with furs.   MADAME DE POMPADOUR

Canada is the only country in the world that knows how to live without an identity.   MARSHALL MCLUHAN

For some reason, a glaze passes over people's faces when you say Canada.
                                                    SONDRA GOTLIEB

A few acres of snow.   VOLTAIRE

CANADIANS

When I was there I found their jokes like their roads—very long and not very good, leading to a little tin point of a spire which has been remorselessly obvious for miles without seeming to get any nearer.
                                                    SAMUEL BUTLER

CANCER

My father died of cancer when I was a teenager. He had it before it became popular.   GOODMAN ACE

—————————— CANDY CORN ——————————

Candy corn is the only candy in the history of America that's never been advertised. And there's a reason. All of the candy corn that was ever made was made in 1911.   LEWIS BLACK

—————————— CAPITAL ——————————

Capital, *n.* The seat of misgovernment.   AMBROSE BIERCE

—————————— CAPITALISM ——————————

Capitalism is a condition both of the world and of the soul. FRANZ KAFKA

—————————— CAPITAL PUNISHMENT ——————————

There is no satisfaction in hanging a man who does not object to it.
                                              GEORGE BERNARD SHAW

The big thieves hang the little ones.   CZECH PROVERB

When I came back to Dublin I was court-martialed in my absence and sentenced to death in my absence, so I said they could shoot me in my absence.
                                                    BRENDAN BEHAN

—————————— CARS ——————————

Is fuel efficiency really what we need most desperately? I say what we really need is a car that can be shot when it breaks down.   RUSSELL BAKER

—————————— CAR ALARMS ——————————

They erupt like indignant metal jungle birds, and they whoop all night. They make American cities sound like lunatic rain forests, all the wildlife affrighted, violated, outraged, shrieking….In a neighborhood of apartment buildings, one such beast rouses sleepers by the hundreds, even thousands. They wake, roll over, moan, jam pillows on their ears and try to suppress the adrenaline. Car thieves, however, pay no attention to the noise.

LANCE MORROW

CAREER

My career is a fascist state. I'm the dictator, the chief of police, the head of the army. Anybody who tries to interfere is put up against the wall and shot.

MICHAEL CAINE

CATS

They smell and they snarl and they scratch; they have a singular aptitude for shredding rugs, drapes and upholstery; they're sneaky, selfish and not particularly smart; they are disloyal, condescending and totally useless in any rodent-free environment.　　JEAN-MICHEL CHAPEREAU

The cat is the only non-gregarious domestic animal.　　FRANCIS GALTON

Cat, *n.* A soft, indestructible automaton provided by nature to be kicked when things go wrong in the domestic circle.　　AMBROSE BIERCE

Curiosity killed the cat, but for a while I was a suspect.　　STEVEN WRIGHT

I can see stopping a car for a dog. But a cat? You squish a cat and go on.

JAMES GALLAGHER

Cats have nine lives. Makes them ideal for experimentation.　　JIMMY CARR

The trouble with a kitten is THAT
Eventually it becomes a CAT

OGDEN NASH

Cats seem to go on the principle that it never does any harm to ask for what you want. JOSEPH WOOD KRUTCH

I am not a cat man, but a dog man, and all felines can tell this at a glance—a sharp, vindictive glance. JAMES THURBER

The only good cat is a stir-fried cat. "ALF"

CELEBRITY

A celebrity is a person who works hard all his life to become well known, then wears dark glasses to avoid being recognized. FRED ALLEN

You can't shame or humiliate modern celebrities. What used to be called shame and humiliation is now called publicity. And forget traditional character assassination. If you say a modern celebrity is an adulterer, a pervert, and a drug addict, all it means is that you've read his autobiography. P. J. O'ROURKE

The nice thing about being a celebrity is that when you bore people, they think it's their fault. HENRY KISSINGER

A celebrity is one who is known to many persons he is glad he doesn't know. H. L. MENCKEN

When everyone is somebody, then no one's anybody. W. S. GILBERT

A sign of celebrity is that his name is often worth more than his services.
DANIEL J. BOORSTIN

CHARM

All charming people, I fancy, are spoiled. It is the secret of their attraction.
OSCAR WILDE

CHASTITY

Chastity: the most unnatural of the sexual perversions.
ALDOUS HUXLEY

We may eventually come to realize that chastity is no more a virtue than malnutrition.
ALEX COMFORT

Chastity always takes its toll. In some it produces pimples; in others, sex laws.
KARL KRAUS

CHARITY

One of the serious obstacles to the improvement of our race is indiscriminate charity.
ANDREW CARNEGIE

CHEERFULNESS

Early morning cheerfulness can be extremely obnoxious.
WILLIAM FEATHER

CHEESE

Poets have been mysteriously quiet on the subject of cheese.
G. K. CHESTERTON

CHESS

Chess is a foolish expedient for making idle people believe they are doing something very clever when they are only wasting their time.

GEORGE BERNARD SHAW

As elaborate a waste of human intelligence as you can find outside an advertising agency. RAYMOND CHANDLER

Chess is seldom found above the upper-middle class: it's too hard.

PAUL FUSSELL

CHICAGO

This vicious, stinking zoo, this mean-grinning, mace-smelling boneyard of a city: an elegant rockpile of a monument to everything cruel and stupid and corrupt in the human spirit. HUNTER S. THOMPSON

CHILDHOOD

Childhood *n.* The period of human life intermediate between the idiocy of infancy and the folly of youth—two removes from the sin of manhood and three from the remorse of age. AMBROSE BIERCE

A happy childhood is poor preparation for human contacts. COLETTE

Nobody gets out of childhood alive. HARLAN ELLISON

CHILDLESSNESS

Childlessness has many obvious advantages. One is that you need not spend two hundred thousand dollars to send anyone to college, or contribute a similar sum to the retirement fund of a stranger who has decided to become a pediatrician. But the principal advantage of the nonparental life-style is that on Christmas Eve, you need not be struck dumb by the three most terrifying words that the government allows to be printed on any product: "Some assembly required."   JOHN LEO

CHILD-PROOF BOTTLE TOPS

Allen Ginsberg said he saw the best minds of his generation destroyed by madness. I have seen the best minds of my generation go at a bottle of Anacin with a ball-peen hammer.   P. J. O'ROURKE

CHILD REARING

One thing they never tell you about child raising is that for the rest of your life, at the drop of a hat, you are expected to know your child's name and how old he or she is.   ERMA BOMBECK

There was a time when we expected nothing of our children but obedience, as opposed to the present, when we expect everything of them but obedience.
ANATOLE BROYARD

Experts say you should never hit your children in anger. When is a good time? When you're feeling festive?   ROSEANNE BARR

CHILDREN

I love children, especially when they cry, for then someone takes them away.
NANCY MITFORD

Of children as of procreation—the pleasure momentary, the posture ridiculous, the expense damnable.   EVELYN WAUGH

If a child shows himself to be incorrigible, he should be decently and quietly beheaded at the age of twelve, lest he grow to maturity, marry, and perpetuate his kind. DON MARQUIS

Children should neither be seen nor heard from—ever again. W. C. FIELDS

Learning to dislike children at an early age saves a lot of expense and aggravation later in life. ROBERT BYRNE

At eight or nine, I suppose, intelligence is no more than a small spot of light on the floor of a large and murky room. H. L. MENCKEN

There are three terrible ages of childhood—1 to 10, 10 to 20, and 20 to 30. CLEVELAND AMORY

The secret of dealing successfully with a child is not to be its parent. MEL LAZARUS

Never have children, only grandchildren. GORE VIDAL

The best way to keep children at home is to make the home atmosphere pleasant—and let the air out of the tires. DOROTHY PARKER

By the time the youngest children have learned to keep the house tidy, the oldest grandchildren are on hand to tear it to pieces. CHRISTOPHER MORLEY

It would seem that something which means poverty, disorder and violence every single day should be avoided entirely, but the desire to beget children is a natural urge. PHYLLIS DILLER

I like children. If they're properly cooked.   W. C. FIELDS

Children are never too tender to be whipped. Like tough beefsteaks, the more you beat them, the more tender they become.   EDGAR ALLAN POE

Insanity is hereditary; you can get it from your children.   SAM LEVENSON

Once you have children, it forever changes the way you bore other people.   BRUCE ERIC KAPLAN

My children weary me. I can only see them as defective adults; feckless, destructive, frivolous, sensual, humorless.   EVELYN WAUGH

A son of my own! Oh, no, no, no! Let my flesh perish with me, and let me not transmit to anyone the boredom and the ignominiousness of life.   GUSTAVE FLAUBERT

Go back to reform school, you little nose-picker.   W. C. FIELDS

Contemporary American children, if they are old enough to grasp the concept of Santa Claus by Thanksgiving, are able to see through it by December 15th.   ROY BLOUNT, JR.

I take my children everywhere, but they always find their way back home.   ROBERT ORBEN

When childhood dies, its corpses are called adults and they enter society, one of the politer names of hell. That is why we dread children, even if we love them. They show us the state of our decay.   BRIAN ALDISS

A child is a curly, dimpled lunatic.　　　　RALPH WALDO EMERSON

What is more enchanting than the voices of young people when you can't hear what they say?　　　　LOGAN PEARSALL SMITH

Children make the most desirable opponents in Scrabble as they are both easy to beat and fun to cheat.　　　　FRAN LEBOWITZ

We are given children to test us and make us more spiritual.
　　　　GEORGE F. WILL

Children are given to us to discourage our better emotions.　　SAKI

My unhealthy affection for my second daughter has waned. Now I despise all my seven children equally.　　　　EVELYN WAUGH

It is almost nicer being a godfather than a father, like having white mice but making your nanny feed them for you.　　　　T. H. WHITE

Human beings are the only creatures that allow their children to come back home.　　　　BILL COSBY

Humans are the only animals that have children on purpose with the exception of guppies, who like to eat theirs.　　　　P. J. O'ROURKE

I don't dislike children, I just don't particularly want to hang around with them a lot. Problem is, neither do their parents.　　　　BILL MAHER

A philosopher told me that, having examined the civil and political order of societies, he now studied nothing except the savages in the books of explorers, and children in everyday life.   NICOLAS CHAMFORT

I have been assured by a very knowing American of my acquaintance in London that a healthy young child, well nursed, is at a year old a most delicious, nourishing and wholesome food, whether stewed, roasted, baked or boiled; and I make no doubt that it will equally serve in a fricassee or a ragout.
JONATHAN SWIFT

Perhaps host and guest is really the happiest relation for a father and son.
EVELYN WAUGH

So all my friends have kids now…which I think is rude.   DAVID CROSS

America's gross national product.   FLORENCE KING

Children are cruel, ruthless, cunning and almost incredibly self-centered. Far from cementing a marriage, children more frequently disrupt it. Child-rearing is on the whole an expensive and unrewarding bore, in which more has to be invested both materially and spiritually than ever comes out in dividends.
NIGEL BALCHIN

I want to have children and I know my time is running out: I want to have them while my parents are still young enough to take care of them.   RITA RUDNER

Children are satisfied with the stork story up to a certain age because the little fartlings are the world's most crustaceous reactionaries; they don't *want* to know, they don't *want* their preconceived opinions toppled.
FLORENCE KING

Never raise your hand to your children; it leaves your midsection unprotected.
ROBERT ORBEN

Children today are tyrants. They contradict their parents, gobble their food, and tyrannize their teachers.
SOCRATES

My husband and I are either going to buy a dog or have a child. We can't decide whether to ruin our carpet or ruin our lives.
RITA RUDNER

Kids. They're not easy. But there has to be some penalty for sex.
BILL MAHER

It is no wonder that people are so horrible when they start life as children.
KINGSLEY AMIS

The trouble with children is that they are not returnable.
QUENTIN CRISP

They grow up so slow.
BRUCE ERIC KAPLAN

——————————————— CHRIST ———————————————

Christ: an anarchist who succeeded. That's all.
ANDRÉ MALRAUX

A parish demagogue.
PERCY BYSSHE SHELLEY

Everyone in the world is Christ and they are all crucified.
SHERWOOD ANDERSON

Christ died for our sins. Dare we make his martyrdom meaningless by not committing them?
JULES FEIFFER

If Christ were here now there is one thing he would not be—a Christian.
MARK TWAIN

CHRISTIAN CHARITY

The Jews and Arabs should settle their dispute in the true spirit of Christian charity.
ALEXANDER WILEY

CHRISTIANITY

Christian, *n.* One who follows the teachings of Christ insofar as they are not inconsistent with a life of sin.
AMBROSE BIERCE

The last Christian died on the cross.
FRIEDRICH WILHELM NIETSCHE

I admire the serene assurance of those who have religious faith. It is wonderful to observe the calm confidence of a Christian with four aces.
MARK TWAIN

I call Christianity the one great curse, the one great intrinsic depravity, the one great instinct of revenge, for which no means are venomous enough, or secret, subterranean and small enough—I call it the one immortal blemish upon the human race.
FRIEDRICH WILHELM NIETZSCHE

What I got in Sunday School…was simply a firm conviction that the Christian faith was full of palpable absurdities, and the Christian God preposterous.
H. L. MENCKEN

Organized Christianity has probably done more to retard the ideals that were its founder's than any other agency in the world.
RICHARD LE GALLIENNE

The Christian religion not only was at first attended with miracles, but even at this day cannot be believed by any reasonable person without one.

DAVID HUME

People in general are equally horrified at hearing the Christian religion doubted, and at seeing it practiced.

SAMUEL BUTLER

The Christian ideal has not been tried and found wanting; it has been found difficult and left untried.

G. K. CHESTERTON

Going to church doesn't make you a Christian any more than going to the garage makes you a car.

LAURENCE J. PETER

I've always figured that if God wanted us to go to church a lot He'd have given us bigger behinds to sit on and smaller heads to think with.

P. J. O'ROURKE

People may say what they like about the decay of Christianity; the religious system that produced green Chartreuse can never really die.

SAKI

——————— CHRISTMAS ———————

I am sorry to have to introduce the subject of Christmas. It is an indecent subject; a cruel, gluttonous subject; a drunken, disorderly subject; a wasteful, disastrous subject; a wicked, cadging, lying, filthy, blasphemous and demoralizing subject. Christmas is forced on a reluctant and disgusted nation by the shopkeepers and the press: on its own merits it would wither and shrivel in the fiery breath of universal hatred; and anyone who looked back to it would be turned into a pillar of greasy sausages.

GEORGE BERNARD SHAW

I believed in Christmas until I was eight years old. I had saved up some money carrying ice in Philadelphia, and I was going to buy my mother a copper-bottomed clothes boiler for Christmas. I kept the money hidden in a brown crock in the coal bin. My father found the crock. He did exactly what I would have done in his place. He stole the money. And ever since then I've remembered nobody on Christmas, and I want nobody to remember me either.

W. C. FIELDS

Christmas is a holiday that persecutes the lonely, the frayed and the rejected.
JIMMY CANNON

Something in me resists the calendar expectation of happiness.
J. B. PRIESTLEY

Next to a circus there ain't nothing that packs up and tears out any quicker than the Christmas spirit.   KIN HUBBARD

The prospect of Christmas appalls me.   EVELYN WAUGH

In the United States Christmas has become the rape of an idea.
RICHARD BACH

Christmas: it's the only religious holiday that's also a federal holiday. That way, Christians can go to their services, and everyone else can sit at home and reflect on the true meaning of the separation of church and state.   SAMANTHA BEE

Christmas is when you have to go to the bank and get crisp money to put in envelopes from the stationery store for tips. After you tip the door-man, he goes on sick leave or quits and the new one isn't impressed.   ANDY WARHOL

Once again we find ourselves enmeshed in the Holiday Season, that very special time of year when we join with our loved ones in sharing centuries-old traditions such as trying to find a parking space at the mall. We traditionally do this in my family by driving around the parking lot until we see a shopper emerge from the mall, then we follow her, in very much the same spirit as the Three Wise Men, who 2,000 years ago followed a star, week after week, until it led them to a parking space.   DAVE BARRY

There is a remarkable breakdown of taste and intelligence at Christmastime. Mature, responsible grown men wear neckties made out of holly leaves and drink alcoholic beverages with raw egg yolks and cottage cheese in them.
                                        P. J. O'ROURKE

Did you ever notice, the only one in *A Christmas Carol* with any character is Scrooge? Marley is a whiner who fucked over the world and then hadn't the spine to pay his dues quietly; Belle, Scrooge's ex-girlfriend, deserted him when he needed her most; Bob Cratchit is a gutless toady without enough get-up-and-go to assert himself; and the less said about that little treacle-mouth, Tiny Tim, the better.   HARLAN ELLISON

Early in life I developed a distaste for the Cratchits that time has not sweetened. I do not think I was an embittered child, but the Cratchits' aggressive worthiness, their bravely borne poverty, their exultation over that wretched goose, disgusted me. I particularly disliked Tiny Tim (a part always played by a girl because girls had superior powers of looking moribund and worthy at the same time), and when he chirped, "God bless us every one!" my mental response was akin to Sam Goldwyn's famous phrase, "Include me out."
                                    ROBERTSON DAVIES

Christians have created a holiday that has become a beast that cannot be fed. Every year, Christmas gets longer and longer and longer, and you don't care, do you? You just take more and more of the calendar for yourself. It's unbelievable. How long does it take you people to shop?! It's beyond belief. It's insane. When I was a kid, Halloween was Halloween, and Santa wasn't poking his ass into it!
                                                                    LEWIS BLACK

Adults can take a simple holiday for children and screw it up. What began as a presentation of simple gifts to delight and surprise children around the Christmas tree has culminated in a woman opening up six shrimp forks from her dog, who drew her name.
                                                                    ERMA BOMBECK

Christmas is an awfulness that compares favorably with the great London plague and fire of 1665–66. No one escapes the feelings of mortal dejection, inadequacy, frustration, loneliness, guilt and pity. No one escapes feeling used by society, by religion, by friends and relatives, by the utterly artificial responsibilities of extending false greetings, sending banal cards, reciprocating unsolicited gifts, going to dull parties, putting up with acquaintances and family one avoids all the rest of the year…in short, of being brutalized by a "holiday" that has lost virtually all of its original meanings and has become a merchandising ploy for color TV set manufacturers and ravagers of the woodlands.
                                                                    HARLAN ELLISON

"Merry Christmas, Nearly Everybody!"   OGDEN NASH

Bah, Humbug!   EBENEZER SCROOGE (CHARLES DICKENS)

CIVILIZATION

Civilization is a limitless multiplication of unnecessary necessities.

MARK TWAIN

The end of the human race will be that it will eventually die of civilization.

RALPH WALDO EMERSON

You're obliged to pretend respect for people and institutions you think absurd. You live attached in a cowardly fashion to moral and social conventions you despise, condemn, and know lack all foundation. It is that permanent contradiction between your ideas and desires and all the dead formalities and vain pretenses of your civilization which makes you sad, troubled and unbalanced. In that intolerable conflict you lose all joy of life and all feeling of personality, because at every moment they suppress and restrain and check the free play of your powers. That's the poisoned and mortal wound of the civilized world.

OCTAVE MIRBEAU

The civilization of one epoch becomes the manure of the next.

CYRIL CONNOLLY

The civilized are those who get more out of life than the uncivilized, and for this the uncivilized have never forgiven them.   CYRIL CONNOLLY

We are born princes and the civilizing process makes us frogs.   ERIC BERNE

You can't say civilization isn't advancing: in every war they kill you in a new way.

WILL ROGERS

I regard everything that has happened since the last war as a decline in civilization.   A. L. ROWSE

One of the indictments of civilizations is that happiness and intelligence are so rarely found in the same person.   WILLIAM FEATHER

Civilization is the distance man has placed between himself and his excreta.
                                                              BRIAN ALDISS

CLASS

Each class preaches the importance of those virtues it need not exercise. The rich harp on the value of thrift, the idle grow eloquent over the dignity of labor.
                                                              OSCAR WILDE

The classes that wash most are those that work least.
                                                              G. K. CHESTERTON

The danger is not that a particular class is unfit to govern. Every class is unfit to govern.   LORD ACTON

CLASSICAL EDUCATION

The advantage of a classical education is that it enables you to despise the wealth which it prevents you from achieving.   RUSSELL GREEN

CLASSICS

Have I uttered the fundamental blasphemy, that once said sets the spirit free? The literature of the past is a bore—when one has said that frankly to oneself, then one can proceed to qualify and make exceptions.
                                              OLIVER WENDELL HOLMES, JR.

A classic is something that everybody wants to have read and nobody wants to read.   MARK TWAIN

--------------------------------- CLEANLINESS ---------------------------------

Cleanliness is almost as bad as godliness.   SAMUEL BUTLER

----------------------------------- CLERGY -----------------------------------

Of learned men, the clergy show the lowest development of professional
ethics. Any pastor is free to cadge customers from the divines of rival sects,
and to denounce the divines themselves as theological quacks.

H. L. MENCKEN

Clergyman, *n.* A man who undertakes the management of our spiritual affairs
as a method of bettering his temporal ones.   AMBROSE BIERCE

Clergyman: a ticket speculator outside the gates of heaven. H. L. MENCKEN

The first clergyman was the first rascal who met the first fool.   VOLTAIRE

I won't take my religion from any man who never works except with his mouth.
CARL SANDBURG

A clergyman is one who feels himself called upon to live without working
at the expense of the rascals who work to live.   VOLTAIRE

------------------------------------ CLUB ------------------------------------

I don't care to belong to a club that accepts people like me as members.
GROUCHO MARX

---------------------------------- COCKTAILS ----------------------------------

Cocktails have all the disagreeability without the utility of a disinfectant.
SHANE LESLIE

A cocktail is to a glass of wine as rape is to love.　　　PAUL CLAUDEL

COCKTAIL PARTIES

The cocktail party has the form of friendship without the warmth and devotion. It is the device for getting rid of social obligations hurriedly en masse, or for making overtures toward more serious social relationships, as in the etiquette of whoring.　　　BROOKS ATKINSON

A hundred standing people smiling and talking to one another, nodding like gooney birds.　　　WILLIAM COLE

COEDS

If all these sweet young things were laid end to end, I wouldn't be the slightest bit surprised.　　　DOROTHY PARKER

COLLEGE FOOTBALL

College football would be more interesting if the faculty played instead of the students—there would be a great increase in broken arms, legs and necks.
H. L. MENCKEN

COMMITTEES

Not even computers will replace committees, because committees buy computers.　　　EDWARD SHEPHERD MEAD

COMMON PEOPLE

God must hate the common people, because he made them so common.
PHILIP WYLIE

COMMUNICATION

Let us make a special effort to learn to stop communicating with each other, so we can have some conversation.   MISS MANNERS (JUDITH MARTIN)

I wish people who have trouble communicating would just shut up.
TOM LEHRER

COMMUNISM

Communism is like one big phone company.   LENNY BRUCE

I never agree with Communists or any other kind of kept men.
H. L. MENCKEN

Communism is the opiate of the intellectuals.   CLARE BOOTHE LUCE

Communism, like any other revealed religion, is largely made up of prophesies.   H. L. MENCKEN

COMPANIONSHIP

I hold that companionship is a matter of mutual weaknesses. We like that man or woman best who has the same faults we have.   GEORGE JEAN NATHAN

COMPUTERS

Buying the right computer and getting it to work properly is no more complicated than building a nuclear reactor from wristwatch parts in a darkened room using only your teeth.   DAVE BARRY

Beware of computer programmers that carry screwdrivers.
LEONARD BRANDWEIN

Programming today is a race between software engineers striving to build bigger and better idiot-proof programs, and the Universe trying to produce bigger and better idiots. So far, the Universe is winning.   RICH COOK

Why is it drug addicts and computer aficionados are both called users?
CLIFFORD STOLL

In all large corporations, there is a pervasive fear that someone, somewhere is having fun with a computer on company time. Networks help alleviate that fear.   JOHN C. DVORAK

Part of the inhumanity of the computer is that, once it is competently programmed and working smoothly, it is completely honest.   ISAAC ASIMOV

Computer dating is fine, if you're a computer.   RITA MAY BROWN

If the automobile had followed the same development cycle as the computer, a Rolls-Royce would today cost one-hundred dollars, get a million miles per gallon, and explode once a year, killing everyone inside.
ROBERT X. CRINGELY

A computer once beat me at chess, but it was no match for me at kick boxing.
EMO PHILIPS

The computer is a moron.   PETER DRUCKER

——————————————— CONFERENCE ———————————————
A conference is a gathering of important people who singly can do nothing, but together can decide that nothing can be done.   FRED ALLEN

QUOTES ON "C" ♦ 115

CONFESSION

Confession is good for the soul only in the sense that a tweed coat is good for dandruff—it is a palliative rather than a remedy.   PETER DE VRIES

Nothing spoils a confession like repentance.   ANATOLE FRANCE

CONGRESS

The American, if he has a spark of national feeling, will be humiliated by the very prospect of a foreigner's visit to Congress — these, for the most part, illiterate hacks whose fancy vests are spotted with gravy, and whose speeches, hypocritical, unctuous and slovenly, are spotted also with the gravy of political patronage, these persons are a reflection on the democratic process rather than of it; they expose it in its underwear.   MARY MCCARTHY

This country has come to feel the same when Congress is in session as when the baby gets hold of a hammer.   WILL ROGERS

It could probably be shown by facts and figures that there is no distinctively native American criminal class except Congress.   MARK TWAIN

Ancient Rome declined because it had a Senate; now what's going to happen to us with both a Senate and a House?   WILL ROGERS

CONGRESSIONAL INVESTIGATIONS

Congressional investigations are for the benefit of photographers.
     WILL ROGERS

CONGRESSMEN

A flea can be taught everything a congressman can.   MARK TWAIN

A palm-pounding pack of preening pols.   WILLIAM SAFIRE

Eighty percent were hypocrites, eighty percent liars, eighty percent serious sinners…except on Sundays. There is always boozing and floozying.…I don't have enough time to tell you everybody's name.

WILLIAM "FISHBAIT" MILLER

Reader, suppose you were an idiot. And suppose you were a member of Congress. But I repeat myself.   MARK TWAIN

———————————— CONSCIENCE ————————————

Conscience is a mother-in-law whose visit never ends.   H. L. MENCKEN

Conscience and cowardice are really the same things. Conscience is the trade-name of the firm.   OSCAR WILDE

The inner voice which warns us that someone may be looking.

H. L. MENCKEN

———————————— CONSCIOUSNESS ————————————

I used to wake up at 4 A.M. and start sneezing, sometimes for five hours. I tried to find out what sort of allergy I had but finally came to the conclusion that it must be an allergy to consciousness.   JAMES THURBER

———————————— CONSERVATIVES ————————————

Conservative, *n.* A statesman who is enamored of existing evils, as distinguished from a liberal, who wishes to replace them with others.

AMBROSE BIERCE

A conservative is a man with two perfectly good legs who, however, has never learned to walk forward. FRANKLIN DELANO ROOSEVELT

They define themselves in terms of what they oppose. GEORGE WILL

A conservative is a man who sits and thinks, mostly sits.
WOODROW WILSON

The most radical revolutionary will become a conservative the day after the revolution. HANNAH ARENDT

--- CONSISTENCY ---

Consistency is the last refuge of the unimaginative. OSCAR WILDE

The only completely consistent people are the dead. ALDOUS HUXLEY

Consistency is a paste jewel that only cheap men cherish.
WILLIAM ALLEN WHITE

Consistency requires you to be as ignorant today as you were a year ago.
BERNARD BERENSON

--- CONSTITUTION ---

Our Constitution protects aliens, drunks and U.S. senators. WILL ROGERS

--- CONTENTED PEOPLE ---

I have not a word to say against contented people, so long as they keep quiet. But do not, for goodness sake, let them go strutting about, as they are so

fond of doing, crying out that they are the true models for the whole species.
JEROME K. JEROME

—————————————— CONTENTMENT ——————————————
Contentment is, after all, simply refined indolence.
RICHARD HALIBURTON

Who is rich? He that is content. Who is that? Nobody.
BENJAMIN FRANKLIN

—————————————— CONVERSATION ——————————————
Conversation is the enemy of good wine and food.
ALFRED HITCHCOCK

If other people are going to talk, conversation becomes impossible.
JAMES MCNEILL WHISTLER

A prating barber asked Archelaus how he would be trimmed. He answered,
"In silence."   PLUTARCH

During the Samuel Johnson days they had big men enjoying small talk; today
we have small men enjoying big talk.   FRED ALLEN

The trouble with her is that she lacks the power of conversation but not the
power of speech.   GEORGE BERNARD SHAW

—————————————— CONVICTIONS ——————————————
Convictions are more dangerous enemies of truth than lies.
FRIEDRICH WILHELM NIETZSCHE

COOKBOOKS

Cookbooks…bear the same relation to real books that microwave food bears to your grandmother's. ANDREI CODRESCU

COOKS

It is no wonder that diseases are innumerable: count the cooks. SENECA

COPY EDITORS

It is wonderful that our society can find a place for the criminally literal-minded. ALICE KAHN

CORPORAL PUNISHMENT

Let's reintroduce corporal punishment in the schools—and use it on the teachers. P. J. O'ROURKE

CORPORATION

Corporation, *n.* An ingenious device for obtaining individual profit without individual responsibility. AMBROSE BIERCE

COSMETIC SURGERY

What does it profit a seventy-eight-year-old woman to sit around the pool in a bikini if she cannot feed herself? ERMA BOMBECK

Anyone who gives a surgeon six thousand dollars for "breast augmentation" should give some thought to investing a little more on brain augmentation. MIKE ROYKO

I have a professional acquaintance whose recent eyelid job has left her with a permanent expression of such poleaxed astonishment that she looks at all times as if she had just read one of my books. FLORENCE KING

THE COUNTRY

The country has charms only for those not obliged to stay there.

ÉDOUARD MANET

It is pure unadulterated country life. They get up early because they have so much to do and go to bed early because they have so little to think about.

OSCAR WILDE

They can have the good old smell of the earth. Nine times out of ten it isn't the good old smell of the earth that they smell so much as the good old smell of chicken feathers, stagnant pools of water, outhouse perfumes, cooking odors from badly designed kitchens and damp wall plaster.

GEORGE JEAN NATHAN

O Lord! I don't know which is the worst of the country, the walking or the sitting at home with nothing to do.   GEORGE BERNARD SHAW

I have no relish for the country; it is a kind of healthy grave.   SYDNEY SMITH

Anybody can be good in the country. There are no temptations there.

OSCAR WILDE

COUPONS

How about all those manufacturers' coupons featuring Exciting Offers wherein it turns out, when you read the fine print, that you have to send in the coupon plus proof of purchase plus your complete dental records by registered mail to Greenland and allow at least eighteen months for them to send you another coupon that will entitle you to twenty-nine cents off your next purchase of a product you don't really want?   DAVE BARRY

COURAGE

Courage is the fear of being thought a coward.　　HORACE SMITH

CRICKET

What is both surprising and delightful is that [baseball] spectators are allowed, and even expected, to join in the vocal part of the game. I do not see why this feature should not be introduced into cricket. There is no reason why the field should not try to put the batsman off his stroke at the critical moment by neatly timed disparagements of his wife's fidelity and his mother's respectability.

GEORGE BERNARD SHAW

CRIME

My husband gave me a necklace. It's fake. I requested fake. Maybe I'm paranoid, but in this day and age, I don't want something around my neck that's worth more than my head.　　RITA RUDNER

CRIMINALS

Criminal: a person with predatory instincts who has not sufficient capital to form a corporation.　　HOWARD SCOTT

It is a fitting irony that under Richard Nixon, *launder* became a dirty word.

WILLIAM ZINSSER

CRITICS AND CRITICISM

Critic, *n.* A person who boasts himself hard to please because nobody tries to please him.　　AMBROSE BIERCE

Critics are like eunuchs in a harem: they know how it's done, they've seen it done every day, but they're unable to do it themselves.　　BRENDAN BEHAN

A critic is a legless man who teaches running.   CHANNING POLLOCK

A critic is a gong at a railroad crossing clanging loudly and vainly as the train goes by.   CHRISTOPHER MORLEY

Has anybody ever seen a drama critic in the daytime? Of course not. They come out after dark, up to no good.   P. G. WODEHOUSE

Drooling, driveling, doleful, depressing, dropsical drips.
          SIR THOMAS BEECHAM

Critics are like pigs at the pastry cart.   JOHN UPDIKE

A book reviewer is usually a barker before the door of a publisher's circus.
          AUSTIN O'MALLEY

A dramatic critic is a man who leaves no turn unstoned.
          GEORGE BERNARD SHAW

For critics I care the five hundred thousandth part of the tythe of a half-farthing.   CHARLES LAMB

Critics are a dissembling, dishonest, contemptible race of men. Asking a working writer what he thinks about critics is like asking a lamppost what it feels about dogs.   JOHN OSBORNE

I had another dream the other day about music critics. They were small and rodentlike with padlocked ears, as if they had stepped out of a painting by Goya.   IGOR STRAVINSKY

There be some men are born only to suck out the poison of books.

BEN JONSON

Criticism is prejudice made plausible.   H. L. MENCKEN

Criticism is a study by which men grow important and formidable at very small expense.   SAMUEL JOHNSON

Criticism is the art wherewith a critic tries to guess himself into a share of the artist's fame.   GEORGE JEAN NATHAN

Reviewing has one advantage over suicide: in suicide you take it out of yourself; in reviewing you take it out of other people.   GEORGE BERNARD SHAW

Having the critics praise you is like having the hangman say you've got a pretty neck.   ELI WALLACH

——————————— CRUISE SHIPS ———————————
If you thought you didn't like people on land …   CAROL LEIFER

——————————— CULT ———————————
A cult is a religion with no political power.   TOM WOLFE

——————————— CULTURE ———————————
Culture is an instrument wielded by professors to manufacture professors, who when their turn comes, will manufacture professors.   SIMONE WEIL

——————————— CURE ———————————
I have a perfect cure for a sore throat: cut it.   ALFRED HITCHCOCK

—————————— CYNICS ——————————

A cynic is a man who, when he smells flowers, looks around for a coffin.
H. L. MENCKEN

Cynic, *n.* A blackguard whose faulty vision sees things as they are, not as they ought to be. AMBROSE BIERCE

Cynicism is the intellectual cripple's substitute for intelligence. It is the dishonest businessman's substitute for conscience. It is the communicator's substitute, whether he is advertising man or editor or writer, for self-respect.
RUSSELL LYNES

A cynic is not merely one who reads bitter lessons from the past, he is one who is prematurely disappointed in the future. SIDNEY HARRIS

What is a cynic? A man who knows the price of everything and the value of nothing. OSCAR WILDE

—————————— CYNICISM ——————————

Cynicism is an unpleasant way of saying the truth. LILLIAN HELLMAN

The power of accurate observation is commonly called cynicism by those who have not got it. GEORGE BERNARD SHAW

Cynicism is not realistic and tough. It's unrealistic and kind of cowardly because it means you don't have to try. PEGGY NOONAN

No matter how cynical you get, it is impossible to keep up. LILY TOMLIN

CALVIN TRILLIN

Sausage-Eating, Slothful Sweetheart

Calvin Trillin was born and raised in Kansas City. He graduated from Yale in 1957, did a hitch in the army, and then joined *Time* magazine. He wrote a column for *The Nation* from 1978 to 1985, which he subsequently collected in two books: *Uncivil Liberties* and *With All Disrespect*. A frequent contributor to *The New Yorker*, he has published several novels and various books on eating. He lives in Greenwich Village.

JW: Your wife has called you a "sausage-eating, slothful crank."
CT: She has. But she also says that down deep I'm really a sweetheart.

JW: A sweetheart, not a curmudgeon?

CT: I've been accused of being amiable. "Good humored" is another accusation that's been made against me.

JW: Then you don't regard yourself as a curmudgeon?

CT: Certainly not. I consider myself a good-natured, sweet-hearted person.

JW: Would you at least say that you have the habit of pointing out unpleasant facts?

CT: Yes, in an amiable way. But I think that's true of not only people who comment on things but it's generally true of reporters, because most people don't remember things the way they happen.

JW: You've suggested that the advance for a book should be at least as much as the cost of the lunch over which it was discussed. Have you received proper recognition for this contribution?

CT: Nobody's ever paid attention to any of my laws. The one about advances was just one of a number of suggestions about the publishing industry. The average trade book has a shelf life of between milk and yogurt, except for books by any member of the Irving Wallace family—they have preservatives. That was supposed to be a New York City ordinance because most of the publishing industry is in New York. I suggested that any novel that weighs over three pounds or deals with more than four generations of the same family should be required to have in the front matter the names of the characters, the page on which they're introduced, their nicknames or pet names, and their sexual proclivities. Nobody took that seriously. After the Watergate books, I suggested that an author who had committed a felony while on the public payroll should be required to donate the royalties to a scholarship fund to send Gypsies to the Harvard Business School. None of these things have ever been taken seriously.

JW: You've also propounded a number of federal laws.

CT: Yes, anybody caught selling macramé in public should be dyed a natural color and hung out to dry. Citizen's arrest for mime. I've never had any of my laws passed or even discussed.

JW: Have you tried lobbying your congressman?
CT: I don't know who my congressman is. We don't have a congressman anymore in the Village. We used to have a congressman, but they took him away. Then for a while we had a congressman who supposedly was the congressman from Staten Island, but the *Village Voice*, all during the "Koreagate" scandal, referred to him as "Democrat, Seoul."

JW: Your first book came out in 1964. Have you been satisfied with the way your books have been handled by your various publishers?
CT: For a while I was what I call an "itinerant loss-leader." I went from publisher to publisher, and if someone said to them, "You just put out things that are going to make a lot of money," they could say, "No, we publish Trillin and he never earns his advance back."

JW: Are there problems in writing satire?
CT: I think there are two problems: The first, of course, is that people take it seriously. The second is that what happens in America is so bizarre, what you write might turn out to be serious compared to what has just happened. That's what I call the Harry Golden Rule, which is named after the late Harry Golden, who used to publish *The Carolina Israelite*. During the fifties, Harry Golden observed that white people in his part of North Carolina didn't mind standing up with black people, they only minded sitting down with them, so he suggested that the way to integrate the schools was to simply take the chairs out and have the kids stand up at their desks. I think he called it, "Harry Golden's Plan for the Vertical Integration of the Schools." About a year later some library was ordered integrated by a federal court and it proceeded to take the chairs out. This is what is called, "being blindsided by the truth," which is a real problem in America. The Harry Golden Rule, properly stated, is that in present-day America it's very difficult, when commenting on events of the day, to invent something so bizarre that it might not actually come to pass while your piece is still on the presses. Certainly *The Nation* readership used to take my stuff too seriously. Occasionally they

would write letters like, "Trillin is usually boring or offensive, and this week he's both."

JW: Do you think the misunderstanding of satire has anything to do with poor reading skills?

CT: No, I think it has to do with just a lack of a sense of humor. Sometimes, of course, we're at fault. Sometimes it's not clear what's real and what isn't because we didn't set it up right.

JW: Do you mind doing book tours?

CT: No, but I have some doubt about how much good they do. You wonder about these people who watch television at four thirty in the afternoon to see various recipes and people play the saw. Why aren't they reading? It's obvious that touring helps books like *How to Remove Your Own Appendix by Thinking You're the Real You,* because they're not actually books. But books that require reading, I'm not so sure.

JW: Do you like California?

CT: There's a theory that almost anything that's fun is going to be ruined sooner or later by people from California. They tend to bring seriousness to subjects that don't deserve it, and they tend to get very good at things that weren't very important in the first place. The example I use is coming across somebody on Venice Beach who had perfected bubble blowing—knew everything about it, produced these huge bubbles, and spoke at length at the tiniest opportunity about what went into a bubble.

JW: Have you taken a position on religious fundamentalism?

CT: I just wrote a column expressing disappointment that one of my phrases hasn't found its way into the political lexicon in this country. The phrase is *deity overload,* the theory that God may be all-powerful and all-knowing but that He is not all-patient. He's got a lot on his plate, and at some point He may look down with disfavor when Pat Robertson asks His blessing for a deal to trade his delegates for the vice presidential nomination.

JW: You've spent vacations in France. Have you had good relations with the French?
CT: One of the problems that Americans have with the French is that Americans think, before they go to France, that French people are basically like Maurice Chevalier. That's their model of French people, and in fact, there was only one Maurice Chevalier and he lived in California. So they go to France expecting to hear someone say, "Sank heaven for leetle girls," and instead they find some really sullen bureaucrat saying, "Grandmoser's maiden name?" and they get irritated. On the other hand, when Americans go to Italy, where a lot of people are still Ezio Pinza, it makes them feel better.

JW: I notice you have cats.
CT: Yes, but I wish we didn't have any cats. I have nothing against them other than the fact that they're useless and destructive and a pain in the ass. Nothing at all. I'm not prejudiced against cats, but these two happen to be particularly dreadful cats, even as cats. They're also noisy cats. They're Siamese and they shout.

JW: Let me ask you about some modern annoyances. How about blow-in cards, those subscription form things that fall out of magazines?
CT: I hardly notice them, probably because I read so many magazines on airplanes.

JW: How about perfumed perfume ads?
CT: I truly hate them. I don't think they should be allowed. It is not a constitutionally protected form of expression; there's nothing in the First Amendment about freedom to stink. That's basically my theory on mime: They've obviously waived their First Amendment rights by refusing to speak.

JW: Do you have problems with car alarms?
CT: We do, at least on Saturday nights, when the Village becomes what we sometimes call "Jerseyated." It's a wonderful time to rob houses in Ridgefield. They're constantly going off around here. I think there should be a definite

rule about car alarms: You should have the right to break the window and turn it off.

JW: Do you run?

CT: No. I suppose the odd jogger looks normal, but runners, people who actually run in marathons, just look pathetic to me. It can't be worth it. They look like those people in the health-food store: gray pallor, stringy little beards, sunken chests. They make you want to call 911.

QUOTES ON "D"

DARK AGES

Perhaps in time the so-called Dark Ages will be thought of as including our own.
                                                                G. C. LICHTENBERG

DARLING

Darling: the popular form of address used in speaking to a person of the opposite sex whose name you cannot at the moment recall.
                                                                OLIVER HERFORD

DATE

Employees make the best dates. You don't have to pick them up and they're always tax-deductible.
                                                                ANDY WARHOL

DAY

Day, *n.* A period of twenty-four hours, mostly misspent.
                                                                AMBROSE BIERCE

It was such a lovely day I thought it a pity to get up.
                                                                W. SOMERSET MAUGHAM

DAY, DORIS

I knew her before she was a virgin.
                                                                OSCAR LEVANT

DEATH

It's not that I'm afraid to die. I just don't want to be there when it happens.
WOODY ALLEN

Sleep is lovely, death is better still, not to have been born is of course the miracle.
HEINRICH HEINE

Those who welcome death have only tried it from the ears up.
WILSON MIZNER

Death will be a great relief. No more interviews.
KATHARINE HEPBURN

DEBT

A man properly must pay the fiddler. In my case it so happened that a whole symphony orchestra had to be subsidized.
JOHN BARRYMORE

DECENCY

Decency…must be an even more exhausting state to maintain than its opposite. Those who succeed seem to need a stupefying amount of sleep.
QUENTIN CRISP

DECISION

Every decision you make is a mistake.
EDWARD DAHLBERG

DELIBERATION

Deliberation, *n.* The act of examining one's bread to determine which side it is buttered on.
AMBROSE BIERCE

DELUSION

The final delusion is the belief that one has lost all delusions.

MAURICE CHAPELAIN

DEMAGOGUE

Demagogue: One who preaches doctrines he knows to be untrue to men he knows to be idiots.

H. L. MENCKEN

DEMOCRACY

A democracy is a government in the hands of men of low birth, no property, and vulgar employments.

ARISTOTLE

Democracy encourages the majority to decide things about which the majority is blissfully ignorant.

JOHN SIMON

The substitution of election by the incompetent many for appointment by the corrupt few.

GEORGE BERNARD SHAW

The bludgeoning of the people, by the people, for the people.

OSCAR WILDE

Democracy is a process by which the people are free to choose the man who will get the blame.

LAURENCE J. PETER

The worship of jackals by jackasses.

H. L. MENCKEN

Democracy becomes a government of bullies, tempered by editors.

RALPH WALDO EMERSON

Democracy gives every man the right to be his own oppressor.

JAMES RUSSELL LOWELL

An aristocracy of blackguards.

LORD BYRON

In every well-governed state wealth is a sacred thing; in democracies it is the only sacred thing.

ANATOLE FRANCE

The whole dream of democracy is to raise the proletarian to the level of stupidity attained by the bourgeois.

GUSTAVE FLAUBERT

Democracy is a device that ensures we shall be governed no better than we deserve.

GEORGE BERNARD SHAW

Apparently, a democracy is a place where numerous elections are held at great cost without issues and with interchangeable candidates.

GORE VIDAL

Democracy is an abuse of statistics.

JORGE LUIS BORGES

The crude leading the crud.

FLORENCE KING

Democracy is the name we give to the people each time we need them.

ROBERT DE FLERS

Democracy means government by discussion, but it is only effective if you can stop people talking.

CLEMENT ATLEE

Democracy consists of choosing your dictators, after they've told you what you think it is you want to hear.

ALAN COREN

Under democracy one party always devotes its chief energies to trying to prove that the other party is unfit to rule—and both commonly succeed, and are right. H. L. MENCKEN

We must abandon the prevalent belief in the superior wisdom of the ignorant. DANIEL J. BOORSTIN

Every government is a parliament of whores. The trouble is, in a democracy, the whores are us. P. J. O'ROURKE

I believe democracy is our greatest export. At least until China figures out a way to stamp it out of plastic for three cents a unit. STEPHEN COLBERT

DEMOCRATS

They say Democrats don't stand for anything. That's patently untrue. We do stand for anything. BARACK OBAMA

DEMOCRATS VS. REPUBLICANS

The Republican and Democratic parties, ancient rivals, do not exist any more as such, there being more fun watching Harvard and Yale. This has brought about a condition where Republican conventions are sometimes attended by Democrats by mistake, and Democratic conventions attended by Republicans on purpose. The only way to tell them apart is by the conditions of the hotel rooms after the convention is over. The Republicans have more gin bottles and the Democrats seem to have gone in more for rye. ROBERT BENCHLEY

The Democrats are the party that says government will make you smarter, taller, richer, and remove the crabgrass on your lawn. The Republicans are the party that says government doesn't work and then they get elected and prove it. P. J. O'ROURKE

The Republicans are the party of bad ideas. The Democrats are the party of no ideas.   LEWIS BLACK

The Democrats seem to be basically nicer people, but they have demonstrated time and again that they have the management skills of celery. They're the kind of people who'd stop to help you change a flat, but would somehow manage to set your car on fire. I would be reluctant to entrust them with a Cuisinart, let alone the economy. The Republicans, on the other hand, would know how to fix your tire, but they wouldn't bother to stop because they'd want to be on time for Ugly Pants Night at the country club.

DAVE BARRY

When you looked at the Republicans you saw the scum off the top of business. When you looked at the Democrats you saw the scum off the top of politics. Personally, I prefer business. A businessman will steal from you directly instead of getting the IRS to do it for him. And when the Republicans ruin the environment, destroy the supply of affordable housing, and wreck the industrial infrastructure, at least they make a buck off it. The Democrats just do these things for fun.   P. J. O'ROURKE

The only difference between the Democrats and the Republicans is that the Democrats allow the poor to be corrupt, too.   OSCAR LEVANT

What is the difference between a Democrat and a Republican? A Democrat blows, and a Republican sucks.   LEWIS BLACK

———————————————— DIAGNOSIS ————————————————

One of the most common of all diseases is diagnosis.   KARL KRAUS

DIARY

Keep a diary and one day it'll keep you.   MAE WEST

DIETS

My soul is dark with stormy riot, Directly traceable to diet.
                              SAMUEL HOFFENSTEIN

I've been on a constant diet for the last two decades. I've lost a total of 789 pounds. By all accounts, I should be hanging from a charm bracelet.
                                   ERMA BOMBECK

DINNER PARTY

The best number for a dinner party is two—myself and a damn good head waiter.   NUBAR GULBENKIAN

DINNER THEATER

"Dinner theater," a way of positively guaranteeing that both food and theater will be amateur and mediocre, which means unthreatening and therefore desirable.   PAUL FUSSELL

DIPLOMACY

The patriotic art of lying for one's country.   AMBROSE BIERCE

The principle of give and take is the principle of diplomacy—give one and take ten.   MARK TWAIN

In archaeology you uncover the unknown. In diplomacy you cover the known.
                              THOMAS PICKERING

Diplomacy is to do and say the nastiest thing in the nicest way.

ISAAC GOLDBERG

I'm convinced there's a small room in the attic of the Foreign Office where future diplomats are taught to stammer.   PETER USTINOV

DISHONESTY

There's one way to find out if a man is honest: ask him; if he says yes, you know he is crooked.   MARK TWAIN

DISNEYLAND

Disneyland is a white pioneer's idea of what America is. Wacky American animals. American conviviality, zappy, zany, congenial and nice, like a parade of demented, bright Shriners.   JONATHAN MILLER

DISTRUST

We have to distrust each other. It's our only defense against betrayal.

TENNESSEE WILLIAMS

Joyous distrust is a sign of health. Everything absolute belongs to pathology.
FRIEDRICH WILHELM NIETZSCHE

DIVORCE

Divorce, *n*. A bugle blast that separates the combatants and makes them fight at long range.   AMBROSE BIERCE

Fission after fusion.   RITA MAE BROWN

Getting divorced just because you don't love a man is almost as silly as getting married just because you do.   ZSA ZSA GABOR

Divorce is a sacred institution between a man and a woman who hate each other.   LEWIS BLACK

For a while we pondered whether to take a vacation or get a divorce. We decided that a trip to Bermuda is over in two weeks, but a divorce is something you always have.   WOODY ALLEN

Remarriage is an excellent test of just how amicable your divorce was.
                                                                    MARGO KAUFMAN

The happiest time of anyone's life is just after the first divorce.
                                                         JOHN KENNETH GALBRAITH

Divorces are made in heaven.   OSCAR WILDE

When a couple decides to divorce, they should inform both sets of parents before having a party and telling all their friends. This is not only courteous but practical. Parents may be very willing to pitch in with complaints, criticism, and malicious gossip of their own to help the divorce along.
                                                                    P. J. O'ROURKE

Whenever I date a guy, I think, is this the man I want my children to spend their weekends with?   RITA RUDNER

DOCTORS

Doctors cut, burn, and torture the sick, and then demand of them an undeserved fee for such services.   HERACLITUS

The art of medicine consists in amusing the patient while nature cures the disease.   VOLTAIRE

They murmured as they took their fees, "There is no cure for this disease."
HILAIRE BELLOC

A doctor's reputation is made by the number of eminent men who die under his care.
GEORGE BERNARD SHAW

God heals, and the doctor takes the fee.
BENJAMIN FRANKLIN

The best doctor is the one you run for and can't find.
DENIS DIDEROT

Doctors are men who prescribe medicines of which they know little, to cure diseases of which they know less, in human beings of whom they know nothing.
VOLTAIRE

Doctors are just the same as lawyers; the only difference is that lawyers merely rob you, whereas doctors rob you and kill you, too.
ANTON CHEKHOV

———————————————— DOGS ————————————————

Dog, *n.* A kind of additional or subsidiary Deity designed to catch the overflow and surplus of the world's worship. The Divine being in some of his smaller and silkier incarnations, takes, in the affection of Woman, the place to which there is no human male aspirant. The Dog is a survival—an anachronism. He toils not, neither does he spin, yet Solomon in all his glory never lay upon a door-mat all day long, sun-soaked and fly-fed and fat, while his master worked for the means wherewith to purchase an idle wag of the Solomonic tail, seasoned with a look of tolerant recognition.
AMBROSE BIERCE

Reading about dogs is almost as bad as having them stand on your chest and lick you.
WILFRID SHEED

The greatest pleasure of a dog is that you may make a fool of yourself with him, and not only will he not scold you, but he will make a fool of himself too.

SAMUEL BUTLER

Histories are more full of examples of the fidelity of dogs than of friends.

ALEXANDER POPE

The average dog is a nicer person than the average person.

ANDREW A. ROONEY

If you pick up a starving dog and make him prosperous, he will not bite you. This is the principal difference between a dog and a man.

MARK TWAIN

The dog has seldom been successful in pulling man up to its level of sagacity, but man has frequently dragged the dog down to his.

JAMES THURBER

To be sure, the dog is loyal. But why, on that account, should we take him as an example? He is loyal to men, not to other dogs.   KARL KRAUS

Has he bit any of the children yet? If he has, have them shot, and keep him for curiosity, to see if it was the hydrophobia.   CHARLES LAMB

─────────────── DOG OWNERS ───────────────

To his dog, every man is Napoleon; hence the constant popularity of dogs.

ALDOUS HUXLEY

I loathe people who keep dogs. They are cowards who haven't got the guts to bite people themselves.   AUGUST STRINDBERG

If you are a dog and your owner suggests that you wear a sweater, suggest that he wear a tail.   FRAN LEBOWITZ

———————————————————— DOUBT ————————————————————

Doubt is not a pleasant condition, but certainty is absurd.   VOLTAIRE

I respect faith, but doubt is what gets you an education.   WILSON MIZNER

The whole problem with the world is that fools and fanatics are always so certain of themselves, but wiser people so full of doubts.

BERTRAND RUSSELL

——————————————————— DRINKING ———————————————————

Alcohol is a very necessary article….It enables Parliament to do things at eleven at night that no sane person would do at eleven in the morning.

GEORGE BERNARD SHAW

An alcoholic is someone you don't like who drinks as much as you do.

DYLAN THOMAS

If the headache would only precede the intoxication, alcoholism would be a virtue.   SAMUEL BUTLER

I called a detox center—just to see how much it would cost: $13,000 for three and a half weeks! My friends, if you can come up with thirteen grand, you don't have a problem yet!   SAM KINISON

Drinking makes such fools of people, and people are such fools to begin with that it's compounding a felony.   ROBERT BENCHLEY

I envy people who drink—at least they know what to blame everything on.
OSCAR LEVANT

I only drink to make other people seem interesting.   GEORGE JEAN NATHAN

Our national drug is alcohol. We tend to regard the use of any other drug
with special horror.   WILLIAM S. BURROUGHS

I have taken more out of alcohol than alcohol has taken out of me.
WINSTON CHURCHILL

So who's in a hurry?
ROBERT BENCHLEY, in response to a warning that drinking is "slow poison"

——————————————————— DRUGS ———————————————————
Reality is a crutch for people who can't cope with drugs.   LILY TOMLIN

I never took hallucinogenic drugs because I never wanted my consciousness
expanded one unnecessary iota.   FRAN LEBOWITZ

Half of the modern drugs could well be thrown out of the window, except
that the birds might eat them.   DR. MARTIN HENRY FISCHER

——————————————————— DUTY ———————————————————
When a stupid man is doing something he is ashamed of, he always declares
that it is his duty.   GEORGE BERNARD SHAW

Duty, *n.* That which sternly impels us in the direction of profit, along the
line of desire.   AMBROSE BIERCE

W. C. FIELDS

A Definite Personality

William Claude Dukenfield was born in Philadelphia in 1880 and was raised above the saloon where his father tended bar. His mother was a strong woman, bitter about her lot in life, and he probably inherited his wisecracking, side-of-the-mouth style from her: She would sit on the porch with her young son and entertain him with a snide, running commentary about passing neighbors.

Contrary to legend, he didn't run away from home after a fight with his father but left under amicable circumstances at the age of eleven to earn his fortune in show business. Inspired by vaudeville performers of the day, he discovered early on what he described as his "fatal facility" for juggling. He taught himself juggling routines and developed brilliant sight gags involving hats, golf clubs, and pool cues through long hours of practice, and eventually earned a reputation as a disciplined professional.

Fields lost his illusions early; after being cheated by unscrupulous booking agents and crooked theater managers, he never again felt financially secure. At the height of his movie career, when he was earning $100,000 a picture, he regularly deposited money in banks all over the country under fictitious names. Because he never revealed the account numbers to anyone and no bank records were found among his possessions, the money was never recovered by his heirs.

He married a showgirl named Harriet Hughes in 1900. They lived together for seven years and produced a son, then separated, never to reconcile. He subordinated his family, his social life, and ultimately his happiness to the demands of his career and turned his personal tragedies into comedy: The characters in his pictures usually include a bratty son, a shrewish wife, a domineering mother-in-law, and a loving daughter (the daughter he never had).

Fields was naturally undemonstrative and easily hurt, so he affected a phony manorial demeanor to conceal his vulnerability. He once told an interviewer that he decided at an early age to become "a definite personality." He strove to be a part of the world but was an outcast. According to Louise Brooks, the former ingenue who wrote perceptively about the Hollywood of the twenties and thirties, Fields "stretched out his hand to Beauty and Love and they thrust it away."

Even his legendary drinking was an outgrowth of his loneliness: He secured the companionship of his fellow vaudeville performers with free whiskey, even though he was himself a teetotaler (as a juggler he didn't want to hurt his timing). But once Fields learned how to drink, he would consume at least a quart of gin a day for the rest of his life.

W. C. Fields played himself in most of his pictures (with the exception of Micawber in *David Copperfield*). He played lovable rogues, bumbling dipsomaniacs, harassed family men plagued by domineering wives and mothers-in-law. He wrote all his pictures under assumed names—Mahatma Kane Jeeves, Charles Bogle, Otis Cribblecross—but seemed incapable of delivering the lines as written.

Fields died on Christmas Day in 1946. Contrary to legend, he isn't buried in Philadelphia; his ashes are in an unmarked urn at Forest Lawn in Hollywood. During his last illness he was confined to a hospital bed, and a visitor was shocked to catch him reading the Bible. "Just looking for loopholes," he explained.

A FLAGON OF FIELDS

Once, during Prohibition, I was forced to live for days on nothing but food and water.

A woman drove me to drink, and I never even had the courtesy to thank her.

I always keep a supply of stimulant handy in case I see a snake, which I also keep handy.

What contemptible scoundrel stole the cork from my lunch?

My illness is due to my doctor's insistence that I drink milk, a whitish fluid they force down helpless babies.

The cost of living has gone up another dollar a quart.

I exercise self-control and never touch any beverage stronger than gin before breakfast.

Anybody who hates dogs and loves whiskey can't be all bad.

QUOTES ON "E"

EARNESTNESS

Earnestness is just stupidity sent to college.   P. J. O'ROURKE

EARTH

Think of the earth as a living organism that is being attacked by billions of bacteria whose numbers double every forty years. Either the host dies, or the virus dies, or both die.   GORE VIDAL

ECONOMISTS

An economist is a surgeon with an excellent scalpel and a rough-edged lancet, who operates beautifully on the dead and tortures the living.

NICOLAS CHAMFORT

An economist is a man who states the obvious in terms of the incomprehensible.   ALFRED A. KNOPF

In all recorded history there has not been one economist who has had to worry about where the next meal would come from.

PETER F. DRUCKER

An economist is an expert who will know tomorrow why the things he predicted yesterday didn't happen today.   LAURENCE J. PETER

If all economists were laid end to end, they would not reach a conclusion.
GEORGE BERNARD SHAW

——————————————— EDITORS ———————————————

Editor: A person employed on a newspaper whose business it is to separate the wheat from the chaff, and to see that the chaff is printed.
ELBERT HUBBARD

An editor should have a pimp for a brother, so he'd have someone to look up to.
GENE FOWLER

——————————————— EDUCATION ———————————————

Education is a state-controlled manufactory of echoes.
NORMAN DOUGLAS

Education...has produced a vast population able to read but unable to distinguish what is worth reading.
G. M. TREVELYAN

It has been said that we have not had the three R's in America, we had the six R's: remedial readin', remedial 'ritin' and remedial 'rithmetic.
ROBERT M. HUTCHINS

I went to school so long ago, *Ethics* was a required course.
H. MYLES JACOB

Education: the inculcation of the incomprehensible into the indifferent by the incompetent.
JOHN MAYNARD KEYNES

Education, *n*. That which discloses to the wise and disguises from the foolish their lack of understanding.
AMBROSE BIERCE

Soap and education are not as sudden as a massacre but they are more deadly in the long run.
MARK TWAIN

Men are born ignorant, not stupid; they are made stupid by education.
BERTRAND RUSSELL

Education is a state-controlled manufactory of echoes.
NORMAN DOUGLAS

We are shut up in schools and college recitation rooms for ten or fifteen years, and come out at last with a bellyful of words and do not know a thing.
RALPH WALDO EMERSON

Society produces rogues, and education makes one rogue cleverer than another.
OSCAR WILDE

Education is a method whereby one acquires a higher grade of prejudices.
LAURENCE J. PETER

I prefer the company of peasants because they have not been educated sufficiently to reason incorrectly.
MICHEL DE MONTAIGNE

How is it that little children are so intelligent and men so stupid? It must be education that does it.
ALEXANDRE DUMAS *fils*

You can't expect a boy to be depraved until he has been to a good school.
SAKI

"Whom are you?" said he, for he had been to night school.   GEORGE ADE

ELECTION

Every election is a sort of advance auction sale of stolen goods.

H. L. MENCKEN

ENEMIES

Enemies to me are the *sauce piquante* to my dish of life.   ELSA MAXWELL

The only thing that will be remembered about my enemies after they're dead is the nasty things I've said about them.   CAMILLE PAGLIA

One should forgive one's enemies, but not before they are hanged.

HEINRICH HEINE

ENGLAND AND THE ENGLISH

England is the most class-ridden country under the sun. It is a land of snobbery and privilege, ruled largely by the old and silly.   GEORGE ORWELL

There is such a thing as too much couth.   S. J. PERELMAN

England has forty-two religions and only two sauces.   VOLTAIRE

The English never smash in a face. They merely refrain from asking it to dinner.   MARGARET HALSEY

The English instinctively admire any man who has no talent and is modest about it.   JAMES AGATE

The English think incompetence is the same thing as sincerity.

QUENTIN CRISP

Curse the blasted jelly-boned swines, the slimy belly-wriggling inverte-
brates, the miserable sodding rotters, the flaming sods, the sniveling,
dribbling, dithering, palsied pulseless lot that make up England today.
They've got white of egg in their veins, and their spunk is that watery it's
a marvel they can breed…Why, why, why, was I born an Englishman!

D. H. LAWRENCE

ENGLISH LANGUAGE

To learn English, you must begin by thrusting the jaw forward, almost clench-
ing the teeth, and practically immobilizing the lips. In this way the English
produce the series of unpleasant little mews of which their language consists.

JOSÉ ORTEGA Y GASSET

ENJOYMENT

People seem to enjoy things more when they know a lot of other people have
been left out of the pleasure. RUSSELL BAKER

EPCOT CENTER

With Epcot Center the Disney corporation has accomplished something I
didn't think possible in today's world. They have created a land of make-
believe that's worse than regular life. P. J. O'ROURKE

EQUALITY

Equality may perhaps be a right, but no power on earth can ever turn it
into a fact. HONORÉ DE BALZAC

That all men are created equal is a proposition to which, at ordinary times,
no sane individual has ever given his assent. ALDOUS HUXLEY

EQUAL OPPORTUNITY

Equal opportunity means everyone will have a fair chance at being incompetent.   LAURENCE J. PETER

ETHICS

Grub first, then ethics.   BERTOLT BRECHT

EVERYTHING

Everything is worth precisely as much as a belch, the difference being that a belch is more satisfying.   INGMAR BERGMAN

Ninety percent of everything is crap.   THEODORE STURGEON

Everything will be forgotten and nothing will be redressed.
                                                      MILAN KUNDERA

EXERCISE

The only possible form of exercise is to talk, not to walk.   OSCAR WILDE

The need of exercise is a modern superstition, invented by people who ate too much and had nothing to think about. Athletics don't make anybody either long-lived or useful.   GEORGE SANTAYANA

I have never taken any exercise except sleeping and resting.
                                                      MARK TWAIN

I get my exercise acting as a pallbearer to my friends who exercise.
                                                      CHAUNCEY DEPEW

The only exercise I get is when I take the studs out of one shirt and put them in another.   RING LARDNER

When I feel like exercising I just lie down until the feeling goes away.
                                                    ROBERT M. HUTCHINS

I think that anyone who comes upon a Nautilus machine suddenly will agree with me that its prototype was clearly invented at some time in history when torture was considered a reasonable alternative to diplomacy.
                                                    ANNA QUINDLEN

The word *aerobics* comes from two Greek words: *aero*, meaning "ability to," and *bics*, meaning "withstand tremendous boredom."   DAVE BARRY

Exercise is bunk. If you are healthy, you don't need it; if you are sick, you shouldn't take it.   HENRY FORD

I believe every human has a finite number of heartbeats. I don't intend to waste any of mine running around doing exercises.
                                                    NEIL ARMSTRONG

——————————— EXISTENCE ———————————
The very purpose of existence is to reconcile the glowing opinion we hold of ourselves with the appalling things that other people think about us.
                                                    QUENTIN CRISP

——————————— EXISTENTIALISM ———————————
Existentialism means that no one else can take a bath for you.
                                                    DELMORE SCHWARTZ

EXPECTATIONS

Blessed is he who expects nothing, for he shall never be disappointed.

JONATHAN SWIFT

EXPERIENCE

Experience is the name everyone gives to their mistakes.   OSCAR WILDE

Experience, *n.* The wisdom that enables us to recognize as an undesirable old acquaintance the folly that we have already embraced. AMBROSE BIERCE

We learn from experience that men never learn anything from experience.

GEORGE BERNARD SHAW

EXPERTS

An expert is a person who avoids small error as he sweeps on to the grand fallacy.   BENJAMIN STOLBERG

An expert is a person who has made all the mistakes that can be made in a very narrow field.   NIELS BOHR

If you believe the doctors, nothing is wholesome; if you believe the theologians, nothing is innocent; if you believe the military, nothing is safe.

LORD SALISBURY

If the world should blow itself up, the last audible voice would be that of an expert saying it can't be done.   PETER USTINOV

GEORGE S. KAUFMAN

The Wittiest Man in America

Geoorge S. Kaufman was one of the most successful and prolific playwrights in the history of Broadway and one of America's greatest wits. He was born George Kaufman on November 16, 1889, in Pittsburgh, to German-Jewish parents. He was raised by a neurotic mother who had lost her first child and was determined to protect George from "germs" by preparing all his food in sterile conditions and preventing him from going outdoors. The pampering instilled in him a lifelong fear of disease and death.

He was a skinny, unathletic, bespectacled kid who responded to the bullying of his schoolmates with quips instead of fists. He wrote stories and poems for his high school paper and, at the age of fourteen, collaborated on a play with another boy. George was a devoted reader of "The Conning Tower," Franklin P. Adams's column in the New York *Evening Mail*, and by the age of fifteen had become a regular contributor to it under the byline "G. S. K." (Kaufman added the middle initial for euphony.)

His father wanted him to be a lawyer, but George was stricken with pleurisy during his first year of college. The doctor prescribed an outdoor job to hasten his recovery, so George was apprenticed to a land surveyor. By his own account he was an inept surveyor and no lover of the outdoors, and was delighted when Adams recommended him for a job writing a humor column at the Washington *Times*. But within a year, he was unemployed: one day he was at his desk at the *Times* when the owner, newspaper mogul Frank Munsey, walked in, took one look at Kaufman, and bellowed, "What's that Jew doing in my city room?" Adams eventually got him a job on the New York *Evening Mail* as a staff writer. He moved from there to the New York *Tribune*, where he began writing theater criticism, and within a few years he became drama editor at the *New York Times*.

In 1917, at the age of twenty-eight, he married Beatrice Bakrow, the daughter of a wealthy Rochester, New York, clothing manufacturer. After their first child was stillborn, they realized they were sexually incompatible and agreed to an "arrangement" whereby each was free to have extramarital affairs but remained devoted to each other in every other way. He was devastated by her sudden death in 1945.

Kaufman's first attempt as a professional playwright was a rewrite of *Someone in the House*, a 1918 play by Larry Evans and Walter Percival. It was a box-office disaster on its own but a flu epidemic didn't help, which prompted Kaufman to write an ad for the show:

BEWARE OF FLU
AVOID CROWDS
SEE "SOMEONE IN THE HOUSE"

He collaborated with Marc Connelly on three plays, beginning with *Dulcy* in 1921. He went on to work with Moss Hart, Edna Ferber, Ring Lardner, Abe Burrows, Herman Mankiewicz, and Howard Dietz. Kaufman's many stage hits included *The Butter and Egg Man*, *The Solid Gold Cadillac*, and *The Man Who Came to Dinner*. He won two Pulitzer Prizes—for *Of Thee I Sing*, the first musical to win a Pulitzer, and *You Can't Take It with You*. For the Marx Brothers he cowrote (with Morrie Ryskind) *Animal Crackers*, *The Cocoanuts*, and *A Night at the Opera*.

Kaufman was tall and lanky, with a prominent nose and thick hair combed into a high pompadour. He was excruciatingly shy: many of his friends and collaborators described his habit of avoiding eye contact by bending down to pick up imaginary pieces of lint from the carpet. He had a cleanliness compulsion, abhorred outward displays of affection, and hated physical contact except, presumably, with his many sexual conquests (the Broadway producer Max Gordon called him a "male nymphomaniac," and he had a brief affair with Mary Astor that erupted into scandal when her estranged husband published her diary in which she described Kaufman's sexual prowess).

He was an insomniac, a hypochondriac, and a pathologically fussy eater: Though he regularly dined in the finest restaurants, he ordered simple food and avoided sauces because he could not be sure of their ingredients.

Kaufman was a soft-spoken, self-deprecating pessimist who was plagued by self-doubt in spite of repeated success. He was insecure about the value of his work and was convinced that each hit would be his last. He thought himself an impostor who would be found out when the current play finally opened.

He was usually wrong. His only real deficiency as a playwright was his reticence about love scenes; he categorically refused to write them, abdicating the responsibility to his collaborators.

His professional generosity was demonstrated in a curtain speech he delivered following the opening of *Once in a Lifetime* (which he wrote with Moss Hart): "I would like the audience to know that eighty percent of this play is Moss Hart." It was probably the other way around, since *Once in a Lifetime* was Hart's first play, and Hart tried to set the record straight in his own curtain speech. Kaufman habitually minimized his own importance in his many collaborative efforts and often refused credit and compensation for his contributions as a playwright, play doctor, and director.

Kaufman was generally polite and considerate, but he had a maniacal hatred for cabdrivers and waiters. He was in a constant state of war with them throughout his adult life. He insisted that waiters took training in ways to exasperate customers, and he treated them accordingly. His mock epitaph for a departed waiter: "God finally caught his eye."

He seldom used four-letter words but could be caustic when provoked by insincerity or stupidity: he once said to a female acquaintance, "You're a birdbrain, and I mean that as an insult to birds." He was not a raconteur but a conversational guerrilla fighter. He would retreat within himself and appear bored and distracted, all the while listening intensely, waiting for the right moment to get off a devastating line.

His dour persona was a fraud. He actually liked people and was generous and compassionate. He cultivated a reputation for penuriousness but was really a soft touch who lent money on the condition the borrower keep quiet about it lest Kaufman's "reputation" be ruined. When Hitler came to power in 1933, he financed the evacuation from Germany of scores of Jews, stood as their financial sponsor when they arrived in the United States, and even supported many of them until they were settled.

During the late fifties he suffered a series of strokes that left him partially paralyzed and blind in one eye. Toward the end of his life he seemed to have come to terms with his fear of death. He died on June 2, 1961.

Moss Hart eulogized him as follows: "The paradox of his nature was that he felt deeply, yet he sheered from any display of emotion. Almost always, it remained unexpressed."

GEORGE S. KAUFMAN
ANECDOTES

At the age of four, his mother told him that an aunt was coming to visit and asked, "It wouldn't hurt to be nice to her, would it?" to which he replied, "That depends on your threshold of pain."

When asked at nine P.M. what he was doing for dinner that evening, he replied, "Digesting it."

During dinner at the Colony, Harpo Marx asked if there was anything you could get there for fifty cents. "Sure," Kaufman answered, "a quarter."

He was piqued by the Marx Brothers' habit of changing his lines. During rehearsals for *Animal Crackers*, Kaufman walked on the stage in mock exasperation and said, "Excuse me for interrupting, but I thought for a minute I actually heard a line I wrote."

At a dinner party he was seated next to a woman who monopolized the conversation all through the meal. By the time the coffee was served, Kaufman could no longer restrain himself. "Madam," he asked, "don't you have any unexpressed thoughts?"

He attended a farewell party in Hollywood for S. N. Behrman, who had just finished writing a screenplay and was returning to New York. Several days later Kaufman ran into Behrman, who had delayed his departure to work on additional dialogue. Kaufman greeted him with, "Ah, forgotten but not gone."

Kaufman was a bridge fanatic who did not suffer incompetent players gladly. When one particularly inept partner asked to be excused to go to the men's room, Kaufman replied, "Gladly—for the first time today I'll know what you have in your hand."

He was partnered with Herman Mankiewicz in a bridge game, and when Mankiewicz made a spectacular blunder, Kaufman exploded. "I know you learned the game this afternoon," he said, "but what *time* this afternoon?"

Another bridge partner, sensing that Kaufman was not pleased with his conduct of the previous hand, asked defensively, "Well, George, how would you have played the hand?"

"Under an assumed name," Kaufman shot back.

During a performance of a very bad play, Kaufman leaned forward and politely asked the lady in front of him if she would mind putting on her hat.

William Gaxton, the star of *Of Thee I Sing*, began to get bored with the part after a long and successful run. During an especially perfunctory performance, Kaufman left the theater and sent him the following telegram: "Watching your performance from the rear of the theater. Wish you were here."

During the run of a play, Kaufman dropped in to monitor a performance. Not at all pleased with what he saw, he placed the following note on the callboard: "Eleven A.M. rehearsal tomorrow morning to remove all improvements to the play inserted since the last rehearsal."

His review of a young tenor, "Guido Nazzo is nazzo guido," began showing up in other notices and was repeated so often that it virtually destroyed the young performer's career. Kaufman was so contrite, he wrote a letter of apology to Mr. Nazzo and offered him a job in a Kaufman musical.

To the author of a badly received play: "I understand your play is full of single entendres."

One of Kaufman's reviews began: "There was laughter in the back of the theater, leading to the belief that someone was telling jokes back there."

In another review he wrote, "I was underwhelmed."

When Kaufman was drama editor at the *New York Times*, a press agent asked, "How do I get our leading lady's name in your newspaper?"

"Shoot her," Kaufman replied.

To the writer of a manuscript replete with spelling errors: "I'm not very good at it myself, but the first rule about spelling is that there is only one *z* in *is*."

A summer-stock producer who had produced a Kaufman play without paying royalties explained, "After all, it's only a small, insignificant theater."

"Then you'll go to a small, insignificant jail," Kaufman answered.

Moss Hart bought an estate in Bucks County, Pennsylvania, installed a swimming pool and planted hundreds of trees. When Kaufman saw it, he said, "This is what God could have done if He'd had money."

After his great success playing Abraham Lincoln on Broadway, Raymond Massey began to assume the character off the stage, affecting Lincolnesque attire, manner, and speech, and prompting Kaufman to observe, "Massey won't be satisfied until someone assassinates him."

Charles Laughton commented that he was successful in the role of Captain Bligh in *Mutiny on the Bounty* because he had come from a seafaring family. "I presume," said Kaufman, alluding to Laughton's portrayal of Quasimodo in *The Hunchback of Notre Dame*, "that you also came from a long line of hunchbacks."

On the television show *This Is Show Business*, a youthful Eddie Fisher complained that girls refused to date him because of his age, and he asked Kaufman's advice.

Kaufman replied, "Mr. Fisher, on Mount Wilson there is a telescope that can magnify the most distant stars up to twenty-four times the magnification of any previous telescope. This remarkable instrument was unsurpassed in the world of astronomy until the construction of the Mount Palomar telescope, an even more remarkable instrument of magnification. Owing to advances and improvements in optical technology, it is capable of magnifying the stars to four times the magnification and resolution of the Mount Wilson telescope.

"Mr. Fisher, if you could somehow put the Mount Wilson telescope *inside* the Mount Palomar telescope, you *still* wouldn't be able to detect my interest in your problem."

Kaufman was fired from *This Is Show Business* on December 21, 1952, when he said on the air, "Let's make this one program where no one sings 'Silent Night.'"

QUOTES ON "F"

───────────── **FAILURE** ─────────────

No one is completely unhappy at the failure of his best friend.

GROUCHO MARX

If at first you don't succeed, failure may be your style.   QUENTIN CRISP

It is not enough to succeed; others must fail.   GORE VIDAL

───────────── **FAITH** ─────────────

Faith, *n*. Belief without evidence in what is told by one who speaks without knowledge, of things without parallel.   AMBROSE BIERCE

Faith may be defined briefly as an illogical belief in the occurrence of the improbable.   H. L. MENCKEN

A casual stroll through the lunatic asylum shows that faith does not prove anything.   FRIEDRICH WILHELM NIETZSCHE

The most common of all follies is to believe passionately in the palpably not true. It is the chief occupation of mankind.   H. L. MENCKEN

FAME

Fame is a vapor; popularity an accident; the only earthly certainty is oblivion.
MARK TWAIN

FAMILIARITY

Familiarity breeds contempt—and children.
MARK TWAIN

Familiarity doesn't breed contempt, it *is* contempt.
FLORENCE KING

FAMILY

When I can do no longer bear to think of the victims of broken homes, I begin to think of the victims of intact ones.
PETER DE VRIES

Sacred family…! The supposed home of all the virtues, where innocent children are tortured into their first falsehoods, where wills are broken by parental tyranny, and self-respect is smothered by crowded, jostling egos.
AUGUST STRINDBERG

The family is a court of justice which never shuts down for night or day.
MALCOLM DE CHAZAL

The family is the ultimate American fascism.
PAUL GOODMAN

A family is but too often a commonwealth of malignants.
ALEXANDER POPE

A married man with a family will do anything for money.
CHARLES DE TALLEYRAND-PÉRIGORD

Having a family is like having a bowling alley installed in your brain.

MARTIN MULL

Home life as we understand it is no more natural to us than a cage is natural to a cockatoo.

GEORGE BERNARD SHAW

The family is a good institution because it is uncongenial.

G. K. CHESTERTON

Happiness is having a large, loving, caring, close knit family in another city.

GEORGE BURNS

I have certainly seen more men destroyed by the desire to have a wife and child and to keep them in comfort than I have seen destroyed by drink or harlots.

WILLIAM BUTLER YEATS

"Family" this and "family" that. If I had a family I'd be furious that moral busybodies are taking the perfectly good word *family* and using it as a code for censorship the same way "states' rights" was used to disguise racism in the midsixties.

JOHN WATERS

FARM

A farm is an irregular patch of nettles bounded by short-term notes, containing a fool and his wife who didn't know enough to stay in the city.

S. J. PERELMAN

FASHION

Never despise fashion. It's what we have instead of God.

MALCOLM BRADBURY

Fashion is a form of ugliness so intolerable that we have to alter it every six months. OSCAR WILDE

Fashions are the only induced epidemics, proving that epidemics can be induced by tradesmen. GEORGE BERNARD SHAW

——————————————— FAST FOOD ———————————————

We were taken to a fast-food café where our order was fed into a computer. Our hamburgers, made from the flesh of chemically impregnated cattle, had been broiled over counterfeit charcoal, placed between slices of artifically flavored cardboard and served to us by recycled juvenile delinquents.
JEAN-MICHEL CHAPEREAU

Scrambled eggs should never be assembled in vatsized proportions.
ROY BLOUNT, JR.

I went into a McDonald's yesterday and said, "I'd like some fries." The girl at the counter said, "Would you like some fries with that?"
JAY LENO

——————————————— FATHERS ———————————————

I grew up to have my father's looks—my father's speech patterns—my father's posture—my father's walk—my father's opinions and my mother's contempt for my father. JULES FEIFFER

Fathers should neither be seen nor heard. That is the only proper basis for family life. OSCAR WILDE

I never got along with my dad. Kids used to come up to me and say, "My dad can beat up your dad." I'd say, "Yeah? When?" BILL HICKS

—————————————— FAVORITES ——————————————

Favorite animal: steak. FRAN LEBOWITZ

Favorite color: I hate colors. IAN SHOALES

—————————————— FBI ——————————————

The FBI is filled with Fordham graduates keeping tabs on Harvard men in
the State Department. DANIEL PATRICK MOYNIHAN

—————————————— FEMINISM ——————————————

The major concrete achievement of the women's movement of the 1970s
was the Dutch treat. NORA EPHRON

Boys don't make passes at female smart-asses.
LETTY COTTIN POGREBIN

How much fame, money, and power does a woman have to achieve on her
own before you can punch her in the face? P. J. O'ROURKE

We will have equality when a female schlemiel moves ahead as fast as a
male schlemiel. ESTELLE RAMEY

Leaving sex to the feminists is like letting your dog vacation at the taxidermist.
CAMILLE PAGLIA

The ironic side effect of women having abandoned their privileged status as
"ladies" is that they are now in danger of being as revolting as men, and
accordingly treated, by men, as nothing special. QUENTIN CRISP

Women are the only exploited group in history to have been idealized into powerlessness.
ERICA JONG

I only know that people call me a feminist whenever I express sentiments that differentiate me from a doormat or a prostitute.
REBECCA WEST

People say to me, "You're not very feminine." Well, they can suck my dick!
ROSEANNE BARR

What's the point of being a lesbian if a woman is going to look and act like an imitation man?
RITA MAE BROWN

Some of us are becoming the men we wanted to marry.
GLORIA STEINEM

When a woman behaves like a man, why can't she behave like a nice man?
DAME EDITH EVANS

I don't understand guys who call themselves feminists. That's like the time Hubert Humphrey, running for President, told a black audience he was a soul brother.
ROY BLOUNT, JR.

FILM

If my film makes one more person miserable, I've done my job.
WOODY ALLEN

FIDELITY

Fidelity *n*. A virtue peculiar to those who are about to be betrayed.
AMBROSE BIERCE

FINANCE

Finance is the art of passing currency from hand to hand until it finally disappears.
ROBERT W. SARNOFF

FINANCIAL NEWS

You know how on the evening news they always tell you that the stock market is up in active trading, or off in moderate trading, or trading in mixed activity, or whatever? Well, who gives a shit?
DAVE BARRY

FINANCIER

A financier is a pawnbroker with imagination.
ARTHUR WING PINERO

FISH

Fish is the only food that is considered spoiled once it smells like what it is.
P. J. O'ROURKE

FISHING

Fishing is a delusion entirely surrounded by liars in old clothes.
DON MARQUIS

Fishing, with me, has always been an excuse to drink in the daytime.
JIMMY CANNON

Fishing…is a sport invented by insects and you are the bait.
P. J. O'ROURKE

There's a fine line between fishing and just standing on the shore like an idiot.
STEVEN WRIGHT

FISHING ROD

A fishing rod is a stick with a hook at one end and a fool at the other.

SAMUEL JOHNSON

FITNESS

The fitness business is about sex and immortality. By toning up the system, you can prolong youth, just about finesse middle age and then, when the time comes, go straight into senility.

WILFRID SHEED

Muscles come and go; flab lasts.

BILL VAUGHAN

FLAMENCO DANCER

A Flamenco dancer is a guy who's always applauding his own ass.

LENNY BRUCE (attributed)

FLATTERY

I hate careless flattery, the kind that exhausts you in your effort to believe it.

WILSON MIZNER

FLOWER CHILDREN

All the flower children were as alike as a congress of accountants and about as interesting.

JOHN MORTIMER

FOOD

There is no love sincerer than the love of food.   GEORGE BERNARD SHAW

Do you know on this one block you can buy croissants in five different places? There's one store called Bonjour Croissant. It makes me want to go to Paris and open a store called Hello Toast.

FRAN LEBOWITZ

The most remarkable thing about my mother is that for thirty years she served the family nothing but leftovers. The original meal has never been found.

CALVIN TRILLIN

I don't like food that's too carefully arranged; it makes me think that [the chef is] spending too much time arranging and not enough time cooking. If I wanted a picture I'd buy a painting.   ANDY ROONEY

Part of the secret of success in life is to eat what you like and let the food fight it out inside.   MARK TWAIN

—————————————— FOOTBALL ——————————————

The game of football is played all over the world. In some countries, such a game may be called a soccer match. In others, a revolution. However, there are several differences between a football game and a revolution. For one thing, a football game usually lasts longer and the participants wear uniforms. Also, there are usually more casualties in a football game. The object of the game is to move the ball past the other team's goal line. This counts as six points. No points are given for lacerations, contusions, or abrasions, but then no points are deducted, either. Kicking is very important in football. In fact, some of the more enthusiastic players even kick the football occasionally.

ALFRED HITCHCOCK

Football combines the two worst features of American life: violence and committee meetings.   GEORGE WILL

If the players were armed with guns, there wouldn't be stadiums large enough to hold the crowds.   IRWIN SHAW

Anybody who watches three games of football in a row should be declared brain dead.   ERMA BOMBECK

FONTS

The more fonts in a document, the less content it has.   GUY KAWASAKI

FORGIVENESS

Always forgive your enemies—nothing annoys them so much.
                                                                    OSCAR WILDE

The stupid neither forgive nor forget; the naive forgive and forget; the wise forgive but do not forget.   THOMAS SZASZ

To err is human; to forgive, infrequent.   FRANKLIN P. ADAMS

FORK

Fork, *n.* An instrument used chiefly for the purpose of putting dead animals into the mouth.   AMBROSE BIERCE

FRANCE AND THE FRENCH

A relatively small and eternally quarrelsome country in Western Europe, fountainhead of rationalist political manias, militarily impotent, historically inglorious during the past century, democratically bankrupt, Communist-infiltrated from top to bottom.   WILLIAM F. BUCKLEY, JR.

France is the only country where the money falls apart and you can't tear the toilet paper.   BILLY WILDER

What I gained by being in France was learning to be better satisfied with my own country.   SAMUEL JOHNSON

I would have loved it—without the French. D. H. LAWRENCE

Ever want to slap an entire country? STEVE LANDESBERG

Everything is on such a clear financial basis in France. It is the simplest country to live in. No one makes things complicated by becoming your friend for any obscure reason. If you want people to like you, you have only to spend a little money. ERNEST HEMINGWAY

Frenchmen are like gunpowder, each by itself smutty and contemptible, but mass them together and they are terrible indeed!
SAMUEL TAYLOR COLERIDGE

The French probably invented the very notion of discretion. It's not that they feel that what you don't know won't hurt you; they feel that what you don't know won't hurt them. To the French lying is simply talking.
FRAN LEBOWITZ

If the French were really intelligent, they'd speak English. WILFRID SHEED

They aren't much at fighting wars anymore. Despite their reputation for fashion, their women have spindly legs. Their music is sappy. But they do know how to whip up a plate of grub. MIKE ROYKO

Every Frenchman wants to enjoy one or more privileges; that's the way he shows his passion for equality. CHARLES DE GAULLE

Germans with good food. FRAN LEBOWITZ

There's something Vichy about the French. IVOR NOVELLO

FREEDOM

When people are free to do as they please, they usually imitate each other.
ERIC HOFFER

The only man who is really free is the one who can turn down an invitation to dinner without giving any excuse.   JULES RENARD

You are free and that is why you are lost.   FRANZ KAFKA

People demand freedom of speech as a compensation for the freedom of thought which they seldom use.   SØREN KIERKEGAARD

FREEDOM OF THE PRESS

Freedom of the press is limited to those who own one.   A. J. LIEBLING

FREE LUNCH

There is no free lunch.   MILTON FRIEDMAN

FREE SPEECH

I agree with everything you say, but I would attack to the death your right to say it.   TOM STOPPARD

FRENCH FRIES

The French fried potato has become an inescapable horror in almost every public eating place in the country. "French fries," say the menus, but they are not French fries any longer. They are a furry-textured substance with the taste of plastic wood.   RUSSELL BAKER

---------------------- FREUD, SIGMUND ----------------------

I think he's crude, I think he's medieval, and I don't want an elderly gentle-man from Vienna with an umbrella inflicting his dreams upon me.

VLADIMIR NABOKOV

Sigmund Freud was a half-baked Viennese quack. Our literature, culture, and the films of Woody Allen would be better today if Freud had never written a word. IAN SHOALES

---------------------- FRIENDSHIP ----------------------

Think twice before you speak to a friend in need. AMBROSE BIERCE

When one is trying to do something beyond his known powers it is useless to seek the approval of friends. Friends are at their best in moments of defeat.

HENRY MILLER

May God defend me from my friends: I can defend myself from my enemies.

VOLTAIRE

It takes your enemy and your friend, working together, to hurt you: the one to slander you, and the other to bring the news to you. MARK TWAIN

Every time a friend succeeds, I die a little. GORE VIDAL

The one thing your friends will never forgive you is your happiness.

ALBERT CAMUS

It is well, when judging a friend, to remember that he is judging you with the same godlike and superior impartiality. ARNOLD BENNETT

A friend who is very near and dear may in time become as useless as a relative.
GEORGE ADE

When a man takes to his bed, nearly all his friends have a secret desire to see him die; some to prove that his health is inferior to their own, others in the disinterested hope of being able to study a death agony. CHARLES BAUDELAIRE

We cherish our friends not for their ability to amuse us, but for ours to amuse them.
EVELYN WAUGH

I like a friend better for having faults that one can talk about.
WILLIAM HAZLITT

Nothing so fortifies a friendship as a belief on the part of one friend that he is superior to the other.
HONORÉ DE BALZAC

Friendship is a common belief in the same fallacies, mountebanks and hobgoblins.
H. L. MENCKEN

Friendship is a very taxing and arduous form of leisure activity.
MORTIMER ADLER

My mother used to say that there are no strangers, only friends you haven't met yet. She's now in a maximum-security twilight home in Australia.
DAME EDNA EVERAGE (Barry Humphries)

—————————————— FUN ——————————————

Most of the time I don't have much fun. The rest of the time I don't have any fun at all.
WOODY ALLEN

The prospect of a long day at the beach makes me panic. There is no harder work I can think of than taking myself off to somewhere pleasant, where I am forced to stay for hours and "have fun."   PHILLIP LOPATE

FUNDAMENTALISTS

There are scores of thousands of human insects who are ready at a moment's notice to reveal the will of God on every possible subject.

GEORGE BERNARD SHAW

FUNERALS

I did not attend his funeral, but I wrote a nice letter saying I approved it.

MARK TWAIN

What bereaved people need is little comic relief, and this is why funerals are so farcical.   GEORGE BERNARD SHAW

The consumer's side of the coffin lid is never ostentatious.

STANISLAW J. LEC

THE FUTURE

The trouble with our times is that the future is not what it used to be.

PAUL VALÉRY

Only one more indispensable massacre of Capitalists or Communists or Fascists or Christians or Heretics, and there we are in the Golden Future.

ALDOUS HUXLEY

If you want a picture of the future, imagine a boot stomping on a human face—forever.   GEORGE ORWELL

QUENTIN CRISP

Courtly Curmudgeon

Quentin Crisp (1908–1999) was born on Christmas Day in Sutton, a middle-class suburb of London. He became aware of his homosexuality at an early age and, in spite of intense family and social pressure, obstinately refused to disguise the fact. At the age of fourteen he was sent to a typically spartan English boarding school (which he describes as a combination monastery and prison) where he first encountered the kind of persecution that would plague him all his life. He worked as a commercial designer and a teacher of tap dancing; wrote books on a variety of subjects including lettering, window dressing, and the English Ministry of Labor; but eventually settled into a thirty-five-year career as an artist's model. His autobiography, *The Naked Civil Servant*, was published in 1968 and was made into a British television play starring John Hurt. Its success vaulted Mr. Crisp into international celebrity. He subsequently published a dozen more books, including *How to Become a Virgin, How to Have a Lifestyle, Doing It with Style* (with Donald Carroll), and *Manners from Heaven.* He became a permanent resident alien in the United States in 1981. He always listed his occupation on income tax forms as "retired waif."

JW: Your manner is deferential, yet the things you write in your books and essays are scathing indictments of humanity.

QC: That's what frightens me. Audiences have been known to say that I'm cynical. Now, as you know from reading the work of Mr. Wilde, a cynic is one who knows the price of everything and the value of nothing, and I certainly have been taught the price of everything, but I wouldn't say that I didn't appreciate the value of things. What I think worries people is that I can't see any point in an endeavor, a ferocious, prolonged endeavor, to set a permanent "relationship" with anybody. That's the bit I can't understand; there I don't see the value and I do see the price.

JW: What is the price of a relationship?

QC: The price is this endless restraint which is asked of you, and the reward is nothing. What have you got in the end of it, unless you have determined to live with somebody rich or more influential than yourself? In fact, that could be a universal law: "The union of two hearts whose incomes are equal is a waste of time."

JW: Where does love come in?

QC: There again, we must first agree what "love" is. Are we of one mind that love is the extra effort we make in our dealings with those whom we cannot like? Because that seems to me the very essence of it. I worry when audiences think this is a joke. It's an aphorism, but it isn't a joke. After all, people like yourself belong to the generation which wanted to redistribute the wealth of the world, and half the world's wealth is love. If our love is given to the brave and the beautiful, they will become the millionaires of love. Then what will happen to love's paupers?

JW: How do you feel about children?

QC: I treat children exactly as though they're people, and I totally refuse to put on that weird voice that people put on: "How are you, Mr. Smith, and how are you, Mrs. Smith, and how are you?" If they think children don't know that they're receiving this nauseous treatment, they're wrong. Very few children want the affection of adults. My parents, at least my mother, imagined that what I wanted was love, while I really wanted abject obedience.

JW: I believe you've written that while your brothers wanted to be footballers, you wanted to be a chronic invalid.

QC: That's right. I was the youngest, and I knew that my life was, in a sense, a losing battle, and I was right. So I thought there might be some way of making a go of failure. If at first you don't succeed, failure may be your style.

JW: How did you endure one bashing after another for all those years?

QC: I was stuck with it. I don't think I could ever have passed myself off as a human being. Long before I ever had the opportunity to dye my hair or pluck my eyebrows—when I was a schoolboy—I was already a lost soul. In England, I never left the house without bracing myself. When you're standing at the bus stop and you see half a dozen young men coming along, you know there will be trouble. It's the way the English are.

JW: You mentioned before that you're working on an article about how to "cure" Christmas.

QC: Even when I was a child, I was embarrassed by Christmas. First of all, it's my birthday. My mother gave me two shillings to buy a present for my father, and my father gave me two shillings to buy a present for my mother,

QUENTIN CRISP ◆ 183

and they both thanked me! I felt a terrible fool. You get presents you're never going to be able to use, and you have to thank people for them, and they thank you for presents they're never going to be able to use. Later in life, when I had invented happiness, I ceased to need festivity. In fact, that's a universal law: "Happy people do not need festivity."

JW: But what's the "cure"?

QC: The cure, of course, is to simply ignore it. You have to put up with about four years of disgrace when you receive Christmas cards and do not send them, but after that you know that the people who send you Christmas cards are doing it to please you and that they don't expect a reply.

JW: Does your attitude about Christmas extend to religion in general; do you subscribe to the idea that more evil has been done in the name of religion than good?

QC: Well, it has done terrifying things. Religious ideas are inflammatory in a way that I find difficult to understand. There are very few wars over the theory of relativity. Very few heated arguments, for that matter. Whereas, in Northern Ireland, they are killing one another over religion. When I told the people of Northern Ireland that I was an atheist, a woman in the audience stood up and said, "Yes, but is it the God of the Catholics or the God of the Protestants in whom you don't believe?"

JW: Do you watch television?

QC: Very little. The programs constantly repeat themselves and one another. No one has yet had the nerve to say, "As we have nothing sensible to tell you between now and eight thirty, please tune in again then."

JW: Do you like punk rock?

QC: I hate it. Long ago I said that all the harm that had come to the world was due to the music, and now someone has arisen and said there will be no more concerts in Central Park because everybody behaved so badly. It seems to me self-evident: All you have to do to restore order to the world is to stop the music. It will mean people start to speak. One of the girls who rings me up actually said, "If I go to a gathering of strangers and there's no music, I'm embarrassed." That means she would have to speak, or at least listen. They like it loud and they like it dark; they don't want to see and they don't want to hear.

JW: Why, do you suppose? Does it have anything to do with the Bomb?

QC: I don't think so, but the Bomb is our only friend. I can't see how anyone can think anything else. We've written the equations on the blackboard, and now we've got down to the bottom right-hand corner and it's wrong. The hermit crab has been on the earth for three million years asking nothing, as far as I know, except a few more hermit crabs. Give the world to them. It's only people who've reduced the situation to this.

JW: Then you think it will end in nuclear destruction?

QC: Yes, and I think it's right. Never in the history of the world has there been a pileup of arms which have not ultimately been used.

JW: Isn't it an unprecedented situation? Individuals have always had to confront their own mortality, but they always had the guarantee of posterity—they could leave their works, their children—but now that's been withdrawn. Couldn't that account for the insanity of the second half of the twentieth century? Couldn't that account for punk rock?

QC: It could, except that the craziness is in the hands of the young, and the young do not think they will die. I can remember, during the [Second World] war, saying to a woman who ultimately became a nun, "I can't even now get used to the fact that I will die," and she said, "Neither can I, but I practice like mad."

JW: Do you believe in an afterlife?

QC: Like most people, I believe not that of which I can be convinced by logic, I believe what my nature inclines me to believe, and the one thing I wouldn't wish on my worst enemy is eternal life. It also makes old age more acceptable: as it's toward the end of the run, you can overact appallingly.

JW: Do you like living in New York?

QC: Yes, I like the people, and I like urban life, even though people are constantly trying to sell me on the countryside. If you want to get out of town occasionally, if fresh air is your lust, fine, but I don't want to spend an hour in the country. I don't long for the countryside, ever. As a child, I didn't even want to go out-of-doors, let alone go to the country. The outside world was alien to me; I wanted to stay home, even a home so wretched.

JW: I take it you're happy to be living in the United States. What's your assessment of the American character?

QC: Americans want to be loved; the English want to be obeyed. In 1963, nothing could have prevented America from ruling the world except what Tennyson called "craven fears of being great." If this building catches on fire and I am the only person who's ever done any fire drill, I must tell you what to do, [or] everybody will die. This is the position in which America now is. As far as I'm concerned, Korea was an undecided war, and Cuba was an undecided war, and then Vietnam. When Vietnam was first mentioned, I said, "Go out there, measure the place up, send back for a bomb the right size, drop it, and say, 'Oh, it slipped.' Just as well, they're only foreigners."

QUOTES ON "G"

—————————————— GAMBLING ——————————————

The gambling known as business looks with austere disfavor upon the business known as gambling.   AMBROSE BIERCE

Gambling promises the poor what property performs for the rich: that is why the bishops dare not denounce it fundamentally.
GEORGE BERNARD SHAW

The urge to gamble is so universal and its practice is so pleasurable, that I assume it must be evil.   HEYWOOD BROUN

I don't gamble online. I've seen too many of my friends get so addicted to poker that they've got no time for Internet porn. And I'm not going to let that happen to me.   JOEL STEIN

—————————————— GANDHI ——————————————

It is alarming and also nauseating to see Mr. Gandhi, a seditious Middle Temple lawyer, now posing as a fakir of a type well known in the East, striding half-naked up the steps of the viceregal palace…to parley on equal terms with the representatives of the king-emperor.
WINSTON CHURCHILL

GAY

"Gay" used to be one of the most agreeable words in the language. Its appropriation by a notably morose group is an act of piracy.

ARTHUR M. SCHLESINGER, JR.

When asked, "Should I tell my mother I'm gay?" I answer, "Never tell your mother *anything*." QUENTIN CRISP

If you think gay is contagious, then you're gay. MARGARET CHO

GENIUS

When a true genius appears in the world you may know him by this sign: that all the dunces are in confederacy against him. JONATHAN SWIFT

GENTILITY

Gentility is what is left over from rich ancestors after the money is gone.

JOHN CIARDI

GENTLEMAN

I am a gentleman: I live by robbing the poor. GEORGE BERNARD SHAW

GERMANY AND THE GERMANS

Germany, the diseased world's bathhouse. MARK TWAIN

Everything that is ponderous, vicious and pompously clumsy, all long-winded and wearying kinds of style, are developed in great variety among Germans.
FRIEDRICH WILHELM NIETZSCHE

German: a good fellow maybe; but it is better to hang him.

RUSSIAN PROVERB

GERMAN REUNIFICATION

I view this in much the same way I view a possible Dean Martin–Jerry Lewis reconciliation: I never really enjoyed their work, and I'm not sure I need to see any of their new stuff. DENNIS MILLER

GIRLS

There are girls who manage to sell themselves, whom no one would take as gifts. NICOLAS CHAMFORT

Any girl can be glamorous. All you have to do is stand still and look stupid. HEDY LAMARR

GLASGOW

The great thing about Glasgow is that if there's a nuclear attack it'll look exactly the same afterwards. BILLY CONNOLLY

GOD

God is the immemorial refuge of the incompetent, the helpless, the miserable. They find not only sanctuary in His arms, but also a kind of superiority, soothing to their macerated egos; He will set them above their betters. H. L. MENCKEN

If God did not exist, it would have been necessary to invent Him. VOLTAIRE

If God created us in his own image we have more than reciprocated. VOLTAIRE

If God were suddenly condemned to live the life which he has inflicted upon men, He would kill himself. ALEXANDRE DUMAS *fils*

The only excuse for God is that he doesn't exist.   STENDHAL

Beware of the man whose God is in the skies.   GEORGE BERNARD SHAW

God seems to have left the receiver off the hook and time is running out.
ARTHUR KOESTLER

Which is it: is man one of God's blunders, or is God one of man's blunders?
FRIEDRICH WILHELM NIETZSCHE

God, that dumping ground of our dreams.   JEAN ROSTAND

If you talk to God, you are praying; if God talks to you, you have schizophrenia.   THOMAS SZASZ

I cannot believe in a God who wants to be praised all the time.
FRIEDRICH WILHELM NIETZSCHE

I do not mind if I lose my soul for all eternity. If the kind of God exists who
would damn me for not working out a deal with Him, then that is unfortunate. I should not care to spend eternity in the company of such a person.
MARY MCCARTHY

For me, the single word "God" suggests everything that is slippery, shady,
squalid, foul and grotesque.   ANDRÉ BRETON

It takes a long while for a naturally trustful person to reconcile himself to
the idea that after all God will not help him.   H. L. MENCKEN

God is the Celebrity-Author of the World's Best-Seller. We have made God into the biggest celebrity of all, to contain our own emptiness.

DANIEL BOORSTIN

God is love, but get it in writing.   GYPSY ROSE LEE

Creator: a comedian whose audience is afraid to laugh.

H. L. MENCKEN

Imagine the Creator as a low comedian, and at once the world becomes explicable.   H. L. MENCKEN

I do not believe in God. I believe in cashmere.   FRAN LEBOWITZ

The impotence of God is infinite.   ANATOLE FRANCE

Perhaps God is not dead; perhaps God is himself mad.   R. D. LAING

If a triangle could speak, it would say that God is eminently triangular, while a circle would say that the divine nature is eminently circular.

BARUCH SPINOZA

God will forgive me; that's his business.   HEINRICH HEINE

He seems to have an inordinate fondness for beetles.   J. B. S. HALDANE

I do not feel obliged to believe that the same God who has endowed us with sense, reason, and intellect has intended us to forgo their use.

GALILEO GALILEI

Why assume so glibly that the God who presumably created the universe is still running it? It is certainly conceivable that He may have finished it and then turned it over to lesser gods to operate. H. L. MENCKEN

Are you there God? It's me, Lewis...and I've got a message for you: YOU'RE AN IDIOT! LEWIS BLACK

I don't know if God exists, but it would be better for His reputation if He didn't. JULES RENARD

If it turns out that there is a God, I don't think that he's evil. But the worst that you can say about him is that basically he's an underachiever. WOODY ALLEN

I respect the idea of God too much to hold it responsible for a world as absurd as this one is. GEORGES DUHAMEL

You must believe in God in spite of what the clergy say. BENJAMIN JOWETT

I read the book of Job last night—I don't think God comes well out of it. VIRGINIA WOOLF

It is the final proof of God's omnipotence that he need not exist in order to save us. PETER DE VRIES

—————————————————— GODS ——————————————————
Whom the mad would destroy, first they make Gods. BERNARD LEVIN

All Gods *were* immortal. STANISLAW J. LEC

Men rarely (if ever) manage to dream up a god superior to themselves. Most gods have the manners and morals of a spoiled child.

ROBERT A. HEINLEIN

The worshiper is the father of the gods.   H. L. MENCKEN

——————————————— GOLDEN RULE ———————————————

The golden rule is that there are no golden rules.

GEORGE BERNARD SHAW

——————————————————— GOLF ———————————————————

Golf is a good walk spoiled.   MARK TWAIN

Golf may be played on Sunday, not being a game within the view of the law, but being a form of moral effort.   STEPHEN LEACOCK

If I had my way, any man guilty of golf would be ineligible for any office of trust in the United States.   H. L. MENCKEN

If you watch a game, it's fun. If you play at it, it's recreation. If you work at it, it's golf.   BOB HOPE

A game in which you claim the privileges of age, and retain the playthings of childhood.   SAMUEL JOHNSON

I regard golf as an expensive way of playing marbles.   G. K. CHESTERTON

Nobody knows exactly how golf got started. Probably what happened was, thousands of years ago, a couple of primitive guys were standing around, holding some odd-shaped sticks, and they noticed a golf ball lying on the grass, and they said, "Hey! Let's see if we can hit this into a hole!" And then they said, "Nah, let's just tell long, boring anecdotes about it instead."

DAVE BARRY

GOOD FELLOWSHIP

What men call good fellowship is commonly but the virtue of pigs in a litter which lie close together to keep each other warm.

HENRY DAVID THOREAU

GOOD LISTENER

A good listener is usually thinking about something else.   KIN HUBBARD

GOODNESS

To be good, according to the vulgar standard of goodness, is obviously quite easy. It merely requires a certain amount of sordid terror, a certain lack of imaginative thought, and a certain low passion for middle-class respectability.

OSCAR WILDE

The good die young—because they see it's no use living if you've got to be good.

JOHN BARRYMORE

On the whole human beings want to be good, but not too good and not quite all the time.   GEORGE ORWELL

It is better to be beautiful than to be good, but it is better to be good than to be ugly.   OSCAR WILDE

GOOD BREEDING

Good breeding consists in concealing how much we think of ourselves and how little we think of the other person.   MARK TWAIN

GOOD DEEDS

No good deed goes unpunished.   CLARE BOOTHE LUCE

GOOD AND EVIL

It is almost impossible systematically to constitute a natural moral law. Nature has no principles. She furnishes us with no reason to believe that human life is to be respected. Nature, in her indifference, makes no distinction between good and evil.   ANATOLE FRANCE

GOOD EXAMPLE

Few things are harder to put up with than the annoyance of a good example.
                                                        MARK TWAIN

GOOD LOOKS

She got her good looks from her father. He's a plastic surgeon.
                                                        GROUCHO MARX

GOSSIP

The only thing worse than being talked about is not being talked about.
                                                        OSCAR WILDE

If you can't say anything good about someone, sit right here by me.
                                            ALICE ROOSEVELT LONGWORTH

GOVERNMENT

A government is the only known vessel that leaks from the top.
                                                        JAMES RESTON

Every government is run by liars and nothing they say should be believed.
                                                        I. F. STONE

Society is produced by our wants and government by our wickedness.
THOMAS PAINE

There's no trick to being a humorist when you have the whole government working for you.
WILL ROGERS

In general, the art of government consists in taking as much money as possible from one class of the citizens to give to the other.
VOLTAIRE

The supply of government exceeds the demand.
LEWIS LAPHAM

Government is an association of men who do violence to the rest of us.
LEO TOLSTOY

Every decent man is ashamed of the government he lives under.
H. L. MENCKEN

Government is too big and important to be left to the politicians.
CHESTER BOWLES

Government expands to absorb revenue—and then some.
TOM WICKER

In rivers and bad governments, the lightest things swim at the top.
BENJAMIN FRANKLIN

I have long contended that, however many zillion dollars the federal government costs us, we get it all back and more in the form of quality entertainment.
DAVE BARRY

Creative semantics is the key to contemporary government; it consists of talking in strange tongues lest the public learn the inevitable inconveniently early.
GEORGE WILL

There never has been a good government.   EMMA GOLDMAN

GRAFFITI

Any academic or literary hustler caught writing that graffiti is a fascinating expression of artistic and cultural creativity [should] be sprayed magenta and left without grants for a year, sentences to be served consecutively.
CALVIN TRILLIN

GRATITUDE

I feel a very unusual sensation—if it is not indigestion, I think it must be gratitude.   BENJAMIN DISRAELI

Gratitude is merely the secret hope of further favors.
FRANÇOIS DE LA ROCHEFOUCAULD

GRIEF

Grief is a species of idleness.   SAMUEL JOHNSON

KARL KRAUS

Word and Substance and Empty Chairs

Karl Kraus, the Viennesse dramatist, critic, and satirist, was born in 1874 in a small Bohemian town near Prague to well-to-do Jewish parents. Three years later the family moved to Vienna, where Kraus spent the rest of his life.

He became a writer when a spinal deformity prevented him from realizing his childhood ambition of entering the theater. He contributed acerbic critical essays to Viennese publications and turned down an offer to join the prestigious Viennese daily, *Neue Freie Presse*, to avoid becoming what he termed a "culture clown."

He continued to publish polemics against the intellectuals, literati, financiers, politicians, poets, and journalists he deemed responsible for the moral bankruptcy of Europe. His avowed object was no less than the preservation of civilization, which he saw imperiled by the cozy relationship between the Austrian press and intellectuals. Kraus was a consummate rhetorician who equated morality with purity of language. ("Word and substance—that is the only connection I have striven for in my life.") He assailed the deliberate corruption of language by special interests and railed against what might be termed the artistic-journalistic complex of the time.

Kraus was acquainted with Sigmund Freud and expressed a fondness for him personally but became obsessed with what he considered the chicanery of psychoanalysis. He attacked Freud and his disciples, whom he dubbed "soul doctors" and "psychoanals." He wrote of Freud's critique of Michelangelo: "Analysis is the *schnorrer's* [beggar's] need to explain how riches come to be; whatever he doesn't possess must have been acquired by swindle; the other merely has the fortune; he, fortunately, *knows*."

In 1899, Kraus founded his own magazine, *Die Fackel (The Torch)*, with which he relentlessly assaulted the corruption and hypocrisy of European society. In it he denounced prison conditions, price fixing, child labor abuses, and the unequal treatment of women. Initially there were other contributors, including August Strindberg and Heinrich Mann, but from 1911 until his death in 1936, Kraus was its sole contributor. ("I no longer have collaborators. I used to be envious of them. They repel those readers whom I want to lose myself.")

Die Fackel contained no paid advertisements and professed indifference to its readers; this announcement appeared regularly on its back cover:

> It is requested that no books, periodicals, invitations, clippings, leaflets, manuscripts or written information of any sort be sent in. No such

material will ever be returned, nor will any letters be answered. Any return postage that may be enclosed will be turned over to charity.

Kraus wrote poetry in which he attempted to objectify his stringent concept of language, and several plays, including *Die letzen Tage der Menschheit (The Last Days of Mankind)* in 1922, which portrayed the disintegration of European society and prophesied the Second World War. From 1910 until his death, he gave numerous public readings of his own works to enthusiastic audiences all over Europe.

His attitude isolated him from all but a few close friends. He slept days and worked nights, and abhorred invasions of his privacy. He recoiled when people accosted him on the street and went to great lengths to avoid human contact. Kraus died of heart failure in June 1936, less than two years before the German *Anschluss*, an event that confirmed his dire predictions for the future of Austrian society. The irony of his work as a satirist was that his contemporaries were so ridiculously self-satisfied, they didn't know they were being savaged.

Kraus was an early champion of the poet and playwright Bertolt Brecht, who said of him: "When the age died by its own hand, he was that hand." Erich Heller appraised him thus: "The satiric radicalism of Karl Kraus is only a defense mechanism of a man ardently in love with the beauty and joy of living."

KARL KRAUS ON THE LIFE
OF A MISANTHROPE

I and my public understand each other very well: it does not hear what I say, and I don't say what it wants to hear.

If I return people's greetings, I do so only to give them their greeting back. Many desire to kill me, and many wish to spend an hour chatting with me. The law protects me from the former.

What torture, this life in society! Often someone is obliging enough to offer me a light, and in order to oblige *him* I have to fish a cigarette out of my pocket.

One's need for loneliness is not satisfied if one sits at a table alone. There must be empty chairs as well. If the waiter takes away a chair on which no one is sitting, I feel a void and my sociability is aroused. I can't live without empty chairs.

KARL KRAUS ON LITERATURE

In the beginning was the review copy, and a man received it from the publisher. Then he wrote a review. Then he wrote a book which the publisher accepted and sent on to someone else as a review copy. The man who received it did likewise. This is how modern literature came into being.

Most critics write critiques which are by the authors they write critiques about. That would not be so bad, but then most authors write works which are by the critics who write critiques about them.

To write a novel may be pure pleasure. To live a novel presents certain difficulties. As for reading a novel, I do my best to get out of it. I have decided many a stylistic problem first by head, then by heads or tails.

Heinrich Heine so loosened the corsets of the German language that today every little salesman can fondle her breasts.

The making of a journalist: no ideas and the ability to express them.

Journalists write because they have nothing to say, and have something to say because they write.

A plagiarist should be made to copy the author a hundred times.

Today's literature: prescriptions written by patients.

KARL KRAUS ON PSYCHOANALYSIS

Psychoanalysis is the disease it purports to cure.

———————

So-called psychoanalysis is the occupation of lascivious rationalists who reduce everything in the world to sexual causes, with the exception of their occupation.

———————

Psychoanalysis: a rabbit that was swallowed by a boa constrictor who just wanted to see what it was like in there.

———————

An analyst turns a man to dust.

———————

Psychoanalysts are father confessors who like to listen to the sins of the fathers as well.

———————

One cleans someone else's threshold of consciousness only if one's own home is dirty.

———————

Most people are sick. But only a few know that this is something they can be proud of. These are the psychoanalysts.

———————

They have the press, they have the stock exchange, and now they have the subconscious!

———————

They pick our dreams as though they were our pockets.

QUOTES ON "H"

HABIT

The fixity of a habit is generally in direct proportion to its absurdity.

MARCEL PROUST

HANUKKAH

When you compare Christmas to Hanukkah, there's no comparison. Christmas is great. Hanukkah sucks! First night you get socks. Second night, an eraser, a notebook. It's a Back-to-School holiday!   LEWIS BLACK

HAPPINESS

Happiness, *n.* An agreeable sensation arising from contemplating the misery of another.   AMBROSE BIERCE

Happiness is not something you experience, it's something you remember.

OSCAR LEVANT

Happiness is an imaginary condition, formerly attributed by the living to the dead, now usually attributed by adults to children, and by children to adults.

THOMAS SZASZ

The only really happy folk are married women and single men.

H. L. MENCKEN

Every man is thoroughly happy twice in his life: just after he has met his first love, and just after he has left his last one.   H. L. MENCKEN

You can be married and bored, or single and lonely. Ain't no happiness nowhere.
CHRIS ROCK

Few people can be happy unless they hate some other person, nation, or creed.
BERTRAND RUSSELL

Men can only be happy when they do not assume that the object of life is happiness.   GEORGE ORWELL

Happiness is the perpetual possession of being well deceived.
JONATHAN SWIFT

I can sympathize with people's pains, but *not* with their pleasure. There is something curiously boring about somebody else's happiness.
ALDOUS HUXLEY

It isn't necessary to be rich and famous to be happy. It's only necessary to be rich.   ALAN ALDA

One of the keys to happiness is a bad memory.   RITA MAE BROWN

Happy is he who causes scandal.   SALVADOR DALI

A person is never happy except at the price of some ignorance.
ANATOLE FRANCE

To be stupid, selfish, and have good health are three requirements for happiness, though if stupidity is lacking, all is lost. GUSTAVE FLAUBERT

HATRED

The more one is hated, I find, the happier one is.

LOUIS-FERDINAND CÉLINE

Now hatred is by far the longest pleasure; Men love in haste, but they detest at leisure. LORD BYRON

It does not matter much what a man hates provided he hates something.

SAMUEL BUTLER

HEADGEAR

Nobody ought to wear a Greek fisherman's
cap who doesn't meet two qualifications:
1. He is Greek.
2. He is a fisherman.

ROY BLOUNT, JR.

HEALTH

The only way to keep your health is to eat what you don't want, drink what you don't like, and do what you'd rather not. MARK TWAIN

It's no longer a question of staying healthy. It's a question of finding a sickness you like. JACKIE MASON

Early to rise and early to bed / Makes a male healthy, wealthy and dead.

JAMES THURBER

HEALTH FOOD

I refuse to spend my life worrying about what I eat. There is no pleasure worth forgoing just for an extra three years in the geriatric ward.

JOHN MORTIMER

What some call health, if purchased by perpetual anxiety about diet, isn't much better than tedious disease.   GEORGE DENNISON PRENTICE

Bread made only of the branny part of the meal, which the poorest sort of people use, especially in time of dearth and necessity, giveth a very bad and excremental nourishment to the body: it is well called *panis canicarius*, because it is more fit for dogs than for men. Health food makes me sick.

CALVIN TRILLIN

HEALTH NUTS

Health nuts are going to feel stupid someday, lying in hospitals dying of nothing.   REDD FOXX

HEART

My heart is pure as the driven slush.   TALLULAH BANKHEAD

HEAVEN

Heaven, as conventionally conceived, is a place so inane, so dull, so useless, so miserable, that nobody has ever ventured to describe a whole day in heaven, though plenty of people have described a day at the seaside.

GEORGE BERNARD SHAW

It is a curious thing…that every creed promises a paradise which will be absolutely uninhabitable for anyone of civilized taste.   EVELYN WAUGH

When I reflect upon the number of disagreeable people who I know have gone to a better world, I am moved to lead a different life.   MARK TWAIN

If I have any beliefs about immortality, it is that certain dogs I have known will go to heaven, and very, very few persons.   JAMES THURBER

In heaven all the interesting people are missing.
                                        FRIEDRICH WILHELM NIETZSCHE

—————————————— HEAVEN AND HELL ——————————————
Men have feverishly conceived a heaven only to find it insipid, and a hell to find it ridiculous.   GEORGE SANTAYANA

—————————————————— HELL ——————————————————
Hell is other people.   JEAN-PAUL SARTRE

When I think of the number of disagreeable people that I know who have gone to a better world, I am sure hell won't be so bad at all.   MARK TWAIN

Maybe there is no actual place called hell. Maybe hell is just having to listen to our grandparents breathe through their noses when they're eating sandwiches.
                                                        JIM CARREY

If there is a hell, it is modeled after Jr. High.   LEWIS BLACK

—————————————————— HISTORY ——————————————————
History, *n*. An account mostly false, of events unimportant, which are brought about by rulers mostly knaves, and soldiers mostly fools.
                                                    AMBROSE BIERCE

History is a set of lies agreed upon.   NAPOLEON BONAPARTE

History repeats itself; that's one of the things that's wrong with history.
                                                        CLARENCE DARROW

We learn from history that we do not learn from history.
                                    GEORGE FRIEDRICH WILHELM HEGEL

History is nothing but a collection of fables and useless trifles, cluttered up
with a mass of unnecessary figures and proper names.   LEO TOLSTOY

On the whole history tends to be rather poor fiction—except at its best.
                                                              GORE VIDAL

History is a bucket of ashes.   CARL SANDBURG

History is nothing but a pack of tricks that we play upon the dead.   VOLTAIRE

History is a nightmare from which we are trying to awaken.   JAMES JOYCE

History would be a wonderful thing—if it were only true.   LEO TOLSTOY

History is bunk.   HENRY FORD

The very ink with which history is written is merely fluid prejudice.
                                                           MARK TWAIN

History teaches us that men and nations behave wisely once they have exhausted all other alternatives.   ABBA EBAN

Events in the past may be roughly divided into those which probably never happened and those which do not matter.   W. R. INGE

We have wasted History like a bunch of drunks shooting dice back in the men's crapper of the local bar.   CHARLES BUKOWSKI

HISTORIAN

Historian: an unsuccessful novelist.   H. L. MENCKEN

HOLIDAYS

Holidays are an expensive trial of strength. The only satisfaction comes from survival.   JONATHAN MILLER

Holidays are often overrated disturbances of routine, costly and uncomfortable, and they usually need another holiday to correct their ravages.   E. V. LUCAS

HOLISTIC

I've decided to skip "holistic." I don't know what it means, and I don't want to know. That may seem extreme, but I followed the same strategy toward "Gestalt" and the Twist, and lived to tell the tale.   CALVIN TRILLIN

HOLLYWOOD

Hollywood is a place where people from Iowa mistake each other for movie stars.   FRED ALLEN

Strip away the phony tinsel of Hollywood and you find the real tinsel underneath.   OSCAR LEVANT

I've been asked if I ever get the DTs; I don't know; it's hard to tell where Hollywood ends and the DTs begin. W. C. FIELDS

Hollywood is a sewer with service from the Ritz Carlton.
WILSON MIZNER

The only "ism" Hollywood believes in is plagiarism.
DOROTHY PARKER

Over in Hollywood they almost made a great picture, but they caught it in time. WILSON MIZNER

In Hollywood, if you don't have happiness, you send out for it. REX REED

Good evening, ladies and gentlemen—and welcome to darkest Hollywood. Night brings a stillness to the jungle. It is so quiet you can hear a name drop. The savage beasts have already begun gathering at the water holes to quench their thirst. Now one should be especially alert. The vicious table-hopper is on the prowl and the spotted back-biter may lurk behind a potted palm.
ALFRED HITCHCOCK

You can take all the sincerity in Hollywood, place it in the navel of a fruit fly and still have room enough for three caraway seeds and a producer's heart.
FRED ALLEN

Hollywood is a great place if you're an orange. FRED ALLEN

Hollywood is like being nowhere and talking to nobody about nothing.
MICHELANGELO ANTONIONI

A dreary industrial town controlled by hoodlums of enormous wealth.
S. J. PERELMAN

Hollywood is a place where they place you under contract instead of under observation.
WALTER WINCHELL

Hollywood—that's where they give Academy Awards to Charlton Heston for acting.
SHIRLEY KNIGHT

In Hollywood a marriage is a success if it outlasts milk.
RITA RUDNER

Hollywood: They only know one word of more than one syllable there, and that is "fillum."
LOUIS SHERWIN

["Tinseltown" is derived from] the German verb *tinzelle*—literally, "to book a turkey into 1,200 theaters and make one's money before word of mouth hits."
CHARLIE HAAS

Ten million dollars worth of intricate and ingenious machinery functioning elaborately to put skin on baloney.
GEORGE JEAN NATHAN

The people here seem to live in a little world that shuts out the rest of the universe and everyone appears to be faking life. The actors and writers live in fear, and nothing, including the houses, seems permanent.
FRED ALLEN

While intelligence is the rule in Hollywood, it tends to be a Hollywood intelligence, which is to say untranslatable, suspicious, uneasy, and parochial—pure Hollywood, country-clublike in its distrust of trained intelligence of an outside kind.
HAROLD BRODKEY

The people are unreal. The flowers are unreal, they don't smell. The fruit is unreal, it doesn't taste of anything. The whole place is a glaring, gaudy, nightmarish set, built up in the desert.   ETHEL BARRYMORE

Hollywood—an emotional Detroit.   LILLIAN GISH

Hollywood is a chain gang and we all lose the will to escape. The links of the chain are forged not with cruelties but with luxuries.   CLIVE BROOK

You get called to L.A. by producers. And by the time you get out there, they sort of forget why they asked you to come.   MICHAEL HERR

Of all the Christbitten places in the two hemispheres, this is the last curly kink in the pig's tail.   STEPHEN VINCENT BENET

In 1940, I had my choice between Hitler and Hollywood, and I preferred Hollywood—just a little.   RENÉ CLAIR

There were times when I drove along the Sunset Strip and looked at those buildings or when I watched the fashionable film colony arriving at some premiere…that I fully expected God in his wrath to obliterate the whole shebang.   S. J. PERELMAN

You can't find any true closeness in Hollywood, because everybody does the fake closeness so well.   CARRIE FISHER

———————————— HOLY ROMAN EMPIRE ————————————
The Holy Roman Empire was neither holy, nor Roman, nor an empire.
                                    VOLTAIRE

HONESTY

Honesty is a good thing, but it is not profitable to its possessor unless it is kept under control.   DON MARQUIS

Honesty is the best policy—when there is money in it.   MARK TWAIN

HOOD ORNAMENTS

Hood ornaments. They were just lovely, and they gave a sense of respect. And they took 'em away because if you can save one human life—that's always the argument—it's worth it, if you can save one human life. Actually, I'd be willing to trade maybe a dozen human lives for a nice hood ornament. I imagine those things really did tend to stick in bicyclists.

MICHAEL O'DONOGHUE

HOPE

Hope in reality is the worst of all evils, because it prolongs the torments of man.
FRIEDRICH WILHELM NIETZSCHE

HOSPITALITY

People are far more sincere and good-humored at speeding their parting guests than on meeting them.   ANTON CHEKHOV

HUMANS

Such is the human race, often it seems a pity that Noah...didn't miss the boat.
MARK TWAIN

The capacity of human beings to bore one another seems to be vastly greater than that of any other animal.   H. L. MENCKEN

Their heart's in the right place, but their head is a thoroughly inefficient organ.   W. SOMERSET MAUGHAM

Most human beings have an almost infinite capacity for taking things for granted.   ALDOUS HUXLEY

There are times when you have to choose between being human and having good taste.   BERTOLT BRECHT

Everyone would like to behave like a pagan, with everyone else behaving like a Christian.   ALBERT CAMUS

Both the cockroach and the bird could get along very well without us, although the cockroach would miss us most.
                JOSEPH WOOD KRUTCH

Render unto Caesar the things that are Caesar's, and unto God the things that are God's; and unto human beings, what?   STANISLAW J. LEC

Human beings, who are almost unique in having the ability to learn from the experience of others, are also remarkable for their apparent disinclination to do so.   DOUGLAS ADAMS

Humanity is a pigsty where liars, hypocrites and the obscene in spirit congregate.   GEORGE MOORE

He who despairs over an event is a coward, but he who holds hopes for the human condition is a fool.   ALBERT CAMUS

We all live in a house on fire, no fire department to call; no way out, just the upstairs window to look out of while the fire burns the house down with us trapped, locked in it.   TENNESSEE WILLIAMS

He who has never envied the vegetable has missed the human drama.
                    E. M. CIORAN

The basic fact about human existence is not that it is a tragedy, but that it is a bore.   H. L. MENCKEN

If I could get my membership fee back, I'd resign from the human race.
                    FRED ALLEN

Don't overestimate the decency of the human race.   H. L. MENCKEN

The chief obstacle to the progress of the human race is the human race.
                    DON MARQUIS

I think computer viruses should count as life. I think it says something about human nature that the only form of life we have created so far is purely destructive. We've created life in our own image.   STEPHEN HAWKING

The nature of men and women—their *essential nature*—is so vile and despicable that if you were to portray a person as he really is, no one would believe you.   W. SOMERSET MAUGHAM

A man never reaches that dizzy height of wisdom that he can no longer be led by the nose.   MARK TWAIN

It is easier to denature plutonium than to denature the evil spirit of man.
                                                            ALBERT EINSTEIN

It is human nature to think wisely and act foolishly.   ANATOLE FRANCE

We're all fucked. It helps to remember that.   GEORGE CARLIN

No doubt Jack the Ripper excused himself on the grounds that it was human nature.   A. A. MILNE

HUMILITY

Humility is no substitute for a good personality.   FRAN LEBOWITZ

HUMOR

Humor is emotional chaos remembered in tranquility.   JAMES THURBER

Humor without malice is like a Pat Boone record on eleven. Malice without humor is like the LAPD.   HENRY ROLLINS

HUNTING

When a man wants to murder a tiger he calls it sport; when a tiger wants to murder him he calls it ferocity.   GEORGE BERNARD SHAW

A sportsman is a man who, every now and then, simply has to out and kill something.   STEPHEN LEACOCK

The English country gentleman galloping after a fox—the unspeakable in full pursuit of the uneatable.   OSCAR WILDE

The fascination of shooting as a sport depends almost wholly on whether you are at the right or wrong end of the gun.   P. G. WODEHOUSE

———————————————— HUSBANDS ————————————————

Husband, *n.* One who, having dined, is charged with the care of the plate.
                                              AMBROSE BIERCE

The husband who wants a happy marriage should learn to keep his mouth shut and his checkbook open.   GROUCHO MARX

Husbands never become good; they merely become proficient.
                                              H. L. MENCKEN

The majority of husbands remind me of an orangutan trying to play the violin.   HONORÉ DE BALZAC

A woman usually respects her father, but her view of her husband is mingled with contempt, for she is of course privy to the transparent devices by which she snared him.   H. L. MENCKEN

Intelligent women always marry fools.   ANATOLE FRANCE

When you see what some girls marry, you realize how they must hate to work for a living.   HELEN ROWLAND

Husbands think we should know where everything is—like the uterus is a tracking device. He asks me, "Roseanne, do we have any Cheetos left?" Like he can't go over to that sofa cushion and lift it himself.

ROSEANNE BARR

When you consider what a chance women have to poison their husbands, it's a wonder there isn't more of it done.   KIN HUBBARD

Husbands are awkward things to deal with; even keeping them in hot water will not make them tender.   MARY BUCKLEY

A husband is what's left of the lover once the nerve has been extracted.

HELEN ROWLAND

Before marriage, a man declares that he would lay down his life to serve you; after marriage, he won't even lay down his newspaper to talk to you.

HELEN ROWLAND

A woman who takes her husband about with her everywhere is like a cat that goes on playing with a mouse long after she's killed it.   SAKI

Marrying a man is like buying something you've been admiring for a long time in a shop window. You may love it when you get it home, but it doesn't always go with everything else in the house.   JEAN KERR

LADY ASTOR: If you were my husband, Winston, I'd put poison in your tea.
WINSTON CHURCHILL: If I were your husband, Nancy, I'd drink it.

Husbands are like fires: they go out when unattended.   ZSA ZSA GABOR

I think every woman is entitled to a middle husband she can forget.
ADELA ROGERS ST. JOHN

American husbands are the best in the world; no other husbands are so generous to their wives, or can be so easily divorced.   ELINOR GLYN

American women expect to find in their husbands a perfection that English women only hope to find in their butlers.   W. SOMERSET MAUGHAM

————————————— HYPOCRISY —————————————

I hope you have not been leading a double life, pretending to be wicked and being really good all the time. That would be hypocrisy.   OSCAR WILDE

We are not hypocrites in our sleep.   WILLIAM HAZLITT

An ounce of hypocrisy is worth a pound of ambition.   MICHAEL KORDA

If hypocrisy were gold, the Capitol would be Fort Knox.   JOHN MCCAIN

PAUL FUSSELL

He Cries at the Indy 500

Paul Fussell (pronounced fusəl) was born in Pasadena, California, in 1924. He received a B.A. from Pomona College in 1947, and an MA and a PhD from Harvard in 1949 and 1952. He has taught at Connecticut College, the University of Heidelberg, Rutgers University, and the University of Pennsylvania. He is the author of numerous books on a wide range of subjects, including *Abroad: British Literary Traveling Between the Wars; The Great War and Modern Memory*, which received the National Book Award in 1976; and *Class*, an insouciant indictment of the American class system.

JW: Are you a curmudgeon?

PF: I don't like the word *curmudgeon.* It implies that there's something wrong with social and cultural criticism, which is the obligation of every educated person. If every educated person is to be a curmudgeon, fine. Certain people have to notice things. There's a great essay by George Orwell called "Why I Write," in which he says that every writer who is honest is motivated by two things: one, the desire to show off; and two, the habit of noticing unpleasant facts. Anybody who notices unpleasant facts in the have-a-nice-day world we live in is going to be designated a curmudgeon.

JW: You see the curmudgeon as a reformer?

PF: Yes, he wants things to be better. Instead of running for Congress, he works through public presentation. He annoys and amuses people in order to bring about social change. The so-called curmudgeon is really an idealist, perhaps even a romantic, sentimental idealist.

JW: I hear a lot about the cynicism and materialism of students these days.

PF: They're the same as they always were. I've been in this trade for thirty-five years, and I don't see much difference. Almost none of them are going to the university for the right reasons, but gradually the best of them wake up. Nobody eighteen has any shape yet, men or women. You're trying to help them see, and you don't know whether you've succeeded until they're thirty-five.

JW: You've said that this is "the worst time since the thirteenth century...the terrorism, the brutality, the contempt for human life, a very vicious place to live, this century." What else do you find contemptible about it?

PF: I think the moment is notable for a general lack of attention to human dignity, which is as bad as it's been since the Renaissance. What I dislike most about the contemporary scene is the way people are treated like animals, which I think we owe to the Second World War—not just the Holocaust but the army, too. Living today is like being in the army: You line up for everything, you queue.

What I hate about contemporary life is a deep, unimaginative contempt for human beings disguised as friendly concern. If it weren't for this fraud, this pretense of friendliness, I could tolerate it easier. I would much rather have people say, "Look, you shit, line up there, we don't give a fuck about you and your mean bank account." There's no reason to be uncomfortable just because those people want you to be uncomfortable. There's too little opposition to this.

JW: Why?

PF: I think most people secretly like being treated badly, perhaps because it makes them feel like part of a great big industrial enterprise, that they're somehow contributing to the modern world.

Another thing that disturbs me is what I call "technological pretension." Every day I spend half an hour to an hour clearing up the mistakes of people I have business relations with—the telephone company, the bank, everybody. I moved recently, and half the people who received the change-of-address card got it wrong because they're so technologically pretentious with their little computer keyboards.

JW: Are you against machines per se?

PF: No, but I'm getting a little bit off them because I don't think they're opening up the good life at all. They're making slaves of people. I got rid of my car, for example. What I'm against is a certain attitude about people that makes machines inevitable. Machines have no sense of humor, and I can't stand to live in a world with no sense of humor, no sense of irony, where everything is literal. That's hell.

JW: In that context you've written that by the next century there will be no difference between the United States and the Soviet Union.

PF: Yes, we're getting closer all the time. I call it "prole drift." It's probably a result of the world population problem—the population of the world has doubled since I was a boy. But intelligence hasn't doubled; sensitivity hasn't doubled; everything that matters hasn't doubled. It's an immense overcrowding. Hence lines and identification numbers are on the increase everywhere, and I think that's worth objecting to. And the two societies are becoming identical in terms of athleticism, the idea of finding national identity in athletic victory. To take advantage of the garrulity of the politician and the politician of the credulity of the journalist. The Soviets happen to be good at chess and weight lifting and we're good at football, but it's the same kind of stupid, mind-blowing imbecility on both sides which is projected as national policy. Two great big, muscle-bound giants with little pea brains on top.

JW: What else disturbs you about contemporary American life?

PF: First-naming by people who have no right to do it. People phone me from Dallas and Houston—they always mispronounce my last name as "fewsell," and that tips me off immediately—and they'll say, "Paul, I'm selling some wonderful oil shares out here and—" Click.

JW: Is the process of having your work published an adversarial relationship?

PF: Very much, and I get angry when editors and publishers try to be my friends. It indicates that they're about to swindle you.

JW: You've written extensively about class. For example, you've said that chess is rarely found above the upper middle class.

PF: I have never known an upper-class person to play chess. Backgammon's their game. Another thing: We've had a young relative staying with us for the past few days which required me to cede her my bathroom and use another one. I was uncomfortable for the entire time, and it reminded me that the upper class never allows itself to be uncomfortable, except on a yacht.

JW: You did a piece for Harper's *about the Indianapolis 500 in which you confessed that you cried when they played "Back Home in Indiana."*

PF: I do it at weddings, too. I think it has to do with my long relation with young people as an observer of their hopes and their beliefs. Seeing someone who really believes in something makes me cry, I don't know why. Out of curiosity, I've visited great Catholic religious centers like Fatima in Portugal and Lourdes in France, although I'm a total religious skeptic myself, as a sort of sociologist of that pathology. It always makes me cry to see the pathos of people who actually believe that drinking holy water is going to cure their polio.

JW: You've done a lot of traveling and travel writing, from which I gather you didn't like Tel Aviv.

PF: I think Tel Aviv is an awful place. It apes the worst things about the United States. It's full of fast food, piped music, and fraudulent friendliness. Everything I hate about the United States, Tel Aviv has in spades. But it's not just Tel Aviv; I could point to many other places in the world that have done this to themselves.

JW: In your book, Abroad, *you say that "anyone who has hotel reservations and speaks no French is a tourist." How do you feel about the French?*

PF: I adore them because they're very honest in their snot. They don't pretend to like anybody but themselves. I love that. I love the French restaurant and the French shop where everyone is addressed as Monsieur or Madame, regardless of their social class. They erect an iron curtain of formality between themselves and other people. I find that I'm happier in an environment like that than in a pseudo-friendly one like the United States. I've never had a French taxi driver try to become my friend.

JW: Whereas here…

PF: Sometimes when I'm in a cruel mood and I'm being driven back from the airport by a taxi driver and he says, "How about those Eagles?" I'll say something like, "What the fuck is this Eagles stuff?" He assumes that because he has me in his cab I have the same interests as he does. I don't demand that he know all about *Samson Agonistes*, yet he demands that I know all about the Eagles.

JW: Aside from that, how do you like living in Philadelphia?

PF: The most accurate thing I can say about Philadelphia, from the point of view of somebody who knows New York and London, is that it's sweet. When I want excitement, I go to New York for a heavy day or evening and then I come back to the dormitory. This is Quietville.

OSCAR LEVANT

Total Recoil

O^{scar} Levant was born in Pittsburgh, Pennsylvania, in 1906, the son of Russian-Jewish immigrants. His parents ran a jewelry store and were music lovers, his father an opera addict, his mother a Tchaikovsky fan.

Levant joked that he tried to run away from home at the age of ten months, and that at the age of ten years, when asked what he wanted to be when he grew up, he replied, "I want to be an orphan." He was an unattractive child with a poor self-image whose high-school classmates awarded him a lemon for being the school's worst dancer (and, typically, he had a pathological aversion to lemons for the rest of his life).

He showed early promise as a pianist, and at sixteen he left home to study music in New York, where he supported himself by giving piano lessons and by playing with dance bands. An appearance in a Broadway musical led to a part in its film version in 1929. He stayed in Hollywood for several years and there met George Gershwin. They became close friends, and Levant virtually abandoned his own career as a composer and became the foremost interpreter of Gershwin's works. He was profoundly shaken by Gershwin's death in 1937.

Levant worked as a songwriter at MGM in the forties and appeared in several movies, often as himself, i.e., a chain-smoking, wisecracking, tortured genius whose normal facial expression was one of amused disgust.

Although he never got past high school, he was knowledgeable on a variety of subjects and was a regular panelist on *Information Please*, a popular forties radio quiz show.

During the fifties and sixties, he appeared sporadically on TV talk shows and stunned viewers with his caustic repartee and frank discussion of his psychiatric problems. He was a manic-depressive, an insomniac, and a hypochondriac. Levant was prey to numerous obsessive rituals: he always buttoned his shirt from the bottom, always stirred his coffee in the same direction four times; when he turned on a water faucet, he tapped it eight times, and when he turned it off, he recited a silent prayer: "Good luck, bad luck, good luck, Romain Gary, Christopher Isherwood and Krisna Menon."

He began taking sleeping pills to control stage fright, and by the end of his life was a walking pharmacopeia. (He once described Demerol as "better than sex.") A veteran analysand, Levant was an in-patient in various psychiatric hospitals, where he was subjected to a variety of "therapies," including shock treatments. (While confined to the psychiatric ward of a Catholic hospital, he complained, "You need a permit from the pope to get two Bufferin here.")

During his career Levant befriended many of the show business greats of his era—he was a close friend and confidant of George S. Kaufman and Groucho Marx—but those who knew him more casually described him best:

> He seems to me to be one of those truly unquenchable human beings in whom the flame of light burns very brightly, but who, just by virtue of that circumstance, finds its strains and tensions the more agonizing; sometimes unbearably so. MALCOLM MUGGERIDGE

> Oscar…is full of contempt for himself. And good neurotic that he is, he is willing to share this contempt with the world. BEN HECHT

> He has no meanness; and it is doubtful if he ever for a moment considered murder. DOROTHY PARKER

Oscar Levant was in constant flight from life, yet he embraced it with a kind of demented joy. He found endless sources of discomfort, annoyance, guilt, and fear, but was capable of laughing at all of them. He wrote three semi-autobiographical books: *A Smattering of Ignorance, The Memoirs of an Amnesiac,* and *The Unimportance of Being Oscar,* which reveal a sensitive, almost tender lunatic who lashed out at everything within his considerable intellectual reach but who always saved the most biting commentary for himself.

His last television appearances were in 1963, on *The Tonight Show,* hosted by Jack Paar. After Levant's death in 1972, Paar closed all his shows with, "Good night, Oscar Levant, wherever you are."

LEVANT ON LEVANT

Under this flabby exterior is an enormous lack of character.

I am no more humble than my talents require.

I'm a self-made man. Who else would help?

I'm a study of a man in chaos in search of frenzy.

When I was young I looked like Al Capone, but I lacked his compassion.

I never read bad reviews about myself, because my friends invariably tell me about them.

I don't drink; I don't like it—it makes me feel good.

I was voted Pill of the Year by the Pharmaceutical Society.

There is a thin line between genius and insanity. I have erased this line.

I was once thrown out of a mental hospital for depressing the other patients.

Instant unconsciousness has been my greatest passion for ten years.

Politics? I could have delivered the mental illness vote in a solid bloc.

If you are created by Dostoevsky, like I am, euphoria comes in handy.

The first thing I do in the morning is brush my teeth and sharpen my tongue.

OSCAR LEVANT
ANECDOTES

He was able to discourse interminably on the subject of his own greatness, and on one occasion subjected Aaron Copland to a lengthy diatribe. Unable to stand it anymore, Copland got up to leave. "Why, Aaron," said Levant, "you're becoming an egomaniac. You used to be able to listen to me all night." Seated at dinner next to an attractive young lady, Levant failed to stifle a yawn. "Am I keeping you up?" she asked.

"I wish you were," he answered.

———————

He had three daughters with his non-Jewish second wife. He referred to his family as the *goyim* and exhorted his children to "finish your martinis before you leave the table."

———————

When introduced to Greta Garbo, Oscar quipped, "Sorry, I didn't catch the name." He later remarked that he had been so overcome by her glamour that all he could do was to stammer the line that ironically has become a prime example of his self-possessed wit.

———————

His first wife subsequently married movie theater tycoon Arthur Loew. At two A.M. on their wedding night, Levant called her and asked, "What's playing at the Loew's State and what time does the feature go on?"

In the late fifties he hosted a local TV show in Los Angeles with his second wife, June, and one night he fell asleep while interviewing a guest. When June tried to nudge him awake, he groused, "Wake me when he's through."

———————————

To an obnoxious acquaintance: "I'm going to memorize your name and throw my head away."

———————————

After dinner at the White House, Levant turned to his wife and said, "Now I suppose we'll have to have the Trumans over to *our* house."

———————————

During a poker game he was told of Judy Garland's latest suicide attempt. "Let's see," he said, dealing a hand, "she's two up on me in suicide attempts, but I'm three up on her in nervous breakdowns. Or is it the other way around?"

GROUCHO MARX

The Dark One

Julius Henry Marx was born in the Yorkville section of Manhattan in 1890 to an unsuccessful Alsatian tailor nicknamed "Frenchie" and an indomitable, archetypal stage mother named Minnie. Groucho was the third of five sons (Leonard, Arthur, Milton, and Herbert later became Chico, Harpo, Gummo, and Zeppo) and was, by his own account, third in his mother's affections. She referred to him as "the dark one."

The origin of his nickname is disputed. It may have come from the practice of wearing a chamois purse around his neck, a "grouch bag," to protect his vaudeville earnings from the hazards of the road, but more likely it was simply an accurate description of his personality.

He began his career at the age of eleven as a boy singer, a member of the Three Nightengales—Groucho, Gummo, and a girl. A series of musical acts (the Four Nightingales, the Six Musical Mascots) barely earned the brothers a living in vaudeville. Groucho worked solo off and on, and was once stranded in Cripple Creek, Colorado, after a disastrous engagement, and had to take a job as a wagon driver until Minnie could send him train fare home. Throughout his early career he encountered tough times and tough audiences. One night in Nacogdoces, Texas, he responded to an especially unruly crowd by announcing, "Nacogdoces is full of roaches."

He started wearing a mustache in an early vaudeville act. One night, late for the curtain, he merely drew it on with greasepaint. The audience didn't seem to notice, so he continued the practice for the rest of his vaudeville career and for most of the Marx Brothers movies. It became his trademark, along with the crouched walk and the leering, rolling eyes. He grew into his stage persona: he didn't wear a real mustache until he reached middle age.

It wasn't until 1924, when Groucho was thirty-four, that the Marx Brothers finally made it to Broadway in a revue called *I'll Say She Is*. The show was a hit, their career skyrocketed, and the following year they displayed their unique brand of slapstick insanity in another stage hit, *The Cocoanuts*, written by George S. Kaufman and Morrie Ryskind.

The Cocoanuts became their first movie. The Marx Brothers made a dozen more films over the next decade, all of which embodied Groucho's utter disrespect for authority. He played a series of punning, lascivious con men with such names as Rufus T. Firefly, Professor Wagstaff, Doctor Hugo Z. Hackenbush, Otis B. Driftwood, Captain Jeffrey T. Spaulding, and J. Cheever Loophole. *A Night in Casablanca* was their last feature film. Groucho said the fun had gone out of moviemaking after the death of Irving Thalberg, the production chief at MGM who had produced *A Night at the Opera* and *A Day at the Races*.

Groucho never graduated from grammar school and regretted his lack of education all his life. He read voraciously to compensate, and secretly wanted to be a writer. He wrote three autobiographical books: *Groucho and Me, Memoirs of a Mangy Lover,* and *The Groucho Letters,* and surrounded himself with what he considered "intellectuals," mostly young writers, quietly helping their careers whenever he could.

From 1950 to 1961, he hosted *You Bet Your Life* on television. Ostensibly a quiz show, it was really a platform for his ad-libs. Contestants were chosen for their ability to act as foils for his slashing wit, and the rules were only loosely observed. He made occasional guest appearances on TV shows during the early seventies and, having enjoyed a renaissance among the baby boom generation, he appeared in a one-man show at Carnegie Hall in 1972 at the age of eighty-two.

Groucho grew increasingly frail and senile, and died in 1977 at the age of eighty-six, having outlived all of his brothers and most of his friends and show business contemporaries.

Groucho Marx was an optimist disguised as a cynic. He was incapable of having a serious conversation, compulsively making fun of everything and everyone. He was always "on." Chico said that he would "insult a king to make a beggar laugh."

GROUCHO MARX
ANECDOTES

After the success of *Cocoanuts*, Groucho bought a house in the suburban Long Island community of Great Neck and inquired about joining a restricted swimming club. The manager told him that the club could not accept his application because of its policy against admitting Jews.

Groucho thought for a moment and asked, "Well, then how about my son? He's only *half* Jewish. Can he go in the water up to his waist?"

David Steinberg recalls dining with Groucho at the Brown Derby. A priest came up to the table and said, "Mr. Steinberg, I'm a fan."

Steinberg immediately said, "Do you know Groucho Marx?"

"Oh, Mr. Marx, I want to thank you for bringing so much joy into the world."

Groucho quickly replied, "I want to thank you for taking so much out."

Groucho was having problems sexually—premature ejaculation. Someone recommended a topical creme guaranteed to prolong erection. When asked later whether it worked, Groucho reported, "I came rubbing the stuff on."

He was invited by Paramount to a screening of *Samson and Delilah*, starring Hedy Lamarr and Victor Mature. At the conclusion of the picture, one of the studio executives asked Groucho how he liked it.

"Well," he replied, "there's just one problem. No picture can hold my interest where the leading man's tits are bigger than the leading lady's."

———————————

A drunken fan careened up to him, slapped him on the back, and said, "Why, you old son of a gun, you probably don't remember me."

Groucho replied, "I never forget a face, but in your case I'll make an exception."

———————————

A guest on his *You Bet Your Life* television show was a woman who had given birth to twenty-two children. "I love my husband," the woman explained sheepishly.

"I love my cigar, too," Groucho said, "but I take it out once in a while."

QUOTES ON "I"

———————————— ICE DANCING ————————————

Ice dancing is not a sport. Take away the skates and the sequins and it's just a public wife-beating. If you saw this happening in a trailer park, you'd call the cops.   BILL MAHER

———————————— IDEAS ————————————

To die for an idea is to set a rather high price on conjecture.
ANATOLE FRANCE

To die for an idea; it is unquestionably noble. But how much nobler it would be if men died for ideas that were true!   H. L. MENCKEN

We use ideas merely to justify our evil, and speech merely to conceal our ideas.
VOLTAIRE

The history of ideas is the history of the grudges of solitary men.
E. M. CIORAN

I can't understand why people are frightened of new ideas. I'm frightened of the old ones.   JOHN CAGE

IDEALISM

Idealism is the noble toga that political gentlemen drape over their will to power.
ALDOUS HUXLEY

Idealism is fine, but as it approaches reality the cost becomes prohibitive.
WILLIAM F. BUCKLEY, JR.

Idealism increases in direct proportion to one's distance from the problem.
JOHN GALSWORTHY

An idealist is one who, on noticing that a rose smells better than a cabbage, concludes that it will also make better soup.   H. L. MENCKEN

I'm an idealist: I don't know where I'm going but I'm on my way.
CARL SANDBURG

When they come down from their ivory towers, idealists are apt to walk straight into the gutter.   LOGAN PEARSALL SMITH

The idealist is incorrigible—if he is turned out of his heaven, he makes an ideal of his hell.   FRIEDRICH WILHELM NIETZSCHE

The idealist walks on his toes, the materialist on his talons.
MALCOLM DE CHAZAL

IDIOT

Idiot, *n.* A member of a large and powerful tribe whose influence in human affairs has always been dominant and controlling.
AMBROSE BIERCE

—————————— IMMACULATE CONCEPTION ——————————

I went to a convent in New York and was fired finally for my insistence that the Immaculate Conception was spontaneous combustion.

DOROTHY PARKER

—————————— IMMORALITY ——————————

Immorality: the morality of those who are having a better time.

H. L. MENCKEN

—————————— IMMORTALITY ——————————

Immortality is the condition of a dead man who doesn't believe he is dead.

H. L. MENCKEN

Millions long for immortality who do not know what to do with themselves on a rainy Sunday afternoon.

SUSAN ERTZ

I don't want to achieve immortality through my work. I want to achieve it through not dying.

WOODY ALLEN

—————————— IMPIETY ——————————

Impiety, *n.* Your irreverence toward my deity.

AMBROSE BIERCE

—————————— INANIMATE OBJECTS ——————————

Inanimate objects are classified scientifically into three major categories—those that don't work, those that break down and those that get lost.

RUSSELL BAKER

—————————— INCOME ——————————

It is better to have a permanent income than to be fascinating.

OSCAR WILDE

─────────────── INFIDELITY ───────────────

I am a strict monogamist: it is twenty years since I last went to bed with two women at once, and then I was in my cups and not myself.

H. L. MENCKEN

Few things in life are more embarrassing than the necessity of having to inform an old friend that you have just got engaged to his fiancée.

W. C. FIELDS

There is one thing I would break up over and that is if she caught me with another woman. I wouldn't stand for that.   STEVE MARTIN

A Code of Honor: Never approach a friend's girlfriend or wife with mischief as your goal. There are just too many women in the world to justify that sort of dishonorable behavior. Unless she's *really* attractive.

BRUCE JAY FRIEDMAN

My boyfriend and I broke up. He wanted to get married, and I didn't want him to.   RITA RUDNER

─────────────── INFLATION ───────────────

Inflation is the one form of taxation that can be imposed without legislation.

MILTON FRIEDMAN

A dollar saved is a quarter earned.   JOHN CIARDI

─────────────── INFORMATION ───────────────

Everybody gets so much information all day long that they lose their common sense.   GERTRUDE STEIN

INSANITY

Insanity: a perfectly rational adjustment to the insane world.

R. D. LAING

INSIDER

You can be a rank insider as well as a rank outsider.   ROBERT FROST

INSINCERITY

What people call insincerity is simply a method by which we can multiply our personalities.   OSCAR WILDE

INSTANT GRATIFICATION

Instant gratification takes too long.   CARRIE FISHER

INTELLECTUALS

Intellectuals are people who believe that ideas are of more importance than values. That is to say, their own ideas and other people's values.

GERALD BRENAN

There are some things only intellectuals are crazy enough to believe.

GEORGE ORWELL

INTELLIGENCE

There is no such thing as an underestimate of average intelligence.

HENRY ADAMS

I would like to take you seriously but to do so would affront your intelligence.

WILLIAM F. BUCKLEY, JR.

INTELLIGENCE SERVICE

An intelligence service is, in fact, a stupidity service.   E. B. WHITE

INTELLIGENTSIA

A large section of the intelligentsia seems wholly devoid of intelligence.
G. K. CHESTERTON

INTERNET

We've heard that a million monkeys at a million keyboards could produce the complete works of Shakespeare; now, thanks to the Internet, we know that is not true.   ROBERT WILENSKY

Why do people keep insisting that I join the twenty-first century? I *live* in the twenty-first century! I just don't want to be bothered by the shitheads on the Internet!   HARLAN ELLISON

My favorite thing about the Internet is that you get to go into the private world of real creeps without having to smell them.   PENN JILLETTE

The Internet is just a world passing around notes in a classroom.
JON STEWART

INTERVIEW

The interview is an intimate conversation between journalist and politician wherein the journalist seeks Journalism which consists largely in saying "Lord Jones died" to people who never knew Lord Jones was alive.

G. K. CHESTERTON

244 • THE BIG CURMUDGEON

──────────────── IRELAND AND THE IRISH ────────────────

Every St. Patrick's Day every Irishman goes out to find another Irishman to
make a speech to.   SHANE LESLIE

Other people have a nationality. The Irish and the Jews have a psychosis.
                                                         BRENDAN BEHAN

──────────────────────── IRONY ────────────────────────

Irony is the hygiene of the mind.   ELIZABETH BIBESCO

DOROTHY PARKER

Just a Little Jewish Girl Trying to Be Cute

Dorothy Rothschild was born in West End, New Jersey, on August 22, 1893, to a Jewish father and a Scottish-American mother who died in her infancy. Her father remarried, and Dorothy was raised by a stepmother who sent her to a Catholic convent school and later to a private finishing school.

In 1917, following her first literary job as a caption writer for *Vogue*, she became a reviewer for *Vanity Fair*, where Robert Benchley was her editor. She was fired on the grounds that her reviews were too tough, and Benchley quit in sympathy. As freelancers, they shared an office for a time, which prompted her famous crack: "If the office had been any smaller, it would have been adultery."

Her marriage to Edwin Pond Parker II of Hartford lasted only a few years, but she continued to use his surname, finding it preferable to her own.

In 1925, she was one of a group of writers who helped Harold Ross found *The New Yorker*, and she became its drama critic in 1927, writing stinging book reviews under the pseudonym "Constant Reader." Her short stories appeared in the magazine until 1955. Parker produced light, satirical verse and pessimistic short stories about loneliness, disillusionment, love gone wrong, and suicide. She was never satisfied with her literary efforts—she strove for truth and purity but never felt she had achieved them. About her verse she once said, "I'm always chasing Rimbauds."

Parker's screenwriting credits include the original version of *A Star Is Born*, and she collaborated on two plays, *Close Harmony* with Elmer Rice and *Ladies of the Corridor* with Arnaud D'Usseau.

In 1933, she married Alan Campbell, an actor-writer eleven years her junior and a homosexual. They went to Hollywood together as screenwriters, were divorced in 1947, and remarried in 1950. When Campbell died in 1963, Parker returned to New York to live out her remaining years.

Her reputation as a wit was based more on her conversational bon mots than on her writing, and it grew to the point that many clever remarks were erroneously attributed to her, even though she scrupulously disavowed them. Conversely, two of her most famous lines have been repeatedly misattributed to others: "You can lead a horticulture but you can't make her think" and "Men seldom make passes at girls who wear glasses" (which is frequently misquoted as "Men never make passes at girls who wear glasses").

Dorothy Parker was the only regular female member of the Algonquin Round Table, and her cynicism extended to the vicious circle itself: "The Round Table thing was *greatly* overrated. It was full of people looking for a free lunch and asking, 'Did you hear the funny thing I said yesterday?'"

She ridiculed what she considered cultural snobbery: When asked if she had attended the most recent performance of the Philharmonic or the latest museum exhibit, Parker's standard reply was, "I've been too fucking busy and vice versa."

Toward the end of her life she had difficulty writing, and missed book review deadlines until she was no longer assigned to write them. But her oral wit remained intact; she still talked brilliantly about her reading material, which remained voluminous and eclectic until her death. But having outlived her fame, Parker became a bitter, alcoholic recluse. She attempted suicide several times and died in 1967 at the age of seventy-four.

Her description of herself is emblematic of her attitude toward the rest of the world: "Boy, did I think I was smart. I was just a little Jewish girl trying to be cute."

DOROTHY PARKER
ANECDOTES

She often vented her contempt for pretension and self-importance on Clare Boothe Luce, and their encounters produced two famous Parkerisms: When told that Luce was always kind to her inferiors, Parker asked, "Where does she find them?"

On another occasion the two women arrived simultaneously at the door of a nightclub. "Age before beauty" was all Luce could muster.

"And pearls before swine," said Parker as she glided through the doorway.

Her husband, Alan Campbell, had just died, and as his body was being removed from the house, a female acquaintance asked Parker if there was anything she could do. "Get me a new husband," she replied.

"Why, that's the most callous, disgusting remark I've ever heard," the woman said.

Parker turned to her and said quietly, "Okay, then run down to the corner and get me a ham and cheese on rye and tell them to hold the mayo."

When a woman told her, "I really can't come to your party, I can't bear fools," Parker answered, "That's strange, your mother could."

On being told that President Calvin Coolidge had just died, she remarked, "How could they tell?"

She is credited with saying at a party, "One more drink and I'll be under the host."

On hearing that a British actress who was notorious for her numerous love affairs had broken her leg, Parker quipped, "She must have done it sliding down a barrister."

Oscar Levant once asked her if she took sleeping pills, and she replied, "In a big bowl with sugar and cream."

She was confined in an oxygen tent after one of several suicide attempts but was sufficiently in possession of herself to ask, "May I have a flag for my tent?"

Parker was hospitalized for alcoholism, and her doctor told her that she would be dead in a month if she did not stop drinking. She looked up at him and whispered, "Promises, promises."

FRAN LEBOWITZ

Manhattan Malcontent

Fran Lebowitz was born in Morristown, New Jersey, in 1950. In 1968, after attending a series of secondary schools without actually graduating, she moved to New York and took a succession of what she calls "cutesy" jobs—waitress, usher, cab driver, and began writing poetry and book and movie reviews. In 1978, after writing columns in *Mademoiselle* and Andy Warhol's *Interview*, she published *Metropolitan Life*, an anthology of biting, aphoristic commentary whose immediate success made her an overnight celebrity. Her second book, *Social Studies*, was published in 1981. Both are collected with a new introduction in *The Fran Lebowitz Reader*.

JW: Do you get to Los Angeles often?

FL: Four, maybe five times a year.

JW: I gather you're not crazy about it.

FL: Actually, I like it much better than I used to, probably because I like New York much less. As New York has gotten duller and duller, L.A. seems less awful. I doubt very much that L.A. has become less awful, it's just that in contrast to New York it seems less awful. You never have to have human contact here; there are very few actual humans to have contact with.

But New York has become so dull. Ed Koch and his Sinclair Lewis boosterism, his "I Love New York" campaign attracted droves of people who don't deserve to live there, people who should live in Atlanta, and it drove out the people who deserve to live there. New York is like Atlanta with very high rents.

JW: Do you ever try to work while you're out here?

FL: I hardly try to work anywhere, and by now I have it down to where I cannot work no matter where I am. In my opinion most writers should do less work and not more, and many of them should move here and not work at all. It would be an advantage to the literary world if most writers stopped writing entirely.

JW: If it's not too personal, how have you been sleeping lately?

FL: I sleep so poorly. I only sleep in the daytime. It's always been that way, even when I was little. I was sent to bed at seven thirty until I was ten, and thought it was normal. I finally asked my mother why she made me go to bed so early and she said, "By seven thirty I couldn't listen to you anymore." My mother was in the house all the time and I followed her around; she was the person I talked at. That was when I was still asking questions instead of giving answers.

JW: Do you remember the point when you stopped asking and started answering?

FL: I had opinions from a young age but mixed them with questions. The only time I ever ask questions now is if I happen to meet a doctor, because I'm a hypochondriac. Other than that I rarely ask questions.

JW: Tell me about your hypochondria.

FL: I never worry about things I could actually get, like from smoking, but I'll be watching TV and they'll be talking about a disease that only seventy-five-year-old Turkish men get and I'll have every symptom.

JW: Do you exercise?

FL: I walk a lot in New York, not for exercise but to get from place to place, and because it's the way of having the least contact with human beings. You have to have a death wish to get in a cab. I take the subway when I'm really late, but I prefer to walk because I don't have to put myself at the mercy of that faceless lunatic who drives the subway or the obviously insane man who's driving the taxicab.

JW: Who doesn't speak English.

FL: Who doesn't speak any known language at all. Every single cab driver in New York has their name spelled in an alphabet that has an *o* with a slash through it. This is not a language I've ever come in contact with. And now they don't let you smoke in cabs. I'm not going to pay all that money so I cannot smoke.

JW: Do you watch much television?

FL: I watch game shows. I was a big fan of *Family Feud*. In fact the high point of my career was having an episode of *Family Feud* dedicated to me on the air. The producer called my agent and said they had noticed how often I said I liked the show and they were going to dedicate a show to me on the air. They did and I watched it, and to me it was the Nobel Prize.

JW: What did you like about the show?

FL: They had teams of families with five people on each team. The most you could win was $5,000 on the daytime version and $10,000 on the night-time version. So say you won $10,000; you had to pay your own way to

California and you had to pay taxes on the money. I figure it cost the average family about $7,500 to win, and I loved watching them jump up and down before they realized they had only won about $500 apiece. I also liked the answers to the questions. It was like going to a mall without having to leave the house. One of my favorite questions they ever had was, "Name five famous American intellectuals" and the first answer from the winning team was "John Kennedy," a well-known intellectual, and it was on the board! In answer to the question, "Name a famous Rudolph," a guy jumped up and yelled, "Rudolph Hitler!"

JW: You once said that to you the ultimate activity was autographing your own book. Do you still enjoy it?

FL: Yes, it's endlessly rewarding. It's a great feeling of accomplishment to have a book in your hand that you wrote. And second of all, you're selling it. Getting money is always a gratifying experience.

JW: What about celebrity in general—does it bother you to be recognized in public, to have your privacy invaded?

FL: Writers don't get that famous; the people who have their privacy invaded are mostly movie stars. Writers get exactly the right amount of fame: just enough to get a good table in a restaurant but not enough so that people are constantly interrupting you while you're eating dinner.

JW: You've been accused of being a snob.

FL: I'm not a snob in the usual sense. I'm not a money snob, I'm not a family snob, I'm a snob in other ways. I'm an elitist. I do not think everyone is created equal. In fact I know they're not. The Constitution doesn't mean that everyone is as good as everyone else, it means that everyone should have the same laws as everyone else. It doesn't mean that everyone's as smart or as cute or as lucky as everyone else. People have distorted the idea of democracy.

JW: Are you a feminist?

FL: No. I'm not opposed to most of the goals or beliefs of feminism, but it doesn't interest me. Not that the things feminists say aren't true, they seem to me to be not only true but so obvious that why would you devote your life to worrying about them? It seems to me the sort of thing that a civilized person wouldn't even bother to mention.

JW: Do you feel that feminism has accomplished anything?

FL: What has changed? Six people have bigger jobs than they would have had. Life has not changed for the average woman except for the worse. Now women have to do not only the jobs that they always had to do because men won't do them—I don't care how many episodes of Phil *Donahue* you watch, men will not do these jobs—they have to do the men's jobs, too. The women who fell for this must be in a fury because they used to have boring lives, and now they still have boring lives but on top of that they have to work forty hours a week. It seems to me you were better off when you only had half these problems.

Probably the salient feature of modern life is the idea that everything can be fixed. It's a fear of bad luck. I call it "the bad facts." These are the bad facts: Men have much easier lives than women. Men have the advantage. So do white people. So do rich people. So do beautiful people. These are the bad facts. You're born, you take a look at yourself; if you're a black woman instead of a white man, your life is ten times harder.

I was recently on the Long Island Expressway going to the airport, surrounded by eleven million people who do this every day. They do this twice a day! And you think to yourself, well, these people obviously feel they're going to live sixty-five thousand years and they figure they might as well spend thirty years sitting in a car. That's how I feel about someone who's an active feminist: you are not going to change anything; if you feel like devoting the little time you have to what I consider a really hopeless cause, you're welcome to do it, but I have no interest in doing it.

JW: You've said that you don't take drugs.

FL: I don't take drugs because I don't feel like dying instantaneously. I stopped when I was nineteen. I never took an hallucinogenic because I never wanted my consciousness expanded one unnecessary iota. I'm sure that being sober all these years accounts for my ill humor.

JW: You're also on record about romantic love.

FL: Romantic love is mental illness. But it's a pleasurable one. It's a drug. It distorts reality, and that's the point of it. It would be impossible to fall in love with someone that you really saw. The second you meet someone that you're going to fall in love with, you deliberately become a moron. You do this in order to fall in love, because it would be impossible to fall in love with any human being if you actually saw them for what they are.

People who get married because they're in love make a ridiculous mistake. It makes much more sense to marry your best friend. You like your best friend more than anyone you're ever going to be in love with. You don't choose your best friend because they have a cute nose, but that's all you're doing when you get married; you're saying, "I will spend the rest of my life with you because of your lower lip." It's amazing that all marriages don't end in divorce. If you can stay in love for more than two years, you're *on* something.

QUOTES ON "J"

JEWS

If my theory of relativity is proven successful, Germany will claim me as a German and France will declare that I am a citizen of the world. Should my theory prove untrue, France will say that I am a German, and Germany will declare that I am a Jew.   ALBERT EINSTEIN

The Jews are a frightened people. Nineteen centuries of Christian love have broken down their nerves.   ISRAEL ZANGWILL

It is extremely difficult for a Jew to be converted, for how can he bring himself to believe in the divinity of...another Jew?   HEINRICH HEINE

JOGGING

It's unnatural for people to run around city streets unless they are thieves or victims. It makes people nervous to see someone running. I know that when I see someone running on my street, my instincts tell me to let the dog out after him.   MIKE ROYKO

JOURNALISM

Journalism justifies its own existence by the great Darwinian principle of the survival of the vulgarist.   OSCAR WILDE

There is much to be said in favor of modern journalism. By giving us the opinions of the uneducated, it keeps us in touch with the ignorance of the community.   OSCAR WILDE

The only qualities for real success in journalism are ratlike cunning, a plausible manner and a little literary ability. The capacity to steal other people's ideas and phrases…is also invaluable.   NICHOLAS TOMALIN

A professional whose business it is to explain to others what it personally does not understand.   LORD NORTHCLIFFE

The First Law of Journalism: to confirm existing prejudice, rather than contradict it.   ALEXANDER COCKBURN

Once a newspaper touches a story, the facts are lost forever, even to the protagonists.   NORMAN MAILER

The public have an insatiable curiosity to know everything. Except what is worth knowing. Journalism, conscious of this, and having tradesman-like habits, supplies their demands.   OSCAR WILDE

Trying to be a first-rate reporter on the average American newspaper is like trying to play Bach's St. Matthew Passion on a ukelele: the instrument is too crude for the work, for the audience and for the performer.

BEN BAGDIKIAN

——————————— JOURNALISTS ———————————
The lowest depth to which people can sink before God is defined by the word *journalist.* If I were a father and had a daughter who was seduced I should not

despair over her; I would hope for her salvation. But if I had a son who became a journalist, and continued to be one for five years, I would give him up.

SØREN KIERKEGAARD

I believe in equality for everyone, except reporters and photographers.

MOHANDAS K. GANDHI

————————————— JUDGES —————————————
Judge: a law student who marks his own papers.   H. L. MENCKEN

Appellate Division judges are whores who became madams.

MARTIN ERDMANN

————————————— JUNK BONDS —————————————
How does something like this happen? How do people spend ten years buying and selling something with *junk* in the name, and then say, "Oh, my God, you mean those weren't good investments? They sounded so *great*! Junk bonds. We thought we couldn't go wrong with a name like that."

JOE BOB BRIGGS

The only time to buy these is on a day with no *y* in it.

WARREN BUFFETT

MIKE ROYKO

A Liberal's Conservative and Vice Versa

Mike Royko (1932–1997), a Pulitzer Prize–winning, nationally syndicated columnist for the *Chicago Tribune*, was born in Chicago in 1932. He attended Wright Junior College, the University of Illinois, and Northwestern University. After serving in the U.S. Air Force during the Korean War, he joined the Chicago *Daily News* in 1952 as a reporter and was assigned a weekly government and political column in 1962. His long-running daily commentary, "Mike Royko," first appeared in the *Daily News* in 1963. He described his role as follows: "My function is to explain things rather than report them."

JW: You've written about the deterioration of manners in movie theaters.

MR: It's the result of television: People are used to talking and they forget that they're not alone when they're in a theater. When I was a kid, I was an usher in a number of theaters and you just told 'em to shut up, and if they didn't shut up, you took 'em out. Today it's anarchy, although I occasionally I go to the movies in a small town in Wisconsin and the kids there are quiet, because for all they know, their uncle may be sitting two rows away. Uncles up there still have crew cuts, half of them are farmers, and they're liable to give the kid a whack in the side of the head. So it's different in smaller communities than it is in a big-city movie theater where, if you tell somebody to shut up, he's liable to pull out a knife.

But it isn't just television, it's also the reason why people are carrying guns in their cars and shooting at somebody who cuts them off, why somebody beat up Dan Rather: people are a lot less inhibited when it comes to being uncivilized. It's the age of the jerk.

JW: In a piece about the "age of the jerk" you wrote that the average politician is a far better man than his average constituent.

MR: That's true. At the very worst, the politician reflects his constituents. In Chicago, we have all these thieves who are aldermen, but they're no worse than the people who elect them. People *do* get the kind of government they deserve.

JW: Aleksandr Solzhenitsyn observed that America has no binding ethic. Do you agree?

MR: The Super Bowl unites us. It's our substitute for war. It's our one unifying element, more so than even the World Series.

JW: I thought baseball was the national pastime.

MR: Baseball isn't violent enough, and the games are too long.

JW: Do you consider yourself a curmudgeon?

MR: I may have certain tendencies. When I started writing my column, I just wanted to give people a laugh. It's pretty hard to do that with nothing but silly subject matter. If you take on more serious subject matter and try to give them a laugh through that, then I guess it's pretty hard to avoid being curmudgeonly.

There's a problem in writing satire: If you publish it in a sophisticated magazine, you can expect readers to know what you're talking about, but if you write for a newspaper or a bunch of newspapers, readers are easily confused.

JW: What do you figure is behind this lack of sensitivity to satire?

MR: There's no laugh track. If we could build in a laugh track, people would know what's funny.

JW: Are you concerned about the decline in the quality of education in this country?

MR: No. We went through a period in this country where everybody thought their kid had to have a college education. The result was we got stuck with a whole generation of overeducated dummies. Guys who should be slicing corned beef are mucking around some corporation making dumb decisions. You've gotta have a certain number of people to pump gas and work in the checkout line. If they don't want to learn to read, if they don't want to go beyond the second year of high school, okay, there'll be a job out there for 'em.

JW: Isn't that an un-American attitude?

MR: Yeah, but the reality is we can't all be white-collar workers, we can't all be executives, and I don't blame the system. I can go through this newsroom and find kids who came out of affluent backgrounds and had the way paid for 'em, but I can also find reporters who came from families of very modest means and had to hustle to make it. The hustlers will make it, even today.

JW: Do conservatives think you're liberal, and do liberals think you're conservative?

MR: More conservatives think I'm liberal than the opposite, but it's close. It's funny what makes somebody a liberal in the conservative mind. I've been against lynching ever since I was a kid, so I guess that makes me a liberal.

Civil rights was really the basis for that whole liberal image I had. I started my column in '63, and the one recurring theme in my column was the civil rights movement. That didn't mean that I agreed with every liberal position—I voted for Eisenhower against Adlai Stevenson and I couldn't stand the Kennedys. People who read the column during the sixties thought I was a Commie. My god, I liked Martin Luther King, Jr. That's the basis for the liberal label.

On the other hand, I did a column in which I figured out what percentage of federal civil service employees are fired in a given year and it's incredible. I can't think of any other work force in America where everybody does their job so well that nobody gets fired. Lawyers get disbarred, doctors get sued for malpractice, but federal bureaucrats are all so good that only one-tenth of one-tenth of one percent ever lose their jobs. Is that a liberal position? Of course not. The real classic liberals want bigger and better federal government. I believe in political patronage because you can fire a patronage worker.

JW: You've advocated public hangings for incompetent bureaucrats.

MR: I've advocated public hangings for a lot of things. Littering, for example. You hear people say, "There's so much mess in the parks." Well, the people who work in the park system don't go around with bushels of litter throwing it around. They don't say, "Okay, guys, here's a hundred pounds of chicken bones, let's throw 'em all over the parks." People are slobs; they won't walk twenty feet to dump their trash in a can. So I advocated the hanging of litterers in the parks. Just leave the bodies up there for a week. Boy, did I hear from people, some who agreed, some who thought I was cruel.

JW: Which disturbed you more?

MR (laughs): The ones who thought I was cruel. I preferred the ones who agreed, even though they thought I was serious. I've advocated public hangings for boom boxes, people who always veer out to the left before they make a right turn, anybody whose name appears in a gossip column in a favorable way more than three times a year. For a while I was in favor of executing politicians who lose elections. People would think twice about running for office. A lot of people agreed with me on that.

JW: You've taken on the National Rifle Association.

MR: I've always defended machine guns on the grounds that I should be able to buy one. I have poor eyesight, and, beyond five feet, I couldn't hit anybody with a pistol. But with a machine gun, you just blast away in the direction of the target and you're bound to hit it. Why should I be deprived of the right to defend my home against Commies and fiends?

JW: Do you jog?

MR: I hate running. I'll run in a game—I'll run about a tennis court or a handball court, but it makes me nervous when I see someone jogging. Dogs'll try to bite you. I did a column about a guy in Chicago who used to carry a bat when he jogged through the parks. Dogs would try to bite him. He used to carry spray stuff and that wasn't effective, so he finally started carrying a bat. One day he hit this dog who was chasing him and broke the dog's leg. The woman who owned the dog had him arrested, he had *her* arrested, and Louisville Slugger put out the "Fido Model" bat.

QUOTES ON "K"

KARMA

What goes around comes around more annoying.   BRUCE ERIC KAPLAN

KENNEDY, TED

Every country should have at least one King Farouk.   GORE VIDAL

KILLING

Kill one man and you are a murderer. Kill millions and you are a conqueror.
Kill all and you are a God.   JEAN ROSTAND

KINDNESS

One can always be kind to people about whom one cares nothing.
OSCAR WILDE

KISSING

The kiss originated when the first male reptile licked the first female reptile, implying in a subtle, complimentary way that she was as succulent as the small reptile he had for dinner the night before.

F. SCOTT FITZGERALD

Lord! I wonder what fool it was that first invented kissing.

JONATHAN SWIFT

To a woman the first kiss is just the end of the beginning but to a man it is the beginning of the end.   HELEN ROWLAND

The first kiss is stolen by the man; the last kiss is begged by the woman.
                                                                                        H. L. MENCKEN

Oh, what lies there are in kisses.   HEINRICH HEINE

Two people kissing always look like fish.   ANDY WARHOL

In love there is always one who kisses and one who offers the cheek.
                                                                                      FRENCH PROVERB

I wasn't kissing her, I was whispering in her mouth.   CHICO MARX

I'd love to kiss you, but I just washed my hair.
             BETTE DAVIS, in *Cabin in the Cotton* (screenplay by Paul Green)

Everybody winds up kissing the wrong person good night.   ANDY WARHOL

KNOWLEDGE

To know all is not to forgive all. It is to despise everybody. QUENTIN CRISP

IAN SHOALES

He's Gotta Go

Merle Kessler was born in 1949, grew up in North Dakota, South Dakota, and Minnesota, and now lives in California. He was a member of Duck's Breath Mystery Theatre, a San Francisco–based comedy group, and is the author of two collections of essays, *I Gotta Go* and *Perfect World*. He is the coauthor, with Dan Coffey, of *The Dr. Science Big Book of Science (Simplified)*. His commentary as the grouchy, fast-talking Ian Shoales was a long-running feature on National Public Radio's *All Things Considered*.

JW: What's been bugging you lately?

MK: Greed, the unbridled greed that's justified in "Lifestyle and Living" columns as being a form of art. Greed has turned into art, and all this talk of Ginnie Maes and Fannie Maes annoys me. "Starter homes." How the hell can you live in a "starter home"? This is like calling your wife your "first wife." It's a very negative way of looking at life.

JW: What about nuclear disarmament?

MK: If I were president, I would throw all our nuclear weapons away. That's why I'll never be elected president.

JW: Ian Shoales has written, "Go ahead and sneer, it's your right." Where exactly does that right come from?

MK: Ian Shoales's job is to have no enthusiasms—except every once in a while, just to prove he's a human being. It's his job to say no in a world where everyone says yes to every lame idea that comes down the pike.

JW: Do you consider yourself a curmudgeon?

MK: No. I consider myself a guy who's trying to make a buck without being stupid.

The funny thing about curmudgeons is that they're mad because life isn't what they wanted it to be. They're expressing a point of view, and even that's rare these days. Someone like Madonna doesn't have a point of view. She's an image, she's High Concept. There's no moral point of view. If you talk about "moral point of view," people look at you like you're crazy. They don't know what that means. If you bring it up, they look at you like, "What're you, a monk or what?" No, I'm just a normal guy who's trying to make a living in show business without dressing in a clown suit.

JW: Let me shoot a few subjects at you: contented people.

MK: There are people who are contented; usually they're aunts and uncles and grandpas. It's kind of a false contentment you see sometimes in places like Marin County. They have this blank look that seems to say, "Since we've taken EST…" Maybe humans aren't meant to be content. Americans seek Nirvana and inner peace and all that stuff, but I don't think it's in our American genes. If you want to be contented, you should be a dog.

JW: Communism.

MK: It's a silly ideology, almost as silly as Mormonism. Most of the tenets of anything are based on really silly premises. Mormons avoided the whole question of Indians and salamanders and gold tablets by creating this intricate and highly successful social structure. Communism avoided the whole question of its viability by killing everybody who wouldn't do things its way.

JW: Children.

MK: My wife and I just had a baby, and there's nothing relaxed about them. They're like these little tense things who scream in order to fall asleep. Just like adults, only more direct.

JW: Any thoughts on the medical profession?

MK: As the technology becomes more and more sophisticated, once they're able to discover more and more things about the fetus, having a baby will be like shopping. You'll be able to select children's careers before they're born: "Looks like a plumber. Better abort."

JW: How about lawyers?

MK: I make fun of lawyers a lot, but actually I've liked every lawyer I've ever met. They're really an unnecessary profession, though. What do they do? They don't produce anything. All they do is guide you through the labyrinth of the legal system that they created—and they keep changing it just in case you start to catch on. It's just like the world of high finance: If you don't understand it, you should stay out of it. I don't understand the law, so I have a lawyer to protect me from it.

JW: Who protects you from the lawyer?

MK: Another lawyer.

JW: How do feel about New York?

MK: It's overpriced, it's dark, it's insular, it has absolutely no idea what's going on in the rest of the country. The only thing it cares about is what it creates itself, and most of that is an illusion. I think its days as a cultural force are numbered. New York is a horrible place.

JW: Los Angeles.

MK: L.A. has the same problem: It pays absolutely no attention to anything except itself.

JW: Liberals.

MK: Their hearts are in the right place, I guess. I just saw this movie, *Atomic Cafe*. There's a part about the Rosenbergs—they didn't give you any *information* about the Rosenbergs, just pictures of them with cellos playing on the sound track. It's just cheap sentimentality not connected to anything, and it bothers me. It's like showing pictures of bludgeoned baby harp seals.

JW: Conservatives.

MK: Showing pictures of bludgeoned baby harp seals and showing pictures of aborted fetuses are the same trick. Conservatives are mainly greedy assholes, and that's their problem. Not *all* of them, but the climate Reagan has created has brought a lot of these scum out of the woodwork.

JW: Then you're not a fan of William F. Buckley?

MK: I think Buckley's a fool who spends too much time caressing dictionaries. Remember when he and Gore Vidal were at the Democratic convention and Vidal called Buckley a crypto-Nazi and Buckley called Vidal a faggot? That's American politics in a nutshell, folks. These are our commentators.

JW: How about Gore Vidal as a writer?

MK: He can be funny, but I don't think much of his writing. He's a much better conversationalist than he is a writer. *Myra Breckinridge* wasn't even good pornography.

JW: He says nobody got it.

MK: Nobody *got* it? Went right over America's head, did it? I must have missed the rhetorical point of the butt-fucking scene.

JW: Psychiatry.

MK: It's a ridiculous profession and it's getting worse. It's becoming almost like palm reading or phrenology. It's been relegated to pop best-sellers and talk shows. The only people that take it seriously are upper-middle-class people who are lonely and can afford to pay someone to listen to them.

JW: Star Wars.

MK: Star Wars is simply a waste of money. It's a Hollywood "High Concept," and there's absolutely no way it can work. It proves again that Reagan doesn't have a brain in his head. A defense policy named for a movie? Give me a break. Sometimes I think America likes Reagan, but they're a little disappointed that they couldn't get Jimmy Stewart.

JW: Tanning.

MK: I don't understand that stuff at all. You go to the beach and you see people just *lying* there. Read a book! Read a magazine! Go swimming! What are you, a plant?

JW: The human race.

MK: I think we'd probably be better off if humans had never existed. Dogs, on the other hand, are perfect creatures.

JW: How so?

MK: Unquestioning loyalty, undying love, they're friendly, they can do tricks. Ian Shoales doesn't have a dog, but Merle Kessler does.

JW: Anything else you'd like to get off your chest?

MK: Lots of things, but it's getting late and, well, I gotta go.

QUOTES ON "L"

LANGUAGE

The great enemy of clear language is insincerity. When there is a gap between one's real and one's declared aims, one turns as it were instinctively to long words and exhausted idioms, like a cuttlefish spurting out ink.

GEORGE ORWELL

I personally think we developed language because of our deep need to complain.

LILY TOMLIN

LAUGHTER

Laughter, while it lasts, slackens and unbraces the mind, weakens the faculties, and causes a kind of remissness and dissolution in all the powers of the soul.

JOSEPH ADDISON

Laughter is nothing else but sudden glory arising from some sudden conception of some eminency in ourselves, by comparison with the infirmity of others, or with our own formerly.

THOMAS HOBBES

Perhaps I know best why it is man alone who laughs; he alone suffers so deeply that he had to invent laughter.

FRIEDRICH WILHELM NIETZSCHE

He who laughs has not yet heard the bad news.

BERTOLT BRECHT

LAW

The law, in its majestic equality, forbids the rich as well as the poor to sleep under bridges, to beg in the streets, and to steal bread.

ANATOLE FRANCE

The penalty for laughing in a courtroom is six months in jail; if it were not for this penalty, the jury would never hear the evidence.   H. L. MENCKEN

Law is a bottomless pit; it is a cormorant, a harpy that devours everything.

JONATHAN SWIFT

Every law is an infraction of liberty.   JEREMY BENTHAM

All laws are an attempt to domesticate the natural ferocity of the species.

JOHN W. GARDNER

The one great principle of English law is to make business for itself.

CHARLES DICKENS

I learned law so well, the day I graduated I sued the college, won the case, and got my tuition back.   FRED ALLEN

LAWSUIT

Lawsuit, *n.* A machine which you go into as a pig and come out of as a sausage.

AMBROSE BIERCE

I was never ruined but twice: once when I lost a lawsuit, and once when I won one.   VOLTAIRE

—————————————— **LAWYERS** ——————————————

Lawyer, *n.* One skilled in the circumvention of the law.

AMBROSE BIERCE

Lawyer: one who protects us against robbery by taking away the temptation.

H. L. MENCKEN

Lawyers are the only persons in whom ignorance of the law is not punished.

JEREMY BENTHAM

If law school is so hard to get through…how come there are so many lawyers?

CALVIN TRILLIN

Lawyers, I suppose, were children once.   CHARLES LAMB

Lawyers are…operators of the toll bridge which anyone in search of justice
must pass.   JANE BRYANT QUINN

The only way you can beat the lawyers is to die with nothing.   WILL ROGERS

An incompetent attorney can delay a trial for months or years. A competent
attorney can delay one even longer.   EVELLE J. YOUNGER

Lawyers and tarts are the two oldest professions in the world. And we always
aim to please.   HORACE RUMPOLE (JOHN MORTIMER)

Lawyers as a group are no more dedicated to justice or public service than a
private public utility is dedicated to giving light.   DAVID MELINKOFF

A group of white South Africans killed a black lawyer because he was black. That was wrong; they should have killed him because he was a lawyer.
WHITNEY BROWN

What's black and white and brown and looks good on a lawyer? A Doberman.
MORDECAI RICHLER

LAZINESS

Laziness is nothing more than the habit of resting before you get tired.
JULES RENARD

LEGOS

Everyone who ever walked barefoot into his child's room late at night hates Legos. I think Mr. Lego should be strung up from a scaffold made of his horrid little pockmarked arch-puncturing plastic cubes.
TONY KORNHEISER

LEISURE

The secret of being miserable is to have the leisure to bother about whether you are happy or not.
GEORGE BERNARD SHAW

LETTERS TO THE EDITOR

Anyone nit-picking enough to write a letter of correction to an editor doubtless deserves the error that provoked it.
ALVIN TOFFLER

LIAR

The aim of the liar is simply to charm, to delight, to give pleasure. He is the very basis of civilized society.
OSCAR WILDE

It is always the best policy to tell the truth, unless, of course, you are an exceptionally good liar.   JEROME K. JEROME

LIBERALS

A liberal is a man who leaves a room when the fight begins.
                                                    HEYWOOD BROUN

The liberals can understand everything but people who don't understand them.
                                                    LENNY BRUCE

Liberal: a power worshipper without power.   GEORGE ORWELL

A liberal is a person whose interests aren't at stake at the moment.
                                                    WILLIS PLAYER

A liberal is a man too broadminded to take his own side in a quarrel.
                                                    ROBERT FROST

Liberals are very broadminded: they are always willing to give careful consideration to both sides of the same side.   ANONYMOUS

Hell hath no fury like a liberal scorned.   DICK GREGORY

LIBERTY

Liberty means responsibility; that is why most men dread it.
                                                    GEORGE BERNARD SHAW

Liberty doesn't work as well in practice as it does in speeches.   WILL ROGERS

Liberty is the right to do whatever the law permits.

BARON DE MONTESQUIEU

LIBRARIANS

On librarians I do speak with prejudice. The profession in general has always seemed to me like the legitimization and financing of an impulse to collect old socks.   JOHN CHEEVER

LIFE

You fall out of your mother's womb, you crawl across open country under fire, and drop into your grave.   QUENTIN CRISP

When you don't have any money, the problem is food. When you have money, it's sex. When you have both, it's health. If everything is simply jake, then you're frightened of death.   J. P. DONLEAVY

For most men life is a search for the proper manila envelope in which to get themselves filed.   CLIFTON FADIMAN

Life is a long lesson in humility.   JAMES M. BARRIE

Life—the way it really is—is a battle not between Bad and Good but between Bad and Worse.   JOSEPH BRODSKY

When we remember we are all mad, the mysteries disappear and life stands explained.   MARK TWAIN

Life would be tolerable but for its amusements.

GEORGE BERNARD SHAW

Not a shred of evidence exists in favor of the idea that life is serious.

BRENDAN GILL

Life is a disease; and the only difference between one man and another is the stage of the disease at which he lives. GEORGE BERNARD SHAW

Life is a sexually transmitted disease and the mortality rate is one hundred percent. R.D. LAING

Life is an effort that deserves a better cause. KARL KRAUS

Life does not cease to be funny when people die any more than it ceases to be serious when people laugh. GEORGE BERNARD SHAW

Life is a hospital in which every patient is possessed by the desire of changing his bed. One would prefer to suffer near the fire, and another is certain he would get well if he were by the window. CHARLES BAUDELAIRE

Life is not so bad if you have plenty of luck, a good physique and not too much imagination. CHRISTOPHER ISHERWOOD

Life is one long process of getting tired. SAMUEL BUTLER

Life is not a spectacle or a feast; it is a predicament. GEORGE SANTAYANA

Why shouldn't things be largely absurd, futile, and transitory? They are so, and we are so, and they and we go very well together. GEORGE SANTAYANA

Life is a predicament which precedes death. HENRY JAMES

Life is a zoo in a jungle.   PETER DE VRIES

Human life is a flash of occasional enjoyments lighting up a mass of pain and misery, a bagatelle of transient experience.
                                        ALFRED NORTH WHITEHEAD

We are all serving a life sentence in the dungeon of life.
                                                    CYRIL CONNOLLY

Life is a constant oscillation between the sharp horns of a dilemma.
                                                    H. L. MENCKEN

Life is a crowded superhighway with bewildering cloverleaf exits on which a man is liable to find himself speeding back in the direction he came.
                                                    PETER DE VRIES

Life is a dead-end street.   H. L. MENCKEN

Life is gamble at terrible odds; if it was a bet you wouldn't take it.
                                                    TOM STOPPARD

Life sucks. Get a fucking helmet, okay?   DENIS LEARY

Life is like an onion: you peel off layer after layer and then you find there is nothing in it.   JAMES GIBBONS HUNEKER

In the great game of human life one begins by being a dupe and ends by being a rogue.   VOLTAIRE

Life is an unbroken succession of false situations.   THORNTON WILDER

Life is divided into the horrible and the miserable. WOODY ALLEN

The first half of our life is ruined by our parents and the second half by our children. CLARENCE DARROW

Life is far too important a thing ever to talk seriously about. OSCAR WILDE

The meaning of life is that it stops. FRANZ KAFKA

Life is judged with all the blindness of life itself. GEORGE SANTAYANA

Life is something to do when you can't get to sleep. FRAN LEBOWITZ

Life is nothing but a competition to be the criminal rather than the victim. BERTRAND RUSSELL

Life is a God-damned, stinking, treacherous game and nine hundred and ninety-nine men out of a thousand are bastards. THEODORE DREISER

People say that life is the thing, but I prefer reading. LOGAN PEARSALL SMITH

LIMOUSINES

Limousines used to be reserved for the ruling class or, on special occasions, for the working class. Today, limousines are like taxicabs with the door handles still intact. ERMA BOMBECK

LITERARY PARTY

A traffic jam of the lost waiting for the ferry across the Styx. DELMORE SCHWARTZ

LITERATURE

Literature: proclaiming in front of everyone what one is careful to conceal from one's immediate circle.   JEAN ROSTAND

Never judge a book by its movie.   J. W. EAGAN

LITIGATION

For certain people, after fifty, litigation takes the place of sex.   GORE VIDAL

LOATHINGS

My loathings are simple: stupidity, oppression, crime, cruelty, soft music.
VLADIMIR NABOKOV

LOGIC

Logic is like the sword: those who appeal to it shall perish by it.
SAMUEL BUTLER

LONDON

London, that great cesspool into which all the loungers of the Empire are irresistibly drained.   ARTHUR CONAN DOYLE

A place you go to get bronchitis.   FRAN LEBOWITZ

London, like a bowl of viscid human fluid, boils sullenly over the rim of its encircling hills and slops messily and uglily into the home counties.   H. G. WELLS

A foggy, dead-alive city like a dying ant-heap. London was created for rich young men to shop in, dine in, ride in, get married in, go to theatres in, and die in as respected householders. It is a city for the unmarried upper class, not for the poor.   CYRIL CONNOLLY

Crowds without company, and dissipation without pleasure.

EDWARD GIBBON

The monstrous tuberosity of civilized life, the capital of England.

THOMAS CARLYLE

In London they don't like you if you're still alive.   HARVEY FIERSTEIN

——————————————— LONG ISLAND ———————————————
How would I describe Long Island? Well, every girl in my neighborhood
looked like Kenny G.   CAROL LEIFER

——————————————— LOS ANGELES ———————————————
It is a geometropolitan predicament rather than a city. You can no more
administer it than you could administer the solar system.

JONATHAN MILLER

L.A. you pass through and get a hamburger.   JOHN LENNON

Double Dubuque.   H. ALLEN SMITH

The Queen of the Angles.   IAN SHOALES

One must never overlook the fact that Los Angeles is an entirely manufactured
city assembled piece by piece beginning in the 1910s and 1920s—the Henry
Ford boom years. Los Angeles without sci-fi caliber infrastructure is not only
unimaginable but impossible. Located nowhere, and lacking any inherent sense
of "thereness," L.A. is like Xerox paper—it becomes whatever is copied on it.

DOUGLAS COUPLAND

Thought is barred in this city of Dreadful Joy, and conversation is unknown.
ALDOUS HUXLEY

I don't really trust people who live where there isn't snow, but Los Angeles is good for the spirit. To see people play volleyball on the beach with no net or out-of-bounds—volleyball as pure experience, exploring person-and-ball relationships.
GARRISON KEILLOR

I mean, who would want to live in a place where the only cultural advantage is that you can turn right on a red light.
WOODY ALLEN

A good part of any day in Los Angeles is spent driving, alone, through streets devoid of meaning to the driver, which is one reason the place exhilarates some people, and floods others with amorphous unease.
JOAN DIDION

I had a colonic irrigation in this clinic in Santa Monica, because people in Los Angeles cannot do anything for themselves, much less take a shit.
MARGARET CHO

Isn't it nice that people who prefer Los Angeles to San Francisco live there?
HERB CAEN

Fall is my favorite season in Los Angeles, watching the birds change color and fall from the trees.
DAVID LETTERMAN

A big hard-boiled city with no more personality than a paper cup.
RAYMOND CHANDLER

There is always something so delightfully real about what is phony here. And something so phony about what is real. A sort of disreputable senility.

NOEL COWARD

I was in Los Angeles, I ordered some coffee and they said "Would you like whole milk, skim milk or soy milk?" and my fist stopped right at his face.

LEWIS BLACK

Everything in Los Angeles is too large, too loud and usually banal in concept...The plastic asshole of the world.   WILLIAM FAULKNER

L.A. is like Vegas—but the losers stay in town.   JERRY SEINFELD

The town is like an advertisement for itself; none of its charms are left to the visitor's imagination.   CHRISTOPHER ISHERWOOD

It's a jolly greedy city. It's a city devoted to pleasure, self-indulgence, prettiness, health, immortality and gracefulness. People are devoting so much time to avoiding death they haven't got much time for leading their life.

JONATHAN MILLER

The chief products of Los Angeles are novelizations, salad, game-show hosts, points, muscle tone, mini-series and rewrites. They export all of these items with the twin exceptions of muscle tone and points, neither of which seems to travel well.   FRAN LEBOWITZ

L.A.: where there's never weather, and walking is a crime. L.A.: where the streetlights and palm trees go on forever, where darkness never comes, like a deal that never goes down, a meeting that's never taken. The city of angels: where every cockroach has a screenplay and even the winos wear roller skates. It's that kind of town.   IAN SHOALES

In Los Angeles, youth is wasted on the middle-aged.   BERTON AVERRE

Los Angeles makes the rest of California seem authentic.
                                              JONATHAN CULLER

I met S. J. Perelman at Gilbert's Books in Hollywood in the '60s—he was back in the Literature section. I asked him, "I thought you hated Los Angeles, yet here you are!" Perelman said, "I come back every twenty years just to renew my disgust."   GARY OWENS

——————————— LOTTERY ———————————
I figure you have the same chance of winning the lottery whether you play or not.   FRAN LEBOWITZ

——————————— LOVE ———————————
Love is like epidemic diseases. The more one fears it the more likely one is to contract it.   NICOLAS CHAMFORT

Love is an exploding cigar we willingly smoke.   LYNDA BARRY

Love ain't nothing but sex misspelled.   HARLAN ELLISON

Love is only a dirty trick played on us to achieve the continuation of the species.
                                        W. SOMERSET MAUGHAM

A constant interrogation.   MILAN KUNDERA

People in love, it is well known, suffer extreme conceptual delusions; the most common of these being that other people find your condition as thrilling and eye-watering as you do yourselves.   JULIAN BARNES

> Oh life is a glorious cycle of song,
> A medley of extemporanea;
> And love is a thing that can never go wrong;
> And I am Marie of Romania.
>   DOROTHY PARKER

Love is the delightful interval between meeting a beautiful girl and discovering that she looks like a haddock.   JOHN BARRYMORE

Love is a word used to label the sexual excitement of the young, the habituation of the middle-aged, and the mutual dependence of the old.
                                             JOHN CIARDI

Just another four-letter word.   TENNESSEE WILLIAMS

Love is the most subtle form of self-interest.   HOLBROOK JACKSON

Love is something that hangs up behind the bathroom door and smells of Lysol.   ERNEST HEMINGWAY

Love is the state in which man sees things most decidedly as they are not.
                                    FRIEDRICH WILHELM NIETZSCHE

The delusion that one woman differs from another.　　H. L. MENCKEN

Love is a perky elf dancing a merry little jig, then suddenly he turns on you with a miniature machine gun.　　MATT GROENING

People who are not in love fail to understand how an intelligent man can suffer because of a very ordinary woman. This is like being surprised that anyone should be stricken with cholera because of a creature so insignificant as the common bacillus.　　MARCEL PROUST

First love is a kind of vaccination which saves a man from catching the complaint a second time.　　HONORÉ DE BALZAC

In the forties, to get a girl you had to be a GI or a jock. In the fifties, to get a girl you had to be Jewish. In the sixties, to get a girl you had to be black. In the seventies, to get a girl you've got to be a girl.　　MORT SAHL

Love is so much better when you are not married.　　MARIA CALLAS

Many a man has fallen in love with a girl in a light so dim he would not have chosen a suit by it.　　MAURICE CHEVALIER

Many a man in love with a dimple makes the mistake of marrying the whole girl.　　STEPHEN LEACOCK

Love is more pleasant than marriage for the same reason that novels are more amusing than history.　　NICOLAS CHAMFORT

By the time you swear you're his,
Shivering and sighing,
And he vows his passion is
Infinite, undying—
One of you is lying.

DOROTHY PARKER

LOVE: A word properly applied to our delight in particular kinds of food; sometimes metaphorically spoken of the favorite objects of all our appetites.
HENRY FIELDING

Once love is purged of vanity, it resembles a feeble convalescent, hardly able to drag itself about.
NICOLAS CHAMFORT

It is a mistake to speak of a bad choice in love, since as soon as a choice exists, it can only be bad.
MARCEL PROUST

The duration of passion is proportionate with the original resistance of the woman.
HONORÉ DE BALZAC

It's possible to love a human being if you don't know them too well.
CHARLES BUKOWSKI

The Art of Love: knowing how to combine the temperament of a vampire with the discretion of an anemone.
E. M. CIORAN

Love, love, love—all the wretched cant of it, masking egotism, lust, masochism, fantasy under a mythology of sentimental postures, a welter of self-induced miseries and joys, blinding and masking the essential personalities in the frozen gestures of courtship, in the kissing and the dating and the desire, the compliments and the quarrels which vivify its barrenness.

GERMAINE GREER

Love is only a dirty trick played on us to achieve the continuation of the species.

W. SOMERSET MAUGHAM

To fall in love you have to be in the state of mind for it to take, like a disease.

NANCY MITFORD

To be in love is merely to be in a state of perceptual anesthesia.

H. L. MENCKEN

When you're in love it's the most glorious two-and-a-half days of your life.

RICHARD LEWIS

Love, in present day society, is just the exchange of two momentary desires and the contact of two skins.

NICOLAS CHAMFORT

Love is two minutes fifty-two seconds of squishing noises. It shows your mind isn't clicking right.

JOHNNY ROTTEN

Love is like an hourglass, with the heart filling up as the brain empties.

JULES RENARD

Love is a springtime plant that perfumes everything with its hope, even the ruins to which it clings.

GUSTAVE FLAUBERT

A temporary insanity curable by marriage.

AMBROSE BIERCE

Love is the desire to prostitute oneself.   CHARLES BAUDELAIRE

The credulity of love is the most fundamental source of authority.
                                                             SIGMUND FREUD

Love is a gross exaggeration of the difference between one person and everybody else.   GEORGE BERNARD SHAW

Love is the victim's response to the rapist.   TI-GRACE ATKINSON

Love: a burnt match skating in a urinal.   HART CRANE

Love is what happens to a man and a woman who don't know each other.
                                                        W. SOMERSET MAUGHAM

Love is a snowmobile racing across the tundra and then suddenly it flips
over, pinning you underneath. At night, the ice weasels come.
                                                             MATT GROENING

Ah, love—the walks over soft grass, the smiles over candlelight, the arguments over just about everything else.   MAX HEADROOM

I can understand companionship. I can understand bought sex in the afternoon. I cannot understand the love affair.   GORE VIDAL

Love as a relation between men and women was ruined by the desire to make
sure of the legitimacy of children.   BERTRAND RUSSELL

When we want to read of the deeds that are done for love, whither do we turn? To the murder column.   GEORGE BERNARD SHAW

The only true love is love at first sight; second sight dispels it.
                                        ISRAEL ZANGWILL

> Every love's the love before
> In a duller dress.
>   DOROTHY PARKER

Love is the triumph of imagination over intelligence.   H. L. MENCKEN

Boy Meets Girl, So What?   BERTOLT BRECHT

Love is like war: easy to begin but very hard to stop.   H. L. MENCKEN

While I have little to say in favor of sex (it's vastly overrated, it's frequently unnecessary, and it's messy), it is greatly to be preferred to the interminable torments of romantic agony through which two people tear one another limb from limb while professing altruistic devotion.
                                        QUENTIN CRISP

It's possible to love a human being if you don't know them too well.
                                        CHARLES BUKOWSKI

When I eventually met Mr. Right I had no idea that his first name was Always.
RITA RUDNER

Tristan and Isolde were lucky to die when they did. They'd have been sick of all that rubbish in a year.
ROBERTSON DAVIES

> When you're away, I'm restless, lonely,
> Wretched, bored, dejected; only
> Here's the rub, my darling dear,
> I feel the same when you are here.
> SAMUEL HOFFENSTEIN

There is always something ridiculous about the emotions of people whom one has ceased to love.
OSCAR WILDE

What is irritating about love is that it is a crime that requires an accomplice.
CHARLES BAUDELAIRE

I know what love is: Tracy and Hepburn, Bogart and Bacall, Romeo and Juliet, Jackie and John and Marilyn....
IAN SHOALES

The happiest moments in any affair take place after the loved one has learned to accommodate the lover and before the maddening personality of either party has emerged like a jagged rock from the receding tides of lust and curiosity.
QUENTIN CRISP

If you love someone, set them free; if they come home, set them on fire.
GEORGE CARLIN

Don't threaten me with love, baby.   BILLIE HOLIDAY

> Your little hands,
> Your little feet,
> Your little mouth—
> Oh, God, how sweet!
> Your little nose,
> Your little ears,
> Your eyes, that shed
> Such little tears!
> Your little voice,
> So soft and kind;
> Your little soul,
> Your little mind!

SAMUEL HOFFENSTEIN

The continued propinquity of another human being cramps the style after a time unless that person is somebody you think you love. Then the burden becomes intolerable at once.   QUENTIN CRISP

Fantasy love is much better than reality love. Never doing it is very exciting. The most exciting attractions are between two opposites that never meet.

ANDY WARHOL

If love is the answer, could you rephrase the question?   LILY TOMLIN

———————————————— LOVE LETTERS ————————————————

It is well to write love letters. There are certain things for which it is not easy to ask your mistress face to face, like money, for instance.

HENRI DE REGNIER

LOVERS

The reason that lovers never weary each other is because they are always talking about themselves. FRANÇOIS DE LA ROCHEFOUCAULD

LUCK

I believe in luck: how else can you explain the success of those you dislike? JEAN COCTEAU

LYING

Lying increases the creative faculties, expands the ego, and lessens the frictions of social contacts. CLARE BOOTHE LUCE

Carlyle said, "A lie cannot live"; it shows he did not know how to tell them. MARK TWAIN

People never lie so much as before an election, during a war, or after a hunt. OTTO VON BISMARCK

ROY BLOUNT, JR.

This Man Is Not a Murderer

The *Sports Illustrated* contributor and author of collections of essays and verse, including *Not Exactly What I Had in Mind*, *One Fell Soup*, and *What Men Don't Tell Women*, wasn't in a terrific mood.

JW: Before we begin, would you please sign this release?
RB: Why do you have to have this?
JW: My publisher requested I have all the interview subjects sign it.
RB (reads and rereads release, then reads aloud): "...releases liability for any activity including [raises voice] invasion of the rights of privacy, libel and

copyright infringement." I'm signing away my rights. I can't do that [winces and laughs derisively].

JW: If that's the only objectionable part of it, just cross it out and initial it.

RB: Okay. [Signs and initials the release.] Why would anybody expect anybody to sign something like this? Nobody wants to sign away their right to sue for libel. I mean, what if you said in the book that I was a murderer?

JW: It's the product of an overzealous lawyer, I guess.

RB: Yeah, the world is full of overzealous lawyers.

JW: Do you consider yourself at all curmudgeonly or misanthropic?

RB (laughs derisively): No. Who would do that?

JW: Well, I grant you that it's uncurmudgeonly to characterize oneself as a curmudgeon, but I'm basing it on some of the things you've written.

RB: Like what?

JW: Like what you wrote about Christmas, for example.

RB: What'd I say about Christmas?

JW: You said that if a kid is smart enough to understand the concept of Santa Claus by Thanksgiving, he'll see through it by December fifteenth.

RB: I never set out to be a curmudgeon.

JW: Okay, let's try something a little closer to home. You've written lots of articles for Sports Illustrated. *What do you think of John McEnroe?*

RB: I think he's a bully, and I don't like bullies. He bullies old, fat men. He's a spoiled kid. Lately maybe he's a burned-out kid. He reminds me of Bobby Fisher, who seemed to me a mixture of baby and tyrant. I think that's an unattractive mixture. He's a petulant, callow bully. But he's a very good tennis player. On the other hand, sports do tend to be dominated by ineffectual, bureaucratic amateurs who don't really know what they're doing. I would be sympathetic to anybody who screams at NCAA officials.

JW: In trying to place you in some sort of curmudgeonly "tradition," I find similarities between your verse and Dorothy Parker's.

RB: I like her verse. It seems to me that it's a kind of anti-Puritanism that was more attractive to me when I was a kid in a Methodist household than it is now. I still like a lot of those lines, but it seems to me sort of mannered now. I still relish a number of her lines, but Mencken really holds up because Mencken had a better time. Mencken liked a lot of things like beer and loose women, and he liked to have a good time.

When I was in high school, I was reading Mencken and I quoted his definition of a Puritan to my mother: "A Puritan is a person who lives in the fear that someone, somewhere, may be having a good time." My mother liked it because she had a sense of humor, but she said, "You know, we're pretty much Puritans ourselves." I was shocked because I'd never faced up to it conceptually that way.

JW: You've written that you don't like the woods because "there's no sin there."
RB: Yeah, I believe in having a sense of sin, a sense of right and wrong. I've never quite understood all the pejorative associations with the word *judgmental*. Obviously you can abuse judgmentalism and you can browbeat people with it, but I think it's wrong *not* to be judgmental. If somebody does something wrong, you have to say it's wrong.

Mark Twain said that the trouble with a lot of Americans was that Puritanism was so solidly established here that you were either Puritan or anti-Puritan and there was no other tradition to hook into, whereas in England you could be a Cavalier or something. There's no real Cavalier tradition in America.

JW: A lot of writers complain about the fact that the market for books is shrinking and it's becoming more and more difficult to get publishers to promote their books.
RB: Every author pisses and moans about his publisher. It's a commercial proposition. It costs an enormous amount of money to advertise books. I'm tired of listening to authors gripe about their publishers—I've done enough

griping and enough listening to get kind of bored with it all. It's the same story over and over: all the things that are wrong with publishing. There *are* a lot of things wrong with publishing, but on the other hand, I remember, when I was a kid growing up in Atlanta, what a narrow selection of books were available. Now you can get any kind of book in the world.

JW: I'd hoped you'd have something nasty to say about publishers.

RB: The reason I stopped complaining about publishers is that it seems to me that if they were better at marketing, if they were certain about the kind of books they wanted, it would be bad for the writer. I mean, you get frustrated with publishers because they don't seem to know how to sell books. It all seems to be a mystery to them, until a book starts selling, and then they advertise it. You wonder who's in charge here, who's selling the book? But if it ceased to be a mystery, it might well become too mechanical. This way you can still slip through the cracks.

Look, if you can make a living being a writer, it's hard to complain. I was down in a little town in Texas one time, writing a story about coon hunts, and I was talking to these guys who were telling me what a wonderful job I had writing for *Sports Illustrated.* And I said, nah, you have to take all these planes and you have to stand in line with your bags and run around the country and it's tiring and you have to stay up late to write the story. One of them said, "I bet it beats runnin' tree saws eight hours a day."

THE CRITICAL CURMUDGEON: ART

The goitrous, torpid and squinting husks provided by Matisse in his sculpture are worthless except as tactful decorations for a mental home.

PERCY WYNDHAM-LEWIS

Just explain to Monsieur Renoir that the torso of a woman is not a mass of decomposing flesh, its green and violet spots indicating the state of complete putrefaction of a corpse.

ALBERT WOLFF

For Mr. Whistler's own sake one ought not to have admitted works into the gallery in which the ill-educated conceit of the artist so nearly approached the aspect of willful imposture. I have seen, and heard, much of Cockney impudence before now; but never expected to hear a coxcomb ask two hundred guineas for flinging a pot of paint in the public's face.

JOHN RUSKIN

Klee's pictures seem to me to resemble, not pictures, but a sample book of patterns for linoleum.

SIR CYRIL ASQUITH

A painting in a museum hears more ridiculous opinions than anything else in the world.

EDMOND DE GONCOURT

Don't pay any attention to what they write about you. Just measure it in inches.

ANDY WARHOL

Every time I paint a portrait I lose a friend.   JOHN SINGER SARGENT

I was going to have cosmetic surgery until I noticed that the doctor's office was full of portraits by Picasso.   RITA RUDNER

After a few months in my parents' basement, I took an apartment near the state university, where I discovered both crystal methamphetamine and conceptual art. Either one of these things are dangerous, but in combination they have the potential to destroy entire civilizations.   DAVID SEDARIS

Performance art is created by thin young men and usually consists of dancerly women taking their clothes off, putting on masks, and dumping blood on each other while a soundtrack screeches out machinery noises.

IAN SHOALES

I hate flowers. I paint them because they're cheaper than models and they don't move.   GEORGIA O'KEEFE

Like most artists who have made an invention of some kind, he [David Hockney] tends to overplay the significance of his own work and goes on about it as though it were a Rosetta Stone, with whose help all representation can be rescued from one-eyed falsehood.   ROBERT HUGHES

CATHY CRIMMINS

The Anti-Mom

Cathy Crimmins's books include *The Secret World of Men: A Girl's-Eye View*, *The Mango Princess*, and *How the Homosexuals Saved Civilization*.

JW: You've been a mother for how long now, eighteen months?
CC: Twenty and a half months, but who's counting?
JW: Don't you like it?
CC: Let's just say I'm not going gentle into that good nitey-nite. When they were giving out mothering skills, I was probably at the movies. I never even learned to cut fruit into pieces. Ever since Kelly could sit up, I've given her a whole apple. She just chews on it and spits it out on the floor and I just

sort of vacuum it up later. For most mothers, day care is a problem. I'm looking for night care, too. Actually, I'm looking for a boarding day-care center. My friends have taken to calling me "The Anti-Mom." You're talking to me on a bad day: I was up driving the Schuylkill Expressway at three o'clock this morning trying to put my insomniac child to sleep.

JW: I gather from some of the things you've written that you didn't enjoy pregnancy, either.

CC: Being pregnant makes you feel like an adolescent girl. First, you're constantly embarrassed about your sexuality, because there it is for everybody to see: "Ha-ha, look at her, she had sex!" Then there's the raging hormones. You're crying one day, laughing the next. You feel ugly and worthless and desperate. If you hated adolescence, I'd advise skipping pregnancy.

But the worst are the Maternity Police. I tell women not to let anybody know they're pregnant until they absolutely must, until they throw up over their boss's desk, because once people realize you're pregnant, the Maternity Police descend on you. You can't smoke, you can't drink, you can't stand there and watch somebody spray a bug dead. I resented that, and I used to sit around in bars drinking a glass of wine just to see how many people would accost me.

And people give you books. My favorite is *Thank You, Dr. Lamaze*, written by Marjorie Karmel, the first American woman to try the Lamaze method. She was always visiting her friends and having martinis in the afternoon while they discussed how in the world they were going to find a doctor who would deliver the baby naturally. They would have three or four cocktails and I thought, *This method is for me! You sip a glass of Chablis as you go into labor!*

JW: What about those warnings against drinking while you're pregnant: "When you take a drink, your baby takes a drink…"

CC: Not a bad idea—somebody to drink with. This stuff is taken to absurd extremes: While I was pregnant I went into a store to buy a pack of cigarettes *for a friend of mine* who was out in the car, and I had to endure a lecture about smoking and pregnancy. It infuriated me.

With my decadent bent, I was a strange candidate for the whole natural childbirth routine. And I've always been a chicken. I would cry hysterically whenever Al pinched my legs during the exercise to simulate labor contractions. He doubted that I could make it through, but I did.

I had an insane desire to give birth in a really groovy fashion. Guess I'm a child of the sixties in that way. Hospitals weren't good enough for me, so I tried this little "birth center" at which you're supposed to write a "birth plan" and "center" yourself. I had "Jacuzzi labor," that's how groovy I am.

The biggest drawback with the birth center is that they make you dispose of your own placenta. They discuss it with you beforehand, so we debated with our friends what we should do with it. One person suggested we drive to the nearest Roy Rogers and throw it in the Dumpster. The birth center suggested planting a tree with the afterbirth under it. We finally compromised: We weren't living at our house because we were renovating (which is another maternity-related illness), so we couldn't plant a tree. So we put it in the freezer. (I never looked at it. The midwife kept trying to get me to look at it, but I said, "No, thanks, I'll just look at my baby here, okay?") I would show visitors the baby, and Al would show them the frozen placenta. We thought of it as a sort of evil twin of our daughter (she has my last name, but the placenta had Al's last name—I promised him). Al finally buried the thing in our backyard when we moved back into the house, but we didn't know what the correct procedure was, whether we should have defrosted it in the microwave first or not, so we buried it frozen. It was a simple ceremony.

JW: And now that the baby's almost two years old, how has motherhood changed you?

CC: Aside from sleep deprivation as a way of life, I haven't really changed at all. I still hate children as I always have and always will, and I don't know why I did this.

JW: Why you had a baby?

CC: Right. I haven't the foggiest notion. I was apparently acting out some biological imperative. A friend of mine says I don't have a single maternal bone in my body, and he's amazed by it because his wife breast-fed their kids until they were twenty years old. But…children irritate me. They get up very early, they're loud, they interrupt, they think they're more important than you. They prevent you from being a child: My little girl has already broken all of my toys. Just this morning I was watching her play with a book of matches, and I said to Al that I should open "Mrs. Cathy's Day Care Center" with open scissors and all the other dangerous things our child seems to find around the house. When she was very small I liked to give her things to play with that would gross other people out, things that *she* just saw as objects. There was a big rubber rat, and a rubber snake. I also liked dressing her in black. My mother was pretty freaked out by that. "Why don't you put a little beret on her and send her to sit in a café in Paris?" she said.

JW: I've never seen a baby dressed in black.

CC: My mother was pushing Kelly down the street in her little town and she had on a little black stretchy thing—this was when she was about six months old—and little kids came up and asked, "Is that a *baby*?" They didn't know that babies could look like that. She looked like Yul Brynner in *The King and I*. That's how I'd dress if I were a baby.

JW: Why did you name her Kelly?

CC: It's my mom's maiden name. Otherwise it borders dangerously on being a bimbo name. Have you ever noticed that bimbo strain of Kellys? There's a bimbo strain and a tomboy strain. It's sort of soap opera-bimbo-name territory. It's what I was supposed to be named, actually. So, I'm just re-creating myself, since it would have been rude to name her Cathy Crimmins, Jr.

JW: Maybe recreating yourself is a reason for having a baby.

CC: Maybe. I've been working on a list of why people have children. I think about it when I'm up in the middle of the night with Kelly. I think, *Wait a minute: People have done this for centuries?* It's hard for me to believe. So I have a list of reasons for having children. One of them is an attraction to Velcro—

JW: Sorry?

CC: All the little kiddie things are made with Velcro so you don't have to tie anything anymore. I also think people have babies because they secretly long for celibacy, or they want to dispose of income without actually dealing with insurance agents or bankers.

Now that I've had one, I think there should be a moratorium. There are just too many people already. Most other things on the planet reproduce and then die right away. I think it would be much better if you just crawled away and died. You *flowered*, and that would be it. My paternal grandmother died in childbirth, and it's not a bad idea. You miss an awful lot of work that way.

JW: What's the connection between having a baby and remodeling?

CC: Remodeling is a mental illness of late pregnancy. It's the nesting instinct. The month before my daughter was born, we had to move out of the house because it was in the demolition stage. When they demo'ed it they discovered that *everything* was wrong with the house. The weight-bearing walls didn't bear weight, the whole house was resting on the sewer pipe so that *any* minute there could be sewage oozing through the floorboards. I was two hundred pounds pregnant, bouncing over planks and saying things like, "Oh, I don't know, I think the vanity should go *there*." I'll never forget the plumber who said—and this is a metaphor for my entire life from then on—the guy said to me, "Geez, Cath, you had a nice house but it turned to shit." That's how I've felt about my life ever since then, basically. I mean, why did I do this? We renovated because I wanted to keep my office, otherwise it would have had to become the baby's room. So right from the start we were in conflict: "You can't have my office. You can have my body, but you can't have my office." The contractors would work for maybe an hour and then they would go away—I assume they were off drinking somewhere—it was like they had beamed up to another planet. They would leave their chain saws all over the stairs and just disappear for days. I would be calling the guy constantly, and when he finally got back to me he would say, "I had very, very personal problems." That was always his excuse: "Very, very personal problems."

JW: Were there any positive experiences at all?

CC: Well, we had a Jewish plumber who was great, but he immigrated to Israel. I often wish I had gone with him.

JW: Do you like living in Philadelphia?

CC: Philadelphia is comfortable. It allows me to fulfill my own mediocrity. It kind of reminds me of Rutgers University, where Ozzie Nelson was one of our wonderful alums. Well, Paul Robeson was, too. (Ozzie Nelson and Paul Robeson are not often mentioned in the same breath.)

What's nice about Philly is you can be a big fish in a small pond—which is great for immediate gratification—and you can still get to New York quickly. I recently interviewed a local bureaucrat who talked about Philadelphia like it's a town-house development: "For me, personally, it's ideally located. It's close to my friends in New York, to my friends in Washington, it's affordable." These are not things for a city to brag about. "Affordable" should be groceries or Toyotas, not cities. I probably resent that attitude even more because in an "affordable" city I live way beyond my means. I'd be in big trouble if I lived in a city that wasn't "affordable."

JW: Have you considered moving?

CC: I *dream* of escaping Philadelphia someday, although I had the chance once and didn't take it. I could have moved to the West Coast and I probably should have, because I think I'm working in a dead form. I should be working in television, I think, but I don't know if I'd fit into that world.

JW: A "dead form"?

CC: As a writer, I've come up against a kind of wall that is starting to exist in America, which is that…there's hardly anything left to parody. Almost anything you try to do satirically comes true within a few months. Life in late-twentieth-century America is just so fucking funny to begin with, so disjointed, so bizarre, so alienating, that there's nothing left to make fun of.

JW: Then what's a satirist to do?

CC: Move to another planet? It's really frightening. I tried *not* writing humor, but I'm like a drug addict. I end up doing these little ribs which become more and more esoteric, and that drastically reduces your audience. I've had people come up to me at book signings and say, "My friend and I have a bet on. Is this a funny book or a serious book?" What can you say? I was brought up to be polite. (My mother was there when I had the baby—she said she couldn't believe that I said "please" and "thank you" during the final stages of labor. "Please get this baby out of me, *please*!" were my final words.) So when someone asks if the book is supposed to be serious or humorous, I'm too polite to say, "You fucking idiot, don't you know that this is a *joke*?" It's happening to me more and more. Almost everything I write, somebody takes seriously.

JW: You've written of your aversion to euphemisms. Have you collected any new ones since you've become a mother?

CC: Yes, there's *play yard*—play pens are no longer cool. You don't have a play *pen* for a kid because a pen suggests imprisonment. *Caregiver* sounds like some kind of caretaker, like you have some huge estate, when actually a caregiver is a babysitter you're paying five bucks an hour. And then there are all those euphemisms for disabilities: *physically challenged, differently abled*—of which a friend of mine who is disabled says, "How am I 'differently abled'? Like, my unique ability is that without a wheelchair I have to drag myself across the floor?" And I've always thought that *special children* is kind of sad, and it disturbs me when the parents of retarded children say, "God gave me this special child because He wanted to test me."

JW: If you had your druthers, how would your life be different?

CC: I want a cold of my own. I want to get a cold, get really, really sick and be the only person in my house with the cold, so that I can get all the attention. Because every time I get a cold, Al gets a cold and then I can't be sick anymore because his cold is always worse. I just want to be injected with the flu virus and go to a motel with room service for a week.

My other goal in life is someday to write a book that I would actually want to read. It's a horrible thing to say, but that's what I'm working for. I don't know if I'll get there during this decade or the next. You see, everything I've made fun of, I've become. I'm afraid to write about anything because within a year I either have the same problem, or I'm doing it. I have become...here's what I have become: a person who has a ceiling-fan repair person. One day when I was waiting for my ceiling-fan repair person, Klaus, I thought, I've hit bottom. How much more complicated can your life be?

THE CRITICAL CURMUDGEON: LITERATURE

For the reader who has put away comic books, but isn't yet ready for editorials in the *Daily News*.

> GLORIA STEINEM, on *Valley of the Dolls* by Jacqueline Susann

---

Too many ironies in the fire.

> JOHN LEONARD, on *Two Sisters* by Gore Vidal

This is not at all bad, except as prose.

> GORE VIDAL, on *The Winds of War* by Herman Wouk

I regard this novel as a work without redeeming social value, unless it can be recycled as a cardboard box.

> ELLEN GOODMAN, on *Message from Nam* by Danielle Steel

It's like going for brain dialysis, this book.

> D. KEITH MANO, on *Ancient Evenings* by Norman Mailer

Hope Ryden writes with great affection about the often maligned coyote; unfortunately, she doesn't write about them with great skill.

> CHARLES SOLOMON

An acquaintance told James Thurber that he'd read a French translation of Thurber's *My Life and Hard Times*, adding, "You know, the book is even better in French!"

"Yes," replied Thurber, "my work tends to lose something in the original."

John Dollar is a novel by Marianne Wiggins, who is now in hiding because she is married to Salman Rushdie. Allah be praised.　　FLORENCE KING

The subtitle of this book is *Some Observations from Both Sides of the Refrigerator Door*, which is appropriate, since it could have been written by a cabbage, either before or after conversion to coleslaw.

RALPH NOVAK, on *Uh-Oh* by Robert Fulghum

This paperback is very interesting, but I find it will never replace a hardcover book—it makes a very poor doorstop.　　ALFRED HITCHCOCK

One never steps twice into the same Auden.　　RANDALL JARRELL

There are two ways of disliking poetry; one way is to dislike it, the other is to read Pope.　　OSCAR WILDE

I do not think this poem will reach its destination.

VOLTAIRE, on Rousseau's "Ode to Posterity"

With the single exception of Homer, there is no eminent writer, not even Sir Walter Scott, whom I can despise so entirely as I despise Shakespeare, when I measure my mind against his.　　GEORGE BERNARD SHAW

Now we sit through Shakespeare in order to recognize the quotations.

OSCAR WILDE

Hamlet is a coarse and barbarous play…One might think the work is a product of a drunken savage's imagination.   VOLTAIRE

Hamlet has been played by five thousand actors—no wonder he is crazy.
                                                              H. L. MENCKEN

Are the commentators on *Hamlet* really mad, or only pretending to be?
                                                              OSCAR WILDE

He had one of the more wicked minds ever going.
                                              TRUMAN CAPOTE, on Mark Twain

---

One must have a heart of stone to read the death of Little Nell by Dickens
without laughing.   OSCAR WILDE

He festooned the dung heap on which he had placed himself with sonnets
as people grow honeysuckle around outdoor privies.
                                              QUENTIN CRISP, on Oscar Wilde

---

You have to be over thirty to enjoy Proust.   GORE VIDAL

He became mellow before he became ripe.
                                  ALEXANDER WOOLLCOTT, on Christopher Morley

---

Mr. Henry James writes fiction as if it were a painful duty.
                                                              OSCAR WILDE

If it must be Thomas, let it be Mann, and if it must be Wolfe let it be Nero,
but never let it be Thomas Wolfe.   PETER DE VRIES

Odets, where is thy sting? GEORGE S. KAUFMAN

He is a bad novelist and a fool. The combination usually makes for great popularity in the U.S. GORE VIDAL, on Aleksandr Solzhenitsyn

---

Capote should be heard, not read. GORE VIDAL

Truman Capote has made lying an art. A *minor* art. GORE VIDAL

That's not writing, that's typing. TRUMAN CAPOTE, on Jack Kerouac

---

He's a second-rate Stephen Birmingham. And Stephen Birmingham is third-rate. TRUMAN CAPOTE, on Louis Auchincloss

---

The House Beautiful is the play lousy. DOROTHY PARKER

Perfectly Scandalous was one of those plays in which all of the actors unfortunately enunciated very clearly. ROBERT BENCHLEY

Number Seven opened last night. It was misnamed by five.
ALEXANDER WOOLLCOTT

There's less here than meets the eye.
TALLULAH BANKHEAD, on a Maeterlinck play

Ouch! WOLCOTT GIBBS, reviewing *Wham!*

I didn't like the play, but then I saw it under adverse conditions—the curtain was up. GEORGE S. KAUFMAN

When I saw *Annie* (at a date's insistence) I had to hit myself on the head afterward with a small hammer to get that stupid "Tomorrow" song out of my head.   IAN SHOALES

If you will only take the precaution to go in long enough after it commences and to come out long enough before it is over, you will not find it wearisome.
GEORGE BERNARD SHAW, reviewing Gounod's *Redemption*

Tonstant Weader fwowed up.
DOROTHY PARKER, reviewing A. A. Milne's *The House at Pooh Corner*

The affair between Margot Asquith and Margot Asquith will live as one of the prettiest love stories in all history.
DOROTHY PARKER, reviewing *The Autobiography of Margot Asquith*

Anybody who doesn't like this book is healthy.
GROUCHO MARX, on Oscar Levant's *The Memoirs of an Amnesiac*

Very nice, but there are dull stretches.
COMTE DE RIVAROL, on a two-line poem

This is not a novel to be tossed aside lightly. It should be thrown with great force.   DOROTHY PARKER

I fell asleep reading a dull book, and I dreamed that I was reading on, so I awoke from sheer boredom.   HEINRICH HEINE

Your manuscript is both good and original; but the part that is good is not original, and the part that is original is not good.   SAMUEL JOHNSON

JOHN WATERS

Things I Hate

Director John Waters's films include *A Dirty Shame*, *Serial Mom*, *Cry-Baby*, *Polyester*, and *Hairspray*.

JW: I'd like to talk about some of the things mentioned in your essay, "101 Things I Hate." Some of your best work, I think.
WATERS: Thank you, but my specialty is saying nice things about things that most people hate, rather than the other way around. That's why my friends call me "John-dhi"—I never like to be unpleasant. But for this interview I'll try to be as mean as possible.

JW: Thanks, I appreciate that. Let's just kind of move from subject to subject, starting with an easy one, just to warm up: mimes.

WATERS: Well, *everyone* hates mimes. Mother Teresa would punch a mime. I hate Mother Teresa now, too, because she joined the pro-lifers. At her age, why can't she just keep on with what she was doing, curing lepers and stuff?

JW: You're the only person I know of who has publicly come out against the Amish.

WATERS: I *hate* the Amish. I hate any religion that forbids you to go to the movies. And I hate them holding up traffic in those carts and talking about "outing the lights" and all that. It's a little too greeting-cardish for me. I feel sorry for the kids.

JW: Among the other things you hate are polyester sheets, roll-on deodorants—

WATERS: I, for one, use spray. It's supposed to be antienvironmental, but I don't believe it. How does spray deodorant make the world end quicker? You could prove it to me and I still wouldn't believe that the world will end one second earlier because I use spray deodorant. As for polyester sheets, I don't even consider them. You sweat and they stick to you. It's like a body bag. If you go to someone's house and they have polyester sheets, you know never to go back.

JW: Do you still hate color photos in newspapers?

WATERS: I'm still not crazy about them. It's the *USA Today* influence. I like *USA Today*, actually, and I get it every day. They started the trend and they seem to be able to do it all right, but it's copied by every local newspaper in the world, and they generally do it very, very badly. If you have an old pair of 3D glasses, just put them on, maybe it will look better.

JW: Do you hate computers?

WATERS: I don't know how to plug the things in. I'm scared of electricity, actually. Every time I plug something in, I think I'm going to die. I'm scared to turn the heat on right now because I'm afraid the house will blow up.

JW: Then you're not a home hobbyist?
WATERS: Are you kidding? My idea of hell would be getting a house you had to fix up.
JW: Pets?
WATERS: I don't mind them if they're *outside*. I like cats because they don't like *you* much. Dogs—I don't need reinforcement ten times a day that I'm an okay person. But I don't wish them evil, you know, I'm not an animal torturer.
JW: You're not fond of the U.S. Postal Service.
WATERS: Well, I love the mail, and my personal mailman is great. But I do get crazed when the mail is late and I have to call the post office. "Are stamps on sale today?" I complain. I also hate those holidays that fall on a Monday where you don't get mail, those fake holidays like Columbus Day. What did Christopher Columbus do, discover America? If he hadn't, somebody else would have and we'd still be here. Big deal.
JW: What kind of mail do you get?
WATERS: It's mostly nice. I've gotten maybe five mean letters in my whole life. A lot of my mail is from kids from small towns who say how great it is to have somebody with their sense of humor. Recently a kid wrote me that Divine was his idol and he wanted to come visit his grave but his mother said, "Oh, no, I'm not taking you to Baltimore to visit the grave of a dead transvestite." I can just hear the mother saying that, and the kid saying, "Why not?"
JW: You've expressed your distaste for "overweight joggers" and walkathons.
WATERS: I don't mind exercise, but it's a private activity. Joggers should run in a wheel—like hamsters—because *I* don't want to look at them. And I really hate people who go on an airplane in jogging outfits. That's a major offense today, even bigger than spandex bicycle pants. You see eighty-year-old women coming on the plane in jogging outfits for comfort. Well, *my*

comfort—my mental comfort—is completely ruined when I see them coming. You're on an airplane, not in your bedroom, so please! And I really hate walkathons. Blocking traffic, people patting themselves on the back. The whole attitude offends me. They have this smug look on their faces as they hold you up in traffic so that they can give two cents to some charity.

JW: You've said that you don't care much for vegetarian restaurants.

WATERS: I don't mind vegetables, I just hate people who won't eat meat and pontificate about it all the time. I'll eat meat, vegetables, anything. The most ludicrous thing I've seen in about five years, and I have proof of this—one of the leaders of one of the animal-rights organizations said this in *New York* magazine and I have the clipping—she said, "Yes, six million Jews were killed in the Holocaust, but this year eight million broiler chickens will be put into roasting ovens." I'm not kidding. She said that and she was dead serious. I can only pray she was Jewish.

JW: That really is…stunning. But getting back to vegetables, do you like sprouts?

WATERS: In a trough, they might be good. On a plate, I'm not too fond of them.

JW: Iceberg lettuce?

WATERS: The polyester of green.

JW: Brussels sprouts?

WATERS: I actually had some recently—I've mellowed on Brussels sprouts.

JW: Really? You once called them "those little balls of hell."

WATERS: Well, they were, the way my mother made 'em.

JW: But you said they're "limp and wilted after a lifetime of being pissed on by birds and other contaminated creatures."

WATERS: Well, that's true, all vegetables have been pissed on. But I guess as we get older we get less demanding about our food.

JW: How about swordfish?

WATERS: Have you ever been in a restaurant where it isn't on the menu?

Yuppies have made swordfish the next endangered species.

JW: Do you still hate nude beaches?

WATERS: I still hate them very much. It's always the worst-looking people who are the most enthusiastic about them. It's always the fattest people with the worst bodies who take their clothes off. I've been to nude beaches and I've never seen the people you *want* to see nude. They're never there.

JW: What don't you like about the telephone?

WATERS: Well, the thing that offends me is a person who gets a weekly paycheck, who is over twenty years old, and you get a busy signal when you dial their number. In this day and age, there's no excuse for that. If you have a weekly paycheck, call waiting is a must. And I hate call waiting because it's so rude, but it's still better than a busy signal. If I ever call someone and get a busy signal, I take them less seriously. Although…I could imagine someone who is extremely confident and says, "Well, it's *their* problem." I'm not that secure.

JW: You've expressed a dislike for dial telephones.

WATERS: I'm all for keeping up with the times technology-wise, especially if you go to stay at somebody's house. You don't want to put long-distance calls on their phone bill, but what can you do? You can dial a credit-card call if you have AT&T, but I try not to give them my money because of how snooty they were twenty years ago. I still remember: You could call up and say, "Fuck you," and they would say, "Thank you, sir." It's like talking to a recording. You could never win. You could say a hundred things and they would only answer you in the six lines they were taught to say. They would never give in. I remember that telephone-company smugness. Don't think they're going to get my business twenty years later. I don't forget.

JW: What about outdoor art murals?

WATERS: Well, I like a few of them. But mostly I hate them, especially the ones funded by government grants. I don't "get" grants anyway. If art is any good, the government wants to stop it, not pay for it. I'm against censorship, but I don't understand all these people who go and try to get a grant. *I* never got a grant. They actually spent money trying to stop my films. Any good art, the government doesn't pay for it. Good art is against the government.

JW: How do you feel about New Age?

WATERS: If I go to a record store or a bookstore and they have a New Age section, I leave immediately. What does New Age mean, anyway? Rotten little crystals? Poor Andy Warhol had a crystal in his pocket when he checked into the hospital—a lot of good it did him.

JW: Do you include astrology under the heading of New Age?

WATERS: New Age is worse than astrology because old hippies are bad enough, but new ones are *really* offensive. People ask me what sign I am and I say, "Feces!" and they change the subject. The only horoscope I've ever liked was one in *Town & Country* that said, "You're going to lose all your money."

JW: Do you like science fiction?

WATERS: No, I've never liked it. But I don't "get" it. I'm not a *buff.* I don't hate it like I hate New Age. I hate Westerns, though. *Hate* is a word we use quite casually here in Baltimore.

JW: And I take it you don't like such American classics as The African Queen *and* The Philadelphia Story.

WATERS: I don't like Katharine Hepburn. Katharine Hepburn gets on my nerves because she's holier than thou. People in Hollywood can't believe that I hate Katharine Hepburn. It's like you committed blasphemy, like you said the meanest thing about Jesus, that's how they act. Oh, please! She's the kind of person I always fled from, an old preppy with an attitude. She thinks she's creating art every time she steps out of her house. She's humor-impaired about herself. She'll say little things to put herself down, but in the way an old WASP does. That's hardly original. And I find the public's awe of her offensive. Maybe that's why I dislike her, how the public sees her and how she flips out and stops any play she's in if someone takes a picture of her. I always wanted to go to one of her performances with a strobe: "Go, Katy baby! Show it! Go, girl!" Like a stripper, just keep strobing her. What could they do—put you on death row? They'd just throw you out. And she'd have a nervous breakdown.

JW: You don't like short subjects.

WATERS: No! Let's just see the movie! I don't have all day to sit there. Nor do I like computer films, even though I'm not sure what they are. I've seen some, but I left too quickly. I had "contempt before investigation," which I'm big on. A friend of mine who's in AA says that they tell you right in the beginning that you can't have contempt. Well, I have contempt all the time. I actually hate something before I know anything about it.

JW: You've criticized the popcorn at movie theaters, too.

WATERS: The butter in the popcorn—well, it's not butter, is it? It tastes like some horrible grease. And you go to the candy counter and the candy sizes are so huge, you need a shopping cart to lug a box of Jujubes back to your seat. A medium Coke is a *vat*.

JW: Do you find the whole experience repugnant?

WATERS: No, I love to go to the movies during the week. It's the weekends I hate because of "dates." I never go to the movies on a Friday night because those people don't go to see the movie, they go to make out. They're the ones who talk the most, and if the movie is the slightest bit unusual or strange the girl goes, "Ewwwww," or "Gross!" all through the sex scenes so he doesn't think she's a whore. I never go on weekends.

JW: Do you watch much TV?

WATERS: No, whenever it's on it's like having somebody in my house that I want to get rid of and they won't leave. I hate the sound of it. All that noise and light coming from a piece of furniture. And I have a huge TV upstairs; I have the biggest TV you can buy. But I only watch it when I have guests, or if there's a war or a video I want to see.

JW: What about the news?

WATERS: No, I don't watch any of it. I know the local weatherman personally and I don't hate him, but I hate the idea that the people who produce the news feel that for anyone to watch a weatherman he has to be a clown. I hate that. I have always had a mild interest in meteorology, but how can you care if it's going to be sunny tomorrow when Bozo the Clown brings you the weather? I'd prefer a serious meteorologist who would tell you how the weather works, not some imbecile cracking jokes.

And another thing: wind-chill factor. Weathermen made that up in the last ten years to disguise the fact that it's the exact temperature you'd expect it to be. If it's thirty degrees, "the wind-chill factor is ten below." It's *not* ten below, it's *thirty*. If the wind is blowing really hard, if it's a *gale-force* wind, the temperature is still thirty degrees, not ten below zero. The wind-chill factor is hype for the weather.

JW: Do you agree with Hunter Thompson that "crack is ruining the drug culture"?

WATERS: I think it's been ruined for a long time. I don't take drugs anymore, but when they asked me to do antidrug spots, I said, "I'm not that much of a hypocrite." I did plenty of drugs when I was young and I'm not sorry about it, but if I had a child I'd be uptight if they took drugs. I had no problems with drugs, but people I took them with are dead from them. The worst drug is the one with smiley face, Ecstasy. Any drug with a smiley face as a symbol has to be bad. It sounds like the most horrible drug I could ever imagine: You wake up and you've invited eight people you hate to dinner. Instead of having a hangover, you have to have eight horrible people sitting in your dining room. I'd rather have a hangover.

JW: You've written extensively about Los Angeles, especially its houses.

WATERS: There's a type of architecture in Los Angeles like nothing I've seen anywhere in the world. The new houses look like modern mausoleums. They fill every inch of the lawn. They look like airports. They're the ultimate in nouveau-riche bad taste. Living in a cold-water flat with dirt floors is classier. I was driving through Trousdale Estates and I actually saw one that had just been knocked down with a wrecker—smoke was coming from where it had just hit the ground. I almost ran off the road from laughing. You see these great Hollywood homes being replaced by things that will end up on post-cards as jokes. Which I'm all for—I'll buy the postcard. I see them and I think, "This makes it more fun to take a drive in L.A. Let's ride around and laugh at the excess and the poor taste of these huge joke houses." And they're even better because you know that the people are dead serious about them.

JW: At the other extreme, you say that Venice Beach is the only place in L.A. that reminds you of the East Coast.

WATERS: Well, I don't "get" the charm of Venice Beach. I have many friends who live there—who pay a fortune to live there—but I think it's mostly hideous and dangerous. To me it's a million-dollar slum, and I like a slum that's cheap. Then it's bohemian. It's too expensive to be a real bohemian in Venice, California.

JW: But you like Muscle Beach.

WATERS: Yes, I like it because it's obvious, it's a temple to exhibitionism and voyeurism, so I'm all for that. I go there to watch the voyeurs because they never think you're looking at them.

JW: Well, we could go on and on, but I'll let you go. Thanks for the interview.

WATERS: Was I mean enough?

THE CRITICAL CURMUDGEON:
THEATER AND FILM

Bernard Shaw has no enemies but is intensely disliked by his friends.

OSCAR WILDE

It is his life work to announce the obvious in terms of the scandalous.

H. L. MENCKEN, on George Bernard Shaw

Mr. Shaw is (I suspect) the only man on earth who has never written any poetry.

G. K. CHESTERTON

He writes his plays for the ages—the ages between five and twelve.

GEORGE JEAN NATHAN, on George Bernard Shaw

His style has the desperate jauntiness of an orchestra fiddling away for dear life on a sinking ship.

EDMUND WILSON, on Evelyn Waugh

If the writing of *This Was a Man* was slow, the production by Basil Dean was practically stationary. The second-act dinner scene between Francine Larrimore and Nigel Bruce made *Parsifal* in its entirety seem like a quick-fire vaudeville sketch.

NOEL COWARD

When Mr. Wilbur calls his play *Halfway to Hell* he underestimates the distance.

BROOKS ATKINSON

Good Fielding, no hit.   KYLE CRICHTON, on a production of *Tom Jones*

[*Last Stop*] is enough to make your flesh crawl—right out of the Ethel Barrymore Theatre.   JOHN CHAPMAN

The play was a great success but the audience was a total failure.
                                                              OSCAR WILDE

Darling, they've absolutely ruined your perfectly dreadful play.
     TALLULAH BANKHEAD to Tennessee Williams, on *Orpheus Descending*

The triumph of sugar over diabetes.
                              GEORGE JEAN NATHAN, on James M. Barrie

---

[William Inge] handles symbolism rather like an Olympic weight lifter, raising it with agonizing care, brandishing it with a tiny grunt of triumph, then dropping it with a terrible clang.
                    BENEDICT NIGHTINGALE, on *Come Back, Little Sheba*

I have nothing against Brecht in his place, which is East Germany.
                                                              CLIVE JAMES

A confusing jamboree of piercing noise, routine roller-skating, misogyny and Orwellian special effects, *Starlight Express* is the perfect gift for the kid who has everything except parents.   FRANK RICH

The sentimental comedy by the Soviet playwright Aleksei Arbuzov is said to have had a great success in its own country. So do fringed lamp shades.
                                                              RICHARD EDER

With *States of Shock*, Sam Shepard appears to have finally attained what he was aiming at all along: total incomprehensibility.   JOHN SIMON

In order to fully realize how bad a popular play can be, it is necessary to see it twice.   GEORGE BERNARD SHAW

It had only one fault. It was kind of lousy.   JAMES THURBER

It is greatly to Mrs. Patrick Campbell's credit that, bad as the play was, her acting was worse. It was a masterpiece of failure.

GEORGE BERNARD SHAW, reviewing *Fedora*

A great actress, from the waist down.

DAME MARGARET KENDAL, on Sarah Bernhardt

She runs the gamut of emotions from A to B.

DOROTHY PARKER, on Katharine Hepburn

The glass eye in the forehead of English acting.

KENNETH TYNAN, on Ralph Richardson

A. E. Matthews ambled through *This Was a Man* like a charming retriever who has buried a bone and can't quite remember where.

NOEL COWARD

Queen of the Nil.   GEORGE JEAN NATHAN, on Tallulah Bankhead

Tallulah Bankhead barged down the Nile as Cleopatra and sank.

JOHN MASON BROWN

She has two expressions: joy and indigestion.
                              DOROTHY PARKER, on Marion Davies

---

There is no sign that her acting would ever have progressed beyond the scope of the restless shoulders and the protuberant breasts; her body technique was the gangster's technique—she toted a breast like a man totes a gun.
                              GRAHAM GREENE, on Jean Harlow

Mr. Muni seemed intent on submerging himself so completely in makeup that he disappeared.   BETTE DAVIS, on *Juarez*

Her familiar expression of strained intensity would be less quickly relieved by a merciful death than by Ex-Lax.   JAMES AGEE, on Ida Lupino

---

One of the most richly syllabled queenly horrors of Hollywood.
                              PAULINE KAEL, on Greer Garson

Miss Stapleton played the part as though she had not yet signed the contract with the producer.   GEORGE JEAN NATHAN, on Maureen Stapleton

---

Alan Ladd has only two expressions: hat on and hat off.   ANONYMOUS

George Raft and Gary Cooper once played a scene in front of a cigar store, and it looked like the wooden Indian was overacting.   GEORGE BURNS

Most of the time Marlon Brando sounds like he has a mouth full of wet toilet paper.   REX REED

Miss Moira Lester speaks all her lines as if they are written in very faint ink on a teleprompter slightly too far away to be read with comfort.

BERNARD LEVIN

A pharaonic mummy, moving on tiny casters, like a touring replica of the Queen Mother.

The Sunday Times of London, on
Elizabeth Taylor in *The Mirror Crack'd*

Just how garish her commonplace accent, squeakily shrill voice, and the childish petulance with which she delivers her lines are, my pen is neither scratchy nor leaky enough to convey.

JOHN SIMON, on
Elizabeth Taylor in *The Taming of the Shrew*

Olivier's idea of introspection was to hood his eyes, dentalize his consonants and let the camera circle his blondined head like a sparrow looking for a place to deposit its droppings.

ROBERT BRUSTEIN, on Laurence Olivier's *Hamlet*

Another dirty shirt-tail actor from New York.

HEDDA HOPPER, on James Dean

Charlton Heston throws all his punches in the first ten minutes (three grimaces and two intonations) so that he has nothing left long before he stumbles to the end, four hours later, and has to react to the Crucifixion. (He does make it clear, I must admit, that he quite disapproves of it.)

DWIGHT MACDONALD, on *Ben Hur*

[William Shatner as] Kirk, employing a thespian technique picked up from someone who once worked with somebody who knew Lee Strasberg's sister.

CLIVE JAMES

She's one of the few actresses in Hollywood history who looks more animated in still photographs than she does on the screen.

MICHAEL MEDVED, on Raquel Welch

Mae West, [in *Myra Breckinridge*] playing a ghastly travesty of womanhood she once played, has a Mae West face painted on the front of her head and moves to and fro like the Imperial Hotel during the 1923 Tokyo earthquake.

JOSEPH MORGENSTERN

Ryan O'Neal is so stiff and clumsy that he can't even manage a part requiring him to be stiff and clumsy.

JAY COCKS

When not emitting one of the clever things Frederic Raphael once said (or else *would* have said, but thought of too late, and so is saying now), [Tom] Conti conveyed introspection by encouraging his eyes to glisten wetly, while smiling with secret knowledge.

CLIVE JAMES

[Charles Grodin] keeps threatening to be funny but he rarely makes it.

PAULINE KAEL

Sylvester Stallone has a face that would look well on a three-toed sloth.

RUSSELL DAVIS

His diction (always bad) is now incomprehensible, as if his ego has grown so big that it now fills his mouth like a cup of mashed potatoes.

JOHN POWERS, on Sylvester Stallone

A testicle with legs.

PAULINE KAEL, on Bob Hoskins

[Judd] Nelson gives a performance with flare: his eyes flare, his nostrils flare, his hair—if such a thing is possible—flares. His tonsils may have been flaring, too, but at least you can't see them. TOM SHALES

Daryl Hannah remains a rotten actress and still looks like a linebacker in a Lorelei wig. JOHN SIMON

Five nice things to say about Steven Seagal: (1) He has very good posture. (2) His ponytail is neatly trimmed. (3) While his acting repertoire is limited, he does a brow furrow Jeremy Irons would kill for. (4) When doing martial-arts maneuvers, he does not emit chickenlike sounds, as Bruce Lee did. (5)...Maybe there are only four. RALPH NOVAK

I like Demi Moore. But that's because I have no taste. JOE QUEENAN

Sarah Brightman couldn't act scared on the New York subway at four o'clock in the morning. JOEL SIEGEL

Helen Hunt won the Oscar by weighing less than the statuette itself.
LIBBY GELMAN-WAXNER (aka Paul Rudnick)

Cecil B. De Mille made small-minded pictures on a big scale. PAULINE KAEL

I learned an awful lot from him by doing the opposite.
HOWARD HAWKES, on Cecil B. De Mille

Cecil B. De Mille returned a script to a screenwriter with the following note: "What I have crossed out I didn't like. What I haven't crossed out I am dissatisfied with."

Since [Jean-Luc] Godard's films have nothing to say, perhaps we should have ninety minutes' silence instead of each of them.   JOHN SIMON

Billy Wilder at work is like two people—Mr. Hyde and Mr. Hyde.
                                                    HARRY KURNITZ

Wilder is a curdled Lubitsch, romanticism gone sour, 78 rpm played at 45, an old-worldling from Vienna perpetually sneering at Hollywood as it engulfs him.   ANDREW SARRIS

A shot that does not call for tracks is agony for dear old Max.
                                          JAMES MASON, on Max Ophuls

------

He perpetually pursues the anticliché only to arrive at anticlimax.
                                        ANDREW SARRIS, on Brian Forbes

------

Blake Edwards is a man of many talents, all of them minor.
                                                    LESLIE HALLIWELL

Several tons of dynamite are set off in this picture—none of it under the right people.   JAMES AGEE, on *Tycoon*

During the making of *Pin-up Girl* Betty Grable was in an early stage of pregnancy—and everyone else was evidently in a late stage of paresis.
                                                            JAMES AGEE

This film needs a certain something. Possibly burial.
                                        DAVID LARDNER, on *Panama Hattie*

This film is the Platonic ideal of boredom, roughly comparable to reading a three-volume novel in a language of which one knows only the alphabet.
JOHN SIMON, on *Camelot*

This long but tiny film.... STANLEY KAUFFMANN, on *Isadora*

Armageddon is an assault on the eyes, the ears, the brain, common sense and the human desire to be entertained. No matter what they're charging to get in, it's worth more to get out. ROGER EBERT

Seagulls, as the film stresses, subsist on garbage, and, I guess, you are what you eat. JOHN SIMON, reviewing *Jonathan Livingston Seagull*

My Dinner with Andre is as boring as being alive. QUENTIN CRISP

I had a colonoscopy once, and they let me watch it on TV. It was more entertaining than *The Brown Bunny*. ROGER EBERT

The Nazi rocket scientist Wernher von Braun played a key role in the development of the V2 rocket, which rained terror on the British civilian population during World War II. After coming to the United States and joining the U.S. rocket program in 1950, von Braun was the subject of a Hollywood movie, *I Aim for the Stars*. Mort Sahl suggested that the title be changed to *I Aim for the Stars, But Sometimes I Hit London*.

[*Gigli* is] such an utter wreck of a movie you expect to see it lying on its side somewhere in rural Pennsylvania, with a small gang of engineers circling and a wisp of smoke rising from the caboose. STEPHEN WHITTY

At this point, there are inflatable toys that are livelier than [Sharon] Stone, but how can you tell the difference? *Basic Instinct 2* is not an erotic thriller. It's taxidermy.   KYLE SMITH

To say [Ralph] Fiennes and [Uma] Thurman don't have the chemistry of [Patrick] Macnee and [Diana] Rigg isn't enough. They don't have the chemistry of Don Adams and Barbara Feldon. They don't have the chemistry of Boris and Natasha.   JEFFREY WESTHOFF, on *The Avengers*

Catwoman doesn't belong on the big screen. It belongs in the litter box or to be scraped off the bottom of our shoes as we head quickly for another theater.
                                                                                                          CONNIE OGLE

[*The Celestine Prophecy*] is arguably as effective as Ambien at inducing sleep, but possible side effects include uncontrollable laughter.   LOU LUMENICK

Glitter [is] the kind of movie only 11-year-old girls who dot their i's with hearts would find bearable.   RENE RODRIGUEZ

[*Little Nicky* is] a movie for people who find pop-up books too intellectually demanding and college keg parties too socially refined.   STEVE TILLEY

Students beware: [*The Scarlet Letter*] is no sub for CliffsNotes. The script takes more liberties with the text than Elizabeth Berkley did with that pole in *Showgirls*.   SUSAN WLOSZCZYNA

What Madonna does [in *Swept Away*] can't properly be called acting—more accurately, it's moving and it's talking and it's occasionally gesturing, sometimes all at once.   RICK GROEN

With no plot, character or dialogue worth experiencing, let alone remembering, [*The Dukes of Hazzard*] merely occupies space on the screen and hopes for the best.
KENNETH TURAN

They should have called [*Pearl Harbor*] "Bore-a, Bore-a, Bore-a."
DESSON THOMSON

3000 Miles to Graceland shouldn't be reviewed in an arts section but rather in that portion of the newspaper dedicated to atrocities, environmental disasters and hate crimes.
SHAWN LEVY

With the release of this wretched film [*Surviving Christmas*], star Ben Affleck takes one more ragged step in what seems his death march from leading man to celebrity game-show guest.
THOMAS PEYSER

The jabbering, meandering, and ossified movie Robert Altman has made from Garrison Keillor's lumbering, affected, and pointless audio curiosity, *A Prairie Home Companion*, is not a movie at all. It's like notes for a movie that was never completed, retrieved from a wastebasket and filmed all night in a broadcast studio before the parking meters ran out of quarters. The result, if you can imagine anything so deadly, is like watching radio.
REX REED

ALEXANDER WOOLLCOTT

The Man Who Came to Dinner

Alexander Wollcott, wit, raconteur, essayist, critic, lecturer, anthologist, was born in Red Bank, New Jersey, in 1887 and grew up in the Phalanx, an experimental commune based on the tenets of Fourierism. He hated his absent father ("The son of a bitch left us dangling from the brink of insecurity over the pit of poverty. What on God's good earth was there for me to love about my father? Or even admire?") but was devoted to his mother. He decided to become a drama critic at the age of ten.

He suffered from a testosterone deficiency, which accounted for his soft skin, round hips, and lack of facial hair. A pudgy, myopic boy, he was teased mercilessly by other children. He immersed himself in books to compensate, and began reviewing them for the Philadelphia *Telegraph* while he was still in high school. After a severe bout of mumps at the age of twenty-two, he spent the rest of his adult life as, in his words, a "semi-eunuch."

Woollcott attended Hamilton College in New York, where his appearance and predilection for dressing in women's clothes made him a social outcast. His response was to exaggerate his differences in the manner of his hero, Oscar Wilde. He was a founding member of the college dramatic club, played all the female leads, and had calling cards printed with the name "Alexandra Woollcott." He would later describe himself as being "half god, half woman."

He volunteered for service in the Great War and was somehow accepted despite his unusual physique (an officer called him "the pregnant mermaid"). Trained as a medical orderly, he was shipped to France, where he quickly wangled a job on the staff of the enlisted-man's newspaper, *Stars and Stripes*. He was soon the paper's top front-line correspondent and became famous both for his impassioned reports and for his uniform, a liberated German officer's coat, a frying pan worn in front for protection, and a shawl across his shoulders.

After the war, he realized his childhood ambition by becoming drama critic for several papers, including the *New York Times*. His critical style was straightforward: If he liked something, he would praise it lavishly and eloquently; if he didn't, he would go to great lengths to sink it. Thus Mark Connelly said that "rancor was Woollcott's only form of exercise," and George Jean Nathan called his style "lump-in-the-throat reviewing." His fellow critic Wolcott Gibbs wrote, "He wasn't exactly hostile to facts, but he was apathetic about them," and Charles Brackett called him "a competent old horror with a style that combined clear treacle and pure black bile."

During the thirties, Woollcott presided over the Algonquin Round Table, a stellar group of wits and raconteurs, of which Edna Ferber wrote:

Their standards were high, their vocabulary fluent, fresh, astringent, tough. Theirs was a tonic influence, one on the other, and all on the world of American letters. The people they could not and would not stand were the bores, hypocrites, sentimentalists and the socially pretentious. They were ruthless toward charlatans, toward the pompous and mentally dishonest. Casual, incisive, they had a terrible integrity about their work and a boundless ambition.

The Algonquin membership included George S. Kaufman, Marc Connelly, Franklin P. Adams, Heywood Broun, Dorothy Parker, Robert Benchley, and Harold Ross, the founder of the *New Yorker*, for which Woollcott wrote his "Shouts and Murmurs" column, a weekly concoction of theatrical anecdotes, gossip, and true-crime murder stories.

Woollcott's several books were compilations of his articles and reviews. One of them, *While Rome Burns*, sold almost 300,000 copies during the depths of the Depression. He wrote two unsuccessful plays, *The Channel Road* and *The Dark Tower* (both of which he later attempted to disown), was the host of a popular radio program, and earned large sums as a peripatetic lecturer. As a critic, he had the reputation of being able to make or break a play and, according to *Publishers Weekly*, also had unprecedented power over book sales: A mere mention of a title on the air could sell thousands of copies.

Radio was his metier. His popular program, *The Town Crier*, opened with the announcer calling out, "Hear Ye, Hear Ye, Hear Ye," after which Woollcott would sign on with "This is Woollcott speaking." Woollcott knew how to hold an audience; he was a born raconteur, his voice magnetic, his timing and microphone technique impeccable.

Woollcott was a closet sentimentalist: He valued family ties and remained close to his relatives, giving them unsparing financial and moral support all his life. He quietly supported his alma mater by helping fellow alumni, donating substantial sums of money, paying the tuition costs of several undergraduates, and waiving his lecture fees for speaking there. Woollcott adopted several charities—he was an early champion of Seeing Eye Dogs for the Blind, and he supported World War I veterans and retired actors—and publicized them both on his radio program and in his columns.

Although he pretended to hate children, Woollcott was kind and generous to those of his friends, and he took a special interest in his two nieces, though his love for them didn't dull his acerbic wit. When one of the girls visited New York at the age of fifteen, Woollcott introduced her to his friends: "This is my niece Polly, who plans to be a prostitute."

In 1924, Woollcott bought Neshobe Island on Lake Bomoseen, Vermont, and turned it into an exclusive club for his friends. It may have been an attempt to re-create his childhood home, the Phalanx, with its extended family. Neshobe became an expensive summer camp for adults. The initiation fee was a thousand dollars and the annual dues were a hundred dollars per person, with nonstop activities including croquet, badminton, fishing, nude swimming, cribbage, and word games. The members included Alice Duer Miller, Howard Dietz, Ruth Gordon, and Beatrice Kaufman. The guests were a who's who of show business, from Noel Coward to Alfred Lunt and Lynn Fontanne, Ethel Barrymore to Harpo Marx, who remarked after seeing Woollcott swimming in the buff: "He looked like something that had gotten loose from Macy's Thanksgiving Day Parade." Woollcott eventually abandoned his riverfront apartment on Fifty-second Street (dubbed "Wit's End" by Dorothy Parker) and moved to Neshobe permanently.

Woollcott's lecture tours put him on the road much of the year, and, given his many acquaintances around the country and his aversion to hotels, he was usually a guest in someone's house. According to all accounts he had no compunction about moving in and taking over. He berated servants, changed the dates on his hosts' social calendars to suit his schedule, and even had one hostess's telephone number changed so he could use the phone without interruption from her friends.

Woollcott was often asked by friends to write letters of recommendation, and, always the practical joker, liked to send them false copies. Thus when S. N. Behrman requested a reference to a prospective landlord, he received a "carbon copy" which read:

> I was astonished to learn that your company was even remotely considering accepting as a tenant such a notorious drunkard, bankrupt, and general moral leper as my miserable friend Behrman.

When George and Beatrice Kaufman requested a letter on behalf of their daughter to the headmistress of an exclusive school, Woollcott sent them a carbon that alleged a series of orgies had taken place in the Kaufmans' home, and which ended, "I implore you to accept this unfortunate child and remove her from her shocking environment." And when Dorothy Parker and her husband, Alan Campbell, were foolish enough to give Woollcott as a credit reference to a department store, he wrote to the store:

> Gentlemen: Mr. Alan Campbell, the present husband of Dorothy Parker, has given my name as a reference in an attempt to open an account at your store. I hope that you will extend this credit to him. Surely Dorothy Parker's position in American letters is such as to make shameful the petty refusals which she and Alan have encountered at many hotels, restaurants, and department stores. What if you never get paid? Why shouldn't you stand your share of the expense?

Woollcott bullied Moss Hart and George S. Kaufman into writing a play in which he could star as himself, and in due course they came up with *The*

Man Who Came to Dinner. The main character is an imperious houseguest who fractures his leg and takes over the household, issuing orders, conducting his social and business affairs—and the affairs of everyone else—from his wheelchair. Woollcott auditioned and lobbied for the part: "I'm perfect for the part," he told Kaufman, "I'm the only man you know who can strut sitting down." Although he was passed over in favor of Monty Woolley for the Broadway production, he was finally given his chance in a 1940 road company. A friend who had seen the play wrote to Woollcott:

> Dear Alec:
> I saw you and your play yesterday and enjoyed both thoroughly except for three unnecessary "God damns" and a half dozen unnecessarily vulgar "wisecracks." If these were deleted, *The Man Who Came to Dinner* would be a rollicking good comedy which I would be glad to recommend to all of my friends without qualification.
>
> T. D. Martin

Woollcott replied:

> My Dear Martin:
> This is to acknowledge your letter of March sixth, which really shocked me. When you speak of "three unnecessary 'God damns'" you imply that there is such a thing as a *necessary* God damn. This, of course, is nonsense. A God damn is never a necessity. It is always a luxury.
>
> Yours very sincerely,
> Alexander Woollcott

On January 23, 1943, Woollcott suffered a fatal heart attack while discussing the question "Is Germany Curable?" on the radio show *The People's*

Platform. He is remembered for his personality, not his literary output. Asked to describe him in one word, George S. Kaufman said, "Improbable." The *New Yorker* noted, "The whole aura of Woollcott was theatrical and delightful, and you approached him as you did the theater—with misgiving but with vast fascination; and you left him as you left a matinee, with dread at emerging from make-believe into a dull side street off Broadway." Walter Winchell said that his reviews were more entertaining than the shows he covered—"even the hits." Walter Lippmann wrote that he had "a piercing eye for sham. He had an acid tongue. But he had gusto, he really liked what he praised, and he cared much more for the men and women he liked than he worried about those he did not like." The actress Margalo Gilmore's assessment of his acting ability could serve as his epitaph: "He wasn't an actor. He was an ego having a lovely time."

WOOLLCOTT SPEAKING

All the things I really like to do are either illegal, immoral, or fattening.

Nothing risqué, nothing gained.

He wrote in reply to a get-well note, "I have no need of your God-damned sympathy....I wish only to be entertained by some of your grosser reminiscences."

To all things clergic I am allergic.

Accosted on the street by an old acquaintance who said, "You remember me, don't you, Alec?" Woollcott quickly replied, "No, I can't remember your name and please don't tell me."

Apologizing to a friend with whom he had quarreled: "I've tried by tender and conscientious nursing to keep my grudge against you alive, but I find it has died on me."

After a disagreement with Harold Ross, Woollcott sent the message: "I think your slogan 'Liberty or Death' is splendid and whichever one you decide on will be all right with me."

Rather than touch any of that slop, I'd just as soon lie face down in a pail of Italian garbage!

———————————

I only posed in public.

———————————

A hick town is one in which there is no place to go where you shouldn't be.

———————————

Woollcott seldom took any exercise more strenuous than croquet. While watching skiers at Sun Valley, he took out a memo pad and wrote, "Remind self never to go skiing."

———————————

His review of a volume of poetry written by a woman entitled *And I Shall Make Music*: "Not on my carpet, lady!"

———————————

Prostitution, like acting, is being ruined by amateurs.

———————————

A broker is a man who takes your fortune and runs it into a shoestring.

———————————

When it was suggested he meet the elderly aunt of an old acquaintance, he replied, "I already know too many people."

———————————

She [Dorothy Parker] is so odd a blend of little Nell and Lady Macbeth. It is not so much the familiar phenomenon of a hand of steel in a velvet glove as a lacy sleeve with a bottle of vitriol concealed in its folds.

———————————

On his first visit to Moss Hart's Bucks County estate, Woollcott wrote in the guest book: "This is to certify that on my first visit to Moss Hart's house I had one of the most unpleasant times I ever spent."

[Harold Ross] looks like a dishonest Abe Lincoln.

Michael Arlen, for all his reputation, is not a bounder. He is every other inch a gentleman.

While on a lecture tour Woollcott received a note from a woman who had performed with him in a play when they were four years old. He scribbled a note to her just before assuming the lectern: "Please have your wheelchair brought around to the stage door after my gibberish is completed."

Asked by Helen Hayes and Charles MacArthur to be godfather at the baptism of their daughter Mary, Woollcott sighed, "Always a godfather, never a god."

THE CRITICAL
CURMUDGEON: MUSIC

There are more bad musicians than there is bad music.   ISAAC STERN

A vile, beastly, rottenheaded, foolbegotten, brazenthroated, pernicious, priggish, screaming, tearing, roaring, perplexing, splitmecrackle, crash-mecriggle, insane, ass of a woman is practicing howling below-stairs with a brute of a singing master so horribly that my head is nearly off.   EDWARD LEAR

After playing the violin for the cellist Gregor Piatigorsky, Albert Einstein asked, "Did I play well?"
  "You played *relatively* well," replied Piatigorsky.

The chromatic scale is what you use to give the effect of drinking a quinine martini and having an enema simultaneously.   PHILIP LARKIN

The sound of a harpsichord—two skeletons copulating on a thin roof in a thunderstorm.   SIR THOMAS BEECHAM

Harpists spend ninety percent of their lives tuning their harps and ten percent playing out of tune.   IGOR STRAVINSKY

I could eat alphabet soup and *shit* better lyrics.
                                        JOHNNY MERCER, on a British musical

Mozart died too late rather than too soon.   GLENN GOULD

Beethoven always sounds to me like the upsetting of a bag of nails, with here and there an also dropped hammer.   JOHN RUSKIN

Art is long and life is short: here is evidently the explanation of a Brahms symphony.   EDWARD LORNE

The banging and slamming and booming and crashing [in *Lohengrin*] were something beyond belief. The racking and pitiless pain of it remains stored up in my memory alongside the memory of the time that I had my teeth fixed.
                    MARK TWAIN

I like Wagner's music better than any other music. It is so loud that one can talk the whole time without people hearing what one says. That is a great advantage.   OSCAR WILDE

Wagner's music is better than it sounds.   MARK TWAIN

I love Wagner, but the music I prefer is that of a cat hung up by its tail outside a window and trying to stick to the panes of glass with its claws.
                    CHARLES BAUDELAIRE

Is Wagner actually a man? Is he not rather a disease? Everything he touches falls ill. He has made music sick.
                    FRIEDRICH WILHELM NIETZSCHE

Leonard Bernstein has been disclosing musical secrets that have been well known for over four hundred years.   OSCAR LEVANT

If the reader were so rash as to purchase any of Béla Bartók's compositions, he would find that they each and all consist of unmeaning bunches of notes, apparently representing the composer promenading the keyboard in his boots. Some can be played better with the elbows, others with the flat of the hand. None require fingers to perform or ears to listen to.

FREDERICK CORDER

Dvorak's *Requiem* bored Birmingham so desperately that it was unanimously voted a work of extraordinary depth and impressiveness, which verdict I record with a hollow laugh, and allow the subject to drop by its own portentous weight.   GEORGE BERNARD SHAW

In the first movement alone, I took note of six pregnancies and at least four miscarriages.

SIR THOMAS BEECHAM, on Bruckner's Seventh Symphony

What can you do with it? It's like a lot of yaks jumping about.

SIR THOMAS BEECHAM, on Beethoven's Seventh Symphony

Sir Thomas Beecham was once asked if he had played any Stockhausen. "No," he replied, "but I have trodden in some."

Rossini would have been a great composer if his teacher had spanked him enough on his backside.   LUDWIG VAN BEETHOVEN

Anton Bruckner wrote the same symphony nine times (ten, actually), trying to get it just right. He failed.   EDWARD ABBEY

Schoenberg is too melodious for me, too sweet.   BERTOLT BRECHT

He'd be better off shovelling snow.

> RICHARD STRAUSS, on Arnold Schoenberg

When told that a soloist would need six fingers to perform his concerto, Arnold Schoenberg replied, "I can wait."

I would like to hear Elliott Carter's *Fourth String Quartet*, if only to discover what a cranky prostate does to one's polyphony.   JAMES SELLARS

Exit in case of Brahms.   PHILIP HALE's proposed inscription over
the doors of Boston Symphony Hall

Why is it that whenever I hear a piece of music I don't like, it's always by Villa-Lobos?   IGOR STRAVINSKY

His music used to be original. Now it is aboriginal.

> SIR ERNEST NEWMAN, on Igor Stravinsky

Claude Debussy played the piano with the lid down.   ROBERT BRESSON

If he'd been making shell-cases during the war it might have been better for music.   MAURICE RAVEL, on Camille Saint-Saëns

---

He has an enormously wide repertory. He can conduct anything, provided it's by Beethoven, Brahms, or Wagner. He tried Debussy's *La mer* once. It came out as *Das Merde*.   ANONYMOUS ORCHESTRA MEMBER, on Georg Szell

---

Someone commented to Rudolph Bing, manager of the Metropolitan Opera, that Georg Szell was his own worst enemy.
  "Not while I'm alive, he isn't!" said Bing.

There was one respect in which Landon Ronald outshone all other conductors. This was in the gleam of his shirtfront and the gloss of his enormous cuffs, out of which peeped tiny, fastidious fingers. He made music sound as if it, too, had been laundered.   JAMES AGATE

Madam, you have between your legs an instrument capable of giving pleasure to thousands—and all you can do is scratch it.
                                    SIR THOMAS BEECHAM to a lady cellist

---

After I die, I shall return to earth as a gatekeeper of a bordello and I won't let any of you enter.   ARTURO TOSCANINI to the NBC Orchestra

---

Already too loud!   BRUNO WALTER, on seeing the orchestra reach for
                              their instruments at the beginning of a rehearsal

---

We cannot expect you to be with us all the time, but perhaps you could be good enough to keep in touch now and again.
                                    SIR THOMAS BEECHAM to a musician during a rehearsal

---

Jack Benny played Mendelssohn last night. Mendelssohn lost.
                                    ANONYMOUS

The great German conductor Hans von Bülow detested two members of an orchestra named Schultz and Schmidt. Upon being told that Schmidt had died, von Bülow immediately asked, "*Und* Schultz?"

Her voice sounded like an eagle being goosed.
                                    RALPH NOVAK, on Yoko Ono

If a horse could sing in a monotone, the horse would sound like Carly Simon, only a horse wouldn't rhyme "yacht," "apricot" and "gavotte."

ROBERT CHRISTGAU

If I had a hammer I'd use it on Peter, Paul and Mary.

HOWARD ROSENBERG

Not content to have the audience in the palm of his hand, he goes one further and clenches his fist.   KENNETH TYNAN, on Frankie Laine

---

When she started to play, Steinway came down personally and rubbed his name off the piano.   BOB HOPE, on Phyllis Diller

---

Yesterday the performance of *Rheingold* took place. From the scenic point of view it interested me greatly, and I was also much impressed by the marvelous staging of the work. Musically it is inconceivable nonsense.

PYOTR ILICH TCHAIKOVSKY

Parsifal is a work of perfidy, of vindictiveness, of a secret attempt to poison the presuppositions of life—a *bad* work....I despise anyone who does not experience *Parsifal* as an attempted assassination of basic ethics.

FRIEDRICH WILHELM NIETZSCHE

I was not able to detect in the vocal parts of *Parsifal* anything that might with confidence be called rhythm or tune or melody; one person performed at a time—and a long time, too—often in a noble, and always in a high-toned, voice; but he only pulled out long notes, then some short ones, then another long one, then a sharp, quick, peremptory bark or two—and so on and so on; and when he was done you saw that the information which he had conveyed had not compensated for the disturbance.   MARK TWAIN

Parsifal—the kind of opera that starts at six o'clock and after it has been going three hours, you look at your watch and it says 6:20.   DAVID RANDOLPH

One can't judge Wagner's opera *Lohengrin* after a first hearing, and I certainly don't intend hearing it a second time.   GIOACCHINO ROSSINI

I liked the opera very much. Everything but the music.
          BENJAMIN BRITTEN, on Stravinsky's *The Rake's Progress*

Her singing reminds me of a cart coming downhill with the brake on.
     SIR THOMAS BEECHAM, on an unidentified soprano in *Die Walküre*

How nice the human voice is when it isn't singing.   RUDOLPH BING

If music be the food of love, shut up.   BRUCE ERIC KAPLAN

FRANK ZAPPA

Drowning in the News Bath

Frank Zappa (1940–1993) is a rock 'n' roll legend.

JW: I've read that you're nocturnal.
FZ: Yes, if left to my own devices I would function exclusively at night and sleep during the day.
JW: What do you have against sunlight?
FZ: Aside from the fact that it can be hazardous to your health, which wasn't always the case, I dislike the feeling that you experience during the daytime, when so many of the world's souls are awake, being industrious. It's a bad

feeling and I don't want to participate. But at night it's a whole different thing. The people who are awake at night are my kind of people. The animals that are awake at night are the better animals: owls, raccoons, bats, the insects that don't want to show off. The ones with the bright colors have to go out in the daytime to get their money's worth, but the nighttime is natural for the drab, beetlelike, sluglike, monastic kinds of life forms. Superior life forms, like silverfish.

JW: You've been quoted as saying that books make you sleepy.

FZ: Yeah, I don't read. People always send me books, but I can't stand them. People ask me to write intros for books, and even when I know the book is great, I can't deal with it. I read about three paragraphs and I start to pass out.

JW: Then how do you get your information?

FZ: I take a "news bath" every afternoon. I've got it down to a science: At four-thirty on Channel 34, which is the Discovery Channel, you tape *Christian Science Monitor;* then you switch over to CNN at five and watch Bernard Shaw make a fool of himself for a little while; then you switch to the local CBS news and hope to see Michael Tuck, who does the most outrageous things on the air. But the fun really starts at six thirty, when you go to Channel 7 to get the very beginning of Peter Jennings and the *ABC News* to find out what their lead story is and start taping that; while the tape is running, immediately flip over to Channel 2 to see what the lead story is going to be on CBS. The way the commercials are staggered on the six-thirty news, if you start with the ABC News you can get the first big chunk before the commercials start. Then, when Jennings goes to a commercial, you immediately switch over to CBS.

JW: What about NBC?

FZ: You skip NBC at this point because Brokaw hardly ever has anything interesting or competitive with the stories on the other networks. You go directly to Channel 2 and pick up another three minutes of news before they go to a commercial. At that point you have to decide whether to give Brokaw his riff or go back to Jennings. You ping-pong back and forth like that, ending up on Channel 7 because their news goes longer than the CBS News. When that half-hour block is over you flip it to Channel 6 for the tail end of *MacNeil/Lehrer*. And when they're done you go back to CNN.

JW: You once said, "The United States is a nation of laws, badly written and randomly enforced," and within the past few years you've battled censorship and have been active in national politics. How do you assess the health of American democracy in the late twentieth century?

FZ: Democracy is one of those things that looks good on paper, but we've come to a crossroads in contemporary America where we really ought to decide, Do we *want* it? When you have a preponderance of people in this country who will willingly accept censorship—in fact, *ask* for it, *demand* it, in the case of the Gulf War—you've got a problem. Asked random questions about the First Amendment and how they would like to have it applied, if you believe in polls at all, the average American wants no part of it. But if you ask, "What if we threw the Constitution away tomorrow?" the answer is "No, that would be bad!" But living under the Constitution is another story altogether.

I've come to the conclusion that there's only one party in this country and it's divided into two parts: Republicans and Republican wannabes. Republicans stand for evil, corruption, manipulation, greed—everything that Americans think is okay after being conditioned to it during the eighties. Republicans stand for all the values that Americans now hold dear. Plus they have more balloons than God, and for a nation raised on cartoons, that tells you something. Anybody with balloons, they're okay. They don't tell you what kind of crippled people had to blow those suckers up.

The Democrats have no agenda, and when they speak on any topic, they want to sound as Republican as possible while still finding a way to retain the pork. I'll be blunt with you: I'm considering running for president as a nonpartisan candidate because I am sick to death of this stuff. The "news bath" is not a warming experience; it makes me deranged for four or five hours a day.

On a show for Bill Moyers called *The Class of the Twentieth Century*, I said that the faces that really belong on Mount Rushmore are J. Edgar Hoover and Joseph McCarthy and Walter Winchell and Hedda Hopper and maybe even Roy Cohn and Michael Milken, because they've had the greatest impact on American society. They have shaped the way things are done in this country. One of the problems with the world in which we live is that people have become accustomed to lies upon lies.

JW: Would you call yourself a misanthrope?

FZ: I have been called a misanthrope, but I prefer "curmudgeon"; it's folksier and less threatening. "Misanthrope" sounds like you'd have to have gone to college to be one.

JW: Are you an irritable person? Are you tough to get along with?

FZ: I hardly ever leave the house, and during the day I hardly ever talk to anybody because I work by myself and just type [music] on the computer. So, if I have to have a conversation with somebody, chances are it's either going to be a member of my family or somebody who works here, and I like all of them. The only other people that I'm with are the journalists who come here to do interviews, and most of them are okay.

JW: Since you don't go out, I don't suppose it bothers you that L.A. has become a zoo.

FZ: That's one of the reasons why I don't go out. L.A. is like a big cancer cell. You get on the plane and you go away for two weeks and when you come back, another globule of something has been added. It just pops up, and you know it's not going to last more than twenty years, because it's made out of twigs and stucco. Every time I have to leave this house and drive down into Hollywood, which is maybe every two or three weeks, there's incremental growth of ugliness upon ugliness. It never ends.

I used to be the major booster of Southern California, at a time when the world thought San Francisco was the aesthetic center of the universe. I always took great umbrage at that because I thought the whole scene up there was a figment of *Rolling Stone*'s imagination. I used to stick up for L.A., but I don't anymore because there's no longer anything going on here aesthetically that's worth defending.

JW: What makes you leave the house?

FZ: There are certain mechanical functions that I can't do in my own studio. I can't do video editing here, so if I have to video edit, I have to leave. If I have an invitation to dinner, I'll go to a restaurant. I've even been to the movies recently. That was a real piece of sociology. I happened to see *Die Hard 2* and it was unbelievable. I was flabbergasted by the audience's response. It made me feel good because the bad guys turn out to be the government and they get their just deserts in the end and the audience loves it. That made me feel good.

JW: When you are out and around, do you encounter much antismoking sentiment?

FZ (lighting a cigarette): Well, I'm not here to impinge on anybody else's lifestyle. If I'm in a place where I know I'm going to harm somebody's health or somebody asks me to please not smoke, I just go outside and smoke. But I do resent the way the nonsmoking mentality has been imposed on the smoking minority. Because, first of all, in a democracy, minorities do have rights. And, second, the whole pitch about smoking has gone from being a health issue to a moral issue, and when they reduce something to a moral issue, it has no place in any kind of legislation, as far as I'm concerned.

JW: But if you look at the studies, sidestream smoke is harmful.

FZ: I'm not buying the data. First of all, it comes to you from the United

States government. If you thought by stamping out all tobacco smoke in the United States you were going to improve the quality of life for everybody in the country, you'd be lunatic. The things that will really harm you, the government won't touch.

JW: For example?

FZ: Dioxin in toilet paper, dioxin in tampons, dioxin in water filters, dioxin in coffee filters, dioxin in tea bags, dioxin in your vegetables because of the runoff from paper plants. Why do they have to bleach paper to make it white, anyway? It seems paltry, punitive, and insignificant to go after smokers, who are not an insignificant minority but about forty-five percent of the population. The way I would deal with the problem is induce more people to smoke, make them the majority and then…kick ass!

JW: Have you ever tried quitting?

FZ: A couple of times. The one time I really tried the hardest was when I had a chest cold and I was in the middle of a tour. We were in Canada and I had to travel every day and sing every night in these cold, hockey rink–type places. I really didn't feel very well and every time I would smoke with this cold, it just made it worse. So I decided to try to quit for a while, and I managed not to smoke for about a week or ten days. Then my sense of smell started coming back and the hotel we were staying at, which *looked* okay, actually smelled very, very bad. Something in the hall—the rugs maybe. In fact, the whole world didn't smell very good, and within a week my cold went away and I was smoking again.

JW: You haven't toured in a while, but you've recently begun "bootlegging the bootleggers." Can you explain how that works?

FZ: I think it is conceptually one of my better plans. Through Rhino [Records], we stole the actual records released by the bootleggers, we used digital technology to clean them up, and we're releasing them in very luxurious packages.

JW: Let me ask you about your tastes as a listener: They've lately been showing the "three tenors" concert on television—Pavarotti, Carreras, and Domingo in Rome. Do you like that kind of music?

FZ: Guys who sing good with an orchestra in the background? I respect what they do, but that style of music is not something that will retain my interest for any period of time. In fact, I am not particularly amused by any television broadcast of serious music, because usually the pictures detract from the music. When I want to hear that kind of music, I want to listen to it—I don't want to look at it.

JW: When you say "that kind of music," do you include Mozart?

FZ: I don't usually listen to Mozart. I like Stravinsky, Varese, Webern, Schoenberg, Bartók, Takemitsu, Messiaen, Penderecki…

JW: How about John Cage?

FZ: I have many John Cage recordings, but I find his writing more interesting than his music.

JW: Do you like rap?

FZ: If it wasn't for rap there would be no poetry in America. I think we went directly from Walt Whitman to Ice-T.

JW: How do you feel about pop romantic songs, ballads, love lyrics?

FZ: I think love lyrics have contributed to the general aura of bad mental health in America. Love lyrics create expectations which can never be met in real life, and so the kid who hears these tunes doesn't realize that that kind of love doesn't exist. If he goes out looking for it, he's going to be a kind of love loser all his life. Where do you get your instructions about love? Your mother and father don't say, "Now, son, now, daughter, here's how love works." *They* don't know, so how can they tell their kids? So all your love data comes to you through the lyrics on Top Forty radio, or, in some instances, in movies or novels. The singer-songwriters who write these lyrics earn their living by pretending to reveal their innermost personal turmoil over the way love has hurt them, which creates a false standard that people use as a guideline on how to behave in interpersonal relationships. "Does my heart feel as broken as that guy's heart?" "Am I loving well?" "Is my dick long enough?"

JW: One of the things that I appreciate about your music is its precision. Are you a taskmaster?

FZ: Well, I'm not murder on them, but I don't let them mess around. Just because it's a rock 'n' roll band is no reason you shouldn't have the same discipline and precision that you ask for in an orchestra—after all, you're handing a guy a paycheck. You try to hire people who can actually play, but even people who can play get lazy. Musicians are unbelievable lazy. And the discipline that you have to create in order to get them to show up on time, to get from place to place in a group—it's a little bit like running an army. Working with live musicians tends to take some of the fun out of life, I won't make any bones about it. You may like the results when you finally listen to it, but it's just like making sausage: not a pretty process.

JW: Would you prefer not to have to rely on it?

FZ: Yes, and that's the way I live now. The things I can do with the synclavier are mind-boggling. It truly does give you the ability, should you choose to do so, to do away with human beings as musical performers. All you've got to do is get a sample of the single note. If you can get a guy to blow one note on the clarinet, he's gone.

JW: Do you miss performing in front of a live audience?

FZ: I used to love going on stage and playing the guitar, but now I don't play unless I've got a reason. Why make your fingers wiggle if you already know what the notes are?

JW: So now you just sit in a room and write music?

FZ: Right. I'm lucky that I've got a wife who likes that I do that and will take care of the mundane stuff while I'm doing it. Without help, I'd be in deep trouble.

JW: What do you see for the future of the planet? For example, how are we going to deal with the population explosion?
FZ: The population has doubled since 1960; it's going to double again before what, 2020? And it's not just that it's doubling, what language is doubling, what skill level, what intelligence level, what education level? And what chemical level? In other words, how many crack babies? They're going to have to be warehoused because they'll have brain damage. They'll be an unemployable work force. And there will be tons of them.

Thank God the yuppies didn't reproduce. Did you ever consider that LSD was really one of the most dangerous drugs ever manufactured because the people who took it turned into yuppies? In the eighties, it was not fashionable to stand up for anything. It was a decade where bending over was the thing you did to get ahead. The way up the ladder was with your mouth attached to the anal orifice of the creature—whatever its denomination—in front of you. It was pushing upward and sucking at the same time as you went up the rungs, with junk bonds spilling out of your pockets and your mind reeling from the LSD experience that you had had in the sixties.

The yuppie lived in a special type of aquarium created for him by the Reagan administration. It was an era when there was enough cash and enough movement up and down in the stock market and enough shady deals that these incompetent little shit-heads were able to make vast amounts of money to buy their Ferraris and snort their cocaine and ruin the economy. Now there's nostalgia for the ability to do that. People wish that the good old days of the eighties would come back. When there was still something to steal.

HAIL TO THE CHIEF

He was ignorant of the commonest accomplishments of youth. He could not even lie.   MARK TWAIN, on George Washington

---

The moral character of [Thomas] Jefferson was repulsive. Continually puling about liberty, equality and the degrading curse of slavery, he brought his own children to the hammer, and made money of his debaucheries.
ALEXANDER HAMILTON

Many persons have difficulty remembering what President Franklin Pierce is best remembered for, and he is therefore probably best forgotten.
RICHARD ARMOUR

He had about as much backbone as a chocolate éclair.
THEODORE ROOSEVELT, on William McKinley

Theodore Roosevelt thought with his hips.   LINCOLN STEFFENS

He hated all pretension save his own pretension.
H. L. MENCKEN, on Theodore Roosevelt

When Theodore attends a wedding, he wants to be the bride, and when he attends a funeral, he wants to be the corpse.
ALICE ROOSEVELT LONGWORTH

Taft meant well, but he meant well feebly.
THEODORE ROOSEVELT, on William Howard Taft

The air currents of the world never ventilated his mind.
WALTER PAGE HINES, on Woodrow Wilson

He writes the worst English that I have ever encountered. It reminds me of a string of wet sponges; it reminds me of tattered washing on the line; it reminds me of stale bean soup, of college yells, of dogs barking idiotically through endless nights. It is so bad that a sort of grandeur creeps into it.
H. L. MENCKEN, on Warren G. Harding

His speeches leave the impression of an army of pompous phrases moving over the landscape in search of an idea. Sometimes these meandering words would actually capture a straggling thought and bear it triumphantly a prisoner in their midst, until it died of servitude and overwork.
WILLIAM MCADOO, on Warren G. Harding

President Harding is a good man who ought to be Lieutenant Governor of Rhode Island.
ROBERT BENCHLEY

Harding was not a bad man. He was just a slob.
ALICE ROOSEVELT LONGWORTH

He looked as if he had been weaned on a pickle.
ALICE ROOSEVELT LONGWORTH, on Calvin Coolidge

He slept more than any other president whether by day or night. Nero fiddled, but Coolidge only snored.
H. L. MENCKEN

He's the greatest man who ever came out of Plymouth, Vermont.

> CLARENCE DARROW, on Calvin Coolidge

If he became convinced tomorrow that coming out for cannibalism would get him the votes he so sorely needs, he would begin fattening a missionary on the White House backyard come Wednesday.

> H. L. MENCKEN, on Franklin D. Roosevelt

A chameleon on plaid.   HERBERT HOOVER, on Franklin D. Roosevelt

---

I'd rather be right than Roosevelt.   HEYWOOD BROUN

Harry Truman proves the old adage that any man can become president of the United States.   NORMAN THOMAS

Harry S Truman, a feisty, plucky native of Missouri…grew up so poor that his family could not afford to put a period after his middle initial.

> DAVE BARRY

I doubt very much if a man whose main literary interests were in works by Mr. Zane Grey, admirable as they may be, is particularly well equipped to be chief executive of this country, particularly where Indian affairs are concerned.

> DEAN ACHESON, on Dwight D. Eisenhower

As an intellectual he bestowed upon the games of golf and bridge all the enthusiasm and perseverance that he withheld from books and ideas.

> EMMET JOHN HUGHES, on Dwight D. Eisenhower

Eisenhower is the only living Unknown Soldier.   ROBERT S. KERR

Roosevelt proved a man could be president for life; Truman proved anybody could be president; Eisenhower proved you don't need to have a president.

KENNETH B. KEATING

The enviably attractive nephew who sings an Irish ballad for the company and then winsomely disappears before the table clearing and dishwashing begin.

LYNDON JOHNSON, on John F. Kennedy

I haven't voted since 1964, when I voted for Lyndon Johnson, the peace candidate.

GORE VIDAL

[Lyndon Johnson] turned out to be so many different characters he could have populated all of *War and Peace* and still had a few people left over.

HERBERT MITGANG

Richard Nixon is a no-good lying bastard. He can lie out of both sides of his mouth at the same time, and even if he caught himself telling the truth, he'd lie just to keep his hand in.

HARRY S TRUMAN

Nixon is the kind of guy who, if you were drowning twenty feet from shore, would throw you a fifteen-foot rope.

EUGENE MCCARTHY (quoted by Mort Sahl)

It is quite extraordinary! Nixon will even tell a lie when it is not convenient to. That is the sign of a great artist.

GORE VIDAL

[Nixon] is the kind of politician who would cut down a redwood tree and then mount the stump to make a speech for conservation.

ADLAI STEVENSON

Richard Nixon inherited some good instincts from his Quaker forebears, but by diligent hard work, he overcame them.   JAMES RESTON

The integrity of a hyena and the style of a poison toad.
HUNTER S. THOMPSON

The Nixon Political Principle: If two wrongs don't make a right, try three.
LAURENCE J. PETER

Richard Nixon impeached himself. He gave us Gerald Ford as his revenge.
BELLA ABZUG

Gerry Ford is a nice guy, but he played too much football without a helmet.
LYNDON JOHNSON

[Gerald Ford] looks like the guy in the science fiction movie who's the first to see "The Creature."   DAVID FRYE

Gerry Ford is so dumb that he can't fart and chew gum at the same time.
LYNDON JOHNSON

Jimmy Carter came from a simple, God-fearing homespun Southern family that was normal in every respect except that many of its members, upon close inspection, appeared to be crazy. After graduating from the U.S. Naval Academy, he served as an officer aboard a nuclear submarine, where, due to an unfortunate radiation leakage, he developed enormous mutant teeth.   DAVE BARRY

Carter is your typical smiling, brilliant, back-stabbing, bullshitting Southern nut-cutter.   LANE KIRKLAND

I would not want Jimmy Carter and his men put in charge of snake control in Ireland. EUGENE MCCARTHY

Jimmy Carter: The only American president in history whose popularity rating dropped below the Prime Rate. KEVIN PHILLIPS

I once called Carter a "chicken-fried McGovern," and I take that back because I've come to respect McGovern. ROBERT DOLE

Sometimes when I look at all my children, I say to myself, "Lillian, you should have stayed a virgin." LILLIAN CARTER

[Jimmy Carter] says his lust is in his heart. I hope it's a little lower. SHIRLEY MACLAINE

[Jimmy Carter] is the only man since my dear husband died to have the effrontery to kiss me on the lips. THE QUEEN MOTHER

An authentic phony. JAMES RESTON, on Ronald Reagan

So shockingly dumb that by his very presence in the office he numbs an entire country. JIMMY BRESLIN, on Ronald Reagan

---

In the heat of a political lifetime, Ronald Reagan innocently squirrels away tidbits of misinformation and then, sometimes years later, casually drops them into his public discourse, like gum balls in a quiche. LUCY HOWARD

Washington couldn't tell a lie, Nixon couldn't tell the truth, and Reagan couldn't tell the difference. MORT SAHL

[Reagan] doesn't die his hair, he's just prematurely orange.   GERALD FORD

That youthful sparkle in his eye is caused by his contact lenses, which he keeps highly polished.   SHEILA GRAHAM, on Ronald Reagan

---

[George H.W. Bush] is the only American statesman whose portrait is an authentic classic of Western Art, being of course by Paul Klee and entitled *The Twittering Machine.*   MURRAY KEMPTON, on George H. W. Bush

---

A cross between Rambo and Mary Poppins.

PETER FENN, on George H. W. Bush

A toothache of a man.   JIM HIGHTOWER, on George H. W. Bush

Every woman's first husband.

BARBARA EHRENREICH and JANE O'REILLY, on George H. W. Bush

The national twit.   MICHAEL KINSLEY, on George H. W. Bush

[George H. W. Bush] has the look about him of someone who might sit up and yip for a Dog Yummie.   MIKE ROYKO

George [H. W.] Bush is Gerald Ford without the pizazz.   PAT PAULSEN

Poor George, he can't help it—he was born with a silver foot in his mouth.
ANN RICHARDS, on George H. W. Bush

My theory is that [George H.W. Bush] has had to tell so many lies—and has such a hard time remembering them—that he sounds dyslexic. GORE VIDAL

According to a new study by a professor at the University of Minnesota., Bill Clinton is considered one of the most intelligent presidents we've ever had, IQ-wise. That's even more impressive if you consider what he was thinking with most of the time.   JAY LENO

Last time I saw Bill Clinton he was swinging on the chandelier in the Oval Office with a brassiere around his head, Viagra in one hand and a Bible in the other, and he was torn between good and evil.

JAMES TRAFFICANT

Talking about Bill Clinton, yesterday the Supreme Court disbarred him, but he's not worried about that, because he's just going to pardon himself.

DAVID LETTERMAN

Nobody likes to be called a liar, but to be called a liar by Bill Clinton is really a unique experience.   H. ROSS PEROT

Yesterday at a White House ceremony, the official portrait of President Clinton was unveiled. Apparently, Clinton's portrait is so realistic that Hillary immediately started yelling at it.   CONAN O'BRIEN

Clinton is saying he's going to model his after-presidential life after Jimmy Carter. He'll be doing a lot of hammering and a lot of nailing, but he ain't building houses.   DAVID LETTERMAN

Unusually incurious, abnormally unintelligent, amazingly inarticulate, fantastically uncultured, extraordinarily uneducated, and apparently quite proud of all these things.   CHRISTOPHER HITCHENS, on George W. Bush

I want to wish a belated birthday to our president. George W. Bush celebrated the big 6-0 on Thursday. When you realize President Bush and Jessica Simpson were born in the same week, maybe there is something to this astrology stuff. JIMMY KIMMEL

The president [George W. Bush] does not like change in his personnel. He likes to keep the same people. I think he got this from having the same third grade teacher year after year. JAY LENO

President Bush's approval rating is not good. A new Gallup poll puts it at just 36 percent which is a new low for his presidency. He is just slightly more popular than herpes now. JIMMY KIMMEL

According to a new poll Laura Bush's popularity rating is 80 percent while President Bush's rating is down to 47 percent. When she heard this Laura said, "Hey, it's just like our grades in college.'" JAY LENO

George W. Bush says he spends sixty to ninety minutes a day working out. He says he works out because it clears his mind. Sometimes just a little too much. JAY LENO

New rule: When President [George W.] Bush meets an autistic teenager, they must wear name tags so we can tell them apart. BILL MAHER

HAIL TO THE VEEP

A rigid, fanatic, ambitious, selfish partisan, and sectional turncoat with too much genius and too little common sense, who will either die a traitor or a madman.   HENRY CLAY, on John C. Calhoun

---

Hang him high as Haman.   ANDREW JACKSON, on John C. Calhoun

A labor-baiting, poker-playing, whiskey-drinking evil old man.
                              JOHN L. LEWIS, on John Nance Garner

---

He was a muddled, totally irrational man, almost incapable of uttering a coherent sentence.   HARRY S TRUMAN, on Henry Wallace

---

Hubert Humphrey talks so fast that listening to him is like trying to read *Playboy* magazine with your wife turning the pages.

                                              BARRY GOLDWATER

A treacherous, brain-damaged old vulture....They don't hardly make 'em like Hubert any more—but just to be on the safe side, he should be castrated anyway.   HUNTER S. THOMSON, on Hubert Humphrey

---

He cries too much.   LYNDON JOHNSON, on Hubert Humphrey

Consider the vice president, George [H. W.] Bush, a man so bedeviled by bladder problems that he managed, for the last eight years, to be in the men's room whenever an important illegal decision was made.   BARBARA EHRENREICH

Quayle was a twink. He got all the way through the sixties without dying from an overdose, being institutionalized by his parents or getting arrested for nude violation of the Mann Act on a motorcycle. At least he was a draft-dodger—although Dan timidly joined the National Guard instead of bravely going to his physical in panty hose.   P. J. O'ROURKE

An empty suit that goes to funerals and plays golf.
                                        H. ROSS PEROT, on Dan Quayle

That's the really neat thing about Dan Quayle, as you must have realized from the first moment you looked into those lovely blue eyes: impeachment insurance.   BARBARA EHRENREICH

Dan Quayle deserves to be vice president like Elvis deserved his black belt in karate.   DENNIS MILLER

As for the look on Dan Quayle's face—how to describe it? Well, let's see. If a tree fell in a forest, and no one was there to hear it, it might sound like Dan Quayle looks.   TOM SHALES

The Secret Service is under orders that if [President] Bush is shot, to shoot Quayle.   JOHN KERRY

How many of you remember President Clinton? You wouldn't have thought it looking at President Clinton that he liked art, but he and his wife Hillary stole about seventy pieces. In fact, the only still life he didn't take was Al Gore.

DAVID LETTERMAN

The man dyes his hair. What does that tell you about him? He doesn't know who he is.

GEORGE W. BUSH, on Al Gore

Vice President Dick Cheney accidentally shot a man during a quail hunt… making seventy-eight-year-old Harry Whittington the first person shot by a sitting veep since Alexander Hamilton. Hamilton, of course, was shot in a duel with Aaron Burr over issues of honor, integrity and political maneuvering. Whittington? Mistaken for a bird.

JON STEWART

Dick Cheney said he felt terrible about shooting a seventy-eight-year-old man, but on the bright side, it did give him a great idea about how to fix Social Security.

BILL MAHER

What a nightmare I had last night. I dreamed I was at a Washington party and I had to choose between Dick Cheney taking me on a hunting trip or Ted Kennedy driving me home.

JAY LENO

LARRY GELBART

Stuck on "Angry"

Larry Gelbart has written comedy for Jack Paar, Sid Caesar, Bob Hope, and Danny Thomas, among others. He was one of the originators of the television version of *M*A*S*H* and served as its principal writer, sometime director, and coproducer during its first four seasons. His screenwriting credits include *Tootsie* and *Oh, God*, and he is the author of two Tony Award–winning Broadway musicals, *A Funny Thing Happened on the Way to the Forum* and *City of Angels*.

JW: Why are movies and television shows so bad?

LG: Motion picture and television executives tend to clone past successes. They actively discourage originality because of the high financial risks of dream making. And all too many members of the creative community are willing to collaborate with them. American mass entertainment has always been based on the bottom line, but now it's increasingly from the bottom of the barrel. The nation's screens—big and small—are awash with films and programming that are more a reflection of dedicated deal making than they are of meaningful filmmaking. Commissions have replaced commitment. Packaging has replaced passion. Whole forests are being devoured to create the pulp that is transformed into printouts of a never ending flow of mindless screenplays that are replays of former screenplays.

It's hard to believe that in just fifty short years, we've gone from Orson Welles's filmic feast (I have a tough time saying *film*—they used to be movies when I was a kid. Film, to me, is what you have on your teeth) to such standardized, trivialized fare. In half a century, we've gone from *Citizen Kane* to candy cane. That's what comes of playing it safe. That's what comes of relying on the kind of market research that asks people whether or not they like a movie that hasn't been made yet, and perhaps never will be if enough of them indicate they won't see it if it ever is. That's what happens when moviemakers take the pulse only of other moviemakers and superimpose the results on an audience they know only as statistics.

JW: Is that why there are so many sequels?

LG: A good many of today's studio decision makers began their executive careers in television—some of them while still attending day school. They were quick to learn that in the world of TV, what pays the rent, theirs *and* the networks', are long-running series. And what is a long-running series but a string of sequels that goes on and on? The same title, the same cast, the same basic plot, week after week, year in and year out. By that yardstick, a movie marquee that boasted *Rocky* and *2010* would not necessarily indicate a double feature.

JW: Haven't there always been movie sequels?

LG: Of course, but hardly in the numbers we see today. They were, for the most part, B pictures. They had none of the bloated importance of today's sequels, which can often decide the fate of the company that has the nerve-wracking distinction of releasing one.

This cinematic senility has transformed Hollywood into a software factory whose product is designed to make a relatively few wealthy while impoverishing our culture. There were two major turning points in the history of American movies: the first, long ago, was when the movies began to talk. And now, in the last decade of the twentieth century, when it's money that talks. Not that it didn't always, but not in such a loud voice as it does today.

JW: But aren't today's movie audiences getting the entertainment they demand?

LG: Well, today's movie audiences are largely television trained, most of them exposed to it almost at birth, learning to watch before they can crawl. And what constitutes their education? What forms their standards? Simple plots, simple problems, everything tied up neatly in twenty-three minutes or forty-eight, or in any case, three minutes before the end of the time slot. Just like real life.

JW: They aim for mediocrity?

LG: With tremendous accuracy. Well, I take that back; I don't think they really *aim* for mediocrity. Some things are made deliberately hokey and bad, but most of the time people are not trying to do junk, they are just trying to do safe material and they wind up with mediocrity.

JW: Why must there always be a happy ending?

LG: The viewers must be kept happy because unhappy viewers aren't in a mood to go out and buy a car or a beer. Or do both at the same time. No involvement, no emotion. The only way you can get any feeling out of your television set is if you touch it when you're wet.

JW: Is that why there are so many feel-good movies?

LG: Feel-good movies, more than anything, mostly make the distributors feel good. They do nothing to reflect or interpret the human condition. And there is, I believe, a group consciousness, some primal need to record our emotions, to remind each other that we *are* each other. That just as we share the same physical fate, so do we share what is in our hearts and our minds. I miss the humanity we once witnessed on the screen.

JW: Did you have problems with network censors in doing M*A*S*H?

LG: The one area where I anticipated trouble, but never received any, made me so grateful that I was able to deal with the rest of it quite rationally. The network never asked us to tone down the political content of the show or the humanism we tried to display. For the first three years, we had the normal amount of stupidity from Program Practices about language, certain situations—one script they absolutely refused to let us film was about two nurses who pretended Hawkeye had made them pregnant. That was the only show they ever said, "No, not at all, not a page of it, not a minute of it." The rest of it was pretty SOP: "Please delete three 'hells,' two 'damns,' and a partridge in a pear tree." They're always worried about sex and sacrilege; no one says "Goddamn" on television. You can say "God" and you can say "damn," but don't ever try to put them together. But they did let us talk about the futility of war; in some very strong ways, it was a political show. You negotiate with them.

JW: Have things gotten better since you did M*A*S*H?

LG: What's gotten a lot better so that it makes things seem a lot worse is communications. We know more about things that used to be kept quiet, we know more about child abuse, we know more about every kind of abuse. Nobody stuck a microphone or a camera in front of Abraham Lincoln's face. Even he probably would have said some foolish things if he had had to provide sound bites for CNN.

I think one of the by-products of the communications explosion is a sort of "corruption fatigue." Someone has called our reaction to all the misery around us "compassion fatigue"—this was when there was all this flooding going on in the U.S. and there was the typhoon in Bangladesh and the Kurds were making their ways—sorry—and all of that. Likewise, I think there's also a corruption fatigue; we've lost our ability to be shocked or enraged by the machinations of politicians. We've been battered with such frequency that we've become indifferent. We're punch drunk with scandal.

JW: You sound like a thwarted idealist.

LG: My idealism is not thwarted, my *hopes* have been thwarted, but then I think everybody's have. The conservatives are unhappy because the country isn't Right enough and the liberals are unhappy because it's getting too Right. No one's happy, but I guess some people are able to put it on whatever passes for the back burner, but I don't have a back burner. Everything's in front. That's my problem. My gauge is stuck on "Anger."

JW: So you see an America in decline?

LG: Which America? The deprived, denied, absolutely whipped black America? Or the terribly wealthy white America? Which America are we talking about? For some Americans, these are the best of times, but not for most. In the past, the lower class could in some way visualize themselves as middle or upper, but now the only way these people can rise above their poverty is through drugs and death and crime. Yes, I think we're in decline. I think we're in decline when Japan can take over the dream factory here, when they can take control of our most popular form of mass entertainment. It's one thing to build a better car and have the public prefer that to an Iacocca product, but it's another thing literally to influence the influence makers. Hollywood has always served its masters.

JW: Hollywood seems all the more important in a world that is spinning out of control.

LG: Yes, because we can't keep up with the backlog, with the inventory of evil. We can't deal with it. The Amazon is still burning, we just don't hear the smoke detectors anymore. No one person is *Time* magazine, with a series of editors handling the various departments of our lives. We're fucking swamped. We turn on the evening news and get the day's toll of child abuse and famine deaths and the murders in the cities and AIDS and crack and...fine, let's switch off and go to the movies. Let's go see the latest Arnold Schwarzenegger movie.

JW: But that's no escape from carnage.

LG: Actually, it is, because in the movies you can die and still be alive. Thelma and Louise can dive into the canyon, but then you have the closing credits and somehow they're still alive. Speaking of which, *Thelma and Louise* showed me for the first time the vast amount of hatred in women for the way they've been treated. If you're a Jew, you understand what it's like to be thought of as less than equal, and if you're a writer you get it even more. A Jewish woman writer, learn how to work a drill press. And if you're a black Jewish woman writer, forget it.

JW: Do you vote?

LG: Yes, I do.

JW: Then you evidently don't feel that it's a de facto disenfranchisement to be forced to vote for merely the lesser of two evils.

LG: I just always vote for the Democratic evil, that's all. I can't vote for the party of Thomas E. Dewey and John Mitchell and George Bush and Ronald Reagan and Richard Nixon. I just can't.

JW: What about Nixon's recent rehabilitation?

LG: I can never understand why the American people buy such bad performers. It's a good thing they're not producers. I don't think he's capable of being "rehabilitated." He's like the uncle in the room we never opened. He still has to do what he does on the sly. You don't see him in a golf cart with George Bush or any of those people, and he hasn't been invited to address the convention. If anything, he's our Rudolf Hess.

JW: You travel quite a bit. I think it was Jay Leno who said that most of the people traveling on airplanes today belong on Greyhound buses. Have you noticed a decline in the quality of travel?

LG: No, because I treat myself very well in the travel department, so I don't really have any complaints. But you know who really hates to fly these days? First-class passengers, because flight attendants assume that everybody in first class is a Frequent Flyer and they don't rush so fast to answer the bell. First class has lost its cachet.

JW: What about some other modern annoyances? Graffiti, for instance. I've been trying to figure out why the sight of it makes my blood pressure jump.

LG: It's messy and it's ugly. As ugly as their lives. Every time I drive into Manhattan from JFK, I think of visitors coming to America and seeing this stuff on the walls and it makes me sick that it's their first impression of us. Graffiti is preliterate. It all comes from the original hand in the cave, somebody saying, "I was here." We've gone from that simple, wondering eloquence of "I was here" to this excremental scribbling. And you wonder, When do they do it, at four in the morning? When do they *do* it?

HOORAY
FOR HOLLYWOOD

He was a short man, almost squat, with a vulpine smirk that told you, as soon as his image flashed onto the screen, that no wife or bankroll must be left unguarded.   S. J. PERELMAN, on Erich von Stroheim

---

The son of a bitch is a ballet dancer.   W. C. FIELDS, on Charlie Chaplin

---

A second-rate bicycle-acrobat who should have kept his mouth shut.
                                      KINGSLEY AMIS, on Charlie Chaplin

---

Making a film with Greta Garbo does not constitute an introduction.
                                      ROBERT MONTGOMERY

When Jean Harlow was introduced to Margot Asquith, she mistakenly pronounced the "t" in Margot, to which Mrs. Asquith replied, "The 't' is silent, as in Harlow."

A face unclouded by thought.   LILLIAN HELLMAN, on Norma Shearer

---

She was divinely, hysterically, insanely malevolent.
                                      BETTE DAVIS, on Theda Bara

She has as much sex appeal as Slim Summerville.
                                        CARL LAEMMLE, on Bette Davis

---

If I ever get my hands on that hag I'll tear every hair out of her mustache.
                                        TALLULAH BANKHEAD, on Bette Davis

---

The best time I ever had with Joan Crawford was when I pushed her down the stairs in *Whatever Happened to Baby Jane.*   BETTE DAVIS

Toward the end of her life she looked like a hungry insect magnified a million times—a praying mantis that had forgotten how to pray.
                                        QUENTIN CRISP, on Joan Crawford

---

A day away from Tallulah [Bankhead] is like a month in the country.
                                        HOWARD DIETZ

The nicest thing I can say about Frances Farmer is that she is unbearable.
                                        WILLIAM WYLER

A character who, if he did not exist, could not be imagined.
                                        S. N. BEHRMAN, on Oscar Levant

---

Pearl is a disease of oysters. Levant is a disease of Hollywood.
                                        KENNETH TYNAN

There is absolutely nothing wrong with Oscar Levant that a miracle can't fix.
                                        ALEXANDER WOOLLCOTT

George Gershwin played good tennis almost by ear.   OSCAR LEVANT

A swaggering, tough little slut.   LOUISE BROOKS, on Shirley Temple

---

The first time I met and embraced Judy Garland, it made pharmaceutical history.   OSCAR LEVANT

Jolson's funeral was widely attended by those who wanted to make sure.
                                                    GEORGE JESSEL

Larry Parks gives me the creeps.   AL JOLSON

Bogart's a helluva nice guy until 11:30 P.M. After that he thinks he's Bogart.
                                                    DAVE CHASEN

The great thing about Errol [Flynn] was that you knew precisely where you were with him—because he *always* let you down.   DAVID NIVEN

When Columbia Pictures boss Harry Cohn died in 1958, Rabbi Magnin of the Wilshire Boulevard Temple was asked to say one good thing about the departed movie mogul. The rabbi thought long and hard and finally said, "He's dead." And Red Skelton explained the large turnout at Cohn's funeral: "It proves what they always say: Give the public what they want and they'll come out for it."

You had to stand in line to hate him.   HEDDA HOPPER, on Harry Cohn

---

Don't worry about Alan…Alan will always land on somebody's feet.
                    DOROTHY PARKER, on her ex-husband Alan Campbell

---

He liked to be the biggest bug in the manure pile.
                                        ELIA KAZAN, on Harry Cohn

Gower Street is paved with the bones of my executive producers.

HARRY COHN

When Louis B. Mayer gave his daughter's husband a high-ranking position at MGM, a wag observed: "The son-in-law also rises."

That French broad likes money.   HARRY COHN, on Claudette Colbert

---

I saw an empty cab pull up and out stepped Sam Goldwyn.

SID GRAUMAN

To Raoul Walsh, a tender love scene is burning down a whorehouse.

JACK L. WARNER

The only Greek tragedy I know is Spyros Skouras.   BILLY WILDER

A man whose few successes were even more distasteful than his many failures.

JOHN SIMON, on Dore Schary

Uncle Carl Laemmle
Has a very large faemmle.
OGDEN NASH, on Hollywood moguls' nepotism

From Poland to Polo in one generation.

ARTHUR MAYER, on Darryl F. Zanuck

He's really Martin Bormann in elevator shoes, with a face-lift by a blind-folded plastic surgeon in Luxembourg.

BILLY WILDER, on Otto Preminger

> Upon my honor
> I saw a madonna
> Sitting alone in a niche
> Above the door
> Of the glamorous whore
> Of a prominent son-of-a-bitch.
>   DOROTHY PARKER, on Marion Davies's dressing room

Wet she's a star, dry she ain't.   FANNY BRICE, on Esther Williams

---

During an elegant dinner party given by the producer (and self-styled gourmet) Arthur Hornblow, Jr., the screenwriter Herman Mankiewicz had a bit too much to drink and abruptly excused himself from the table. When he returned, looking greatly relieved, he casually reported to his host, "Don't worry, Arthur, the white wine came up with the fish."

Michael Wilding's in love with himself, but he's not sure if it's reciprocated.
                                                        RICHARD BURTON

She looked as if butter wouldn't melt in her mouth—or anywhere else.
                                        ELSA LANCHESTER, on Maureen O'Hara

---

Clark Gable's ears make him look like a taxicab with both doors open.
                                                        HOWARD HUGHES

He's the kind of guy who, if you say, "Hiya, Clark, how are ya?" is stuck for an answer.   AVA GARDNER, on Clark Gable

---

Lolly was possessed by a fiendish, auntielike excitement when on the trail of a hot "exclusive," and would sit at her telephone all night long if necessary, interpreting the denials of those she was interrogating as the great horned owl interprets the squeaking of distant mice.

PAUL O'NEIL, on Louella Parsons

Her virtue was that she said what she thought, her vice that what she thought didn't amount to much.   PETER USTINOV, on Hedda Hopper

---

I think he'd do well to spend a summer on a ranch.

GARY COOPER, on Anthony Perkins

Burt Lancaster! Before he can pick up an ashtray, he discusses his motivation for an hour. Just pick up the ashtray and shut up!   JEANNE MOREAU

There have been times when I've been ashamed to take the money. But then I think of some of the movies that have given Olivier cash for his old age, and I don't feel so bad.   STEWART GRANGER

George Sanders had a face, even in his twenties, which looked as though he had rented it on a long lease and had lived in it for so long he didn't want to move out.   DAVID NIVEN

An over-fat, flatulent, sixty-two-year-old windbag, a master of inconsequence now masquerading as a guru, passing off his vast limitations as pious virtues.

RICHARD HARRIS, on Michael Caine

Peter O'Toole looks like he is walking around just to save funeral expenses.

JOHN HUSTON

Paul Newman has the attention span of a lightning bolt.

ROBERT REDFORD

Miss Georgia and Mr. Shaker Heights.

> GORE VIDAL, on Joanne Woodward and Paul Newman

A walking X-ray.

> OSCAR LEVANT, on Audrey Hepburn

Working with Julie Andrews is like being hit over the head with a Valentine card.

> CHRISTOPHER PLUMMER

A professional amateur.

> LAURENCE OLIVIER, on Marilyn Monroe

Working with her is like being bombed by watermelons.

> ALAN LADD, on Sophia Loren

She has no charm, delicacy or taste. She's just an arrogant little tail-twitcher who's learned to throw sex in your face.

> NUNNALLY JOHNSON, on Marilyn Monroe

I've stayed in his house, and he has bored me to death. He tells the *sa-a-ame* stories he's been telling for years, and all I ever heard were his records, which he played *over* and *over* again.

> PHYLLIS MCGUIRE, on Frank Sinatra

I wish Frank Sinatra would just shut up and sing.

> LAUREN BACALL

A dope with fat ankles.

> FRANK SINATRA, on Nancy Reagan

[Nancy Davis] projects the passion of a Good Humor ice cream: frozen, on a stick, and all vanilla.

> SPENCER TRACY

Glassy-eyed and overdressed, [she] always looks as if she has just been struck by lightning in a limousine.   MARK CRISPIN MILLER, on Nancy Reagan

---

When he's late for dinner, I know he's either having an affair or is lying dead in the street. I always hope it's the street.
JESSICA TANDY, on her husband, Hume Cronyn

I once shook hands with Pat Boone and my whole right side sobered up.
DEAN MARTIN

Miss United Dairies herself.   DAVID NIVEN, on Jayne Mansfield

---

Zsa Zsa Gabor is inscrutable, but I can't vouch for the rest of her.
OSCAR LEVANT

I thought I might win [an Oscar] for *The Apartment*, but then Elizabeth Taylor had her tracheotomy.   SHIRLEY MACLAINE

Elizabeth Taylor is so fat, she wears stretch kaftans.   JOAN RIVERS

Poor Ingrid [Bergman]: She speaks five languages and can't act in any of them.
JOHN GIELGUD

I always knew Frank would end up in bed with a boy.
AVA GARDNER, on Frank Sinatra's marriage to Mia Farrow

A woman went to a plastic surgeon and asked him to make her like Bo Derek. He gave her a lobotomy.   JOAN RIVERS

He was insatiable. Three, four, five times a day was not unusual for him, and he was able to accept telephone calls at the same time.

JOAN COLLINS, on Warren Beatty

He's the type of man who will end up dying in his own arms.

MAMIE VAN DOREN, on Warren Beatty

Am I just cynical, or does anyone else think the only reason Warren Beatty decided to have a child is so he can meet babysitters?

DAVID LETTERMAN

To the unwashed public, [Joan Collins] is a star. But to those who know her, she's a commodity who would sell her own bowel movement.

ANTHONY NEWLEY

Jane Fonda…is so obsessed with remaining inhumanly taut by working out ninety-two hours a day that it took her more than a decade to notice that she was married to a dweeb.   DAVE BARRY

I'd really like to work with [Barbra Streisand] again, in something appropriate. Perhaps *Macbeth*.   WALTER MATTHAU

Working with Cher is like being in a blender with an alligator.

PETER BOGDANOVICH

A bag of tattooed bones in a sequined slingshot.   MR. BLACKWELL, on Cher

---

Cher…has had so much cosmetic surgery that, for ease of maintenance, many of her body parts are attached with Velcro.   DAVE BARRY

He has so many muscles that he has to make an appointment to move his fingers.   PHYLLIS DILLER, on Arnold Schwarzenegger

---

She is her biggest fan. If Kathleen Turner had been a man, I would have punched her out long ago.   BURT REYNOLDS

Whenever I know that an artist is trying to raise my consciousness, I have flashbacks of Jane Fonda, Sissy Spacek, and Jessica Lange lecturing Congress about the realities of farm life.   BRAD HOLLAND

Not greatly gifted, not deeply beautiful, Madonna tells America that fame comes from *wanting* it badly enough. And everyone is terribly good at badly wanting things.   MARTIN AMIS

The only thing Madonna will ever do like a virgin is give birth in a stable.
                              BETTE MIDLER

I acted vulgar. Madonna *is* vulgar.   MARLENE DIETRICH

I love my job, and, with the exception of Kim Basinger, most of the people I work with.   JEFFREY KATZENBERG

I'll never put Tom Cruise down. He's already kinda short.   DON SIMPSON

I've had a few sakes, driven down Sunset, had wild fantasies—but I didn't pull over and say, "Give me a blowjob!"   PIERCE BROSNAN, on Hugh Grant

---

And who can forget Mel Gibson in *Hamlet*? Though many have tried.
                              HARRY ANDREWS

Mel Gibson's *Hamlet*? Now I've seen everything. Except Mel Gibson's Hamlet.
ROBERT MITCHUM

Gwyneth Paltrow is quite pretty in a British, horsey sort of way.
JULIA ROBERTS

Here comes Ashley Judd in her no-yeast-infection-here Oscar gown.
LIBBY GELMAN-WAXNER (a.k.a. Paul Rudnick)

OSCAR WILDE

Everything to Declare

Oscar Fingal O'Flahertie Wills Wilde was born in 1854 in Dublin at 21 Westland Row, but, typically, he claimed to have arrived at 1 Merrion Square, a better address. His father was an eminent surgeon and amateur archaeologist, and his flamboyant mother contributed patriotic poems to the nationalist journal *The Nation* under the pen name "Speranza." She once admonished a visitor who described an acquaintance as being "respectable": "You must never employ that description in this house. It is only tradespeople who are respectable."

Wilde attended Magdalen College, Oxford, where he eliminated his Irish accent and cultivated a penchant for the Pre-Raphaelites, a disdain for conventional morality, and the image of a fop. (He was already a dandy at the age of thirteen: in his first letter to his mother from boarding school he asked for two flannel shirts, one violet and one crimson.) As an undergraduate he gained a reputation for his epigrams and for his outlandish behavior. He briefly considered converting to Catholicism (when asked his religion he would reply, "I don't think I have any—I'm an Irish Protestant"), and became a disciple of Walter Pater, embracing the doctrine of Aestheticism, the view that aesthetic values take precedence over moral ones. Wilde won the Newdigate prize for his poem "Ravenna" in 1878 and published his first collection of poems in 1881.

From Oxford he went down to London, where he soon acquired a large circle of influential friends, including the actress Lillie Langtry ("I would rather have discovered Lillie Langtry than to have discovered America"). The Prince of Wales asked to meet him, and although Wilde denied the gossip that he walked the streets of London carrying a lily, he boasted that he had made the world *believe* that he did.

Wilde embarked on a lecture tour of the United States in 1882. When he arrived in America aboard the S.S. *Arizona*, a customs officer asked if he had anything to declare, and Wilde replied, "I have nothing to declare but my genius." After his American tour he went to Paris, where he wrote a play, had his hair curled, and met Émile Zola, who in toasting him said, "Mr. Wilde will have to reply in his barbarous tongue." Wilde answered instead in perfect French: "I am Irish by birth, English by race, and as Mr. Zola says, condemned to speak the language of Shakespeare."

He met Constance Lloyd in 1883; they married in 1884, settled in London, and eventually had two sons, Cyril in 1885 and Vivian in 1886, the same year in which Wilde stopped having intercourse with his wife because of a recurrence of the syphilis he had contracted from a prostitute at Oxford. He had his first homosexual encounter soon thereafter and developed the penchant for young male prostitutes that would continue for the rest of his life. He played the part of a conventional husband but, like the characters in his plays, was not what he appeared to be.

Wilde published a novel, *The Picture of Dorian Gray*, and a collection of children's stories, *The Happy Prince*, in 1891, and then wrote a series of successful plays, including *Lady Windermere's Fan* (1892), *A Woman of No Importance* (1893), and his masterpiece, *The Importance of Being Earnest* (1895). From the successful opening of his play *Lady Windermere's Fan* (after which he made a curtain speech while scandalously smoking a cigarette), his legend grew.

A brilliant conversationalist, Wilde coined numerous aphorisms, many of which found their way into his comedies. In fact, the plays were essentially vehicles for his epigrams: "I can't describe action," he said. "My people sit in chairs and chatter." The sheer number and quality of his bon mots prompted Dorothy Parker to lament:

> If with the literate I am
> Impelled to try an epigram
> I never seek to take the credit
> We all assume that Oscar said it.

In 1891, Wilde met the young Lord Alfred Douglas, "Bosie," the son of the Marquis of Queensberry, and they began a long and tempestuous affair. After Wilde's refusal to stop seeing his son, Queensberry called at Wilde's London club and left a card addressed to "Oscar Wilde posing Somdomite [*sic*]." When Wilde sued for libel, Queensberry pleaded and proved justification, and thereby won the case. Wilde was then prosecuted under English criminal laws against homosexuality, and was convicted and sentenced to two years at hard labor. He later said, "The two great turning points in my life were when my father sent me to Oxford and when Society sent me to prison." Upon his release in 1897, broken by the harsh prison treatment in body if not in spirit, he exiled himself to France, where he lived in poverty and obscurity under the alias Sebastian Melmoth, after the hero of a Gothic novel who sells his soul for the promise of prolonged life.

He published *The Ballad of Reading Gaol* in 1898; and *De Profundis*, a bitter indictment of Lord Douglas and an apologia for his own conduct, was published posthumously in 1905.

A keen observer of human folly, Wilde skewered the hypocrisy of Victorian society on the sharp point of his elegant wit. He was arrogant, audacious, self-absorbed, but was also kind and generous and quick to laugh at himself. In the end he was a bona fide tragic figure: noble, heroic, and self-destructive. His biographer Richard Ellmann believed that Wilde struggled to "save what is eccentric and singular from being sanitized and standardized, to replace a morality of severity with one of sympathy." Wilde summed himself up in a remark to André Gide: "Would you like to know the great drama of my life? It is that I've put my genius into my life; I've only put my talent into my works."

He died in Paris in 1900, at the age of forty-six, unrepentant: "A patriot put in prison for loving his country loves his country. A poet put in prison for loving boys loves boys." Unable to pay the medical bills for his last illness, he said, "I am dying as I have lived, beyond my means." And, wit to the end, of the shabby wallpaper in his deathbed sickroom he remarked: "One of us had to go."

WILDE ON WOMEN

No woman should ever be quite accurate about her age. It looks so calculating.

One should never trust a woman who tells one her real age; a woman who would tell one that would tell one anything.

As long as a woman can look ten years younger than her own daughter, she is perfectly satisfied.

Thirty-five is a very attractive age; London society is full of women who of their own free choice remained thirty-five for years.

No woman should have a memory. Memory in a woman is the beginning of dowdiness.

Women have a wonderful instinct about things. They can discover everything except the obvious.

A man can be happy with any woman as long as he does not love her.

Women give men the very gold of their lives. But they invariably want it back in small change.

Between men and women there is no friendship possible. There is passion, enmity, worship, love, but no friendship.

The history of women is the history of the worst form of tyranny the world has ever known. The tyranny of the weak over the strong. It is the only tyranny that lasts.

Women are never disarmed by compliments. Men always are. That is the difference between the sexes.

I am afraid that women appreciate cruelty, downright cruelty, more than anything else. They have wonderfully primitive instincts. We have emancipated them, but they remain slaves looking for their masters all the same. The only way to behave to a woman is to make love to her, if she is pretty, and to someone else, if she is plain.

Women, as some witty Frenchman once put it, inspire us with the desire to do masterpieces, and always prevent us from carrying them out.

A woman will flirt with anybody in the world as long as other people are looking on.

There is nothing in the world like the devotion of a married woman. It is something no married man knows anything about.

THERE'LL ALWAYS
BE AN ENGLAND (ALAS)

A family with the wrong members in control—that, perhaps, is as near as one can come to describing England in a phrase.   GEORGE ORWELL

There are only two classes in good society in England: the equestrian classes and the neurotic classes.   GEORGE BERNARD SHAW

English cuisine is generally so threadbare that for years there has been a gentleman's agreement in the civilized world to allow the Brits preeminence in the matter of tea—which, after all, comes down to little more than the ability to boil water.   WILFRID SHEED

I did a picture in England one winter and it was so cold I almost got married.   SHELLEY WINTERS

A fundamental difference between the U.S. and Britain is in Britain, no one will talk unless he has a reason and in America, no one will stop talking unless he has a reason.   CLIVE JAMES

Trousers—it's such a stumbling word. It epitomizes the British bumbling and inability to be streamlined and coherent. In the States they have pants and jeans, but in England we still have trousers.   ROGER RUSKIN SPEAR

The national sport of England is obstacle racing. People fill their rooms with useless and cumbersome furniture, and spend the rest of their lives trying to dodge it.   HERBERT BEERBOHM TREE

This is a very horrible country, England. We invented the Macintosh, you know. We invented the flasher, the voyeur. That's what the press is about.
                                        MALCOLM MCCLAREN

So little, England. Little music. Little art. Timid. Tasteful. Nice.
                                                ALAN BENNETT

I would like to live in Manchester, England. The transition between Manchester and death would be unnoticeable.   MARK TWAIN

In England…education produces no effect whatsoever. If it did, it would prove a serious danger to the upper classes, and would probably lead to acts of violence in Grosvenor Square.   OSCAR WILDE

If England treats her criminals the way she has treated me, she doesn't deserve to have any.   OSCAR WILDE

The Englishman has all the qualities of a poker except its occasional warmth.
                                            DANIEL O'CONNELL

The English are not a very spiritual people, so they invented cricket to give them some idea of eternity.   GEORGE BERNARD SHAW

We English are good at forgiving our enemies; it releases us from the obligation of liking our friends.   P. D. JAMES

You should study the Peerage....It is the best thing in fiction the English have ever done.
OSCAR WILDE

I like the English. They have the most rigid code of immorality in the world.
MALCOLM BRADBURY

One matter Englishmen don't think in the least funny is their happy consciousness of possessing a deep sense of humor.
MARSHALL MCLUHAN

An Englishman does everything on principle: he fights you on patriotic principles; he robs you on business principles; he enslaves you on imperial principles.
GEORGE BERNARD SHAW

Englishwomen's shoes look as if they had been made by someone who had often heard shoes described but who had never seen any.
MARGARET HALSEY

I think it is owing to the good sense of the English that they have not painted better.
WILLIAM HOGARTH

The most dangerous thing in the world is to make a friend of an Englishman, because he'll come sleep in your closet rather than spend ten shillings on a hotel.
TRUMAN CAPOTE

If you eliminate smoking and gambling, you will be amazed to find that almost all an Englishman's pleasures can be, and mostly are, shared by his dog.
GEORGE BERNARD SHAW

It is quite untrue that English people don't appreciate music. They may not understand it but they absolutely love the noise it makes.

SIR THOMAS BEECHAM

Even today, well-brought-up English girls are taught by their mothers to boil all veggies for at least a month and a half, just in case one of the dinner guests turns up without his teeth.   CALVIN TRILLIN

The English find ill-health not only interesting but respectable and often experience death in the effort to avoid a fuss.   PAMELA FRANKAU

There is something remarkably and peculiarly English about the passion for sitting on damp seats watching open-air drama...only the English have mastered the art of being truly uncomfortable while facing up to culture.

SHERIDAN MORLEY

From every Englishman emanates a kind of gas, The deadly choke-damp of boredom.   HEINRICH HEINE

The English have no respect for their language. It is impossible for an Englishman to open his mouth without making some other Englishman despise him.   GEORGE BERNARD SHAW

Americans want to be loved; the English want to be obeyed.

QUENTIN CRISP

DAVE BARRY

Passages

Dave Barry is a nationally syndicated columnist. His books include *Dave Barry Talks Back*, *Dave Barry Turns 40*, and *Dave Barry's Money Secrets*.

JW: Dave, you're a member of the baby-boom generation, and the things you write about tend to mirror the experiences of your contemporaries.
DB: Yes, being born in 1947 was the smartest marketing decision I ever made.
JW: Your work has a "Dave Barry's Passages" aspect, dealing with everything from birth and childhood to middle age and what you call "geezerhood." For example, you've complained that they've changed the rules on having a baby.

DB: Yes, it's really alarming to me what they've done. The old system of having a baby was much better than the new system, the old system being characterized by the fact that the man didn't have to watch. In the new system you not only have to watch, you have to sit around in a room with people you don't even know and openly discuss things like the uterus. I'm against it. A lot of good people were born under the old system—I was, Dwight Eisenhower was.

JW: What about the delivery itself?

DB: When our son was born, I sort of focused on my wife's head. Basically there were two parts of my wife in the delivery room, the head and everything else. The everything else part, there were hundreds of people involved. People we had never seen before. They brought in, like, *tour buses* of people. "Over here, take a look at this." I don't know what was going on in there, but my wife was—my wife's head was—making some pretty awful noises. And when we brought Robert home from the hospital, I was surprised at his output as opposed to his input. You can put one ounce of beets into the child, and the child will keep putting stuff out for days—from several orifices. It's kind of like the miracle of cold fusion.

JW: How old is Robert now?

DB: He's ten. I'm amazed how much little boys are like poltergeists: You don't see them do it, but they'll stand in the middle of a room—one little boy—and there'll be noise from everywhere, things flying off shelves—and you don't know how they do it. And their attention spans are very limited—comparable to a gnat's. No, gnats are probably a lot better. I'd rather take a group of gnats to a skating rink for a birthday party than a group of ten-year-olds. On Robert's last birthday I took him and a group of his friends to one of those go-cart tracks. Watching them out there I felt like calling the state legislature to warn them not to issue them driver's licenses under any circumstances. For God's sake, keep these people away from vehicles.

JW: And you've still got the teenage years to look forward to.

DB: And everybody tells me they're worse. But I've noticed that one thing about parents is that no matter what stage your child is in, the parents who have older children always tell you the next stage is worse. I could picture great-great-grandparents saying, "How old is your child? Eighty-seven? Wait till he's eighty-nine. You wouldn't believe it."

JW: What about the financial burden of being a parent?

DB: Every third day, you read an article that says by the time *your* kid wants to go to college, it's going to cost you more than the national debt. What do people do, stop eating for four years?

JW: And you've pointed out that hair gel alone will run you thousands of dollars.

DB: It's scary when your child stops dressing exactly the way you tell him to and starts developing fashion concepts of his own. They have the same taste in fashion that they have in TV viewing. And of course, underlying all your anguish about this is the knowledge that you did all the same things to your own parents and therefore you have no right to dictate your child's haircut. So he got one of those haircuts that looks like there's a sea urchin clinging to his head.

JW: Does he have an earring?

DB: No, God, please, *shhh, shhh.* And the thing is, if I try to be cool and tell him he can get an earring, he'll get a *nose* ring. Or by the time my son is in high school it will be nose bones, or something like that. It'll be just like when I came home with long hair: We'll have to sit around at Thanksgiving and pretend that my son doesn't have a nose bone.

JW: In one of your books you confess to being increasingly worried about the condition of your gums. Is that a sign of middle age?

DB: I would say so, yes. That and the fact that gradually, without noticing it, you turn into a Republican and judge everything on the basis of whether or not it will increase your taxes. And for me another sign is saying things to my son that I thought were hilarious when my father said them to me: "Don't do that, you'll put somebody's eye out!" But if you put on a scale all the things you cared about when you were twenty-one and all the things you care about now, the two key elements being sex and gums, the scales would slowly tip in the favor of gums, the older you get. I think probably by the time I'm sixty or sixty-five, I'll have joined a religion based on gums, I'll be so concerned about them. See, the dental profession has really let us down. Everything they ever told us was a lie and it—how old are you, Jon?

JW: I'm your age, Dave.

DB: Well, then you know. All that time we brushed seventy-three minutes after every meal and thought our teeth would be in great shape, they never told us about flossing. They never even mentioned it. We brushed and brushed with an effective decay-preventive dentifrice, but we never flossed. And now everybody our age has enormous tooth problems. Right?

JW: Right, and it becomes an obsession. Do you have an Interplak?

DB: I don't have an Interplak, but I've got a WaterPik.

JW: I'm afraid you're using outmoded technology.

DB: What's an Interplak?

JW: Well, whereas the WaterPik shoots water, apparently...

DB: Yes, it's a WaterPik. If it shot kerosene, it would be a KerosenePik.

JW:...the Interplak is actually an electrified toothbrush.

DB: Oh yes, I've seen ads for that. It looks like an electric toothbrush to me. Big deal.

JW: Except that thousands of tiny bristles...

DB: I know, there's a patented action, right?

JW: Right.

DB: I bet you also buy the new razor blade with alum on it. Every six months they improve the shaving experience. I've been meaning to do a column about shaving breakthroughs for years. I go way, way back to when they first started doing safety razor commercials. They keep coming up with those incredible shaving breakthroughs, but shaving is still a pain in the butt.

JW: Do you remember when they introduced the Wilkinson Sword Blade? It was going to revolutionize shaving.

DB: And now everybody has the one with two blades: The first blade pulls the whiskers up—

JW:…and the second blade snaps the whiskers off! But to get back to aging, you've written that the midlife crisis is generally triggered when a male realizes one day that he has devoted his entire life to something he hates.

DB: Which is true of almost every guy I know, though some of them haven't admitted it to themselves yet. Most of them are successful and worked very hard to get there. It's like, when they were twenty-two they said, "What do I really, really hate? I'm going to become that." Particularly lawyers. You'd think there would be enough advance warning: No one likes lawyers, so why would you deliberately set out to be one? It's like saying, "I'm going to be a leper when I grow up." And yet all these people go out and pay money to go to law school, and then they become really depressed about it and they have midlife crises. I'm the only person I know who hasn't had one.

JW: Why do you think you've been spared?

DB: I've been really busy. Also, I just tend to be late. I'm just getting to puberty.

JW: Do you have any advice for women whose husbands are going through midlife crisis?

DB: The key here is understanding. If the husband wants to drive a fancy sports car, let him drive a fancy sports car. If he wants to wear gold jewelry, let him wear gold jewelry. If he wants to see other women, shoot him in the head. Women don't seem to have midlife crises, and I still don't understand why that is. They just keep battling away. Maybe women are intelligent enough to accept that they're actually getting older, so they try a new makeup—

JW: While driving.

DB: Here in Miami, women actually have plastic surgery while driving.

JW: Another part of growing older is investing your money for retirement, so

404 ♦ THE BIG CURMUDGEON

you've taken it upon yourself to explain various investment vehicles, including the stock market.

DB: It's a proven Investment Concept, the stock market. Basically you give your money to a stockbroker, who takes some of it right away, so right there we see that your money is going to work. And then he buys stock, which is identified in code in the newspaper. Every day you look it up and you see things like, "The stock market is off today, as many large investors found spots on their underwear." And you watch it some more and it goes down and down and then you call the stockbroker and he sells it and he keeps some more money. And that's your stock market, as far as I can tell. I don't know anybody who has ever made money on the stock market.

JW: You did a great public service by publishing the self-test questionnaire from the life insurance institute.

DB: Right. The test consists of three questions: "(1) How much insurance do you have? (2) You need more. (3) We'll send somebody over right now." That's always been the way it's been with my life insurance. I've never had my life insurance guy call to say, "Dave, you've got too much life insurance. Let's cut back on it. I'm going to mail *you* some money, Dave."

JW: And how does Social Security work?

DB: It's a great idea. Basically the way it works is they take money away from you and they give it to older people, including older people who are so wealthy they use the money to buy sun hats for their racehorses. The idea here is to transfer as much wealth as possible from you to somebody else, which is the idea of, as far as I can tell, the entire government. The theory is that when you become an old person, this program will work for you. The problem is that since you didn't have any children—you couldn't afford it because you were giving all your money to old people buying sun hats for their racehorses—there won't *be* any young people to support you, so the entire system will be depending on, like, seventeen kids working at Burger King.

JW: And then there are the joys of retirement like golf, fishing…

DB: A great sport, golf. I tried it once, until I ran out of balls, which was somewhere around the first or second tee. I didn't think it was possible for you to swing your club in one direction and have the ball, in defiance of all the laws of physics that I'm familiar with, go in pretty much the opposite direction. The really great thing about golf—and this is the reason why a lot of health experts like me recommend it—you can drink beer and ride in a cart while you play. I just don't get the part about the clubs and the ball. So maybe I'll just do the cart and the beer end of it. Kind of like a specialist.

JW: You can drink beer while fishing too, can't you?

DB: Absolutely. And there again, the mistake a lot of people make is they actually put fishing equipment in the boat, which creates the danger that you'll actually wind up with a fish in the boat with you, and some of those things will kill you. I don't want to suggest that fishermen are stupid, but have you ever seen what they put on the hook expecting fish to bite it? It's not food, it's the most digusting thing in the world. I was actually scuba diving once and saw bait. We were in a reef area where people were fishing nearby, and this hook with bait on it drifted down—and the fish were almost laughing! They all probably would have liked to have evolved little hands so they could hold their little bellies.

JW: What else is there to look forward to upon retirement?

DB: The joys of geezerhood. Geezer fashion, for example. There's a geezer look that we see a lot down here in Miami. For one thing, you want to show a lot of armpit. I don't think there's anything more visually appealing to other people than an old guy's armpit. Old guys like to wear big, baggy undershirts. And Bermuda shorts that would easily hold not only the guy but seven or eight Labrador retrievers—comfortably—cinched up as high as possible— nice and tight up around the chest area. And of course, a guy's got to have knee socks and a pair of wingtips. And a hat. Your older guy should wear a hat at all times, in the bed, in the shower. The hat identifies him when he's driving, by the way. Whenever you're behind a person going eight miles an hour on an interstate, the guy will always be wearing a hat. Now, a geezer wants to drive as slow as possible. A true geezer driver will pick a speed ahead of time, say, seventeen miles an hour, and drive that speed under all conceivable conditions, no matter where, no matter what. With the turn signal on. A geezer will put the turn signal on when he buys the car and then just leave it on until he trades it in.

JW: Is there a standard geezer car?

DB: The geezer car is actually three to four normal-size cars welded together. It should be much bigger than anything else on the road, or even the road itself. The hood should be so big that it's impossible for the driver to tell what lane he's in, sometimes even what zip code he's in, by merely looking out the window. Planes could take off and land on the hood of the geezer car.

JW: Among your favorite subjects is Miami, where you've lived with your wife and son for several years. I gather you're still adjusting to life there.

DB: Well, you're permanently adjusting to Miami because entire new populations wash ashore every day here. It's a challenge for most Americans to visit Miami because it's bilingual. I still don't know what the other language is besides Spanish. To me, that's the adventure of it. It's a lot like being in a foreign country in that you're always trying to figure out what exactly is going on. I like it.

JW: You seem obsessed by the insects there.

DB: Yeah, well, *you* say I'm obsessed by the insects, but that's because you don't, on your way to work every morning—and I'm only talking about walking across my backyard—confront spiders that in any other area would be registered with the department of motor vehicles. Or I'll just be walking along and reach for the doorknob and there will be a grasshopper the size of a Weimaraner sitting on it, just saying, "Yeah, go ahead. Touch me, buddy. Yeah, go ahead, touch me."

JW: As a successful author, you've had to do those grueling book tours. Do you like to travel?

DB: Absolutely not. Especially air travel. First, it should be a law that the pilot has to be older than me. Also, why do they go to all that trouble to make sure you don't have a weapon and then give you a dinner roll that you could easily kill a person with?: "Take this plane to Cuba or I'm going to hit you with this roll." And how do they get the crying babies on there? It's got to be an incredible logistical problem to get a crying baby on every plane you ever take. I've been on flights where they've had to hold the plane until the crying baby arrived: "Sorry, we're going to have to wait here ten minutes, the crying baby isn't here yet." There's a crying-baby facility at every airport, and they bring extras in on really busy days. But sometimes you have a breakdown in the system, the baby won't cry, and you have to get another one.

JW: How do they ensure the baby will be seated directly behind you?

DB: They use the computer to do that.

JW: And what about the confusing fares?

DB: You can have 380 people on an aircraft going to the same place and no two of them will have paid the same fare. This is a product of deregulation, under which anybody who can produce two forms of identification is allowed to own an airline. People who used to be in the concrete business are buying airlines: "Do we need all four engines running *all* the time? Can't we cut back on that? And why can't the pilots serve the drinks?" And under deregulation, they've been obliged to lower the average IQ of the passengers, which is clear from the way they find their seats, or fail to find their seats. Have you ever watched people get on airplanes? They're holding a thing that clearly says, "Seat 3A" and they stare at it and stare at it, and some malignant force from another planet tells them, "Go sit in Seat 8F." And then everyone on the plane has to change.

JW: Do you have a favorite seat on the plane?

DB: Yes, I like to sit in a seat in first class—without paying for it.

JW: In your history of the United States, Dave Barry Slept Here, *you changed the way history will be taught for generations to come. It involves the dates—*

DB: Yes, over the years I got tired of reading story after story about how American students are stupid. Every year they'd say, "We're even stupider than we were last year. Now we're not only behind the Japanese and the Germans and the French, we're actually behind a lot of species of animals." So I asked myself, What can we do? Obviously the kids aren't capable of learning more, and we can't get smarter kids, so let's make history dumber. One of the problems with history when I was a kid was that it was very poorly organized in the sense that you had all these different dates. Whoever thought this system up was just not thinking about the kids. So I developed a system where every date would be October eighth. You can't miss with this system. The children always know it was October eighth. Even July Fourth falls on October eighth.

JW: With the only important date being October eighth, what does that do to your holidays?

DB: That's a good question! Well, one way to deal with it, we could just have no other holidays at all and then have an enormous party on October eighth, and not go back to work again until, like, May ninth. That would be a good way to handle it.

JW: Why did you choose October eighth?

DB: It's my son's birthday. We ought to extend the same principle to math. Think how easy math would be if the answer were always 4. Not to toot my own horn, but I think I ought to get the Nobel Prize for this.

JW: Speaking of prizes, how did you react to winning a Pulitzer?

DB: I figured it was just one more indication of the nation's drug problem. When we get to this point, you have to ask yourself, "Shouldn't we all just move to Australia?"

QUOTES ON "M"

MAINE

As Maine goes, so goes Vermont.   JAMES A. FARLEY

THE MAJORITY

Whenever you find that you are on the side of the majority, it is time to reform.
MARK TWAIN

MALE BONDING

Can't anything be done about that klunky phrase *male bonding*? What kind of people invent phrases like *male bonding*? Can't anything be done about them, like cutting off their research grants or making them read Keats until they pick up a little respect for the felicitous phrase?   RUSSELL BAKER

MAN

A man is the sum of his ancestors; to reform him you must begin with a dead ape and work downward through a million graves.   AMBROSE BIERCE

It is even harder for the average ape to believe that he has descended from man.
H. L. MENCKEN

Why did Nature create man? Was it to show that she is big enough to make mistakes, or was it pure ignorance?   HOLBROOK JACKSON

The proof that man is the noblest of all creatures is that no other creature has ever denied it.   G. C. LICHTENBERG

Man is a rational animal who always loses his temper when called upon to act in accordance with the dictates of reason.   ORSON WELLES

Man is an intelligence in servitude to his organs.   ALDOUS HUXLEY

Man is the only animal that can remain on friendly terms with the victims he intends to eat until he eats them.   SAMUEL BUTLER

I believe the best definition of man is the ungrateful biped.
                                        FYODOR DOSTOEVSKY

Man is a clever animal who behaves like an imbecile.   ALBERT SCHWEITZER

The earth has a skin and that skin has diseases; one of its diseases is called man.
                        FRIEDRICH WILHELM NIETZSCHE

Man is a hating rather than a loving animal.   REBECCA WEST

Man is a dog's ideal of what God should be.   HOLBROOK JACKSON

What is a man? A miserable little pile of secrets.   ANDRÉ MALRAUX

Perhaps the only true dignity of man is his capacity to despise himself.
                                        GEORGE SANTAYANA

Man is a puny, slow, awkward, unarmed animal.   JACOB BRONOWSKI

What is man, when you come to think upon him, but a minutely set, ingenious machine for turning, with infinite artfulness, the red wine of Shiraz into urine?   ISAK DINESEN

───────────────────────── MANKIND ─────────────────────────

I hate mankind, for I think myself one of the best of them, and I know how bad I am.   SAMUEL JOHNSON

If all mankind were to disappear, the world would regenerate back to the rich state of equilibrium that existed ten thousand years ago. If insects were to vanish, the environment would collapse into chaos.

EDWARD O. WILSON

I love mankind; it's people I can't stand.   CHARLES SCHULTZ

───────────────────────── MANNERS ─────────────────────────

Manners are especially the need of the plain. The pretty can get away with anything.   EVELYN WAUGH

To succeed in the world it is not enough to be stupid, you must also be well-mannered.   VOLTAIRE

───────────────────────── MARRIAGE ─────────────────────────

Marriage succeeds love as smoke does a flame.   NICOLAS CHAMFORT

The conception of two people living together for twenty-five years without having a cross word suggests a lack of spirit only to be admired in sheep.

ALAN PATRICK HERBERT

I love being married. It's so great to find that one special person you want to annoy for the rest of your life. RITA RUDNER

We were happily married for eight months. Unfortunately, we were married for four and a half years. NICK FALDO

If variety is the spice of life, marriage is the big can of leftover Spam. JOHNNY CARSON

Passion and marriage are essentially irreconcilable. Their origins and their ends are mutually exclusive. Their co-existence in our midst constantly raises insoluble problems, and the strife thereby engendered constitutes a persistent danger for every one of our social safeguards. DENIS DE ROUGEMENT

The only charm of marriage is that it makes a life of deception necessary for both parties. OSCAR WILDE

Marriage, *n.* The state or condition of a community consisting of a master, a mistress and two slaves, making in all, two. AMBROSE BIERCE

Marriage is a triumph of habit over hate. OSCAR LEVANT

He marries best who puts it off until it is too late. H. L. MENCKEN

Marriage always demands the greatest understanding of the art of insincerity possible between two human beings. VICKI BAUM

I couldn't see tying myself down to a middle-aged woman with four children, even though the woman was my wife and the children were my own. JOSEPH HELLER

Someone once asked me why women don't gamble as much as men do, and I gave the commonsensical reply that we don't have as much money. That was a true but incomplete answer. In fact, women's total instinct for gambling is satisfied by marriage.　　　　　　　　　GLORIA STEINEM

The days just prior to marriage are like a snappy introduction to a tedious book.　　　　　　　　　　　　　　　　　　WILSON MIZNER

BARBARA WALTERS: You've been married forty-two years. What makes your marriage work?
ROBERT MITCHUM: Lack of imagination, I suppose.

No man, examining his marriage intelligently, can fail to observe that it is compounded, at least in part, of slavery, and that he is the slave.
　　　　　　　　　　　　　　　　　　　　H. L. MENCKEN

All tragedies are finished by death; all comedies are ended by a marriage.
　　　　　　　　　　　　　　　　　　　　LORD BYRON

When two people are under the influence of the most violent, most insane, most delusive, and most transient of passions, they are required to swear that they will remain in that excited, abnormal and exhausting condition until death do them part.　　　　　　　GEORGE BERNARD SHAW

The trouble with wedlock is that there's not enough wed and too much lock.
　　　　　　　　　　　　　　　　　　CHRISTOPHER MORLEY

The chain of wedlock is so heavy that it takes two to carry it—sometimes three.
　　　　　　　　　　　　　　　　　　ALEXANDRE DUMAS *père*

Marriage is like paying an endless visit in your worst clothes.

J. B. PRIESTLEY

Marriage is popular because it combines the maximum of temptation with the maximum of opportunity.　　GEORGE BERNARD SHAW

A ceremony in which rings are put on the finger of the lady and through the nose of the gentleman.　　HERBERT SPENCER

A kind of cosmic, bored familiarity in which everyone watches television and lives and lets live.　　MICHAEL NOVAK

The surest way to be alone is to get married.　　GLORIA STEINEM

A friendship recognized by the police.　　ROBERT LOUIS STEVENSON

One should always be in love. That is the reason one should never marry.

OSCAR WILDE

Marriage is an adventure, like going to war.　　G. K. CHESTERTON

Marriage is the only adventure open to the cowardly.　　VOLTAIRE

Marriage makes an end of many short follies—being one long stupidity.

FRIEDRICH WILHELM NIETZSCHE

In olden times sacrifices were made at the altar—a practice which is still continued.　　HELEN ROWLAND

I don't think I'll get married again. I'll just find a woman I don't like and give her a house.   LEWIS GRIZZARD

Courtship to marriage, as a very witty prologue to a very dull play.
WILLIAM CONGREVE

The dread of loneliness is greater than the fear of bondage, so we get married.
CYRIL CONNOLLY

Marriage: a souvenir of love.   HELEN ROWLAND

I got married the second time in the way that, when a murder is committed, crackpots turn up at the police station to confess the crime.
DELMORE SCHWARTZ

Marriage is an arrangement by which two people start by getting the best out of each other and often end by getting the worst.
GERALD BRENAN

Marriage is an alliance entered into by a man who can't sleep with the window shut, and a woman who can't sleep with the window open.
GEORGE BERNARD SHAW

Love is an ideal thing, marriage a real thing; a confusion of the real with the ideal never goes unpunished.   JOHANN WOLFGANG VON GOETHE

A man in love is incomplete until he is married. Then he is finished.
ZSA ZSA GABOR

Nothing to me is more distasteful than that entire complacency and satisfaction which beam in the countenances of a newly married couple.

CHARLES LAMB

The most happy marriage I can picture…would be the union of a deaf man to a blind woman.

SAMUEL TAYLOR COLERIDGE

Since the law prohibits the keeping of wild animals and I get no enjoyment from pets, I prefer to remain unmarried.

KARL KRAUS

I come from a big family. As a matter of fact, I never slept alone until I was married.

LEWIS GRIZZARD

We sleep in separate rooms, we have dinner apart, we take separate vacations—we're doing everything we can to keep our marriage together.

RODNEY DANGERFIELD

It was a perfect marriage. She didn't want to and he couldn't.

SPIKE MILLIGAN

I know nothing about sex, because I was always married.　ZSA ZSA GABOR

No man is regular in his attendance at the House of Commons until he is married.

BENJAMIN DISRAELI

Never get married while you're going to college; it's hard enough to get a start if a prospective employer finds you've already made one mistake.

KIN HUBBARD

It destroys one's nerves to be amiable every day to the same human being.
BENJAMIN DISRAELI

I married beneath me—all women do. NANCY ASTOR

Politics doesn't make strange bedfellows—marriage does.
GROUCHO MARX

A book in which the first chapter is written in poetry and the remaining chapters in prose. BEVERLEY NICHOLS

Even the God of Calvin never judged anyone as harshly as married couples judge each other. WILFRID SHEED

Marriage is a bargain, and somebody has to get the worst of the bargain.
HELEN ROWLAND

Something like the measles; we all have to go through it.
JEROME K. JEROME

Take it from me, marriage isn't a word—it's a sentence. KING VIDOR

Marriage is the alliance of two people, one of whom never remembers birthdays and the other who never forgets them. OGDEN NASH

There are two kinds of marriages: where the husband quotes the wife, and where the wife quotes the husband. CLIFFORD ODETS

Marriage is based on the theory hat when a man discovers a brand of beer exactly to his taste he should at once throw up his job and go to work in the brewery.   GEORGE JEAN NATHAN

We would have broken up except for the children. Who were the children? Well, she and I were.   MORT SAHL

He married a woman to stop her getting away. Now she's there all day.
                                                    PHILIP LARKIN

MARTYRDOM

It is often pleasant to stone a martyr, no matter how much we admire him.
                                                    JOHN BARTH

Martyrdom is the only way in which a man can become famous without ability.   GEORGE BERNARD SHAW

A thing is not necessarily true because a man dies for it.   OSCAR WILDE

Martyrdom covers a multitude of sins.   MARK TWAIN

There is a certain impertinence in allowing oneself to be burned for an opinion.   ANATOLE FRANCE

Great persecutors are recruited among martyrs whose heads haven't been cut off.   E. M. CIORAN

MASTURBATION

Don't knock masturbation—it's sex with someone I love.   WOODY ALLEN

The good thing about masturbation is that you don't have to dress up for it.
TRUMAN CAPOTE

MEANINGFUL

The word *meaningful* when used today is nearly always meaningless.
PAUL JOHNSON

THE MEDIA

The media. It sounds like a convention of spiritualists.   TOM STOPPARD

MEDICAL PROFESSION

We have not lost faith, but we have transferred it from God to the medical profession.   GEORGE BERNARD SHAW

MEDICINE

Medicine, *n.* A stone flung down the Bowery to kill a dog in Broadway.
AMBROSE BIERCE

MEDIOCRITY

Some men are born mediocre, some men achieve mediocrity, and some men have mediocrity thrust upon them.   JOSEPH HELLER

Women want mediocre men, and men are working hard to become as mediocre as possible.   MARGARET MEAD

THE MEEK

Pity the meek, for they shall inherit the earth.   DON MARQUIS

The meek shall inherit the earth, but not the mineral rights.   J. PAUL GETTY

MEETINGS

Meetings are indispensable when you don't want to do anything.
JOHN KENNETH GALBRAITH

Meetings are an addictive, highly self-indulgent activity that corporations and other large organizations habitually engage in only because they cannot actually masturbate.
DAVE BARRY

MEMORANDUM

A memorandum is written not to inform the reader but to protect the writer.
DEAN ACHESON

MEMORY

Why is it that our memory is good enough to retain the least triviality that happens to us, and yet not good enough to recollect how often we have told it to the same person?
FRANÇOIS DE LA ROCHEFOUCAULD

Nothing fixes a thing so intensely in the memory as the wish to forget it.
MICHEL DE MONTAIGNE

I can remember when the air was clean and sex was dirty.
GEORGE BURNS

MEN

All men are frauds. The only difference between them is that some admit it. I myself deny it.
H. L. MENCKEN

The average man does not know what to do with his life, yet wants another one which will last forever.
ANATOLE FRANCE

The only thing worse than a man you can't control is a man you can.

MARGO KAUFMAN

Men are genetically inferior to women.

ANDREA LYNNE

The male is a domestic animal which, if treated with firmness and kindness, can be trained to do most things.

JILLY COOPER

Most men do not mature, they simply grow taller.

LEO ROSTEN

I refuse to consign the whole male sex to the nursery. I insist on believing that some men are my equals.

BRIGID BROPHY

Giving a man space is like giving a dog a computer: The chances are he will not use it wisely.

BETTE-JANE RAPHAEL

I require three things in a man: He must be handsome, ruthless, and stupid.

DOROTHY PARKER

Plain women know more about men than beautiful ones do.

KATHARINE HEPBURN

Give a man a free hand and he'll run it all over you.

MAE WEST

Don't accept rides from strange men—and remember that all men are as strange as hell.

ROBIN MORGAN

Once you know what women are like, men get kind of boring. I'm not trying to put them down. I mean I like them sometimes as people, but sexually they're dull.

RITA MAE BROWN

I only like two kinds of men: domestic and imported.   MAE WEST

To a smart girl men are no problem—they're the answer.   ZSA ZSA GABOR

The men who really wield, retain, and covet power are the kind who answer bedside phones while making love.   NICHOLAS PILEGGI

Men hate to lose. I once beat my husband at tennis. I asked him, "Are we going to have sex again?" He said, "Yes, but not with each other."
ERIC RUDNER

RITA RUDNER

No man is a hero to his wife's psychiatrist.   ERIC BERNE

Macho does not prove mucho.   ZSA ZSA GABOR

———————————— MEN AND WOMEN ————————————
The main difference between men and women is that men are lunatics and women are idiots.   REBECCA WEST

Women represent the triumph of matter over mind, just as men represent the triumph of mind over morals.   OSCAR WILDE

———————————— MENCKEN'S LAW ————————————
Whenever A annoys or injures B on the pretense of saving or improving X, A is a scoundrel.   H. L. MENCKEN

———————————— METHOD ACTING ————————————
Method acting? There are quite a few methods. Mine involves a lot of talent, a glass and some cracked ice.   JOHN BARRYMORE

METRIC SYSTEM

The metric system did not really catch on in the States, unless you count the increasing popularity of the nine-millimeter bullet.　　DAVE BARRY

MIAMI

We had elected to move voluntarily to Miami. We wanted our child to benefit from the experience of growing up in a community that is constantly being enriched by a diverse and ever-changing infusion of tropical diseases. Also they have roaches down there you could play polo with.　　DAVE BARRY

God's waiting room.　　JOHN LEGUIZAMO

MIAMI BEACH

Miami Beach is where neon goes to die.　　LENNY BRUCE

MIDDLE AGES

We owe to the middle ages the two worst inventions of humanity—gunpowder and romantic love.　　ANDRÉ MAUROIS

MIDDLE CLASS

In the middle classes, where the segregation of the artificially limited family in its little brick box is horribly complete, bad manners, ugly dresses, awkwardness, cowardice, peevishness and all the pretty vices of unsociability flourish like mushrooms in a cellar.

GEORGE BERNARD SHAW

The middles cleave to euphemisms not just because they're an aid in avoiding facts. They like them also because they assist their social yearnings toward pomposity. This is possible because most euphemisms permit the speaker to multiply syllables, and the middle class confuses sheer numerousness with weight and value.   PAUL FUSSELL

MILITARY INTELLIGENCE

Military intelligence is a contradiction in terms.   GROUCHO MARX

MILITARY JUSTICE

Military justice is to justice what military music is to music.
                                                    GEORGES CLEMENÇEAU

MISSIONARIES

When the missionaries came to Africa they had the Bible and we had the land. They said, "Let us pray." We closed our eyes. When we opened them we had the Bible and they had the land.   BISHOP DESMOND TUTU

Missionaries are going to reform the world whether it wants to or not.
                                                              OSCAR WILDE

Our noble society for providing the infant Negroes in the West Indies with flannel waistcoats and moral pocket handkerchiefs.
                                                         CHARLES DICKENS

Missionaries, my dear! Don't you realize that missionaries are the divinely provided food for destitute and underfed cannibals? Whenever they are on the brink of starvation, Heaven in its infinite mercy sends them a nice plump missionary.   OSCAR WILDE

MISUNDERSTANDING

It is by universal misunderstanding that all agree. For if, by ill luck, people understood each other, they would never agree.

CHARLES BAUDELAIRE

MODERATION

Moderation is a fatal thing: nothing succeeds like excess.   OSCAR WILDE

MODERN ARCHITECTURE

The [Birmingham, England] Central Library looks like a place where books are incinerated, not kept.   PRINCE OF WALES

MODERN ART

Skill without imagination is craftsmanship and gives us many useful objects such as wickerwork picnic baskets. Imagination without skill gives us modern art.   TOM STOPPARD

MONEY

Make money and the whole nation will conspire to call you a gentleman.

GEORGE BERNARD SHAW

Money, to be worth striving for, must have blood and perspiration on it—preferably that of someone else.   WILSON MIZNER

I'm tired of love, I'm still more tired of rhyme, but money gives me pleasure all the time.   HILAIRE BELLOC

The chief value of money lies in the fact that one lives in a world in which it is overestimated.   H. L. MENCKEN

Money cannot buy
The fuel of love
but it is excellent kindling.

W. H. AUDEN

When it is a question of money, everybody is of the same religion.   VOLTAIRE

It is a kind of spiritual snobbery that makes people think they can be happy without money.   ALBERT CAMUS

Those who have some means think that the most important thing in the world is love. The poor know that it is money.   GERALD BRENAN

The two most beautiful words in the English language are "check enclosed."
DOROTHY PARKER

People will swim through shit if you put a few bob in it.
PETER SELLERS

Virtue has never been as respectable as money.   MARK TWAIN

To be clever enough to get a great deal of money, one must be stupid enough to want it.   G. K. CHESTERTON

Money cannot buy health, but I'd settle for a diamond-studded wheelchair.
DOROTHY PARKER

——————————— MONROE, MARILYN ———————————
A vacuum with nipples.   OTTO PREMINGER

She was good at playing abstract confusion in the same way a midget is good at being short. CLIVE JAMES

———————————————— MONOGAMY ————————————————
Monogamy is so weird. Like when you know their name and stuff.
MARGARET CHO

———————————————— MOORE, MICHAEL ————————————————
If you're going to dedicate your career to ranting about the excesses of American capitalism, you probably shouldn't weigh 450 pounds.
GREG GIRALDO

———————————————— MORALITY ————————————————
There is no moral precept that does not have something inconvenient about it.
DENIS DIDEROT

Morality is the weakness of the mind. ARTHUR RIMBAUD

Go into the street and give one a man a lecture on morality and another a shilling, and see which will respect you most. SAMUEL JOHNSON

Bourgeois morality is largely a system of making cheap virtues a cloak for expensive vices. GEORGE BERNARD SHAW

Morality is the theory that every human act must be either right or wrong, and that 99 percent of them are wrong. H. L. MENCKEN

Morality consists in suspecting other people of not being legally married.
GEORGE BERNARD SHAW

Morality is a disease which progresses in three stages: virtue—boredom—
syphilis. KARL KRAUS

Morality is simply the attitude we adopt toward people we personally dislike.
OSCAR WILDE

The inflation of cruelty with a good conscience is a delight to moralists—
that is why they invented hell. BERTRAND RUSSELL

Moral indignation is jealousy with a halo. H. G. WELLS

———————————— MORAL CERTAINTY ————————————
Moral certainty is always a sign of cultural inferiority. The more uncivilized the
man, the surer he is that he knows precisely what is right and what is wrong. All
human progress, even in morals, has been the work of men who have doubted
the current moral values, not of men who have whooped them up and tried to
enforce them. The truly civilized man is always skeptical and tolerant, in this field
as in all others. His culture is based on "I am not too sure." H. L. MENCKEN

———————————— MORNING ————————————
Getting out of bed in the morning is an act of false confidence.
JULES FEIFFER

The average, healthy, well-adjusted adult gets up at seven thirty in the morning feeling just plain terrible. JEAN KERR

———————————— MOTHER ————————————
Mother is the dead heart of the family, spending father's earnings on consumer goods to enhance the environment in which he eats, sleeps, and watches
television. GERMAINE GREER

Why do grandparents and grandchildren get along so well? They have the same enemy—the mother. CLAUDETTE COLBERT

———————————— MOTHER-IN-LAW ————————————

I know a mother-in-law who sleeps with her glasses on, the better to see her son-in-law suffer in her dreams. ERNEST COQUELIN

A mother-in-law dies only when another devil is needed in hell. FRANÇOIS RABELAIS

If you must choose between living with your mother-in-law and blowing out your brains, don't hesitate—blow out hers. VICTORIEN SARDOU

———————————— MOVIES ————————————

Movies are one of the bad habits that have corrupted our century. They have slipped into the American mind more misinformation in one evening than the Dark Ages could muster in a decade. BEN HECHT

The movies are the only business where you can go out front and applaud yourself. WILL ROGERS

There's only one thing that can kill the movies, and that's education. WILL ROGERS

It is my indignant opinion that ninety percent of the moving pictures exhibited in America are so vulgar, witless and dull that it is preposterous to write about them in any publication not intended to be read while chewing gum. WOLCOTT GIBBS

MTV

MTV is to music as KFC is to chicken.   LEWIS BLACK

MURALS IN RESTAURANTS

The murals in restaurants are on a par with the food in museums.
PETER DE VRIES

MUSEUMS

Visiting museums bastardizes the personality just as hobnobbing with priests makes you lose your faith.   MAURICE VLAMINCK

MUSIC

Of all noises, I think music is the least disagreeable.   SAMUEL JOHNSON

There are two kinds of music—good music and bad music. Good music is music that I want to hear. Bad music is music that I don't want to hear.
FRAN LEBOWITZ

Extraordinary how potent cheap music is.   NOEL COWARD

Classical music is the kind we keep thinking will turn into a tune.
KIN HUBBARD

A good deal of classical music is, today, the opium of the good citizen.
GEORGE STEINER

Music makes one feel so romantic—at least it always got on one's nerves—which is the same thing nowadays.   OSCAR WILDE

I hate music, especially when it's played.   JIMMY DURANTE

The public doesn't want new music; the main thing it demands of a composer is that he be dead. ARTHUR HONEGGER

Music is the refuge of souls ulcerated by happiness. E. M. CIORAN

The chief objection to playing wind instruments is that it prolongs the life of the player. GEORGE BERNARD SHAW

Musical people always want one to be perfectly dumb at the very moment when one is longing to be absolutely deaf. OSCAR WILDE

Let a short Act of Parliament be passed, placing all street musicians outside the protection of the law, so that any citizen may assail them with stones, sticks, knives, pistols, or bombs without incurring any penalites.

GEORGE BERNARD SHAW

I hate music. There's too much music everywhere. It's horrible stuff, the most noise conveying the least information. Kids today are violent because they have no inner life; they have no inner life because they have no thoughts; they have no thoughts because they know no words; they know no words because they never speak; and they never speak because the music's too loud.

QUENTIN CRISP

Assassins! ARTURO TOSCANINI to his orchestra

MUSICOLOGIST

A musicologist is a man who can read music but can't hear it.

SIR THOMAS BEECHAM

FLORENCE KING

Go Away

Florence King's books include the autobiographical *Confessions of a Failed Southern Lady, With Charity Toward None: A Fond Look at Misanthropy,* and *STET, Damnit!* She lives in Virginia.

JW: Do you consider yourself a curmudgeon? A misanthrope? A reactionary?
FK: I have been a misanthrope for as long as I can remember, but I didn't know it because I never heard the word until I read Moliere's *Le Misanthrope* in college. As a child I simply thought of myself as "different." As an adolescent I preferred "aloof," and as a young adult going through my Ayn Rand

stage I called myself "objective." When the Randian heat wore off I settled for "loner." The beginning of self-knowledge came when I discovered Shakespeare's *Timon of Athens*, who won my heart because he had "Go Away" carved on his tombstone—just the sort of thing I would do. I looked Timon up in Plutarch's *Lives* and found that *misanthrope* was also an English word—up till then I thought it was French. All misanthropes are curmudgeons, but all curmudgeons are not misanthropes. I'm the real McCoy. I agree with Sartre that "hell is other people," but I also agree with Jonathan Swift, who said, "I hate and despise the animal called Mankind, but I like the occasional Tom, Dick, and Harry." A reactionary? Of course; misanthropy is by definition an illiberal stance. It's the only means left to be against everything Martin Sheen is for.

JW: You've written a book about misanthropy.

FK: Firsthand, behind-the-scenes information is the kind America likes. Not unmindful of other portions of the equine anatomy, we are the land of the horse's mouth. Alcoholics write books about alcoholism, drug addicts write books about drug addiction, madams write books about madaming, so I wrote a book about misanthropy.

JW: You've been called "the thinking man's redneck"…

FK: The thinking man desperately needs a redneck, so it might as well be me.

JW: You appear on the cover of one of your books, brandishing a semiautomatic pistol. What are you, some kind of gun nut?

FK: Not really. I'm not the hobby type, and God knows I'm not the outdoors type. I simply like guns because you can't shoot people without them. Criminals have declared war on America and I have declared war on criminals. Anybody who messes with me had better be prepared to carry his ass home in a bucket.

JW: On the back cover of the same book, it says that you don't suffer fools gladly. What are the consequences of that attitude, to both you and the fools?

FK: The consequences to the fools? I don't suffer fools and I like to see fools suffer. The consequences to me? "He who tells the truth must have one foot in the stirrup." Old Armenian proverb.

JW: Do you regret not having married and had children?

FK: At this point in my life I would rather be dead than married. Occasionally in my naive youth, I thought it would be nice to be married so I could have regular sex without a lot of distraction and bother, but as time went on, it began to dawn on me that marriage was the least efficient source of what I wanted. As for not having had children, let's put it this way: My hero is Good King Herod. I have never understood child molestation because, in order to molest a child, you have to be in the same room with a child, and I don't know how perverts stand it.

JW: You've referred to radical left-wing female gay rights activists as a "gang of muff-diving Druids." What do you have against them?

FK: They have so politicized sex that it's gone from raucous to caucus.

JW: You've been critical of yuppies in a variety of ways. For example, you've likened yuppie nutrition to a mortification of the flesh. What are they trying to atone for?

FK: Those who have lost their characters have nothing left but their bodies to make them feel like good people. Intense, obsessive interest in health, nutrition, and exercise arouses my suspicions. I distrust anybody who worries too much about such things. I take my leaf from Seneca: "Scorn pain. Either it will go away or you will."

JW: Has the American male changed since 1978, when you published He: An Irreverent Look at the American Male?

FK: He's no longer a wimp, he's a state-of-the-art pussy. Molly Yard should be declared a common scold and subjected to the ducking stool. That woman looks like a stubbed toe and behaves like a little old tennis shoe among ladies.

JW: What else is wrong with America today?

FK: We worship education but hate learning. We worship success but hate the successful. We worship fame but hate the famous. We are a nation of closet misanthropes, which is why I decided to "come out," so to speak. There's no national glue holding us together because somebody put too much pluribus in the unum. Our fabled Great Diversity is so divisive that every president is forced to be a fence-straddling "moderate"—we literally make a strong man weak.

JW: What can we do about it?

FK: Nothing. We'll have to wait until it collapses and then start all over again. It won't be long now.

JW: You've defined democracy as "the crude leading the crud." What form of government would you prefer?

FK: I believe in absolute monarchy and the divine right of kings. One thing I like about Bloody Mary: She never nagged her subjects about lung cancer. I would much rather be at the mercy of someone with the power to say, "Off with her head!" than be nibbled to death by a bureaucratic duck.

JW: If called upon, would you "support, protect, and defend" the Constitution of the United States?

FK: The Constitution as written and intended no longer exists, so I can't very well support it. I would fight to restore it, to wrest it from the clutches of ACLU types who are using it as a cover for their collectivist-egalitarian agenda.

JW: Where do you stand on prayer and sex education in the schools?

FK: I'm for prayer in the schools because ritual and ceremony are calming and civilizing, and the little fartlings should be tamped down whenever possible. I am against sex ed in schools because sex is more fun when it's dirty and sinful.

JW: You've been variously critical of agents, publishers, and editors, from which I gather that you're not enamored of the publishing business.

FK: I'm enamored of my agent, Mel Berger, who is one of the few people in the world for whom I feel warm affection—he's Tom, Dick, and Harry rolled into one. I also like my publisher and my editor. It's copy editors I hate because I've been burned by them too often, like the one who thought the Cavaliers and Roundheads were football teams, or the one who found my opinions too strong and softened them by adding "alas and alack." The bitch rewrote me. Most copy editors are freelancers and female, which is a large part of the problem. More and more women want a flexible work-at-home arrangement so they can take care of their kids, but if they expect me to feel compassion for them, they have their Florences mixed up: I'm King, not Nightingale, and I don't want my manuscript competing with a screaming brat because I know which gets priority. Ideally, copy editors should fit the description in Mary McCarthy's *The Group:* "Old maids mostly, with a pencil behind their ear and dyspepsia. We've got a crackerjack here, Miss Chambers. Vinegary type." Obviously a job for me, which is why I do my own.

JW: How do you feel about doing author tours to promote your books?

FK: Being a citizen of the Republic of Nice, the person I most admire and wish to emulate is the man who died on the *Dick Cavett Show.* I forget his name but it doesn't matter; to a veteran of book-promotion tours who has walked through the valley of the shadow of Happy Talk, he will go down in history as the Man Who Got Even. I will never go on the *Today Show.* I'd rather corner them in a dungeon and pull the caps off their teeth. The only thing I have in common with those people is a sofa.

JW: You review books for a number of publications, including the American Spectator. *What are your critical ground rules?*

FK: I believe books should be reviewed for their literary, not political, content. I am proud of my own adherence to this rule. I have raved three liberal feminists—Susan Brownmiller, Andrea Dworkin, and Kate Millett—and panned a fellow conservative: Ben Stein. Felix Unger thinks it's fun to be neat; I think it's fun to be fair. The simplest rule of reviewing is the one most often ignored: A review must say (1) what the book is about, and (2) what the reviewer thinks of it. The writer I hate most is Robert Fulghum, author of *All I Really Need to Know I Learned in Kindergarten* and *It Was on Fire When I Lay Down on It*. Titles like these are immensely popular with people-lovers, so if I ever write *As Soon As I Figure Out How to Make a Sword Out of This Friggin' Plowshare* you will know I have gone soft.

JW: What do you find offensive in reviews of your own books?

FK: I can't stand confused, inarticulate people who have trouble getting to the point, especially when they're reviewing a book of mine. Nothing irritates me more than a reviewer who uses my navel for his navel-gazing.

JW: Why have you given up writing for women's magazines?

FK: I discovered I'm not really a woman; there's just an "F" on my driver's license. These things happen.

JW: Do you have any advice to young writers?

FK: Reject the bohemian image of the writer; there is nothing creative about decadence and squalor. Be neat and organized in your workroom and your materials; outward disorder leads to inner chaos. Beware of writer groupies; the writer's self-sufficiency and bent for solitude attract insecure types whom I call the Love people. Their unconscious motivation is the destruction of the Work people. Either kick them out of your life or don't admit them in the first place, because they will become jealous of your work. These are the individuals who phone you every day to make sure you still love them, so you are always being forced into the position of telling them that you never did.

JW: You've written about the beneficial effects of going through menopause. Do you have any advice for other women regarding "the change"?

FK: You will lose your sex drive, but every magazine article, talk show, and self-help book will assure you that you're as horny as ever. Pay no attention to them, it's just another American conspiracy.

JW: What are some other "American conspiracies"?

FK: There is an American conspiracy that says everyone is highly sexed, but everyone is not. It takes a certain bandit persona to go at everything with real élan, and most people simply aren't like that. Speaking in another context, George Orwell said: "The great mass of human beings are not acutely selfish. After the age of about thirty they abandon individual ambition—in many cases, indeed, they almost abandon the sense of being individuals at all—and live chiefly for others, or are simply smothered under drudgery." Another American conspiracy of more recent vintage holds that women are as highly sexed as men. This is the insane side of equality: everybody's got a right to climb the walls and live in torment. Women have a cyclical sex drive that leaves us quiescent for most of the month. Moreover, the female sex drive is sixty percent vanity, thirty percent curiosity, and ten percent physical. I didn't masturbate until I was seventeen—find me the man who can make that statement. My chief sexual fantasy involved showering together, and I was compelled to visualize it so that no water splashed on the floor and messed up my nice clean bathroom. Find me the man who would give a damn about the mess even in real life, never mind fantasy.

JW: Are you a good housekeeper?

FK: You could eat off my floor, but I can't guarantee the table: I write on it.

JW: When you receive a letter from a stranger, what form of salutation do you prefer: Dear Miss King; Dear Ms. King; Dear Florence King; Dear Florence?

FK: Dear Miss King.

JW: Why?

FK: Because I'm a spinster. My whole life has been a feminist statement, so I don't need Ms. to prove who I am. As for Dear Florence King, it makes me feel as if they want all of me, and nobody ever gets that.

JW: Do you watch television?

FK: I watch old movies—it's interesting to gauge my present reactions and compare them to my original reactions when I saw the movies for the first time as a child or a young woman. And of course I watch baseball, the Orioles mostly. I don't watch any sitcoms; judging from the previews I see while I'm watching something else, they are all sit and no com. I never laugh at sight gags; my idea of wit is a verbal thrust or an oblique understatement such as Noel Coward's definition of a gentleman: "A man who can play the bagpipes, but doesn't." I loved *Upstairs, Downstairs*, but I am not an unquestioning devotee of *Masterpiece Theatre*: some of them are terribly boring. *Fall of Eagles* because it was about the history of the belle epoque, which I wish I'd lived in. And anything about FDR, because the socialist sonofabitch was the personification of my childhood.

JW: Are you religious?

FK: I believe in reincarnation and can't wait to see who I'm going to be next. I hope I'll be male and a major-league baseball player. I'm not religious in the conventional sense; as an Episcopalian child I thought trinity meant going to church three times a year, but I approve of religion and think society needs it. As Napoleon said: "Religion is necessary because it keeps the poor people from killing the rich people." A certain opulence of imagination draws me to the old Latin-and-incense Roman Catholicism, and the doctrine of papal infallibility appeals to the exhausted American in me: Debate must stop somewhere if the mind and society are to have peace.

JW: Do you sleep well?

FK: Like a goddam baby.

QUOTES ON "N"

NARCISSIST

A narcissist is someone better-looking than you are.　　　GORE VIDAL

NASA

Some agencies have a public affairs office. NASA is a public affairs office
that has an agency.　　　JOHN PIKE

NATION

A nation is a society united by delusions about its ancestry and by common
hatred of its neighbors.　　　W. R. INGE

NATIONALISM

Every nation ridicules other nations, and all are right.

ARTHUR SCHOPENHAUER

Every nation thinks its own madness normal and requisite; more passion and
more fancy it calls folly, less it calls imbecility.　　　GEORGE SANTAYANA

NATURE

Nature is a hanging judge.　　　ANONYMOUS

Now, nature, as I am only too well aware, has her enthusiasts, but on the
whole, I am not to be counted among them. To put it rather bluntly, I am

not the type who wants to go back to the land; I am the type who wants to go back to the hotel.   FRAN LEBOWITZ

Nature: that lovely lady to whom we owe polio, leprosy, smallpox, syphilis, tuberculosis, cancer.   STANLEY N. COHEN

Just because something happens in nature doesn't make it *natural.*
                    SAMANTHA BEE

—————————————— NECESSITY ——————————————
"Necessity is the mother of invention" is a silly proverb. "Necessity is the mother of futile dodges" is much nearer the truth.
                    ALFRED NORTH WHITEHEAD

—————————————— NEIGHBORS ——————————————
I was much distressed by next-door people who had twin babies and played the violin; but one of the twins died, and the other has eaten the fiddle—so all is peace.   EDWARD LEAR

—————————————— NETWORK EXECUTIVES ——————————————
Dealing with network executives is like being nibbled to death by ducks.
                    ERIC SEVAREID

—————————————— NEVER ——————————————
Is never good for you?   ROBERT MANKOFF

—————————————— NEW JERSEY ——————————————
New Jersey looks like the back of an old radio.   JOSH GREENFELD

The Holland Tunnel was built so commuters can go to New Jersey without being seen.
FRED ALLEN

NEWS

News is what people want to keep hidden; everything else is publicity.
BILL MOYERS

NEWS ANCHORS

Do you know what White House correspondents call actors who pose as reporters? Anchors.
JAY LENO

NEWS EXECUTIVES

Fake news executives are nicer than real news executives, though real news executives are funnier than fake news executives. They don't know they're being funny.
STEPHEN COLBERT

NEWS NETWORKS

On an average day seven minutes of news happens. Yet there are currently three full-time, twenty-four-hour news networks.
JON STEWART

NEWSPAPER

Trying to determine what is going on in the world by reading newspapers is like trying to tell the time by watching the second hand of a clock.
BEN HECHT

Newspapers have degenerated. They may now be absolutely relied upon.
OSCAR WILDE

A newspaper is a device unable to discriminate between a bicycle accident and the collapse of civilization.
GEORGE BERNARD SHAW

A newspaper consists of just the same number of words, whether there be any news in it or not. HENRY FIELDING

The average newspaper, especially of the better sort, has the intelligence of a hillbilly evangelist, the courage of a rat, the fairness of a prohibitionist boob-jumper, the information of a high school janitor, the taste of a designer of celluloid valentines, and the honor of a police-station lawyer.

H. L. MENCKEN

——————————— NEW YEAR'S EVE ———————————

The proper behavior all through the holiday season is to be drunk. This drunkenness culminates on New Year's Eve, when you get so drunk you kiss the person you're married to. P. J. O'ROURKE

——————————— NEW YORK ———————————

New York: Where everyone mutinies but no one deserts.

HARRY HERSHFIELD

Prison towers and modern posters for soap and whiskey.

FRANK LLOYD WRIGHT

New York is the only city in the world where you can get deliberately run down on the sidewalk by a pedestrian. RUSSELL BAKER

The city of right angles and tough, damaged people. PETE HAMILL

The nation's thyroid gland. CHRISTOPHER MORLEY

If a day goes by and I haven't been slain, I'm happy. CAROL LEIFER

I love New York. I've got a gun.   CHARLES BARKLEY

I love New York City. I reason I live in New York City because it's the loudest city on the planet Earth. It's so loud I never have to listen to any of the shit that's going on in my own head.   LEWIS BLACK

It is one of the prime provincialities of New York that its inhabitants lap up trivial gossip about essential nobodies they've never set eyes on, while continuing to boast that they could live somewhere for twenty years without so much as exchanging pleasantries with their neighbors across the hall.

LOUIS KRONENBERGER

New York Taxi Rules:
1. Driver speaks no English.
2. Driver just got here two days ago from someplace like Senegal.
3. Driver hates you.   DAVE BARRY

Some people say Paris is more esthetic than New York. Well, in New York you don't have time to have an esthetic because it takes half the day to go downtown and half the day to go uptown.   ANDY WARHOL

On a New York subway you get fined for spitting, but you can throw up for nothing.   LEWIS GRIZZARD

A marriage, to be happy, needs an exterior threat. New York provides that threat.   GARRISON KEILLOR

New York: the only city where people make radio requests like "This is for Tina—I'm sorry I stabbed you."   CAROL LEIFER

New York has more commissioners than Des Moines, Iowa, has residents, including the Commissioner for Making Sure the Sidewalks Are Always Blocked by Steaming Fetid Mounds of Garbage the Size of Appalachian Foothills, and, of course, the Commissioner for Bicycle Messengers Bearing Down on You at Warp Speed with Mohawk Haircuts and Pupils Smaller Than Purely Theoretical Particles. DAVE BARRY

No other city in the United States can divest the visitor of so much money with so little enthusiasm. In Dallas, they take away with gusto; in New Orleans, with a bow; in San Francisco, with a wink and a grin. In New York, you're lucky if you get a grunt. FLETCHER KNEBEL

When we moved to New York we had to get rid of the children. Landlords didn't like them and, in any case, rents were so high. Who could afford an apartment big enough to contain children? RUSSELL BAKER

This muck heaves and palpitates. It is multidirectional and has a mayor. DONALD BARTHELME

—————————————— NOBEL PRIZE ——————————————
I can forgive Alfred Nobel for having invented dynamite, but only a fiend in human form could have invented the Nobel Prize. GEORGE BERNARD SHAW

Nobel Prize money is a lifebelt thrown to a swimmer who has already reached the shore in safety. GEORGE BERNARD SHAW

The Nobel is a ticket to one's own funeral. No one has ever done anything after he got it. T. S. ELIOT

NOISE

The amount of noise which anyone can bear undisturbed stands in inverse proportion to his mental capacity.   ARTHUR SCHOPENHAUER

NONCONFORMITY

Woe to him inside a nonconformist clique who does not conform with nonconformity.   ERIC HOFFER

NOVEMBER

November, *n*. The eleventh twelfth of a weariness.   AMBROSE BIERCE

NUCLEAR WAR

There will be no nuclear war. There's too much real estate involved.
      FRANK ZAPPA

JOHN LEO

Wanted by the Niceness Police

John Leo is a contributing editor and columnist for *U.S. News & World Report* and the author of four books: *How the Russians Invented Baseball and Other Essays of Enlightenment*, *Two Steps Ahead of the Thought Police*, *Incorrect Thoughts: Notes on Our Wayward Culture*, and *Islam: The Truth Revealed: A Clear Look at the Muslim Religion*.

JW: I'd like to talk about what you've called "hypersensitive minorities…"
JL: I think this is the age of great touchiness. Everybody is in the business of burnishing their image and hammering anybody who gets in the way. A

couple of guys complained that one of my columns was antigay, and I pointed out that the same column had a crack about Catholics, Arabs, fat people,
thin people, and Native Americans. Only they didn't notice that. They were
a perfect illustration of how incredibly touchy everybody is these days. You
can't attack anybody. We have "niceness police" all around us.

JW: Is everything sacred?

JL: What isn't? WASPS? Are they the only fair game left? I used to think that
middle-aged white businessmen were the only ones left, but then someone
complained that there were too many middle-aged-white-businessman villains on TV. So there's nobody to pick on anymore. We'll have to have villains
with Martian last names, because obviously you can't use an *ethnic* last name,
and everybody can't be called "Green" and "Smith." And while we're on the
subject, I should tell you that every time a street gang is portrayed it has to
be perfectly integrated; it's got to have blacks, Puerto Ricans, and whites,
because otherwise someone might get the idea that people hang around in
ethnic groups of their own. We can't have that! The best example of this was
The Long Hot Summer with Don Johnson. The mob calling for his lynching was the only totally integrated lynch mob ever seen in America. Now,
why blacks would be in a lynch mob in the South is obscure, except that the
producers felt uncomfortable having an all-white mob. What it comes down
to is you're never going to see a black shoeshine guy or a homosexual villain.
We're going for mainstream, white-bread, middle-aged, middle-size villains.

JW: Is this new touchiness confined to Hollywood?

JL: Not at all: In a campaign against political incorrectness, Smith College
recently warned its freshpersons about ten dangerous "isms." In that spirit I would propose my own list of political taboos. To the big three of *racism,
sexism,* and *heterosexism,* I would add *ageism,* bias against seniors by the
temporarily young, and *ableism,* bias against the "physically challenged"
and "differently abled" (formerly the "disabled" or "handicapped") by the

"temporarily abled." "Blind to the truth" would be an example of ableist language; stairs would be an example of ableist architecture. And there's *speciesism*, the doctrine that people are somehow more valuable than mice or insects. A philosopher of animal rights named Peter Singer writes that "speciesists allow the interests of their own species to override the greater interests of members of other species." A person swatting a mosquito would thus be a speciesist. So would a bird eating an insect, a snake eating a bird, a jackal eating a snake, or a lion eating Peter Singer.

JW: Was it an example of some sort of "ism" when the Federal Aviation Administration banned blind persons from sitting next to the exits on airliners?

JL: Yes, it was a blatant case of "sightism," the belief that visually impaired people cannot do as well as sighted people at all tasks.

JW: And there must be "isms" based on appearance.

JL: Lots of them: *Lookism* is the belief that some people are easier on the eyes than others, which creates an unacceptable hierarchy based on mere appearance. There's *sizeism*, the prejudice against the differently sized. Thus articles on dieting and overeating are biased. And there's *birthmarkism*, the refusal to see that it is not birthmarks that are unsightly but rather the society that frowns upon them. Ted Kennedy, Jr., wrote to the *Boston Globe* to complain about an article on birthmark treatment techniques when actually, he pointed out, "our attitude is the problem, and that can never be corrected surgically." It goes beyond appearance: "Inappropriately directed laughter" has been banned at the University of Connecticut, hence *laughism*. Micky Kaus of the *New Republic* wrote that while growing a beard, he was disinvited by a cable TV show out of *blatant shavism*. And a Boston-based group of militant lesbians, pointing out that some women are especially sensitive to odors, argued that social events "should be advertised as scent-free, and sniffers posted at the entrance to ensure that all who enter are in compliance." This is nothing short of *scentism*. I suppose splashing on some Old Spice would combine scentism and shavism into *aftershavism*. You've got to be careful out there.

JW: Is this all part of what you've called the "relentless manufacture of new rights"?

JL: Absolutely. As a cursory reading of almost any newspaper will show, American politics is awash in rights talk. We have criminal rights, computer rights, animal rights, children's rights, victim's rights, abortion rights, privacy rights, housing rights, the right to know the sex of fetus, the right to own AK-47s for hunting purposes, the right not to be tested for AIDS, and the right not to inform anyone that we may be infected. Recently we have acquired the right to die, and according to some rather imaginative theorists, a damaged fetus has "a right not to be born." Mental patients used to have a right to treatment, but now that they have been dumped on the streets, they have an ACLU-protected right to no treatment and, therefore, the right to die unhelped in alleys. According to the ACLU, airline pilots have a right not to be randomly tested for alcohol, leaving passengers with an implied right to crash every now and then.

And speaking of alcohol, have you noticed that whereas you used to be just a drunk, now you are "alcohol disabled"? Almost everybody is clamoring to *become* handicapped. A woman in Virginia was arrested for trying to poison her two-year-old son by mixing mouse poison with breakfast cereal and ice cream, and the defense was that she is suffering from "Munchausen's syndrome by proxy." Now, Munchausen's syndrome is a mental disorder in which people mutilate themselves to elicit attention. So to get this woman into the Munchausen's syndrome, it had to be by "proxy" since she had attempted to harm not herself but her child. The devil made her put the mouse poison in the ice cream. That's the "manufacture of disability." We do that more and more.

JW: Are things any better at the university level?

JL: I think the universities are suffering from a breakdown that goes back to the sixties, when they gave up the in loco parentis approach and allowed the kids to start running the university. Now they're regretting it because a lot of the kids are antifemale, antiblack, and so forth, so you have friction all the time. Instead of trying to build a community, they're trying to become niceness police. For example, they want to bar certain words. So now if a male student has an argument with a female student and it gets heated and he calls her a bitch, he can be taken up on charges or expelled, which is an absolutely preposterous suspension of free speech.

JW: Another disturbing trend in American society is the shrinking of attention spans. Life grows increasingly less linear, sequences and story lines are disappearing from newspaper and magazine stories and even comic strips, political discourse degenerates further into sound bites. There's even a radio psychiatrist in L.A. who takes you through five years of therapy in five minutes...

JL: And the price is right, too. It's all true about attention spans. And it's beginning to affect our politics because the easily understood things are becoming our major issues. Everybody goes nuts over animal rights because the issue can be explained to a three-year-old in eight seconds, but no one gives a damn about the S&Ls—it's five hundred billion dollars lost, but no one can understand it. We talk about the instantly graspable, emotional issues that a moron can understand. Things that make good "visuals." A tormented animal or a burnt flag is terrific—it gets you emotionally.

JW: Some of the "visuals" employed by the animal-rights movement are indeed compelling, but where do you come down on the issue itself?

JL: I'm of two minds about it. First of all, I think the anticruelty people are absolutely right: There's a lot of pointless cruelty to animals, particularly to develop perfumes and powders, and that seems unconscionable. The part I don't like is the emotional "feel-good" aspect of it, the implication that you can feel morally superior and wonderful and engaged worrying about the torment of a dog, the way you would never be engaged about the much more vivid torment of actual human beings that goes on without anyone picketing against it. There's a kind of moral one-upmanship about it. You get to feel superior to the woman who wears dead minks.

JW: You've also complained about the spread of advertising. In one column you described taking the world's shortest cab ride because when you got in the taxi there was a ticker tape showing a commercial.

JL: The only response you can have when you're being sold something nine inches from your face inside the cab is: "Let me out of here!" The only other thing you could do is destroy it, but I didn't have a crowbar with me. It's getting worse and worse. The ad slogan has to cut through the clutter, which means that plain English creates more clutter for people like you and me. They have ads now on hot dogs. You buy a hot dog and there will be a commercial for some other product on the hot dog.

JW: On the wrapper?

JL: On the *skin*. Edible. You're eating the commercial. Someone wrote and told me they have them on the inside of men's room doors—talk about captive audiences. They're putting ads everywhere they can think of: life guard platforms, golf carts, tee markers, golfer's cards, parking meters, bus shelters. They'll put them on anything they can.

JW: Even the names of sporting events: There's the "Sunkist Fiesta Bowl," the "John Hancock Sun Bowl"—what's next?

JL: The Preparation-H Bowl.

JW: But are there any encouraging signs? Disney recently announced that they wouldn't allow commercials in theaters where their movies are shown.

JL: But Disney plants the ads in their own movies: *Roger Rabbit* had an ad for Lucky Strikes embedded in it. Why get pious and say you're going to protect your viewers from having to watch ads when the ads are already in your movies? What they mean is, *we'll* handle the ads inside our product, thank you very much, and we don't want anybody putting ads around us because we don't get paid for them.

JW: How about perfumed perfume ads?

JL: You open a magazine and an incredible stench comes floating out. There are five or six naked narcissists posing languidly and this yellow gas comes up toward your nostrils. You need a gas mask.

JW: All aimed at the baby boomers, the most affluent segment of society, fewer than half of whom follow public affairs or read a daily newspaper.

JL: It seems to me that the whole electorate is in the business of going to sleep as rapidly as possible. Look at the whole census thing: No one returned his form. But that may be a protest against junk mail. There are so many stupid things in the mail, saying "Important Thing about the Environment," while it's really a pitch for some club or something. People just heave that stuff out. If you look at the dismal census response and the small voter turnout and nobody reading anything important, you find a somnolent public. I think people are just in shock about change, and the easiest way to resist that shock is to insert your head in the sand and keep it there until you grow old.

JW: And we seem to be getting increasingly jaded when it comes to entertainment.

JL: That's certainly true when it comes to rock bands, whose sacred mission is to offend as many parents as possible. Which is an increasingly arduous assignment in a culture growing cruder by the day. Ozzy Osbourne had to bite the head off a living bat, thus risking the wrath of animal-rights people *and* rabies at the same time. God knows what the next generation will have to do. Autopsies on TV? It's getting harder and harder to gross us out.

JW: Standards are eroding all over the place. You did a piece about increasing use of the f word. Who are the worst offenders?

JL: I don't know if [Los Angeles Dodger Manager] Tom Lasorda is the all-time champion, but he's certainly in the finals. He once used the word forty-four times in a minute and a half during a visit to the mound. Now, I figure that if you use it forty-four times every time you change pitchers, with an average of three pitching changes a game, you would use it a million times in a year—just while standing on the mound. I think that whoever has the patent on the f word sure owes most of their livelihood to Tom Lasorda's use of it.

JW: You're an avid baseball fan, and you've compiled a list of favorite baseball clichés, and I'd like you to translate a few of them. "He came to play," for instance.

JL: A guy with no talent at all, you can always say he "came to play" or he "gives 110 percent," or you can call him a "scrappy player." A "scrappy player" is a player with no known skills at all who is not legally dead. If he moves at all, he's "scrappy." "Scrappy" people tend to leave the big leagues after one year because it takes more than "scrappiness" now. What else? A "great natural athlete." Darryl Strawberry is "a great natural athlete." "A great natural athlete" is someone with wonderful talent and ability who doesn't use them at all. If he has a great arm and great hitting ability but hits .220, strikes out, and can't catch a fly ball, you say he has "great natural ability." "We can hold our own with any team in this league" means we will be lucky to have a .500 season; if we win as many as we lose, it will be a truimph of the human spirit because we have no ability whatsoever. "This year we will be working on fundamentals" means there's no hope. We can't do anything right. "We're rebuilding" means we need eight, maybe nine more players in the starting lineup. "This is a rebuilding year" translates to "we're going to try to teach them which base to run to if they get a hit."

JW: How about "This is a team to watch"?

JL: Only if you've already seen everything else on TV and every movie ever made.

JW: You've written about your passion for another "sport," bird-watching. How did you get involved?

JL: One day you just look up and you say, "Holy smoke, I never noticed *that* thing before." And then you discover it's a mourning dove, a really beautiful bird. Then you start *chasing* them, and before you know it you're *collecting* them. It's the grown-up version of a little boy's attempt to collect every base-ball card. It becomes a kind of hunting game in which you begin to notice the beautiful things around you. And it gets you away from the humdrum of daily life. It's an obsession: I know a lot of birders who divorced nonbird-ers and then married birders. You have to organize your life around birding, including your wife, or otherwise your new wife will think you're as nuts as your old one did. You have to make sure that you have matched obsessions in the family.

JW: How obsessive are you?

JL: A couple of years ago I went to Attu. Attu is the last Aleutian Island, clos-er to Tokyo than it is to Anchorage. It's way out in the middle of nowhere. They drop you there, and if you get sick, hard luck. There's nothing on the island. You get stuck there for three weeks in the most primitive conditions. There's nothing to do. You sleep in a room with nineteen of your closest friends, all of whom are either coughing or snoring or both. You put up with this because of the chance that you might see five or six "Asian specialties." The big-time birders go there—sometimes every year, sometimes twice a year—with the hope of seeing maybe one bird that they haven't seen before to add to their lifetime list. That is truly obsessive.

JW: "Lifetime list"?

JL: Lifetime *North American* list. Attu is really an Asiatic island, but techni-cally it's part of Alaska, so any Asian bird that flies over it can be counted on your North American list. So you spend five thousand dollars and three unbearable weeks to see a bird you could see two minutes outside Paris, just so you can get it on your North American list. My idea of a great birding chase is one where you can drive right to the top of the mountain, hop out, see the bird, and jump right back into air-conditioned comfort. But every once in a while some idiotic bird will position itself at the bottom of some enormous canyon so that you have to go down to get it. It's a four-hour descent and then you have to climb back up with the sun in your face and there's no water and you're climbing and—you just want a helicopter at that point. I once tried to drive down into something called California Gulch in an '87 Buick. No one had ever tried that before, because California Gulch is a sheer rock face. We're sitting there, maybe a foot and a half from the edge, and this fellow says, "John, maybe we should get out now." I said, "Perhaps you're right." So we went out and got the bird.

JW: Are there differences between women birders and men birders?

JL: There are a lot of very successful and competitive female birders, but I think by and large the sexual differences do assert themselves. I noticed that of the people who send in their life list to the American Birding Association, about ninety percent are male. I guess it's because the collecting, the drivenness, the hunting instinct, tends to be male, whereas women are more automatically drawn to the beauty and flight and freedom of birds and then only secondarily do they amass their list. Whereas the male will drive five hundred miles, look up at the bird, say, "That's it," write it down on his list, and completely miss the beauty of it.

JW: With men it's a form of acquisitiveness?

JL: Yes, it's non-financial avarice. You want every bird, to have and to hold.

QUOTES ON "O"

OAKLAND, CALIFORNIA

The trouble with Oakland is that when you get there, there isn't any there there.
GERTRUDE STEIN

The trouble with Oakland is that when you get there, it's there.

HERB CAEN

OBITUARIES

I have never killed a man, but I have read many obituaries with great pleasure.
CLARENCE DARROW

He died alone with his family.   BRUCE ERIC KAPLAN

OBSCENITY

Obscenity is what happens to shock some elderly and ignorant magistrate.
BERTRAND RUSSELL

Obscenity is whatever gives a judge an erection.   ANONYMOUS

OK

I'm not OK, you're not OK, and that's OK.   WILLIAM SLOANE COFFIN

OLD

A man is as old as the woman he feels.

GROUCHO MARX

OPEN MIND

If you leave the smallest corner of your head vacant for a moment, other people's opinions will rush in from all quarters.

GEORGE BERNARD SHAW

OPERA

Opera, *n.* A play representing life in another world whose inhabitants have no speech but song, no motions but gestures, and no postures but attitudes.

AMBROSE BIERCE

How wonderful opera would be if there were no singers.

GIOACCHINO ROSSINI

The opera…is to music what a bawdy house is to a cathedral.

H. L. MENCKEN

Going to the opera, like getting drunk, is a sin that carries its own punishment with it, and that a very severe one.

HANNAH MOORE

If a thing isn't worth saying, you sing it.

PIERRE AUGUSTIN CARON DE BEAUMARCHAIS

No opera plot can be sensible, for people do not sing when they are feeling sensible.

W. H. AUDEN

Opera is when a guy gets stabbed in the back and instead of bleeding, he sings.

ED GARDNER

One goes to see a tragedy to be moved; to the opera one goes either for want of any other interest or to facilitate digestion. VOLTAIRE

An unalterable and unquestioned law of the musical world required that the German text of French operas sung by Swedish artists should be translated into Italian for the clearer understanding of English-speaking audiences.
EDITH WHARTON

Opera in English is, in the main, just about as sensible as baseball in Italian.
H. L. MENCKEN

I do not mind what language an opera is sung in so long as it is a language I don't understand. SIR EDWARD APPLETON

People are wrong when they say that the opera isn't what it used to be. It *is* what it used to be. That's what's wrong with it. NOEL COWARD

——————————— OPERA STAR ———————————
When an opera star sings her head off, she usually improves her appearance.
VICTOR BORGE

——————————— OPTIMISM ———————————
Optimism is the madness of maintaining that everything is right when it is wrong. VOLTAIRE

Optimism: the noble temptation to see too much in everything.
G. K. CHESTERTON

Optimism, *n.* The doctrine or belief that everything is beautiful, including what is ugly. AMBROSE BIERCE

Optimism is the content of small men in high places.

F. SCOTT FITZGERALD

The place where optimism flourishes most is the lunatic asylum.

HAVELOCK ELLIS

The basis of optimism is sheer terror. OSCAR WILDE

Optimist, *n.* A proponent of the doctrine that black is white.

AMBROSE BIERCE

The optimist thinks that this is the best of all possible worlds, and the pessimist knows it. J. ROBERT OPPENHEIMER

An optimist is a man who has never had much experience. DON MARQUIS

I find nothing more depressing than optimism. PAUL FUSSELL

ORCHESTRA

Orchestras only need to be sworn at, and a German is consequently at an advantage with them, as English profanity, except in America, has not gone beyond a limited technology of perdition. GEORGE BERNARD SHAW

OTHER PEOPLE

Most people are other people. Their thoughts are someone else's opinions, their lives a mimicry, their passions a quotation. OSCAR WILDE

OXFORD

Oxford: a sanctuary in which exploded systems and obsolete prejudices find shelter and protection after they have been hunted out of every corner of the world.   ADAM SMITH

I was a modest, good-humored boy; it is Oxford that has made me insufferable.   MAX BEERBOHM

———————————— OYSTERS ————————————

Oyster, *n.* A slimy, gobby shellfish which civilization gives men the hardihood to eat without removing its entrails! The shells are sometimes given to the poor.
AMBROSE BIERCE

I will not eat oysters. I want my food dead. Not sick, not wounded, dead.
WOODY ALLEN

ROBERT BENCHLEY

I May Be Wrong…

Robert Benchley once proposed his own autobiographical sketch to *Current Biography*. "Born on the Isle of Wight, September 15, 1807, shipped as cabin boy on the *Florence J. Marble* in 1815, wrote *A Tale of Two Cities* in 1820, married Princess Anastasie of Portugal in 1831 (children: Prince Rupprecht and several little girls), buried in Westminster Abbey in 1871."

Robert Charles Benchley was actually born in Worcester, Massachusetts, in 1889, to Maria Jane Moran Benchley and Charles Benchley. He showed early comedic tendencies when he recited these lines during his first year at Phillips Exeter Academy:

My mother-in-law has lately died;
For her my heart doth yearn.
I know she's with the angels now
'Cause she's too tough to burn.

He attended Harvard College, where he was a member of Hasty Pudding and where, as editor of the *Lampoon*, he published a parody of *Life*, the first in what would be a long series of *Lampoon* magazine parodies. Two years after graduating from Harvard in 1912, he married his childhood sweetheart, Gertrude Darling. The Benchleys eventually had two sons, Nathaniel and Robert Jr., prompting Benchley to remark of sex, "We tried it twice and it worked both times."

By 1915, he was a city reporter for the New York *Tribune*, where Franklin P. Adams was his sponsor and his coworkers included George S. Kaufman and Heywood Broun. By his own admission, Benchley was "the worst reporter, even for his age, in New York City." His problem was the inability to ask questions he considered indelicate. He thus welcomed an invitation to join the staff of the *Tribune Magazine*, where he wrote book reviews and features on New York life. In 1919, he was hired as managing editor of *Vanity Fair*, where he met the diminutive Dorothy Parker and the six-foot seven-inch Robert E. Sherwood. Benchley said that when the three of them walked down the street together they looked like a "walking pipe organ." When they resigned enmasse from *Vanity Fair* in 1920, Sherwood embarked on his career as a playwright, and Benchley and Parker shared a freelance office.

Benchley was the theater critic for *Life* from 1920 to 1929, and wrote a column in the *New Yorker* under the pseudonym "Guy Fawkes" from 1929 to 1940. His theater criticism was exacting but not cruel. He had rigorous standards, but he often inserted the disclaimer "I may be wrong."

He was a charter member of the Algonquin Round Table, along with Alexander Woollcott, Marc Connelly, and Edna Ferber. In 1922, Benchley wrote and performed a satirical monologue entitled "The Treasurer's Report" in a revue put on by members of the Round Table. Irving Berlin and Sam Harris were in the audience and signed Benchley to perform it in their Broadway production, *The Music Box Review*. The show ran for nine months, and in 1928, "The Treasurer's Report" was made into the first all-talking motion picture, establishing Benchley as a national celebrity. He went on to write, produce, and star in some forty movie "shorts," including *The Courtship of the Newt, How to Figure the Income Tax,* and *How to Sleep*, which won an Oscar in 1935. He also had many small movie parts in which he played a character much like himself, and he once advertised in *Variety* for "society drunk" roles.

He was an expert procrastinator ("Anybody can do any amount of work, so long as it isn't the work he is supposed to be doing"), and whenever a writing assignment was overdue he displayed a positive genius for finding something else to do instead. Thus he once labeled all the spice jars in the pantry rather than complete an important piece. And according to his son, Nathaniel, his ability to evade the task at hand could go to even greater extremes:

> Once, he had been trying to start a piece but couldn't get it under way, so he went down the corridor to where a poker game was in progress, just to jolt his mind into starting up. Some time later, he returned to his room, sat down to the clean sheet of paper in the typewriter, and pecked out the word "The." This, he reasoned, was as safe a start as any, and might possibly break the block. But nothing else came, so he went downstairs and ran into a group of Round Table people, with whom he passed a cheerful hour or so. Then, protesting that he had to work, he went back upstairs, where the small, bleak "The" was looking at him out of the

expanse of yellow paper. He sat down and stared at it for several minutes, then a sudden idea came to him, and he finished the sentence, making it read "The hell with it," and got up and went happily out for the evening.

Though he published fifteen books of humorous essays, including the best-selling *Of All Things*, he was plagued by professional self-doubt. He desperately wanted to be a serious writer, but his sense of humor kept getting in the way. He feared he was wasting his time in frivolity, and he regarded whatever he was working on a temporary detour from the *real* work, which he could never manage to do. "It took me fifteen years to discover that I had no talent for writing," he said, "but I couldn't give it up because by that time I was too famous."

Benchley had a puritanical streak. During Prohibition, he would accompany his friends to speakeasies and lecture them on the evils of drink. But he eventually succumbed to the spirit of the times (perhaps reasoning that if the government was so opposed to drinking, it must have some redeeming value), and he began to drink with the zeal of a convert. When a friend warned him that alcohol was "slow poison," Benchley replied, "So who's in a hurry?" His drinking got progressively worse through the twenties and thirties, and he died in 1945, at the age of fifty-six, of a cerebral hemorrhage.

Both James Thurber and E. B. White considered Benchley the finest American humorist since Mark Twain, and Stephen Leacock judged him "the most finished master of the technique of literary fun in America." His gentle humor came from his sense of outraged decency, but he was generous to others and he stood up for causes he considered worthy. Dorothy Parker called him "a kind of saint."

QUINTESSENTIAL BENCHLEY

Why don't you get out of that wet coat and into a dry martini?

Drinking makes such fools of people, and people are such fools to begin with, that it's compounding a felony.

A man showed a supposedly unbreakable watch to Benchley and Dorothy Parker in a speakeasy. They promptly shook it, slammed it on the bar, and stamped on it. The dismayed owner picked it up, put it to his ear and exclaimed, "It stopped."

"Maybe you wound it too tight," said Benchley.

Asked whether he knew the six-foot seven Robert E. Sherwood, Benchley climbed on a table, reached to the ceiling with one hand, and said, "Why, I've known Bob Sherwood since he was this high."

A great many people have come up to me and asked how I manage to get so much work done and still keep looking so dissipated.

I do most of my work sitting down; that's where I shine.

Tell us your phobias, and we will tell you what you are afraid of.

I haven't been abroad in so long that I almost speak English without an accent now.

Six days after Charles Lindbergh's triumphant landing at Le Bourget, Benchley sent a cable to a friend in Paris: ANY TIDINGS OF LINDBERGH? LEFT HERE WEEK AGO. AM WORRIED.

Benchley came out of a Manhattan restaurant and said to a uniformed man at the door, "Would you get me a taxi, please?"

"I'm sorry," replied the man, "I'm an admiral in the United States Navy."

"All right," said Benchley, "then get me a battleship."

An ardent supporter of the hometown team should go to a game prepared to take offense, no matter what happens.

In America there are two classes of travel—first class, and with children. Drawing on my fine command of the language, I said nothing.

QUOTES ON "P"

PAINTING

Painting, *n*. The art of protecting flat surfaces from the weather and exposing them to the critic.

AMBROSE BIERCE

PALEY, WILLIAM

He looks like a man who has just swallowed an entire human being.

TRUMAN CAPOTE

PANAMA

It's not like they make or grow anything. The whole country is based on international banking and a canal the United States can take back any time it wants with one troop of Boy Scouts.

P. J. O'ROURKE

PARANOIA

A paranoid is a man who knows a little of what's going on.

WILLIAM BURROUGHS

I envy paranoids; they actually feel people are paying attention to them.

SUSAN SONTAG

Even paranoids have real enemies.

DELMORE SCHWARTZ

PARENTHOOD

There are times when parenthood seems nothing but feeding the mouth that bites you.   PETER DE VRIES

There may be some doubt as to who are the best people to have charge of children, but there can be no doubt that parents are the worst.
GEORGE BERNARD SHAW

The only people who seem to have nothing to do with the education of the children are the parents.   G. K. CHESTERTON

Some people seem compelled by unkind fate to parental servitude for life. There is no form of penal servitude worse than this.   SAMUEL BUTLER

The Jewish man with parents alive is a fifteen-year-old boy and will remain a fifteen-year-old boy until they die.   PHILIP ROTH

Parents were invented to make children happy by giving them something to ignore.   OGDEN NASH

They fuck you up, your mum and dad....   PHILIP LARKIN

PÂTÉ

It scored right away with me by being the smooth, fine-grained sort, not the coarse, flaky, dry-on-the-outside rubbish full of chunks of gut and gristle to testify to its authenticity.   KINGSLEY AMIS

PATIENCE

Patience, *n.* A minor form of despair, disguised as a virtue. AMBROSE BIERCE

You must first have a lot of patience to learn to have patience.

STANISLAW J. LEC

---------------------------------- PATRIOTISM ----------------------------------

Patriotism is the last refuge of a scoundrel.   SAMUEL JOHNSON

In Dr. Johnson's famous dictionary, patriotism is defined as the last resort of a scoundrel. With all due respect to an enlightened but inferior lexicographer, I beg to submit that it is the first.   AMBROSE BIERCE

Patriotism is the willingness to kill and be killed for trivial reasons.

BERTRAND RUSSELL

When you hear a man speak of his love for his country, it is a sign that he expects to be paid for it.   H. L. MENCKEN

"My country, right or wrong" is like saying, "My mother, drunk or sober."

G. K. CHESTERTON

Patriotism is a pernicious, psychopathic form of idiocy.

GEORGE BERNARD SHAW

Patriotism is the virtue of the vicious.   OSCAR WILDE

Patriotism is often an arbitrary veneration of real estate above principles.

GEORGE JEAN NATHAN

Patriotism is your conviction that this country is superior to all other countries because you were born in it.   GEORGE BERNARD SHAW

Love makes fools, marriage cuckolds, and patriotism malevolent imbeciles.
PAUL LEAUTAUD

A patriot must always be ready to defend his country against his government.
EDWARD ABBEY

—————————————— PEACE ——————————————

Peace, *n*. In international affairs, a period of cheating between two periods of fighting. AMBROSE BIERCE

—————————————— PENIS PIERCING ——————————————

I question not only those who are getting their penis pierced, but also those who are doing the piercing. I mean, this is what you're doing for a living? God, your parents have to be pissed. ADAM CAROLLA

—————————————— PEOPLE ——————————————

It is absurd to divide people into good and bad. People are either charming or tedious. OSCAR WILDE

When there are two conflicting versions of the story, the wise course is to believe the one in which people appear at their worst. H. ALLEN SMITH

The devil is an optimist if he thinks he can make people meaner.
KARL KRAUS

People who have no faults are terrible; there is no way of taking advantage of them. ANATOLE FRANCE

The world is populated in the main by people who should not exist.
GEORGE BERNARD SHAW

How I hate the attitude of ordinary people to life. How I loathe ordinariness! How from my soul I abhor nice simple people, with their eternal price-list. It makes my blood boil.   D. H. LAWRENCE

People come up to me and say, "What's wrong?" Nothing. "Well, it takes more energy to frown than it does to smile." Yeah, well, it takes more energy to point that out than it does to leave me alone.   BILL HICKS

People could make the world a nice place to live…if there weren't so goddamn many of them.   CLAYTON HEAFNER

People will buy anything that is one to a customer.   SINCLAIR LEWIS

People (a group that in my opinion has always attracted an undue amount of attention) have often been likened to snowflakes. This analogy is meant to suggest that each is unique—no two alike. This is quite patently not the case. People…are quite simply a dime a dozen. And, I hasten to add, their only similarity to snowflakes resides in their invariable and lamentable tendency to turn, in a few warm days, to slush.   FRAN LEBOWITZ

There are more fools in the world than there are people.
                              HEINRICH HEINE

─────────────────── THE PEOPLE ───────────────────
The people are that part of the state that does not know what it wants.
                    GEORGE FRIEDRICH WILHELM HEGEL

Once the people begin to reason, all is lost.   VOLTAIRE

The people are to be taken in very small doses.

RALPH WALDO EMERSON

You can fool too many of the people too much of the time.

JAMES THURBER

—————————— PERSONAL QUESTIONS ——————————
Once upon a time a chap in Virginia, I believe it was, pressed me publicly on the recurrence of adulterous triangles in my earlier novels. Had I myself been a vertex in such a triangle? "Only once," I told him: "with your mother."

JOHN BARTH

—————————— PESSIMISM ——————————
A pessimist is a man who has been compelled to live with an optimist.

ELBERT HUBBARD

Pessimist: one who, when he has the choice of two evils, chooses both.

OSCAR WILDE

A pessimist thinks everybody is as nasty as himself, and hates them for it.

GEORGE BERNARD SHAW

A pessimist is a person who has had to listen to too many optimists.

DON MARQUIS

I guess I just prefer to see the dark side of things. The glass is always half empty. And cracked. And I just cut my lip on it. And chipped a tooth.

JANEANE GAROFALO

My pessimism extends to the point of even suspecting the sincerity of other pessimists.   JEAN ROSTAND

—————————————— PHD ——————————————
Where there are two PhDs in a developing country, one is head of state and the other is in exile.   EDWIN HERBERT SAMUEL

—————————————— PHILADELPHIA ——————————————
Philadelphia: all the filth and corruption of a big city; all the pettiness and insularity of a small town.   HOWARD OGDEN

Philadelphia, a metropolis sometimes known as the City of Brotherly Love, but more accurately as the City of Bleak November Afternoons.
                                        S. J. PERELMAN

They have Easter egg hunts in Philadelphia, and if the kids don't find the eggs, they get booed.   BOB UECKER

—————————————— PHILANTHROPY ——————————————
Philanthropy is the refuge of rich people who wish to annoy their fellow creatures.   OSCAR WILDE

Take egotism out, and you would castrate the benefactors.
                                  RALPH WALDO EMERSON

Giving away a fortune is taking Christianity too far.
                                  CHARLOTTE BINGHAM

PHILOSPHERS

All are lunatics, but he who can analyze his delusions is called a philosopher.
AMBROSE BIERCE

There is only one thing a philosopher can be relied upon to do, and that is to contradict other philosophers.
WILLIAM JAMES

If you wish to understand a philosopher, do not ask what he says, but find out what he wants.
FRIEDRICH WILHELM NIETZSCHE

PHILOSOPHY

Philosophy, *n*. A route of many roads leading from nowhere to nothing.
AMBROSE BIERCE

Those who lack the courage will always find a philosophy to justify it.
ALBERT CAMUS

Our quaint metaphysical opinions, in an hour of anguish, are like playthings by the bedside of a child deathly sick.
SAMUEL TAYLOR COLERIDGE

Philosophy teaches us to bear with equanimity the misfortunes of others.
OSCAR WILDE

Philosophy is an unusually ingenious attempt to think fallaciously.
BERTRAND RUSSELL

I think I think; therefore, I think I am.
AMBROSE BIERCE

PHONOGRAPH

Phonograph, *n.* an irritating toy that restores life to dead noises.

AMBROSE BIERCE

PHOTOGRAPHER

The photographer is like the cod, which produces a million eggs in order that one may reach maturity. GEORGE BERNARD SHAW

PLASTIC SURGERY

It used to be said that by a certain age a man had the face that he deserved. Nowadays, he has the face he can afford. MARTIN AMIS

One popular new plastic surgery technique is called lipgrafting, or "fat recycling," wherein fat cells are removed from one part of your body that is too large, such as your buttocks, and injected into your lips; people will then be literally kissing your ass. DAVE BARRY

PLATITUDE

Platitude: an idea (a) that is admitted to be true by everyone, and (b) that is not true. H. L. MENCKEN

PLEASANTRIES

Nothing is as irritating as the fellow who chats pleasantly while he's overcharging you. KIN HUBBARD

PLEASURE

Pleasure, *n.* The least hateful form of dejection. AMBROSE BIERCE

Illusion is the first of all pleasures. OSCAR WILDE

I despise the pleasure of pleasing people that I despise.

MARY WORTLEY MONTAGU

One of the simple but genuine pleasures in life is getting up in the morning and hurrying to a mousetrap you set the night before.   KIN HUBBARD

POETS

In the case of many poets, the most important thing for them to do…is to write as little as possible.   T. S. ELIOT

A poet more than thirty years old is simply an overgrown child.

H. L. MENCKEN

Poets, like whores, are only hated by each other.   WILLIAM WYCHERLEY

POETRY

I know that poetry is indispensable, but to what I could not say.

JEAN COCTEAU

All bad poetry springs from genuine feeling.   OSCAR WILDE

I think that one possible definition of our modern culture is that it is one in which nine-tenths of our intellectuals can't read any poetry.

RANDALL JARRELL

Poetry is a religion without hope.   JEAN COCTEAU

Poetry and consumption are the most flattering of diseases.

WILLIAM SHENSTONE

Blank verse, *n.* Unrhymed iambic pentameters— the most difficult kind of English verse to write acceptably; a kind, therefore, much affected by those who cannot acceptably write any kind.   AMBROSE BIERCE

Free verse is like free love; it is a contradiction in terms.
                                                   G. K. CHESTERTON

Poetry is nobody's business except the poet's, and everybody else can fuck off.
                                                      PHILIP LARKIN

─────────────────── POLITENESS ───────────────────
Politeness…is fictitious benevolence.   SAMUEL JOHNSON

Politeness, *n.* The most acceptable hypocrisy.   AMBROSE BIERCE

That roguish and cheerful vice, politeness.
                                        FRIEDRICH WILHELM NIETZSCHE

─────────────── POLITICAL CORRECTNESS ───────────────
Political correctness is just tyranny with manners.   CHARLTON HESTON

Being politically correct means always having to say you're sorry.
                                                    CHARLES OSGOOD

We'll be right back to the politically correct program called "The Good, the Bad, and the Beauty Impaired."   COLIN MOCHRIE

─────────────────── POLITICIANS ───────────────────
A good politician is quite as unthinkable as an honest burglar.
                                                      H. L. MENCKEN

One has to be a lowbrow, a bit of a murderer, to be a politician, ready and willing to see people sacrificed, slaughtered, for the sake of an idea, whether a good one or a bad one.   HENRY MILLER

Take our politicians: They're a bunch of yo-yos. The presidency is now a cross between a popularity contest and a high school debate, with an encyclopedia of clichés the first prize.   SAUL BELLOW

Politics and the fate of mankind are formed by men without ideals and without greatness. Those who have greatness within them do not go in for politics.
                                                                        ALBERT CAMUS

In order to become the master, the politician poses as the servant.
                                                                   CHARLES DE GAULLE

The secret of the demagogue is to make himself as stupid as his audience so that they believe they are as clever as he.   KARL KRAUS

Anybody that wants the presidency so much that he'll spend two years organizing and campaigning for it is not to be trusted with the office.
                                                                       DAVID BRODER

A politician is a person with whose politics you don't agree; if you agree with him he is a statesman.   DAVID LLOYD GEORGE

I once said cynically of a politician, "He'll double-cross that bridge when he comes to it."   OSCAR LEVANT

Have you ever seen a candidate talking to a rich person on television?
                                                                       ART BUCHWALD

The dirty work at political conventions is almost always done in the grim hours between midnight and dawn. Hangmen and politicians work best when the human spirit is at its lowest ebb. RUSSELL BAKER

If a politician found he had cannibals among his constituents, he would promise them missionaries for dinner. H. L. MENCKEN

If you want to find a politician free of any influence, you can find Adolf Hitler, who made up his own mind. EUGENE MCCARTHY

A candidate for office can have no greater advantage than muddled syntax; no greater liability than a command of the language. MARYA MANNES

New Rule: Stop saying you're resigning because you want to spend more time with your family or because you want to return to the private sector, or because of your health. That's all just code for "I'm about to be indicted." BILL MAHER

The saddest life is that of a political aspirant under democracy. His failure is ignominious and his success is disgraceful. H. L. MENCKEN

My choice early in life was either to be a piano player in a whorehouse or a politician. And to tell the truth, there's hardly any difference. HARRY S TRUMAN

The volume of political comment substantially exceeds the available truth, so columnists run out of truth, and then must resort to imagination. Washington politicians, after talking things over with each other, relay misinformation to Washington journalists, who, after intramural discussion, print it where it is thoughtfully read by the same politicians, who generally believe it. It is the only successful closed system for the recycling of garbage that has ever been devised. JOHN KENNETH GALBRAITH

Nine politicians out of ten are knaves who maintain themselves by preying on the idiotic vanities and pathetic hopes of half-wits. H. L. MENCKEN

Ninety eight percent of the adults in this country are decent, hardworking, honest Americans. It's the other lousy two percent that get all the publicity. But then, we elected them. LILY TOMLIN

Here richly, with ridiculous display,
The politician's corpse was laid away.
While all of his acquaintance sneered and slanged,
I wept; for I had longed to see him hanged.

HILAIRE BELLOC

Unfortunately, politicians have the Paul Masson theory of government—
"We will deal with no problem before its time." MERVIN FIELD

Ninety percent of the politicians give the other ten percent a bad name.
HENRY KISSINGER

Politicians are interested in people. Not that this is always a virtue. Fleas are interested in dogs. P. J. O'ROURKE

———————————— POLITICS ————————————
Politics, *n.* Strife of interests masquerading as a contest of principles.
AMBROSE BIERCE

Politics is the diversion of trivial men who, when they succeed at it, become important in the eyes of more trivial men.   GEORGE JEAN NATHAN

Being in politics is like being a football coach; you have to be smart enough to understand the game, and dumb enough to think it's important.
                                                EUGENE MCCARTHY

The standard of intellect in politics is so low that men of moderate mental capacity have to stoop in order to reach it.   HILLAIRE BELLOC

All politics are based on the indifference of the majority.   JAMES RESTON

Politics is not the art of the possible. It consists in choosing between the disastrous and the unpalatable.   JOHN KENNETH GALBRAITH

It makes no difference who you vote for—the two parties are really one party representing four percent of the people.   GORE VIDAL

Nothing is so admirable in politics as a short memory.
                                            JOHN KENNETH GALBRAITH

It is dangerous for a national candidate to say things that people might remember.   EUGENE MCCARTHY

Politics is the art of looking for trouble, finding it whether it exists or not, diagnosing it incorrectly, and applying the wrong remedy.
                                                    ERNEST BENN

Politics is the skilled use of blunt objects.   LESTER B. PEARSON

Nothing can so alienate a voter from the political system as backing a winning candidate.   MARK B. COHEN

I have never found in a long experience of politics that criticism is ever inhibited by ignorance.   HAROLD MACMILLAN

Politics is perhaps the only profession for which no preparation is thought necessary.   ROBERT LOUIS STEVENSON

The more you observe politics, the more you've got to admit that each party is worse than the other.   WILL ROGERS

Politics makes estranged bedfellows.   GOODMAN ACE

THE POOR

We who are liberal and progressive know that the poor are our equals in every sense except that of being equal to us.   LIONEL TRILLING

The poor don't know that their function in life is to exercise our generosity.
                                                        JEAN-PAUL SARTRE

It is only the poor who are forbidden to beg.   ANATOLE FRANCE

PORNOGRAPHY

I don't think pornography is very harmful, but it is terribly, terribly boring.
                                                            NOEL COWARD

My reaction to porno films is as follows: After the first ten minutes, I want to go home and screw. After the first twenty minutes, I never want to screw again as long as I live.   ERICA JONG

POSTERITY

Leaving behind books is even more beautiful—there are far too many children.
MARGUERITE YOURCENAR

Posterity is as likely to be wrong as anybody else.   HEYWOOD BROUN

Posterity is just around the corner.   GEORGE S. KAUFMAN

POWER

If absolute power corrupts absolutely, does absolute powerlessness make you pure?   HARRY SHEARER

PRAYER

Pray, *n.* To ask the laws of the universe be annulled on behalf of a single petitioner confessedly unworthy.   AMBROSE BIERCE

I squirm when I see athletes praying before a game. Don't they realize that if God took sports seriously He never would have created George Steinbrenner?
MARK RUSSELL

Forgive, O Lord, my little jokes on Thee, and I'll forgive Thy great big joke on me....Forgive me my nonsense as I also forgive the nonsense of those who think they talk sense.   ROBERT FROST

PREGNANCY

If pregnancy were a book they would cut the last two chapters.
NORA EPHRON

PREJUDICE

I am free of all prejudices. I hate everyone equally.   W. C. FIELDS

I don't like principles. I prefer prejudices.   OSCAR WILDE

A great many people think they are thinking when they are merely rearranging their prejudices.   WILLIAM JAMES

──────────────── PRESIDENCY ────────────────

The men the American people admire most extravagantly are the most daring liars; the men they detest most violently are those who try to tell them the truth. A Galileo could no more be elected President of the United States than he could be elected Pope of Rome. Both high posts are reserved for men favored by God with an extraordinary genius for swathing the bitter facts of life in bandages of soft illusion.   H. L. MENCKEN

The best reason I can think of for not running for president of the United States is that you have to shave twice a day.   ADLAI STEVENSON

If I were the president, I'd bring some *life* to the White House. The theme of my administration would be summarized by the catchy and inspirational phrase: "Hey, the Government Is Beyond Human Control, So Let's at Least Have Some Fun with It."   DAVE BARRY

We need a president who's fluent in at least one language.   BUCK HENRY

If presidents don't do it to their wives, they do it to the country.   MEL BROOKS

Any American who is prepared to run for president should automatically, by definition, by disqualified from ever doing so.   GORE VIDAL

These presidential ninnies should stick to throwing out baseballs and leave the important matters to serious people.   GORE VIDAL

When I was a boy I was told that anybody could become President; I'm beginning to believe it.   CLARENCE DARROW

In my lifetime, we've gone from Eisenhower to George W. Bush. We've gone from John Kennedy to Albert Gore. Now if that's evolution, I believe that in about twelve years, we're going to be voting for plants.   LEWIS BLACK

As democracy is perfected, the office of president represents, more and more closely, the inner soul of the people. On some great and glorious day the plain folks of the land will reach their heart's desire at last and the White House will be adorned by a downright moron.   H. L. MENCKEN

—————————————— **PRINCIPLES** ——————————————

You can't learn too soon that the most useful thing about a principle is that it can always be sacrificed to expediency.   W. SOMERSET MAUGHAM

Principles have no real force except when one is well fed.   MARK TWAIN

It is easier to fight for one's principles than to live up to them.
                                                         ALFRED ADLER

I like persons better than principles and I like persons with no principles better than anything else in the world.   OSCAR WILDE

When a man says he approves of something in principle, it mean he hasn't the slightest intention of putting it into practice.   OTTO VON BISMARCK

—————————————— **PRIVACY** ——————————————

Privacy—you can't find it anywhere, not even if you want to hang yourself.
                                                         MENANDER

PRIZES

The Pulitzer Prize was awarded to Saul Bellow for fiction only after Bellow had won the Nobel Prize, which must have seemed like being given a cup of warmed-over instant coffee twenty minutes after having drunk the world's most expensive cognac.   JOSEPH EPSTEIN

PROCRASTINATION

Never put off until tomorrow what you can do the day after tomorrow.
MARK TWAIN

PROCREATION

Any man who, having a child or children he can't support, proceeds to have another should be sterilized at once.   H. L. MENCKEN

PRODUCER

"Nervous producer" is a redundancy. So is "complaining producer."
MORLEY SAFER

PROFANITY

Under certain circumstances, profanity provides a relief denied even to prayer.
MARK TWAIN

There ought to be a room in every house to swear in.   MARK TWAIN

PROGRESS

What we call progress is the exchange of one nuisance for another nuisance.
HAVELOCK ELLIS

All progress is based upon a universal innate desire on the part of every organism to live beyond its income.   SAMUEL BUTLER

Progress celebrates Pyrrhic victories over nature and makes purses out of human skin.   KARL KRAUS

Progress is the mother of problems.   G. K. CHESTERTON

Progress was all right. Only it went on too long.   JAMES THURBER

Usually, terrible things that are done with the excuse that progress requires them are not really progress at all, but just terrible things.
                                                                                          RUSSELL BAKER

—————————————— PROMISCUITY ——————————————
A promiscuous person is someone who is getting more sex than you are.
                                                                                          VICTOR LOWNES

—————————————— PROSPERITY ——————————————
Everything in the world may be endured except continued prosperity.
                                                                    JOHANN WOLFGANG VON GOETHE

—————————————— PROTESTANTISM ——————————————
Definition of Protestantism: hemiplegic paralysis of Christianity—and of reason.   FRIEDRICH WILHELM NIETZSCHE

The chief contribution of Protestantism to human thought is its massive proof that God is a bore.   H. L. MENCKEN

—————————————— PSYCHIATRY ——————————————
Why should I tolerate a perfect stranger at the bedside of my mind?
                                                                                          VLADIMIR NABOKOV

The relation between psychiatrists and other kinds of lunatic is more or less the relation of a convex folly to a concave one.   KARL KRAUS

Psychiatry enables us to correct our faults by confessing our parents' shortcomings.   LAURENCE J. PETER

I suspect that our own faith in psychiatry will seem as touchingly quaint to the future as our grandparents' belief in phrenology seems now to us.
                                        GORE VIDAL

If the Prince of Peace should come to earth, one of the first things he would do would be to put psychiatrists in their place.   ALDOUS HUXLEY

—————————— PSYCHOANALYSIS ——————————

Psychotherapy: the theory that the patient will probably get well anyhow, and is certainly a damned ijjit.   H. L. MENCKEN

Psychoanalysis makes quite simple people feel they're complex.   S. N. BEHRMAN

Let the credulous and the vulgar continue to believe that all mental woes can be cured by a daily application of old Greek myths to their private parts.
                                        VLADIMIR NABOKOV

Psychoanalysis is confession without absolution.   G. K. CHESTERTON

I once asked Woody Allen how his psychoanalysis was going after twenty-five years. He said, "Slowly."   JOHN CLEESE

Freud is the father of psychoanalysis. It has no mother.   GERMAINE GREER

I just want to make one brief statement about psychoanalysis: "Fuck Dr. Freud."
OSCAR LEVANT

––––––––––––––––––– PSYCHOBABBLE –––––––––––––––––––

To err is dysfunctional, to forgive codependent.   BERTON AVERRE

I will not bond. I will not share. I refuse to nurture.   DENIS LEARY

––––––––––––––––––– THE PUBLIC –––––––––––––––––––

The public is a ferocious beast: One must either chain it up or flee from it.
VOLTAIRE

The public is wonderfully tolerant. It forgives everything except genius.
OSCAR WILDE

The public will believe anything, so long as it is not founded on truth.
EDITH SITWELL

The public is a fool.   ALEXANDER POPE

––––––––––––––––––– PUBLIC FIGURES –––––––––––––––––––

Today's public figures can no longer write their own speeches or books, and there is some evidence that they can't read them either.   GORE VIDAL

––––––––––––––––––– PUBLIC OPINION –––––––––––––––––––

Public opinion, in its raw state, gushes out in the immemorial form of the mob's fear. It is piped into central factories, and there it is flavored and colored, and put into cans.   H. L. MENCKEN

One should respect public opinion insofar as is necessary to avoid starvation and keep out of prison, but anything that goes beyond this is voluntary submission to an unnecessary tyranny. BERTRAND RUSSELL

PUBLIC RESTROOM

When you walk into the public restroom, why is everything fucking wet?
DANE COOK

PUBLIC TELEVISION

Public Television: where a hundred people work so thirty can watch.
PHIL HENDRIE

PUBLISHER

One of the signs of Napoleon's greatness is the fact that he once had a publisher shot. SIEGFRIED UNSELD

PUNCTUALITY

Punctuality is the virtue of the bored. EVELYN WAUGH

PUNNING

Hanging is too good for a man who makes puns; he should be drawn and quoted. FRED ALLEN

PURITANISM

The Puritan hated bear-baiting, not because it gave pain to the bear, but because it gave pleasure to the spectators. THOMAS BABINGTON MACAULAY

Puritanism…helps us enjoy our misery while we are inflicting it on others.
MARCEL OPHULS

There is only one honest impulse at the bottom of Puritanism, and that is the impulse to punish the man with a superior capacity for happiness.

H. L. MENCKEN

PUBLISHERS

As repressed sadists are supposed to become policemen or butchers, so those with irrational fear of life become publishers.   CYRIL CONNOLLY

I could show you all society poisoned by this class of person—a class unknown to the ancients—who, not being able to find any honest occupation, be it manual labor or service, and unluckily knowing how to read and write, become the brokers of literature, live on our works, steal our manuscripts, falsify them, and sell them.   VOLTAIRE

MARGO KAUFMAN

Redhead

Margo Kaufman (1953–2000) was a widely published columnist, the Hollywood correspondent for *Pug Talk*, and a frequent commentator on National Public Radio. Her books include *Clara: The Story of the Pug Who Ruled My Life*, *This Damn House: My Subcontract with America*, and a collection of columns, *1 800 Am I Nuts?*

JW: You've done magazine and newspaper columns on a variety of issues. For example, you recently tackled the recession from an unusual perspective.
MK: This is going to sound awful but, the worse the economy, the harder

it gets for pets. Because a pet is a high-expense item. It's not so bad for the first six to eight years, when the pet is still cute; but when the pet gets older, then the pet becomes an economic factor. Every time you take an old pet to the vet, you're looking at a minimum of $100. Vets are like cab drivers—you're at their mercy. You can't budget, say, $50 for the pet this month because if the pet should suddenly get an itch, you're looking at $300 in an instant. You're struggling to pay your MasterCard and your mortgage and you're not buying new clothes—you're not doing anything for yourself, and suddenly your pet gets an eye infection and it's $40 a month for the drops. [My pug] Stella's drops are $40 a month, but can she see me? Nooooo. She can't see anything that isn't edible, but just to keep her little eyes clear and mucus-free, forty bucks a month.

JW: Have you considered—

MK: The vet absolutely refuses to put the dog to sleep. I have two pugs and I love them and I've been a very good mother and they've had a glorious life, but they're both thirteen years old and it's rough. Stella has bad arthritis and she can't walk much farther than the mailbox, which is right outside the door. She basically sleeps all day, except the twenty minutes when she's eating. But the vet refuses to put her to sleep as long as she's "still interested in her dish." This dog would come up from the grave to eat. My vet says there are "still things we could try." He doesn't want to try anything under $200.

JW: Have you thought of changing vets?

MK: What am I going to do? Pick up the phone, call around, and go, "Hi. Will you kill my dog?"

JW: What exactly is it about pugs that appeals to you?

MK: They're living proof that God has a sense of humor.

JW: Some people find them a bit unattractive.

MK: I think they're cute. They look like little gargoyles or gremlins. I think the pug's charm is its aesthetic quality. Anywhere a pug is, a pug makes you smile. If a pug's on a sofa, it looks ornamental. When you take them out-side, they're like lawn art. You take the pug to the country, you put the pug in the desert, you walk it on the beach, it's money in the bank of good cheer.

JW: But how are they as pets?

MK: They have a Jewish princess personality, squared. My pugs have the greatest sense of entitlement of anything I've ever known. I wish I were a pug. I wish I had their personality. They don't have any idea that they should do anything in exchange for what they get. I always try to be a good sport, and it's my worst quality. The pug is never a good sport.

JW: You wrote a piece recently in which you said that there are certain things you don't want to hear about—

MK: I don't want to know if people are bulimic, I really don't. I went out to lunch with a friend and she told me she was bulimic. What was I supposed to say, "Let's go in the ladies' room and throw up together"? I've always had a weak stomach, and if somebody gets sick, I get sick, too. So when she got up in the middle of lunch and went to the bathroom, what was I supposed to think? I'll never invite her to dinner again.

A friend of mine is seeing a guy who goes to a different "anonymous" group every day, and she says it's a wonder he still knows his last name. I think it's wonderful that all these people are getting help, but do I need to know about it? I never drank, so why do I have to sober up vicariously? I realize it's fashionable to be a drug addict or a drunk or a sexaholic, but I'd rather be out of that loop.

Sensitive men are also a problem. My nightmare is that my husband will want to go to a Robert Bly seminar. The day he starts telling me how he feels...

JW: You don't want him to share his feelings? I thought that was what women want.

MK: Women only want men to share certain feelings, like how they feel about us, if it's positive: "Honey, you're the most wonderful person in the world and

I couldn't live without you." Women analyze everything to death—every emotional nuance. If men did that, it would be a nightmare. Think about when a guy has a cold: A woman's cold and a man's cold are not the same thing. A woman's cold is a minor complaint. A woman's cold is a cheap excuse to get out of sex. But a man's cold is pneumonia. A man's cold requires major intervention. A woman gets a cold, the flu, the guy goes out and works on the car. A man gets a cold and it's the end of the world. Now imagine that attitude, only with feelings. It's asking for trouble. I also think it's a mistake to expect a man to understand your feelings or give you any kind of emotional support.

JW: Are there any instances in which men are good at expressing their feelings?

MK: Yes, when they get "head-pop." Men go through cycles where their head gets larger and larger. When a man is involved in an exciting project, his head becomes larger and larger and he gets very full of himself. Then, one day someone says something negative to him—it can be really minor, like "I don't like that report," or "I don't like the way you put the commas in that sentence," and the guy's head pops. You can chart your relationship with a man by how big his head is on a given day. Like the phases of the moon. In the early stages, when the head is just beginning to puff up, you can really make progress, but when the head gets big again, you have to wait until it pops and then start over. Unfortunately, the head always re-inflates.

I think the best way to communicate with a man is just to tell him what you want. Women expect guys to be mind readers, but they don't run on the same program. For example, women all know what to say to each other: You call any woman and you say, "I'm not feeling very cute now, I'm bloated and I have cramps," the woman will say exactly the right thing. *Any* woman—pick one off the street. Say this to a man and he will always say the wrong thing. If you say, "I'm bloated and I have cramps," he'll say, "Yeah, you do look a little puffy." Men never know what to say. They don't know their own feelings, so how could they know yours?

JW: Is that because of the male ego?

MK: The male ego knows no bounds, and I want one desperately. I would give anything for one. Anything that happens to a man is the most important thing in the world. It doesn't matter what you do, it doesn't matter what happens to you—it's not as important as what happens to him. You cannot win. You can never be more *x*—fill it in—than a guy. You can't be happier, sadder, more depressed, more successful, busier, sicker. It seems to be a survival mechanism, and I don't mean it as a criticism, I mean it almost in admiration.

JW: Do you like sports?

MK: Mostly as a male soporific. I was trained by my mother to be a good date, which meant I learned the basics of all the popular sports. I think women make a big mistake complaining about sports, because with sports you always know exactly where your husband/boyfriend/lover is: in front of the TV. They're not doing anything harmful, they're sitting there peacefully for an hour, hour and a half.

I'm sort of fascinated by trash sports, like tractor pulling or dwarf tossing. Are people really that bored? There's cat chasing, where sky divers throw the cat out of the plane and try to catch it. And hacky sack, where the brain-dead kick around a beanbag. Or mountain biking: You go out on a trail for a nice hike and there they are, huffing and puffing. They completely ruin it for hikers. On the way up they look like little rats on a treadmill, and then they come speeding down at you at about ninety miles an hour. They wear those stupid pants that no one in America looks good in. To be a mountain biker you have to have serious spandex. It's amazing: Women who rejected the panty girdle are now happily encasing themselves like sausage.

JW: Why do they wear them?

MK: Just to show they can. It's like wearing a hat. If you put a hat on, you get a certain number of points for just having the guts to wear it.

JW: Do you like to shop?

MK: For me, shopping is a transcendental experience. It can cure anything, as long as you shop for the right reasons. Like, you're depressed, you're happy, you're sad, you're uncomfortable, you're afraid, you're a success, you're a failure. See, the only thing in life you can control is your wardrobe. You can't control your friends and you can't control your house and you can't control your career—but as long as the cleaner returns it, you have complete control over what you put on your back in the morning.

JW: What about shopping for things other than clothes?

MK: I think it's strange how expensive and ugly things are. It's not so much sticker shock, it's aesthetic shock. I mean, who decided that appliances in America should be wood grain? *Simulated* wood grain. Who wants an oak toaster? Do they have wood-grain Xerox machines? Of course not. Then why are all kitchen appliances wood grain? Is it supposed to conjure up the hearth?

I think bad taste should be a felony. They should arrest whoever invented "decorator colors." A decorator color is a color that is not found in nature. Like avocado, there's nothing that's avocado, not even an avocado.

JW: And food shopping?

MK: I hate markets, except for Gelson's [an upscale supermarket chain in Southern California]. That's God's market. I like to go, get the few items I need, and leave. My premarriage refrigerator was just fruit, bagels, frozen yogurt, and Diet Coke. But my husband is a maniac. When we were first married, he would go to four different markets to find the cheapest peach. It made me insane. And when I put the toilet paper in the cart, he would multiply the squares times the price times the *ply* and put it back on the shelf. Life is too short to count the squares on the toilet paper. Now we've been together long enough that if I go to the market with him, I only buy the sanctified brands—the ones he has preordained the cheapest.

And he has another interesting habit: Whenever we're about to get in the checkout line he disappears in search of the elusive whatever, which means that I have to unload all the groceries and check them through. Invariably all the items are rung up, he's still not back, the person behind me is hitting my shins with their cart, it's freezing in the market, they're playing the instrumental version of "Yellow Submarine," and he's nowhere to be found. So I have him paged. I do it all the time now. It's great. He just slinks right over. He's much better about sticking with me since I started the paging system.

JW: Is he any better in restaurants?

MK: Well, I'm a boring eater, I always order the same thing, and he's really adventurous. Whenever he's mad at me—you know how there's one accusation in every marriage that gets pulled out when everything else fails?—the charge he throws at me is "You don't like Mexican food." The ultimate indictment. I'm sorry, honey, but I just don't wake up in the middle of the night with a hankering for flautas. Everybody is so damned sophisticated about food these days. The other night we went to a *Yucatán* Mexican restaurant! Is this necessary? Suddenly people who can't find Mexico on a map know the difference between chorizos and chimichanga. And people judge you by what you order for lunch. You might as well shoot yourself if you order a chef's salad, and if you order meat in some circles, you're doomed. It's best to order something you can't pronounce, or something raw. Raw always scores big points. For lunch, it used to be either a hamburger, the deli, or Chinese. Now it's Ethiopian food.

JW: Overnight houseguests are another problem. How do you handle them?

MK: I won't have them. My sister spent the night recently and she had the audacity to take a shower in my bathroom. I'm not good in the morning—nothing positive has ever happened to me before noon. So when I woke up and I went to the bathroom and saw that she was there, I wanted to cut her heart out. Houseguests are just too much trouble. Does anybody really want somebody staying in their house? If you live in a big house and have servants, okay, I can understand it. But if you live in a single-family dwelling, a houseguest is a problem. The only exception is if you're in some kind of dysfunctional relationship where you need a buffer. Those people *like* houseguests. Ever notice that when the marriage is breaking up they invite you to stay with them for weeks? "We don't care, you can have our bed."

JW: And then there's the ultimate domestic inconvenience, remodeling.

MK: A nightmare. It's like houseguests to the twenty-eighth power. Strangers come into your house with saws. There you are, in *your* territory, and strangers are there with all these destructive instruments and you have no idea whether they know what they're doing. They come and they demolish and they track dirt and they make a lot of noise and, in the end, it's never quite right. But you don't care anymore because you're beaten down and broke. And I work at home, so I'm all alone. My husband always says, "Honey, I'm going to the office. They're going to raze the house today, but don't worry, it won't be intrusive." That's what my husband always says, "It won't be intrusive." Which means I won't be able to do anything remotely normal for a year.

Home remodeling is the epitome of a lose-lose situation. Oh, you *might* get one of those *Architectural Digest* results—maybe. But it still won't be exactly what you wanted. It will look good in the magazine because they'll come and put flowers everywhere and arrange the ashtrays at ninety-degree angles, but if you really think about it, when you see those houses that have been redone, you don't know what the people thought they were going to get. And you don't know the miserable life they led while they were doing it. You don't know whether they're in debt for the rest of their lives, or whether they're still speaking to each other. The problem with home remodeling is one word: dream. When you get your car fixed, you don't expect your dream car. When you get your teeth fixed, you don't expect your dream teeth. But when you remodel, you expect your dream house.

JW: And you've written about your neighbors in Venice [California].

MK: My neighbors are very strange. I remarked to one of them the other day that I hadn't seen him for a while, and he said, "Me and Sally and the baby have moved down the street." I said, "Oh, is Sally your wife?" (I didn't know him that well.) And he said, "No, she's sort of my friend." "And the baby, is it yours?" "Well, I'm not sure, it could be." Then I asked him why he was wearing a wedding ring, and he replied that he had married this Vietnamese girl so she could get her green card but now she's in New Zealand. The scariest part about it is, that was a normal conversation in my neighborhood. My husband has lived in Venice for a long time, and he doesn't think anybody is strange. We had this woman next door—a nutcase—who had a cat named Spot. Every day she would put Spot in a little basket and lower him into our yard, which he was using as a litter box. She would stand on her balcony watching him dig up our flowers crooning, "Spot, Spot." It drove me nuts. My husband, of course, thought she was just lonely—the male rationale for all weird female behavior—and told me I should be nicer to her. I actually felt guilty.

Then one day I heard the shot. There was a woman all dressed for success—with the unmistakable carmine talons of a real estate agent—bleeding in our driveway. Our neighbor, Lonely Girl, had shot her in the leg because she was seeing her ex-husband. I know that doesn't make sense, but nothing about the neighbor ever did. The paramedics were working on the victim and her purse started ringing. She said, "Get it, get the phone." The paramedic said, "Lie down, you're in shock." She said, "I'm in escrow."

The neighbor stood on the balcony and called to my husband. She said, "I shot her." He said, "Don't tell me." The police took her away. I got stuck feeding the cat.

JW: Aside from neighbor problems, do you like working at home?
MK: Yes, but it has its drawbacks. For one, nobody believes you're ever doing anything. They think you just sit around all day and eat bonbons. They call you at any time and expect you to talk, expect you to take them

to the airport, pick up the cleaning, do the laundry. If you work in an office, you have a secretary and office workers and a Xerox machine, all these ego props to enhance your sense that you're really working, that what you do is absolutely vital. So, when the person who works in an office says, "I had a terrible day, the copier didn't work, Sylvia broke up with her boyfriend, the phones went down," these are perceived to be terrible tragedies. But if you say, "I've had nine rejections in the last twenty-five minutes," the reply is, "Did you get to the cleaners?"

I once had a job in an office where I did absolutely nothing. I went there every day but there was nothing for me to do. I would just sit there. I finally had to quit because it was making me homicidal. Then I began to work at home again, where I was doing much more work, but it was perceived that I had left my "real" job. That's how it is: If you say you work at home, people think you're a failed real estate agent. Not that I think being a writer is a career people respect. Almost everyone thinks they could write if only they had the time. People think they can do it, so they don't really think what you do is anything special. They think you're getting away with something.

JW: You do a lot of travel writing, most recently about something you call "vacation bravado."

MK: When people go on vacation, they do things they would never do at home. If somebody were to say to you, "Hey, let's climb a volcano!" at home, you would look at them like they were crazy. But if you're in another country, up you go! And when you get there, there's a crowd of people all dressed alike: The women in cute little shorts, the guys with cameras. Have you seen that Reebok commercial where they climb the pyramid in Guatemala? This gorgeous woman going *boing, boing, boing,* right up to the top? Well, I was *at* that pyramid, and women aren't going *boing,* they're clinging to the sides and begging their husbands not to take their picture till they get to the bottom.

So far I have been convinced on vacation to climb a volcano and a pyramid and to ride a donkey down a canyon. The only thing in my defense, I haven't para-sailed. Can you imagine being a human kite in your own neighborhood? You'd never do it. People will do anything for the pictures. They risk their lives for the Fotomat.

JW: What about the perils of getting there in the first place?

MK: I don't like buses. To ride a bus is to wonder how you're going to die. Is the bus going to break down? Is the driver going to run it off a cliff? Is the guy in the next seat going to stab you? Are you going to get off the bus somewhere you shouldn't and never be heard from again? Think about it. Think of the form of transportation where there's the most mass death. Bus.

JW: But you do like to travel, and you like to get off the beaten track, judging by your recent travel pieces about Thailand and Indonesia.

MK: There's no such thing as off the beaten track anymore. Anywhere you go, they have it marketed. Thailand is more marketed than most places. Thailand is Disneyland. Go to any part of Thailand and they have *rides*: a ride on a raft, a ride on an elephant, a trip to a butterfly farm. And when you land in Bali, after being on the plane for twenty-four hours, the first thing you see is a Colonel Sanders. There's no place in the world where you can't get Coca-Cola. They may not have indoor plumbing, but all the shops have stacks of beer and cigarettes.

JW: What's your policy on hotel rooms?

MK: I love luxury hotels, but I'm married to someone who would stay in a youth hostel. We've gradually reached a compromise: I don't pick where we go and I don't pick how we get there, but I've retained veto power on the accommodations. Call me fussy, but I demand clean sheets and a private bathroom.

JW: Do you travel light?

MK: Not really, but my husband does. But a funny thing about people who travel light: They invariably travel with someone like me who's lugging around a set of Vuitton luggage. My husband leaves with one little bag, but he puts anything he might need in my suitcase. And he's always buying things—stone carvings, jackets, rugs—and putting them in my suitcase. People who travel light make me nervous. People who travel light are the same people who will say to you with a straight face, "Honey, do you have an inflatable pillow? Do you have a book light?"

JW: Does he at least give you credit for carrying all the stuff?

MK: No. When I'm going to, let's say, a malaria kingdom, I first go to the doctor and get every medication I might possibly need, and my doctor sends me away with prescriptions for anything that could possibly happen in the jungle. And my husband accuses me of carrying around a small pharmacy. But in Thailand he got dysentery—for a man it's dysentery, for a woman it's diarrhea—and I suddenly realized I had the medicine for it. What a wonderful moment when he crawled over and begged for it.

JW: One last question: how do you feel about bottle redheads?

MK: I wish they would round up all these fake redheads. They're everywhere. I used to be the only redhead in my dance class, but now there are all these women with hair the color of Ethan Allen furniture. Cherrywood. Mahogany. These fake redheads did not pay their dues. They never got called "Freckles" or "Carrot Top." They never had to swim with a T-shirt to avoid getting sunburned. They weren't constantly asked by sleazy men on the street, "Where did you get that red hair from?" "Is it real?" And now they all walk around with this hot-shit attitude, which no real redhead has. Real redheads are incredibly direct and usually very nice. These fake redheads are everywhere. Yesterday my sister called to say she was thinking of dyeing her hair red. I warned her that it would seriously affect our relationship. Am I done?

ABSENT FRIENDS

Her features did not seem to know the value of teamwork.   GEORGE ADE

She was a professional athlete—of the tongue.   ALDOUS HUXLEY

She's descended from a long line her mother listened to.   GYPSY ROSE LEE

Nature played a cruel trick on her by giving her a waxed moustache.
ALAN BENNETT

She looked as if she had been poured into her clothes and had forgotten to
say "when."   P. G. WODEHOUSE

The finest woman that ever walked the streets.   MAE WEST

She's been on more laps than a napkin.   WALTER WINCHELL

When he dances he's all feet and when he stops he's all hands.
ARTHUR SHEEKMAN

Although he is a very poor fielder, he is a very poor hitter.   RING LARDNER

If not actually disgruntled, he was far from being gruntled.
P. G. WODEHOUSE

He may be a son-of-a-bitch, but he's our son-of-a-bitch.

FRANKLIN D. ROOSEVELT

He can compress the most words into the smallest ideas of any man I ever met.

ABRAHAM LINCOLN

He had occasional flashes of silence that made his conversation perfectly delightful.

SYDNEY SMITH

There are grammatical errors even in his silence.

STANISLAW J. LEC

He continued to be an infant long after he ceased to be a prodigy.

ROBERT MOSES

He had delusions of adequacy.

WALTER KERR

He is a sheep in sheep's clothing.

WINSTON CHURCHILL

I've just learned about his illness. Let's hope it's nothing trivial.

IRVIN S. COBB

He was like a cock who thought the sun had risen to hear him crow.

GEORGE ELIOT

He has all the virtues I dislike and none of the vices I admire.

WINSTON CHURCHILL

He doesn't know the meaning of the word fear, but then again he doesn't know the meaning of most words.

ANONYMOUS

He knew the precise psychological moment when to say nothing.
OSCAR WILDE

He fell in love with himself at first sight and it is a passion to which he has always been faithful.
ANTHONY POWELL

His words leap across rivers and mountains, but his thoughts are still only six inches long.
E. B. WHITE

No one can have a higher opinion of him than I have, and I think he's a dirty little beast.
W. S. GILBERT

He is not only dull himself, he is the cause of dullness in others.
SAMUEL JOHNSON

Some cause happiness wherever they go; others whenever they go.
OSCAR WILDE

She always tells stories in the present vindictive.
TOM PEACE

Remember, men, we're fighting for this woman's honor, which is more than she ever did.
GROUCHO MARX, in *Duck Soup*

You could throw her in the river and skim ugly for three days.
ANONYMOUS

In order to avoid being called a flirt, she always yielded easily.
CHARLES DE TALLEYRAND-PÉRIGORD

Called upon to eulogize an acquaintance he detested, Voltaire at first refused but was finally persuaded to say a few words: "I have just been informed that he is dead. He was a hardy patriot, a gifted writer, a faithful friend and an affectionate husband and father—provided he is really dead."

His imagination resembled the wings of an ostrich. It enabled him to run, though not to soar. THOMAS BABINGTON MACAULAY

He has Van Gogh's ear for music. BILLY WILDER

She's afraid that if she leaves, she'll become the life of the party.
GROUCHO MARX

She was a singer who had to take any note above A with her eyebrows.
MONTAGUE GLASS

He was a gentleman who was generally spoken of as having nothing a year, paid quarterly. ROBERT SMITH SURTEES

His mind is so open that the wind whistles through it.
HEYWOOD BROUN

He hasn't an enemy in the world—but all his friends hate him.
EDDIE CANTOR

His mother should have thrown him away and kept the stork. MAE WEST

If brains was lard, he couldn't grease a pan.
BUDDY EBSEN, in *The Beverly Hillbillies*

He's a fine friend. He stabs you in the front.

LEONARD LOUIS LEVINSON

The louder he talked of his honor, the faster we counted our spoons.

RALPH WALDO EMERSON

I don't like her. But don't misunderstand me: My dislike is purely platonic.

HERBERT BEERBOHM TREE

He's the only man I ever knew who had rubber pockets so he could steal soup.

WILSON MIZNER

His lack of education is more than compensated for by his keenly developed moral bankruptcy.

WOODY ALLEN

I feel so miserable without you, it's almost like having you here.

STEPHEN BISHOP

QUOTES ON "Q"

QUOTATIONS

Quotation, n: The act of repeating erroneously the words of another.
AMBROSE BEIRCE

The ability to quote is a serviceable substitute for wit.
W. SOMERSET MAUGHAM

Stay at home in your mind. Don't recite other people's opinions. I hate quotations. Tell me what you know.
RALPH WALDO EMERSON

The surest way to make a monkey out of a man is to quote him.
ROBERT BENCHLEY

It is unbecoming for young men to utter maxims.
ARISTOTLE

Most people are other people. Their thoughts are someone else's opinions, their lives a mimicry, their passions a quotation.
OSCAR WILDE

A facility for quotation covers the absence of original thought.
DOROTHY L. SAYERS

Be careful; with quotations, you can damn anything.
ANDRÉ MALRAUX

It's better to be quotable than to be honest.   TOM STOPPARD

Most anthologists…of quotations are like those who eat cherries…first picking the best ones and winding up by eating everything.
                                        NICOLAS CHAMFORT

CARRIE FISHER

Aghast in Her Own House

Carrie Fisher is the author of *The Best Awful, Delusions of Grandma, Surrender the Pink,* and *Postcards from the Edge,* as well as numerous short stories and screenplays. She is also known for her portrayal of Princess Leia in the Star Wars pictures.

CF (Entering the room): So I had a dream last night in which someone spoke the words "Aghast in her own house," and then I dreamed I was on the bottom of the pool, drowning, and I didn't have any toes! You need those toes to spring up to the surface, you know.

JW: Do you put your dreams into your novels?

CF: I usually can't remember them; what's left I certainly plumb, I suppose is the word, but I really have trouble remembering them.

JW: Because of the drugs?

CF: I couldn't say. I actually remember things much more vividly that happened when I was *on* drugs than anything when I was off them. I always made it a point to remember, in case someone asked, "Are you on acid?" "I am *not* on acid and to prove it I will tell you what you're wearing and what you're thinking and how you feel."

JW: I get the impression that you don't entirely regret your experience with what, acid and Percodan?

CF: I had a good time.

JW: Why such a strange combination?

CF: Percodan, I needed; acid, I liked. First everything hurts and then nothing makes sense. I wanted it either melted down or blown away. Medicine: "Take two of these and you'll feel better." Well, if two make me feel better, eight will make me feel fantastic, and sixteen will make me feel nothing at all. There's a great line of Jerry Garcia's: "It cuts away care." I mean, could any of us care less? Yes, if properly medicated, you could care far less. And then it comes crashing back.

JW: No free lunch?

CF: No, and quite a piper to have to pay.

JW: And you did and—

CF: Here I am in the House that Acid Decorated.

JW: Did you rely exclusively on your own drug experiences in writing Postcards from the Edge?

CF: Not entirely. People told me stuff. I was Joan of Narc, the patron saint of the addict. Just after I got divorced I went on a wine date with this very funny writer who said that he'd read my book and felt that we'd gone out before and had split up because of something I did, but that he had forgiven me and so now we could go out again. People think that everything I write is hyperautobiographical, which is so and not so. I have friends who still think I shot heroin because Alex [a character in *Postcards from the Edge*] did. I guess it's inevitable, so you might as well have fun with it. I once facetiously said I was going to write about a lesbian grandmother who seduces her whole family, and the press took me seriously. They thought I was talking about my Grandma Red! Fortunately, she thought it was funny, so I'm relieved. I "outed" her at the age of eighty.

JW: You've been outed yourself.

CF: Yes, they outed Penny Marshall and me! Both of us talk so much, I can just imagine the moment it happened: "Will you shut up already about scouting locations? I'll go down on you if you just—where's your vibrator? What, we're going to have to hear about the casting thing again? Just lay down!" I've always thought that sex is about *contact*, and that I could achieve conversationally what most people achieve carnally, so why go through all that messiness? Why put myself, at five-one and a half, up against somebody who's going to be taller than I am? I mean, let's face it, I'm going to be at a disadvantage. *They* fuck and *you* get fucked. It's psychologically and philosophically incorrect for me. But then I come from a long line of short, frigid women. But if I were a lesbian, maybe I could find a girl my height. I've always said that I wanted to find myself before somebody bigger did. Which isn't hard at five-one and a half. Before I left for India, Treat Williams said to me, "I hope you find what you're looking for." And I hope I don't have to take it back and get it in my size.

JW: Didn't you sort of find yourself when you got off drugs? In fact, don't you credit rehab with saving your life?

CF: I credit overdose. I credit dramatic incident that very graphically tells you, "This isn't working." I credit that with *getting* to rehab, and rehab was unfortunately one of the most interesting things that ever happened to me. Which says something about my life. I would never have met people like that. And I was humiliated. It really tears you down. Which is good. I'd spent a good five years telling you I wasn't a drug addict, that I was tired, that I was on antihistamines, that I was anything but an addict. In rehab I began to watch that denial process. It's the same mechanism that functions when you're in a destructive relationship. You just watch while your brain vomits up the piece of news of why you're not really doing what you are in fact doing.

JW: What about the "higher power" aspect?

CF: I believe in God and strong turbulence. I also call my mother, who says, "Well, you've had a good life." Thanks, Mom. I love the idea of God, but it's not stylistically in keeping with the way I function. I would describe myself as an enthusiastic agnostic who would be happy to be shown that there is a God. I can see that people who believe in God are happier. My brother is. My dad is, too. But I *doubt.* I mean, come on, we're really going to go to Heaven? Even if we are, I don't have anything to wear. So I don't completely get the higher-power thing, but I know it's helped friends of mine enormously, so I would never try to tear it down.

JW: What did you think of the Just Say No campaign?

CF: If I hadn't been taking drugs already, it would have made me start immediately. You can't say to teenagers, "It's bad. We only did it because we were stupid and it wasn't fun." It was fun, and they know we're lying.

JW: Didn't you once say that humor is your armor because you actually take things very seriously?

CF: That's my most hilarious gag. I think everything is very, very heavy, so I joke about everything. The worse the situation, the better the gag. I had a friend staying with me who had AIDS, and we had lots of laughs.

JW: Is nothing sacred?

CF: No. Are you kidding? Death? You drag out the big artillery for death.

The worst thing that could happen to me would be to lose my sense of humor.

JW: Have you ever lost it?

CF: Yes, when I broke up with my ex-husband. I didn't make a joke for a couple of days. People were waiting around on the outskirts of my personality for the superstructure to re-occasion itself. But you can observe your own lack of humor and eventually that becomes funny. You feel sorry for yourself, and that's funny. You can't stay there anymore.

JW: Are you a moody person?

CF: I'm annoyed most of the time.

JW: Are you athletic?

CF: No. I make myself exercise, but I don't like much movement at all. If talking were aerobic, I'd be the thinnest person in the world.

JW: You've been quoted as saying that you feel particularly qualified on two subjects, drugs and relationships, and since you've already demonstrated your expertise on the subject of drugs, I'll ask you to pontificate a little about relationships. First of all, do you think they're easier for men?

CF: Yes, of course. Men get their identity from their work, women get their identity from their men. If a woman gets a good job, it's great, but better still because she might meet a great guy—fight her way to the top and then meet a richer guy who will take care of her while she has babies. Whenever you hear of two people breaking up, the man has usually instigated it—there are of course exceptions to this rule—but the man has generally scouted another sexual location prior to the split-up, and if he's a powerful man, in five seconds he can be in a relationship with any one of a vast array of women.

JW: Is life easier for men?

CF: Well, it's longer for women, but only at the bad end. I wish we got our seven extra years up front, or in the middle somewhere. We look worse faster. Wrinkles on men is character; on women, it's "Oh, *shit*!" And men are fertile forever. You can be Hugh Hefner at sixty and have a baby with a twenty-one-year-old and it's not seen as vampiric. But if a woman does it, it's pathetic.

JW: Is sex better for women?

CF: I don't know about that. There are some women who have something, I've heard, like a "multiple orgasm," like firecrackers going off all throughout their system, and they can have a series of orgasms if they are set up right. I can't confess to this tendency myself. In general, I think it's true that women fuck to love and men love to fuck. When *we* do it, we're hoping he'll call us and love us. When they do it, they're just doing it. It's biological for them and it's emotional for us.

JW: What about romance?

CF: I heard a great definition of it: "Not founded in reality." Romance is based on uncertainty, so when you don't know where you stand and you're waiting for somebody to sort of define the direction, which is usually the male, that's romance. Romance is searing uncertainty, which creates sexual excitement, which is only there for as long as you're not settled in. When certainty kicks in, sex fades out. If marriage is based on romance, it's over. That tends to shock people. A girlfriend of mine left her boyfriend because he didn't ask her to waltz or something, or he didn't hold her chair out, and I thought, *You'll* have a great life.

JW: Do you think people expect too much from their relationships?

CF: I don't know, but I don't see the point of constantly having your relationship in a line through every situation. What are you going to bring to it if you're always in it? I once said to Paul at a party, "Please don't stand next to me, people will think we're salt-and-pepper shakers." But that's the bad part of me; I didn't grow up with a family that was ever around me, so I got very invested in entertaining myself. I used to make up stories about furniture. Telling myself little jokes, making the best of not too bad of a time. I was alone.

JW: And you read a lot.

CF: The first drug. It blocks out the world. They could tear the house down and I would be playing with my hair, my tongue out, reading. To this day I read like a horse. I bring the book up to my face like a feedbag. My family used to call me a bookworm—and they meant it in a derogatory way—they said it like "Jew"—like that *Jew* part of the family that we never see. So, I don't rely on other people for my experience, but I'm sensitive, and if you start criticizing my behavior, judging me, then I have to get your approval back, because I have a problem with people being mad at me. The one thing I've figured out from twenty years of therapy is that I must have decided that [my father] Eddie Fisher was very mad at me, personally.

JW: You once said that you were "born of a golden womb," and you've talked about being photographed by Modern Screen *when you were three days old. So, my question is—*

CF: Do I have a soul left?

JW: No, my question is, What do you think of when you pass the guy on Sunset who sells the Maps to the Stars Homes?

CF: I wonder how they get the addresses. We were on it when I was little and when the tourists came, if they had a movie camera we would stand still, and if they had a still camera, we'd move.

JW: Do you observe any sort of celebrity code of conduct?

CF: Yes, absolutely. It's funny because you don't know there is one till you see someone breaking it. If I'm out with Meryl [Streep], *I'm* the moat. If people come up to her, I must deflect them; if they come up to both of us, I must deflect them. I still get treated as Princess Leia, or lately it's "You're my favorite writer," or even "I loved your Madonna interview."

JW: Do you have a preference as to how you'd like to be recognized?

CF: As a writer. I loved doing those movies, but if you liked them, tell George [Lucas]. That's not my accomplishment. I was there. It was a great party, but it wasn't my house. The book thing is my party.

JW: I'd like to mention a few names and just get some quick reactions: Julia Phillips.

CF: I heard that she said my book is like me: "Tiny, witty and eager to be loved." You want to say, "What, we should *all* try to get everyone to hate us?"

JW: Ron Reagan.

CF: I still want to do more on Julia Phillips.

JW: Go ahead.

CF: That's okay. Who *is* Ron Reagan? Is he a ballet dancer? A talk-show host? I do respect the fact that it's hard to be somebody's kid. Patti Davis called me to get some advice about *Mother*. She was going to go after *Mother*. I said, Well, do it, but be a little bit funny. It's not like it's going to be a shock. "Really? Nancy's not nice? Oh, my God, that's so weird! I thought she was just adorable with those tiny shoulders and that big helmet hair."

JW: Mr. Blackwell.

CF: I made his Worst Dressed list, which I think is hilarious. But is that a career? You set yourself up as the discerning measure of all fashion based on what? What does *he* wear? Where does he come from? Who the fuck is he? I know there are answers to these questions, but I don't want them.

JW: Arnold Schwarzenegger.

CF: Oh, the name alone. What does that name mean? I saw him at this [George] Bush dinner (I wasn't invited, I went with [David] Geffen). Arnold's a Republican. A Republican bodybuilder. For the same reasons that Reagan was president, Schwarzenegger is our biggest star.

JW: Bret Easton Ellis.

CF: Sweet guy. Adorable. So what if he's written a book about headless women being fucked in the neck: "Honey, don't interrupt me right now, I'm reading about someone being sodomized while their brains are lying on the floor. Just one sec, okay? It's poetry."

JW: Jerry Lewis.
CF: Terrible hair.
JW: Oprah Winfrey.
CF: I saw the Oprah Winfrey show only once, on a trip to Omaha, and I've never watched it again. The theme was abused children who finally couldn't take it anymore and murdered their parents. She's talking to this young woman whose father had raped her every day for her whole life and she finally got a gun. Then he came to rape her again. Oprah Winfrey says, "What happened the day you murdered your father?" And the woman says, "I said that I didn't want to talk about the particulars of that." Oprah looks at the camera and the audience and goes, "You're on a show about children who murdered their parents and you don't want to talk about that?" Oprah does a look like, "Hey, you're here to sell beef and you don't want to talk about the burger you had?" Talk about cold. Talk about not having a soul.
JW: David Letterman.
CF: He has no life, from what I understand. I said to him on the air, "My sense of this is, I get nervous coming on the show, you get nervous when the show ends." He said, "You're not far off from the truth," and then he changed the subject. He will not talk to you in the halls because if you say, "Hello," you're wasting it. He wants it all saved up. The only thing that's important is when the camera's on. The guy isn't interested in people, he's interested in the show.
JW: Cher.
CF: She's a little long in the tubes to be prancing around naked in public. I'm sorry, but that's the way it is. I don't make up the facts, I just report them.
JW: Gore Vidal.
CF: There are certain people who are elder statesmen in the community of letters, and I occasionally meet these people and I just try not to fawn. Actually, the best person for that is [William] Styron, who I gave that little toy

that says, "Fuck you, fuck you, fuck you. Eat shit, eat shit, eat shit. You're an asshole. Love and Kisses." Hilarious. He's a genius. He once said, "I'd call her a cunt, but she lacks the depth and the charm." Genius. Maybe you should interview him.

JW: Ali MacGraw?

CF: Well, she's does this makeup commercial I watch all the time. They do it like it's a talk show. My fantasy is that I'm watching the show and people come in and I go, "Shhh, shhh, wait, I love this part about highlighting."

JW: Sam Donaldson.

CF: He doesn't move his face when he talks. His eyes are like shark eyes. Dead.

JW: Jesse Jackson.

CF: Fun to watch being interviewed. He'll answer any question because he's genuinely interested in himself. He loves himself, and I love to watch people who love themselves. It's like watching a great bath. But I don't care for all that weeping. I don't believe anybody should weep in public. And people should weep in private only if they have a note from their doctor saying they have some kind of fever or are vomiting uncontrollably. It's wrong to weep in public. There's no justification for it unless your husband has been murdered in a motorcade. There are only a very few extenuating circumstances in which there should be any lachrymal license whatsoever.

JW: Norman Mailer.

CF: Well, he asked for $50,000 to do the Madonna interview [for *Rolling Stone*] and they wouldn't go for it. $50,000! I did it for $3,500 and they printed it twice.

JW: Prince.

CF: I like Prince. I think he's really good. He's sleeping with all these gorgeous white women and never talking about it himself but getting *them* to talk about it and ruin their careers in the South.

JW: Jack Nicholson.

CF: He's fun because he doesn't make sense. I told him recently at a party that he should sleep with me so that I could write about it. I got him to think about it for a couple of minutes.

JW: Warren Beatty.

CF: He claims that I came on to him in London. Now, I've never come on to anyone. I'm sure I said to him, "Come on, Warren, I didn't give my virginity to you, so let's do it now." And he took it seriously, because humor is not Warren's strongest suit. He must think of me as a failure. His one failure.

JW: You've said that you declined his offer to relieve you of your virginity when you made Shampoo *together.*

CF: Right, I chose reality over anecdote. I didn't want to be at the receiving end of his technique.

JW: Spike Lee.

CF: Get a sense of humor! It makes total sense that the first hot black director we have is angry and racist, because there have been so many racist white directors, and we never talk about that. And I can see that it would be difficult to be both funny and that angry. But his interviews are so heavy. Lighten up, Spike, you got the job. He's a powerful guy. In fact, he would be a great boyfriend for me. Torture, black eyes. Can you imagine? I'm the wife Spike Lee deserves. A white woman, which he says he would never be with, so let's get someone really white. I am Spike Lee's Wife from Hell. I'm white and weird and I won't pay enough attention to him. If he does any more of those angry interviews, I'm going to write him and see if he wants the wife he deserves.

QUOTES ON "R"

RACISM

Why hate someone for the color of their skin when there are much better reasons to hate them? DENIS LEARY

I don't care if you think I'm a racist as long as you think I'm a thin racist. SARAH SILVERMAN

RADIO

Radio: the triumph of illiteracy. JOHN DOS PASSOS

Radio: death in the afternoon and into the night. ARTHUR MILLER

Radio is a bag of mediocrity where little men with carbon minds wallow in sluice of their own making. FRED ALLEN

I don't hold with furniture that talks. FRED ALLEN

RAT RACE

The trouble with the rat race is that even if you win, you're still a rat. LILY TOMLIN

REACTIONARY

A reactionary is someone with a clear and comprehensive vision of an ideal world we have lost. KENNETH MINOGUE

READING

No place affords a more striking conviction of the vanity of human hopes than a public library.   SAMUEL JOHNSON

REAGAN LIBRARY

Prepare yourself for some bad news: Ronald Reagan's library just burned down. Both books were destroyed. But the real horror: He hadn't finished coloring either one of them.   GORE VIDAL

REALITY

Reality is nothing but a collective hunch.   LILY TOMLIN

REFORM

The only way to reform some people is to chloroform them.

THOMAS C. HALIBURTON

REFORMERS

All reformers, however strict their social conscience, live in houses just as big as they can pay for.   LOGAN PEARSALL SMITH

RELATIONSHIPS

It is explained that all relationships require a little give and take. This is untrue. Any partnership demands that we give and give and at the last, as we flop into our graves exhausted, we are told that we didn't give enough.

QUENTIN CRISP

Almost all of our relationships begin and most of them continue as forms of mutual exploitation, a mental or physical barter, to be terminated when one or both parties run out of goods.   W. H. AUDEN

RELATIVES

Relations are simply a tedious pack of people who haven't got the remotest knowledge of how to live, nor the smallest instinct about when to die.

OSCAR WILDE

RELIGION

Religion consists in a set of things which the average man thinks he believes and wishes he was certain.
MARK TWAIN

All religions are founded on the fear of the many and the cleverness of the few.
STENDHAL

You never see animals going through the absurd and often horrible fooleries of magic and religion. Only man behaves with such gratuitous folly. It is the price he has to pay for being intelligent but not, as yet, quite intelligent enough.
ALDOUS HUXLEY

Most religions do not make men better, only warier.   ELIAS CANETTI

The idea of a good society is something you do not need a religion and eternal punishment to buttress; you need a religion if you are terrified of death.
GORE VIDAL

Since the whole affair had become one of religion, the vanquished were of course exterminated.
VOLTAIRE

Randomness scares people. Religion is a way to explain randomness.
FRAN LEBOWITZ

Religion is the fashionable substitute for belief.   OSCAR WILDE

Religion: It's given people hope in a world torn apart by religion.
                                                          JON STEWART

We must respect the other fellow's religion, but only in the sense and to the extent that we respect his theory that his wife is beautiful and his children smart.   H. L. MENCKEN

Religion is the venereal disease of mankind.   HENRI DE MONTHERLANT

Religion is the masterpiece of the art of animal training, for it trains people as to how they shall think.   ARTHUR SCHOPENHAUER

Where it is a duty to worship the sun it is pretty sure to be a crime to examine the laws of heat.   JOHN MORLEY

Truth, in matters of religion, is simply the opinion that has survived.
                                                          OSCAR WILDE

Religion is a monumental chapter in the history of human egotism.
                                                          WILLIAM JAMES

Religion has the best bullshit story of all time. Think about it. Religion has convinced people that there's an invisible man…living in the sky…who watches everything you do every minute of every day. And the invisible man has a list of ten specific things he doesn't want you to do. And if you do any of these things, he will send you to a special place, of burning and fire and smoke and torture and anguish for you to live forever, and suffer, and burn, and scream, until the end of time. But he loves you. He loves you. He loves you and he needs money. GEORGE CARLIN

We have just enough religion to make us hate, but not enough to make us love one another. JONATHAN SWIFT

There is not enough religion in the world to destroy the world's religions. FRIEDRICH WILHELM NIETZSCHE

The cosmos is a gigantic fly-wheel making 10,000 revolutions a minute. Man is a sick fly taking a dizzy ride on it. Religion is the theory that the wheel was designed and set spinning to give him the ride. H. L. MENCKEN

There's no bigger atheist than me. Well, I take that back. I'm a cancer screening away from going agnostic and a biopsy away from full-fledged Christian. ADAM CAROLLA

I'm a born-again atheist. GORE VIDAL

—————————————— REPORTER ——————————————
Reporter, *n.* A writer who guesses his way to the truth and dispels it with a tempest of words. AMBROSE BIERCE

—————————————— REPUBLICANS ——————————————
In this world of sin and sorrow there is always something to be thankful for; as for me, I rejoice that I am not a Republican. H. L. MENCKEN

Republicans are the party that says government doesn't work, and then they get elected and prove it. P. J. O'ROURKE

REPUTATION

One can survive everything, nowadays, except death, and live down every-thing except a good reputation.   OSCAR WILDE

RESPECT

There was no respect for youth when I was young, and now that I am old, there is no respect for age. I missed it coming and going.   J. B. PRIESTLEY

RESPECTABILITY

I have always thought respectable people scoundrels, and I look anxiously at my face every morning for signs of my becoming a scoundrel.
                    BERTRAND RUSSELL

The more things a man is ashamed of, the more respectable he is.
                    GEORGE BERNARD SHAW

REVOLUTION

Revolution, *n.* In politics, an abrupt change in the form of misgovernment.
                    AMBROSE BIERCE

With the exception of capitalism, there is nothing so revolting as revolution.
                    GEORGE BERNARD SHAW

A revolution is interesting insofar as it avoids like the plague the plague it promised to heal.   DANIEL BERRIGAN

Revolutions have never lightened the burden of tyranny, they have only shift-ed it to another shoulder.   GEORGE BERNARD SHAW

Revolution is a trivial shift in the emphasis of suffering.   TOM STOPPARD

Every revolution evaporates and leaves behind only the slime of a new bureaucracy.   FRANZ KAFKA

―――――――――――――― THE RICH ――――――――――――――

What is the matter with the poor is poverty; what is the matter with the rich is uselessness.   GEORGE BERNARD SHAW

It is the wretchedness of being rich that you have to live with rich people.   LOGAN PEARSALL SMITH

Prior to the Reagan era, the newly rich aped the old rich. But that isn't true any longer. Donald Trump is making no effort to behave like Eleanor Roosevelt as far as I can see.   FRAN LEBOWITZ

Someday I want to be rich. Some people get so rich they lose all respect for humanity. That's how rich I want to be.   RITA RUDNER

Every man thinks God is on his side. The rich and powerful know he is.   JEAN ANOUILH

The rich aren't like us, they pay less taxes.   PETER DE VRIES

―――――――――――― THE RIDICULOUS ――――――――――――

Look for the ridiculous in everything and you find it.   JULES RENARD

―――――――――――― RIGHT AND WRONG ――――――――――――

Any preoccupation with ideas of what is right and wrong in conduct shows an arrested intellectual development.   OSCAR WILDE

RIVERA, GERALDO

If Geraldo Rivera is the first journalist in space, NASA can test the effect of weightlessness on weightlessness.　　　　ANONYMOUS

ROCK JOURNALISM

Most rock journalism is people who can't write interviewing people who can't talk for people who can't read.　　　　FRANK ZAPPA

ROGERS, WILL

This bosom friend of senators and congressmen was about as daring as an early Shirley Temple movie.　　　　JAMES THURBER

ROMANCE

When one is in love one always begins by deceiving oneself, and one always ends by deceiving others. This is what the world calls a romance.

OSCAR WILDE

Romance should never begin with sentiment. It should begin with science and end with a settlement.　　　　OSCAR WILDE

Romance, like the rabbit at the dog track, is the elusive, fake, and never attained reward which, for the benefit and amusement of our masters, keeps us running and thinking in safe circles.　　　　BEVERLY JONES

RUSSIA

Ideas in modern Russia are machine-cut blocks coming in solid colors; the nuance is outlawed, the interval walled up, the curve grossly stepped.

VLADIMIR NABOKOV

BEDFELLOWS

EARL OF SANDWICH: Sir, I do not know whether you will die on the gallows or of the pox.
JOHN WILKES: That will depend, my lord, on whether I embrace your principles or your mistress.

He is a man of splendid abilities, but utterly corrupt. Like rotten mackerel by moonlight, he shines and stinks.
JOHN RANDOLPH, on Edward Livingston

He is a self-made man who worships his creator.
JOHN BRIGHT, on Benjamin Disraeli

The difference between a misfortune and a calamity is this: If Gladstone fell in the Thames, that would be a misfortune. But if someone fished him out again, that would be a calamity.
BENJAMIN DISRAELI

Lord Birkenhead is very clever, but sometimes his brains go to his head.
MARGOT ASQUITH

He could not see a belt without hitting below it.
MARGOT ASQUITH, on David Lloyd George

Mr. Lloyd George…spoke for a hundred seventeen minutes, in which period he was detected only once in the use of an argument.   ARNOLD BENNETT

David Lloyd George did not care in which direction the car was travelling, so long as he remained in the driver's seat.   LORD BEAVERBROOK

When they circumcised Herbert Samuel they threw away the wrong bit.
DAVID LLOYD GEORGE

Neither of his colleagues can compare with him in that acuteness and energy of mind with which he devotes himself to so many topics injurious to the strength and welfare of the state.
WINSTON CHURCHILL, on Stafford Cripps

Decided only to be undecided, resolved to be irresolute, adamant for drift, solid for fluidity, all-powerful to be impotent.
WINSTON CHURCHILL, on Stanley Baldwin

One could not even dignify him with the name of stuffed shirt. He was simply a hole in the air.   GEORGE ORWELL, on Stanley Baldwin

---

Neville Chamberlain looked at foreign affairs through the wrong end of a municipal drainpipe.   WINSTON CHURCHILL

Listening to a speech by Chamberlain is like paying a visit to Woolworth's. Everything is in its place and nothing above sixpence.   ANEURIN BEVAN

[Chamberlain has] the mind and manner of a clothesbrush.
HAROLD NICOLSON

I thought he was a young man of promise, but it appears he was a young man of promises. A. J. BALFOUR, on Winston Churchill

---

He mistakes verbal felicities for mental inspiration.
ANEURIN BEVAN, on Winston Churchill

When I am right, I get angry. Churchill gets angry when he is wrong. We are angry at each other much of the time. CHARLES DE GAULLE

In defeat unbeatable; in victory unbearable.
WINSTON CHURCHILL, on Field Marshal Montgomery

[Clement Atlee] reminds me of nothing so much as a dead fish before it has had time to stiffen. GEORGE ORWELL

Mr. Attlee is a very modest man. But then he has much to be modest about.
WINSTON CHURCHILL

He is forever poised between a cliché and an indiscretion.
HAROLD MACMILLAN, on Anthony Eden

He was not only a bore, he bored for England.
MALCOLM MUGGERIDGE, on Anthony Eden

No one who knows Mr. Randolph Churchill and wishes to express distaste for him should ever be at a loss for words which would be both opprobrious and apt. EVELYN WAUGH

He immatures with age. HAROLD WILSON, on Tony Benn

La Pasionaria of middle-class privilege.
DENIS HEALEY, on Margaret Thatcher

She sounded like the Book of Revelations read out over a railway station address system by a headmistress of a certain age wearing calico knickers.
CLIVE JAMES, on Margaret Thatcher's television technique

She is democratic enough to talk down to anyone.
AUSTIN MITCHELL, on Margaret Thatcher

An artlessly sincere megalomaniac.   H. G. WELLS, on Charles de Gaulle

---

In Pierre Elliott Trudeau, Canada has at last produced a political leader worthy of assassination.   IRVING LAYTON

His mind was like a soup dish, wide and shallow; it could hold a small amount of nearly everything, but the slightest jarring spilt the soup into somebody's lap.   IRVING STONE, on William Jennings Bryan

---

You really have to get to know Dewey to dislike him.
ROBERT A. TAFT, on Thomas E. Dewey

Dewey looks like the bridegroom on the wedding cake.
ALICE ROOSEVELT LONGWORTH

I fired MacArthur because he wouldn't respect the authority of the president. I didn't fire him because he was a dumb son of a bitch, although he was.
HARRY S TRUMAN

I studied dramatics under him for twelve years.
                    DWIGHT D. EISENHOWER, on Douglas MacArthur

---

Mr. John Foster Dulles—the world's longest-range misguided missile.
                                            WALTER REUTHER

John Connally's conversion to the GOP raised the intellectual level of both
parties.   FRANK MANKIEWICZ

Compared to Imelda Marcos, Marie Antoinette was a bag lady.
                                            STEPHEN SOLARZ

He is neither a strategist, nor is he schooled in the operational art, nor is he
a tactician, nor is he a general, nor is he a soldier. Other than that, he's a
great military man.
            GENERAL NORMAN SCHWARTZKOPF, on Saddam Hussein

Smooth is an inadequate word for Dulles. His prevarications are so highly
polished as to be aesthetically pleasurable.   I. F. STONE

He gave a fireside speech and the fire went out.
                    MARK RUSSELL, on Henry "Scoop" Jackson

He would have made a very good bartender.
                            GORE VIDAL, on Teddy Kennedy

His campaign sounded a note of the bogusly grand. [Gary] Hart is [John F.]
Kennedy typed on the eighth carbon.   LANCE MORROW

Dukakis is Greek for *Mondale*.   JAY LENO

Susan Estrich, the left-leaning tower of pissantry who served as Michael Dukakis's campaign manager in the 1988 presidential race.

FLORENCE KING

Henry Kissinger…became the nation's top foreign-policy strategist despite being born with the handicaps of a laughable accent and no morals or neck.

DAVE BARRY

The Billy Carter of the British monarchy.…

ROBERT LACY, on Princess Margaret

Jesse Jackson is a man of the cloth. Cashmere.   MORT SAHL

Such an active lass. So outdoorsy. She loves nature in spite of what it did to her.   BETTE MIDLER, on Princess Anne

---

She walks like a duck with a bad leg.

RICHARD BLACKWELL, on the Duchess of York

Barbara Bush reads *House and Garden* for fashion tips.   JUDY TENUTA

P. J. O'ROURKE

Why I Am a Republican

P. J. O'Rourke is the H. L. Mencken Research Fellow at the Cato Institute and a frequent panelist on NPR's *Wait, Wait…Don't Tell Me!* His books include *Modern Manners, Holidays in Hell, Parliament of Whores,* and *Peace Kills: America's Fun New Imperialism.*

JW: You've characterized the S&L scandal, agricultural subsidies, and even Social Security as manifestations of Americans' greed.
PJO'R: The problem with Social Security is that people want to get more out of it than they put in. The problem behind the problem is the sense of

entitlement that seems to be overwhelming our society. Things that used to be privileges have become rights. People feel entitled to free medicine, free retirement benefits, every kind of disaster relief, protection from bad luck and from bad weather, and on and on, never asking themselves, "What have I done for society that would make society want to do anything for me? What have I even tried to do?" It's one thing to talk about crippled war veterans, whose sense of entitlement is justified, but why must society fix things for teenage drug addicts? If members of society want to help others who have gotten themselves in trouble or have simply had bad luck, that's great, that's Christian charity. But what makes people think that the rest of society is obliged, or should be forced by law, to help them every time they screw up?

JW: Well, what does make them think that?

PJO'R: I don't know, but I think newspapers and magazines, the media in general, encourage people to think this way.

JW: And lawyers?

PJO'R: Lawyers certainly do. But with lawyers there's usually some measure of logic—much as I detest the abuse of litigation, especially in liability cases—there's some measure of logic in it, even though that logic is often strained. But there is no measure of logic in someone saying, "Well, I've got myself addicted to heroin, so the nation, the government, the taxpayers, owe me a program to get over my addiction."

JW: Or, "The government owes me a subsidy to operate my farm."

PJO'R: Precisely. It's important to remember that most of these subsidies do not go to poor people; the majority go to the middle class. Our modern federal government is spending almost $5,000 a year on every person in America. The average American household of 2.64 people thus receives almost $13,000 worth of federal benefits, services, and protection per annum. These people would have to have a family income of $53,700 to pay as much in taxes as they get in goodies. Only 18.5 percent of the population has that kind of money. And only 4.8 percent of the population file income tax returns showing more than $50,000 in adjusted gross income. Ninety-five percent of Americans are on the mooch.

JW: Is that how the federal budget deficit got so big?

PJO'R: It got so big because in a democracy people can vote benefits for themselves and vote not to pay taxes for them. People simply want all this stuff for less than it costs. That's all there is to it. Lawmakers are doing nothing but responding to their constituencies.

JW: The whores are us?

PJO'R: The whores are us, although I must say that there are certain kinds of lawmakers—liberals, I call them—who egg those constituencies on: "Isn't there more stuff you would like? What have we forgotten? Dental care, that's it. Wouldn't you like some free dental care, too?"

JW: And you've suggested that the growing number of old people are a big part of the problem.

PJO'R Yes! All of a sudden there are geezers and duffers and biddies everywhere you look. There didn't used to be this many old people. I remember when it was just the occasional coot on a porch rocker waxing nostalgic about outdoor plumbing. Now they're all over the place—arteriosclerosing around on the racquetball courts, badgering skydiving instructors for senior-citizen discounts, hogging the Jacuzzi at the singles apartment complex. They're even taking over pop music. I went to see the Who last summer, and a bunch of old farts were playing in the band.

JW: But how do old people contribute to the budget deficit?

PJO'R: About thirty percent of the federal budget is now spent on "older Americans." As the antediluvian segment of the population continues to grow, we'll be spending more and more on them. The over-fifty-fives are the only age group in the country that will get significantly larger in the next century. By 2030, a fifth of the nation will be old, and lots of the old will be ancient. In fact, the eighty-five-plus bunch, according to the Census Bureau, is the nation's fastest-growing group. There will be between fifteen and thirty million of them by the mid-2000s. Yet though they may be alive, they won't be doing much living. Last year a Harvard Medical School research project examined thousands of geriatric Bostonians and found double the previously estimated incidence of Alzheimer's. Nearly half of those over eighty-five had signs of the disease. Medicare already costs taxpayers $100 billion per annum, with thirty percent of that money spent on treatment in the last year of patients' lives.

JW: The future of the baby boom isn't pretty.

PJO'R: The baby boom is rapidly turning into the Senescence Swell. Those of us born between 1946 and 1964 constitute one-third of the total U.S. population. And we're already worse than our parents. We're the most vapid, screw-noodled, grabby, and self-infatuated generation in history. Imagine what we'll be like in forty years—wearing roller skates in our walkers, going to see Suzanne Vega in Atlantic City, grumbling that our heart-lung machines have gone condo, and buying Ralph Lauren cashmere colostomy bags.

JW: You're not mad about Europeans, or "Euro-Weenies," as you've called them, and I gather that you don't enjoy traveling in Europe.

PJO'R: Say what you will about "land of opportunity" and "purpled mountains majesty above the fruited plain," our forebears moved to the United States because they were sick to death of lukewarm beer—and lukewarm coffee and lukewarm bathwater and lukewarm mystery cutlets with mucky-colored mushroom cheese junk on them. Everything in Europe is lukewarm except the radiators. You could use the radiators to make party ice. But nobody does. I'll bet you could walk from the Ural Mountains to the beach at Biarritz and not find one rock-hard, crystal-clear, fist-size American ice cube. Ask for whiskey on the rocks, and you get a single gray, crumbling leftover from some Lilliputian puddle freeze plopped in a thimble of Scotch (for which you're charged like sin). And the phones don't work. They go "blat-blat" and "neek-neek" and "ugu-ugu-ugu." No two dial tones are alike. The busy signal sounds as if the phone is ringing. And when the phone rings you think the dog farted.

The Europeans can't figure out which side of the road to drive on, and I can't figure out how to flush their toilets. Do I push the knob or pull it or twist it or pump it? And I keep cracking my shins on that stupid bidet thing. (Memo to Europeans: Try washing your *whole* body; believe me, you'd smell better.) Plus there are ruins everywhere.

I've had it with these dopey little countries and all their poky borders. You can't swing a cat without sending it through customs. Everything's too small. The cars are too small. The beds are too small. The elevators are the size of broom closets. Even the languages are itty-bitty. Sometimes you need two or three just to get you through till lunch.

JW: Let me bring you back to a domestic issue: You've been critical of the War on Drugs. I assume you think we're losing.

PJO'R: We've already lost.

JW: Why?

PJO'R: A modern arrest requires a stack of forms as thick as a Sunday *New York Times* "Arts and Leisure" section, and filling them out is as complicated as buying something at Bloomingdale's with an out-of-state check. A modern conviction requires just as much effort and tedium in court. The average D.C. cop, for example, spends twenty days of his month testifying or waiting to do so. The end result of the dangers, annoyances, delays, boredom, and paper shuffling that go into a bust is...nothing. The perp's turned loose. Mostly the perp is turned loose right there in the precinct house. Mere possession of coke usually gets you a citation, a ticket, like you'd turned left on red with your nose. Get caught selling to the UCs, the undercover policemen, and you might have to stay in jail until tomorrow morning.

You can't walk one block in any city in America without wackos and soaks spitting up in your pants cuffs and homeless vagabonds gnawing the tassels off your Foot-Joys. You can't stop at a stoplight without getting squeegeed in the kisser by practitioners of beggary—the most rapidly expanding sector of America's economy. One out of five American children are growing up needy, and fifty-three percent of those kids have nothing for a dad except a blind, microscopic, wiggle-tailed gamete that hasn't held a job since it got to the womb. Drugs are an improvement on some of these problems. Who wouldn't rather have a couple of plump, flaky lines on a mirror and half a disco biscuit than lead the life these people are leading? Drugs are the answer, after all, to the question "How can I get high as a kite?" or "How can I make money without working?"

JW: *Are you saying that drugs are just a symptom?*

PJO'R: Drugs are just a symptom. We all know that. "Drugs are just a symptom." Well, blindness is "just a symptom" of river fever. And having your genitals swell to the size of a Geo Tracker is just a symptom of elephantiasis. And death is just a symptom of AIDS. Even without reading *Time* or watching *Nightline*, just with what I can see with my own eyes, I think the symptom is bad enough to treat. Consider the "mushrooms," for instance. "Mushrooms" is slang for kids and old people who get shot down under dealer crossfire. When the poor, damn mushrooms have a nickname, that's a bad symptom—a symptom worth treating. And if we're serious about treating the symptoms, maybe we'll begin to get an inkling of what the hell disease we've got.

JW: *So what are we going to do about drugs?*

PJO'R: We can get hysterical about them. That's always been fun. I can remember the antediluvian age of drug hysteria, when the occasional bebop musician's ownership of a Mary Jane cigarette threatened to turn every middle-class American teenager into a sex-crazed car thief. This particular hysteria proved well founded. Every middle-class American teenager did try marijuana and did become sex-crazed, although no more car-thievish than usual. Then there was LSD, which was supposed to make you think you could fly. I remember it made you think you couldn't stand up, and mostly it was right. The much predicted heavy precipitation of wingless adolescents—which caused many people to move their cars out from under trees near hippie pads—failed to materialize.

The early seventies heroin craze likewise petered out before emptying the nation's scout camps and Hi-Y chapters. And by the time PCP came along to make kids psychotic, kids were acting so psychotic anyway, who could tell the difference? The only unifying theme in these drug scares seemed to be an American public with a strong subconscious wish to get rid of its young people.

Marijuana is self-punishing; it makes you acutely sensitive, and in this world, what worse punishment could there be? Heroin turns people into amoral scuzzballs. But a heroin addict who gets his fix is well behaved or dead—and you can't get better behaved than that. And a heroin addict who doesn't get his fix is helpless. I lived on the Lower East Side during New York City's smack phase, and one night a big guy with a knife tried to rob me. This would have been frightening if he hadn't been half a block away and shaking so badly he couldn't move. "Come here and give me all your money!" he yelled. "No," I shouted back. I left him to work it out on his own.

JW: What about crack?

PJO'R: I've smoked freebase, which is the couture version of crack. It felt great. Actually, it felt too great. It reminded me of that experiment that you read about in college psychology textbooks, about the rat that had the electrode inserted directly into the pleasure center of his brain, and then he pushes the little lever that activates the electrode, and he keeps pushing it and pushing it and pushing it—until you have to read about him in a college psychology textbook. I didn't feel like smoking freebase twice.

Crack is a drug for those who are already fucked up. In fact, getting fucked up is for those who are already fucked up. Crack-cocaine use has shown few signs of spreading to this nation's well blessed. County fairs will not be filled with bruised and bleeding Holsteins because 4-H members went into milking frenzies while smoking rock. There isn't going to be a sudden dearth of nuclear physicists because Asian kids are selling their homework to buy vials.

We're not serious about the drug trouble in this country. We're not serious about the trouble causing the drug trouble. We're not serious about anything. We've got a welfare system that pays you to have illegitimate children but takes away your medical benefits if you get a job. We've got big-city property laws where if you buy a piece of rental property, you're punished with a price freeze, but if you wreck a piece of rental property, no force on earth can evict you. When somebody screams obscenities at imaginary tormentors and takes a crap on your front steps, you can't get that person committed to a mental institution. But walk through the park after eight P.M. and all your friends call you crazy. We are not a serious nation.

JW: How do you regard the new generation of journalists?

PJO'R: The journalists in my day, not even going back to *Front Page* times, were cynical, hard-drinking, often not very well educated people, but people who could write drunk or write sober and write quickly. Now journalists have turned into a nest of do-gooders. They're a bunch of laptop-tickling, nonsmoking, nondrinking, macrobiotic-looking, twinkly little twerps. I see them all over the world. They were all over the place in the Gulf War. They're completely electronically plugged in, always playing around with modems and things. On the convoy into Kuwait, in the middle of the night, we ran over shrapnel and got flat tires, and it was wonderful to see these kids suddenly confronted with the material world. Something that they couldn't scroll up on, something that didn't have a password key. They didn't have the slightest goddamned idea how to change a tire. They couldn't tell gasoline from diesel oil. Useless in the real world. Kind of hard to equate these people with Mike Royko.

JW: Why are they like that?

PJO'R: It's the fault of *All the President's Men.* I had never met a journalist who had been to journalism school previous to about four years after that movie. And then all of them had been to journalism school. What goes on in journalism school? It takes ten minutes to teach somebody to write a pyramid lead. What else is there to know? Except everything in the world, of course, which takes twenty years of hard work. Whenever I speak to college journalism or writing classes I tell them, "I've only got two things to say to you. If you want to write, write. The only way to learn how to do it is by doing it. And the other thing is read." It's amazing how many of these kids you meet who don't read. If you want to write, you have to first read.

JW: Are today's journalists representative of their generation?

PJO'R: In general, no. When I lecture on college campuses, it's like going back to pre-1965 college. The kids are in fraternities and sororities, they sort of care about their classes and are a little worried about their careers, but not too much. They love to drink beer. They're nice. They're kids, not monsters from space like we were. I like them. But young journalists, especially television ones, are awful. Television has become the career of choice for extremely ambitious, talent-free individuals.

JW: Can you explain the difference between Republicans and Democrats?

PJO'R: It's really very simple: If you think about God, he's obviously a Republican. He's a middle-aged, even elderly, white male. He's quite stern, definitely into rules and regulations, very legalistic. He holds people responsible for their actions. He holds the mortgage on literally everything on earth. He's very well connected socially and politically—it's very difficult to get into God's heavenly country club. It's obvious from the number and condition of the poor on the earth that God is not terribly interested in their material well-being. He's a Republican.

Santa Claus is obviously a Democrat. Santa Claus is jolly, he works very hard for charity. He may know everything about everybody, but he never uses it. He's kind to animals. He gives everybody everything they want without thought of a quid pro quo. He's a great guy. But unfortunately, he doesn't exist.

THE DIFFERENCE BETWEEN MEN AND WOMEN

In love women are professionals, men are amateurs. FRANÇOIS TRUFFAUT

A woman's a woman 'til the day she dies, but a man's a man only as long as he can. MOMS MABLEY

When a man and a woman die, as poets sung,
His heart's the last part moves, her last, the tongue.
BENJAMIN FRANKLIN

A woman's guess is much more accurate than a man's certainty.
OSCAR WILDE

All men laugh at the Three Stooges and all women think that the Three Stooges are assholes. JAY LENO

Women are never disarmed by compliments. Men always are. That is the difference between the sexes. OSCAR WILDE

Of the two lots, the woman's lot of perpetual motherhood, and the man's of perpetual babyhood, I prefer the man's. GEORGE BERNARD SHAW

You never see a man walking down the street with a woman who has a little pot belly and a bald spot.   ELAYNE BOOSLER

Men play the game; women know the score.   ROGER WODDIS

Women eat while they are talking; men talk while they are eating.
                                        MALCOLM DE CHAZAL

A successful man is one who makes more money than his wife can spend.
A successful woman is one who can find such a man.   LANA TURNER

Women represent the triumph of matter over mind, just as men represent
the triumph of mind over morals.   OSCAR WILDE

A tranquil woman can go on sewing longer than an angry man can go on
fuming.   GEORGE BERNARD SHAW

Women aren't embarrassed when they buy men's pajamas, but a man buying a nightgown acts as though he were dealing with a dope peddler.
                                                    JIMMY CANNON

Man makes love by braggadocio, and woman makes love by listening.
                                                    H. L. MENCKEN

Women, as they grow older, rely more and more on cosmetics. Men, as they grow older, rely more and more on a sense of humor.   GEORGE JEAN NATHAN

No male can beat a female in the long run because they have it over us in
sheer, damn longevity.   JAMES THURBER

LEWIS BLACK

A Little Bitter

Standup comedian Lewis Black is probably best known as the apoplectic commentator on *The Daily Show with Jon Stewart*. A graduate of the University of North Carolina and the Yale School of Drama, he's the author of more than forty plays and the best-selling book, *Nothing's Sacred*.

JW: Do you mind being called a curmudgeon?
LB: Not at all. I don't get "the happy thing."
JW: How about "misanthrope"?
LB: "Misanthrope" is good, too. Actually, there's a young film director who

wants to do a modern version [of Molière's *The Misanthrope*] with me in the title role. It takes place in L.A., which is just perfect.

JW: Not crazy about Los Angeles?

LB: I'm fine there as long as I'm working. Otherwise I get psychotic.

JW: You're an East Coast kind of guy.

LB: Yeah, I live in New York and grew up in Silver Spring, Maryland.

JW: What's your most vivid childhood memory?

LB: Hiding under the desk in case of nuclear attack. The whole idea of going into your basement with your family—which is the way my parents were going to deal with it—I just kept thinking, I'm not going to spend two weeks in the basement with these people eating canned peaches! If I figured that out at the age of 10 or 11, what were the adults thinking?

The other thing I remember vividly was watching the neighborhood sprawl all over the place. We lived across from where my father worked, the Naval Ordinance Lab. We were one of the first neighborhoods out there. I remember there was a farm at the end of our street, but within ten years the farm was gone and they'd built houses everywhere. Then the malls sprang up, bam bam bam bam bam. When I went back twenty years ago and took a long drive around the area, everything had been filled in.

JW: Were you a religious family?

LB: We didn't go to Friday night services, but I went to Hebrew school and I was bar mitzvah'd. I was kind of attracted to the whole thing…until I started hanging out more and more with Jews and I realized you can only hang out with a few of them. Too many is too much. I like a mix. And some of the religious stuff just didn't appeal to me. I have friends who've returned to it, but I never got any real comfort from it. I've always had a certain sense of spirituality, but any formal expression seems to be *nuts*. But we had one of the great rabbis of the twentieth century until I was 12, and it was well worth listening to him take that stuff and make sense of it. He used the Old

Testament as a blueprint for social action. He'd read from *Isaiah* how Shmuel and Huchie did A and B and he'd flip it into why we should help Negroes! I'm like, Holy fuck, how'd he do that?! He was so good at it, I began to think it would be a great job to stand up there every week and tell these fuckers off!

JW: You actually considered becoming a rabbi?

LB: I actually did consider it. But then he left and a new guy came in and he was a putz, at least by comparison. Funny: His son is also a rabbi and at his father's funeral he apparently quoted from my book, which was nice. Anyway, by the time I was 13, I was starting to fade, and by the time I was 15 and confirmed I was out of there.

JW: In your act you talk about your problem with Hanukkah.

LB: The problem with Hanukkah is that it occurs next to Christmas and in comparison makes us look retarded. Why would you put your holiday up against that holiday? Don't tell me you couldn't switch it if you wanted to— nobody cares. Put it in early June! Then Christians would pay attention. The whole idea of putting up the menorah next to a Christmas tree…what *planet* are you on? Look, I realize what it represents and hoo-hah, but it's just a bunch of candles! If you've got a Christmas tree and a menorah side by side, which one are you going to look at? The menorah is only good for about three nights anyway. On the fourth night you ask your parents, "Are we gonna light the menorah?" and they go, "No, go look at the pilot light." The dreidel is only good for testing how bright your kid is. If you spin it in front of him and he pays attention for more than five seconds he's not going to be good in math. And the gifts! It's a pen and pencil set, then socks, an eraser…it's a back-to school holiday! But you go next door and it's *Let's Make A Deal*. The Christians have enough cartons to build a homeless village. They're getting X-Boxes and we're getting two apples.

JW: What about Thanksgiving?

LB: When I was a kid we ate and drank and passed out on Thanksgiving. Nobody woke us up and said, "Let's go *shopping*!" I actually go to Macy's every year, which is really stupid. I wake up the day after Thanksgiving and trundle down to Macy's to watch people go berserk. It's *spectacular*. I rarely people-watch, but it's my favorite place. No self-respecting Jew would buy shit before Christmas, when it's the most expensive. Put a note card in the box: "You're getting a toaster."

JW: You were born in 1948, which makes you a baby boomer. How do you assess your generation?

LB: All that was required of us was to legalize marijuana, and we couldn't do it! I don't smoke it anymore, but come *on*! It was the one thing you figure we could have gotten done. And look at the two Presidents from our generation: It's like, "a blow job isn't sex" and "it depends on what the definition of 'is' is," and a guy who gets really good jobs because of his family and every time he fucks up, his family has to bail him out. It's beyond belief! The baby boomers fucked up everything that was given us, and what did we put in its place? Spas and health clubs. The major thing that we'll leave on the planet is the concept of style over substance. I'm a little bitter about it.

JW: The older generation always complains that the world is going to hell in a hand basket. Is that what we have, or is there a quantum difference now?

LB: I was just thinking about that the other day. This period is like living under Millard Fillmore or Warren G. Harding. There's a level of government incompetence that's positively shocking, a level that was unimagined until now. These are the assholes who said they wanted to "dismantle government." What do you want people to do, *putz*? It's called *jobs*. I don't give a shit if they're just sitting there all day. They used to fill the jobs with qualified, experienced people. Everybody worked for the government in my neighborhood. My best friend's dad worked for the Agency for International Development for, like, twenty years. But now these clueless political appointees have those jobs, and they're a bunch of fuckups!

JW: Which is why we still don't have solar energy...

LB: How do we not have solar energy by now? If President Kennedy could decide that we would get to the moon in ten years and we *got* to the moon in ten years, you can't tell me that we couldn't have done solar by now if we'd really tried. We can't have solar, but we can have an *iPod*? We've got a thing the size of a credit card that can show movies, but solar energy—that's impossible. We're a great country, but we don't apply the greatness to anything that really matters.

JW: Are we still capable of mounting a concerted technological effort, given the sorry state of our educational system?

LB: I think so, because percentage-wise, the best of the best is still as good as it was. The top one percent or the top five percent are still capable. It just requires focus. We still have Westinghouse Scholars who can figure out the electromagnetic ratio of clams to oysters.

JW: The news is getting more and more absurd. Is that a curse or a blessing for a comic?

LB: It's a real problem for a comic to find a more absurd position than what's actually happening. If Mark Foley is involved with helping us figure out how to deal with sexual predators and he's a sexual predator, how am I supposed to top that? A lot of the time I tell the audience that I'm too tired to think of anything. I wake up in the morning and start reading the newspaper and something strikes me. And then I have to calm down. Like this morning I read in Maureen Dowd's [*New York Times*] column that [House Speaker Nancy] Pelosi picked Silvestre Reyes to chair the House Intelligence Committee. At a press conference announcing his appointment, the guy could not answer whether Al-Qaeda is Sunni or Shia. (They're Sunni, by the way.) Or the frozen embryo thing. Frozen embryos aren't *alive*! They're *frozen*!

What part of that don't you assholes understand? You show me in the Bible where anybody refrigerated anything. Some Kansas cocksucker got upset over the fact that they throw these embryos out so he wants to *adopt* them. Right: I've got three in my freezer that I'm raising; every once in a while I open the door and yell at them. And of course I'm going to take them as a tax write-off.

For the amount of information we get every day, we don't get any information at all. The news doesn't help you understand anything. Like that scroll they put on the bottom [of the TV screen]. I think it's given me ADD!

JW: Might the Internet help?

LB: Maybe, if we can stop these people from *blogging*. There's a great line Barry Levinson has my character say in *Man of the Year*: if you put two people side by side on television, and one is a homicidal maniac and the other is a genius, because they're both on television, they're equals. That's even more true of bloggers. *Anybody* can have a blog.

JW: But isn't that pure democracy?

LB: Yes, at its most heinous and frightening level. The shakeout is going to be something extraordinary.

JW: What about the absence of outrage on the part of the public, the lack of reverberation of momentous events?

LB: The lack of reverberation, at least from the perspective of a comic working clubs all over the country and seeing what people are up to, is due to the number of people with two jobs. They have no *time*. They're just barely surviving.

JW: What's your "demographic"?

LB: The youngest fans I have are ten and it goes to the eighties. Now there's been a jump in the black portion of my audience and the gays have started coming. I've also been getting more military, starting even before the Iraq war—and now it's massive. A guy gave me his purple heart! It's extraordinary. There are even Republicans who show up! It's a real cross-section.

JW: Where do you place yourself on the ideological spectrum. I assume you're not a neocon.

LB: Nobody really knows what a neoconservative is except that when they watch *The Matrix*, they believe it's real.

JW: Are you a liberal?

LB: Liberals have disappeared. They've been cowed into submission. No, while I'm conservative on some things and liberal on others, I'm really a socialist. Which kind of *fucks* me. Thirty years ago, I had a recreation center to go to in the summer. It was open eight hours a day and everybody had access to it. We still had a very good volunteer fire department that was adequately funded—we had all these government services. Now we've reached the point where people don't want to pay property taxes to fund schools because they don't have children! Oh really? Well, then you have to *leave*. There has to be a contract among the people who live here. You create public spaces, you create things so there's a real reason to go to work so your kid will get A, B, C, and D. The contract is broken. For example, there's a piece in the paper today about the "breakthrough" in public housing in New York. They're going to build 120,000 new units by 2013. A hundred and twenty thousand in a city of nine million? YOU FUCKIN' DICKS! That's the best we can do?

JW: Is there any real hope unless we take the money out of the electoral process?

LB: No, I don't think so. And these guys don't want to take it out. They need too much money to run and they're running constantly and it's the big flaw in the system. The other problem is greed. It gets worse every year. Cheney gets a $40 million balloon from Halliburton and then Halliburton gets all the Iraq projects. Does nobody see a connection?

JW: You've offered a solution—a modest proposal—for electing the president...

LB: The winner of *American Idol* throws a dart at a board. Whatever city it hits, you immediately put a monkey on a plane, fly him over it, push him out, and he parachutes down to the ground. The first person whose hand he grabs is the next president. Here's another one: If America's economy is inexorably tied to Santa's ass, then I say we elect him president. It'll be Christmas all year round, so the Christians will be happy—it's the only time these pricks are *ever* happy. Then you'll have this big fat son-of-a-bitch president with a white beard who answers every question with "Ho, ho, ho."

JW: Were you surprised at the invitation to speak at the Congressional Correspondents' dinner?

LB: I was astonished, because I'm not really on the radar for these people. The guy who picked me came and saw my set and really liked me. He said we'd just have to clean it up. Which I really didn't mind, because it's a good exercise. Besides, I don't have the time or energy to argue with these cocksuckers over what a satirist can and cannot say. They asked me to come and entertain that group of clowns, and that's what I did. They're the tightest-assed group of people on earth. I once performed a Tom Daschle fundraiser—a friend of mine who knew Daschle asked me to do it. It's not the kind of thing I usually do, but I'm glad I went because I got to sit next to Ann Richards. Anyway, this was at the height of Pat Buchanan being nuts—he kind of swings back and forth between lucid and insane. I said, "I don't know why you people even listen to him because I know he's nuts because most people laugh by expelling air—'ha ha ha'—but he laughs by *inhaling*. What you hear is actually the sound of his own asshole sucking him in." Four people in the audience laughed, including Ann Richards. And I got livid. I looked at them and said, "You have got to be kidding me! I've been in front of Republicans who laughed at that joke, mixed audiences—there's no audience I've ever stood in front of that didn't laugh at that joke. And then you wonder why you people are out of *touch*? Do you know you're Democrats? Are you all his best *friend*?"

JW: Those football rants you do on television…are you really a fan?

LB: It's the perfect televised sport: continuous movement, it changes every second, it's amped up…I *love* football. I'm sick. Football provides us a place where we can scream anything we want. I like to go to the games and every so often yell, "MY LIFE *SUCKS!*" Football also produces great hatred. There's Cleveland and Pittsburgh and they *hate* each other. Or Duke and UNC: You wonder how the Serbs and Croats got in this position? I went to Chapel Hill, and though two of my closest friends went to Duke, it's the only real hatred I have. I *hate* Duke. I watch their games to see them *lose*. Even if it's in the finals and they're representing the ACC, *I do not care,* for they are *evil.*

JW: What about the Super Bowl?

LB: It destroyed the game. They stop for two weeks, they interview everybody…I don't care where these people *come from* or what their *hobbies* are. And the commercials are like mystery stories! You don't even know what they're selling until the very end. Three rabbits are on a log, one of them goes home and hangs himself—buy a bike! Plus, the Super Bowl isn't played at a time of day when football is normally played.

JW: But there's Monday Night Football *and* Sunday Night Football…

LB: The only way to watch football at night is the way I did recently. We went to a buffet at a strip club in Houston where the game was on. This is the concept of heaven for American males and the perfect way to watch football: You have your buffet, you have a drink, you watch a play…and then look at tits.

JW: Speaking of which, what did you make of Janet Jackson's "wardrobe malfunction" at the 2004 Super Bowl?

LB: Every news station was like, "Holy God! Did you see what happened at the halftime show yesterday? Janet Jackson's breast was exposed! It was horrifying! Let's take a look at it. It was terrible. Let's look at it again. It was disgusting! Can we see the tit again?" The Goodyear blimp flew over and we got a shot of the tit right from the blimp: Let's look at that tit! It's 5:02, we haven't seen the tit since 5. Let's look at that again!" And then Congress... Which doesn't do *shit*...! Stops on a dime! "Holy God! Did you see the tit?! Let's talk about the tit!" And they locked themselves in and they probably got huge pictures of the tit so they could get a closer look at the tit. "You see how big that tit is? It's insane how big that tit is!" They spent so much time looking at that tit, I actually thought Osama bin Laden was hiding in it. And then one by one, they came on TV to pontificate about how we're going into a moral sewer, about how this image of a breast at a family half-time show was not only "disgusting," it was "disturbing," it was "shocking," it was "indecent." But I thought, It's just a *tit*! None of those adjectives *apply*.

JW: What's the difference between you and your onstage character?

LB: The character onstage is me if I'm in Los Angeles for more than a day. Otherwise I'm much more relaxed than the character. I can get pretty wound up, but I don't have the kind of anger that I used to have. Well, I've still got it, but I don't let it rip. But I was out with some friends in New Orleans recently and there was this woman—this may be why I don't get laid—and she said that she thought that Bush really is a religious and sincere man. I went *nuts*. Certain buttons just set me off. Or if I'm watching *Meet the Press* or *Face the Nation*, where you actually see these people as they are and they can't sound-bite it, that's when I *really* become the guy onstage. I can't abide it.

THE WAR BETWEEN
MEN AND WOMEN

The first time Adam had a chance, he laid the blame on women.

NANCY ASTOR

A man who has never made a woman angry is a failure in life.

CHRISTOPHER MORLEY

Heinrich Heine bequeathed his estate to his wife on the condition that she marry again, because, according to Heine, "There will be at least one man who will regret my death."

Girls have an unfair advantage over men: If they can't get what they want by being smart, they can get it by being dumb.　　　YUL BRYNNER

NOEL COWARD: Why Edna, you look almost like a man in that suit.
EDNA FERBER: So do you, Noel, so do you.

It is assumed that the woman must wait, motionless, until she is wooed. That is how the spider waits for the fly.　　　GEORGE BERNARD SHAW

When men and women agree, it is only in their conclusions; their reasons are always different.　　　GEORGE SANTAYANA

In the sex war, thoughtlessness is the weapon of the male, vindictiveness of the female.   CYRIL CONNOLLY

Never go to bed mad. Stay up and fight.   PHYLLIS DILLER

When women discovered the orgasm it was, combined with modern birth control, perhaps the biggest single nail in the coffin of male dominance.
                                                                EVE FIGES

MALE HECKLER: Are you a lesbian?
FLORYNCE KENNEDY: Are you my alternative?

The concern that some women show at the absence of their husbands does not arise from their not seeing them and being with them, but from the apprehension that their husbands are enjoying pleasures in which they do not participate, and which, from their being at a distance, they have not the power of interrupting.   MICHEL DE MONTAIGNE

BESSIE BRADDOCK: Winston, you're drunk!
WINSTON CHURCHILL: Bessie, you're ugly. But tomorrow I shall be sober.

I don't believe man is woman's natural enemy. Perhaps her lawyer is.
                                                          SHANA ALEXANDER

She was so glad to see me go, that I have almost a mind to come again, that she may again have the same pleasure.   SAMUEL JOHNSON

On a visit to the United States, Winston Churchill attended a luncheon where fried chicken was served. When he politely asked the hostess, "May I have more breast?" she scolded him: "Mr. Churchill, in America we say 'white meat' or 'dark meat.'" The next day Churchill sent the woman an orchid with the following note: "Madam, I would be much obliged if you would pin this on your white meat."

Most hierarchies were established by men who now monopolize the upper levels, thus depriving women of their rightful share of opportunities for incompetence.   LAURENCE PETER

Between men and women there is no friendship possible. There is passion, enmity, worship, love, but no friendship.   OSCAR WILDE

GUY KAWASAKI

Computer Curmudgeon

Guy Kawasaki was born in Honolulu, Hawaii, in 1954. After attending Iolani School, he earned a BA in psychology from Stanford and an MBA from UCLA. In the mid-1980s, he brought the practice of evangelism to the high-tech industry when, as Apple's chief evangelist, he helped create a market for the new Macintosh desktop computer. After leaving Apple he became CEO of ACIUS, which produced the 4th Dimension database program, and cofounded Fog City Software. He is currently a managing director of Garage Technology Ventures, a Silicon Valley venture capital firm, as well as a husband, father, speaker, and hockey addict. He's the author of eight books, including *The Computer Curmudgeon, Rules for Revolutionaries,* and *The Art of the Start.*

JW: When you published The Computer Curmudgeon *in 1992, you defined "electronic mail" as "a method for receiving messages you cannot understand, from people you don't know, concerning things you don't care about." Is that still true fifteen years later?*

GK: Yes, in fact, more true than ever. E-mail is too cheap because it doesn't require enough time, effort, or expense to create and send. Hence, the relationship between sender and receiver is asymmetric: easy/cheap for sender, hard/expensive/pain-in-the-ass for receiver.

Unfortunately young people—i.e., people with more time than money, have created even worse things for old people—i.e., people with more money than time. The worst example is creation of a class of people called "bloggers." These are folks with nothing to say writing for people with nothing to do.

JW: Does that apply to you and the people who read your blog?

GK: Did Ambrose Bierce consider himself devilish? For sure it applies to me. It may or may not apply to my readers.

A tiny number of the people who read my blog are clueless. My favorites are the ones who complain about four things: the top-ten format; the bulleted-list format; the long length of my posts; and my plugs for stuff that I like. This is akin to going into a sushi bar and complaining that it serves raw fish. That's what a sushi bar does. Long top tens, bulleted lists, essays, and evangelism are what I do.

I especially love the people who threaten to stop reading my blog unless I stop doing one of those four things. Let me get this straight: You're going to stop reading my *free* blog? I hope they have a SCUBA (Self-Contained Underwater Bozo Apparatus) tank because they won't be able to hold their breath long enough.

JW: What about bloggers?

GK: The more popular a person thinks he is in the blogosphere, the thinner his skin and the thicker his hypocrisy. This should be exactly the opposite: the higher you go the thicker the skin and thinner the hypocrisy. The more a blogger uses the pronoun "I," the less he has to say. Many bloggers apparently believe that people not only give a shiitake about everything they say, but that these people are hanging on to every word.

There are three kinds of bloggers: human news bots (is this an oxymoron?), ranters, and essayists. Each kind is an art form. The third category, the essayists, might be the most difficult kind of blogging, and unfortunately it's the category I aspire to. It's a good thing I have eight books to plagiarize.

JW: Then why do you blog? It can't be for the money.

GK: No, it's hard to make money blogging because advertising revenues just don't amount to much. But there are other significant rewards—like helping people change the world. Here's a little story for you: At eleven P.M. a few weeks ago, my wife asked me, "What are you doing?" I wish I could have said, "Making money." Instead I told her, "I'm changing the world, fifteen thousand people at a time." To which she deadpanned, "Oh, you're blogging again…"

JW: You've also tried to change the way people e-mail. What are some of your current dos and don'ts?

GK: First of all, craft your subject line. Your subject line is a window into your soul, so make it a good one. It has to get your message past the spam filters, so take out anything about sex and money-saving special offers. Then, it must communicate that your message is highly personalized. For example, "Love your blog," "Love your book," and "You skate well for an old man," always work on me.

Also, limit your recipients. As a rule of thumb, the more people you send an e-mail to, the less likely any single person will respond to it, much less perform any action that you requested. If you're going to ask a large group of people to do something, then at least use blind carbon copies. That way, not only will the few recipients think they're important, you won't burden the whole list with everyone's e-mail address. Nor will you reveal everyone's e-mail address inadvertently.

JW: Anything else?

GK: Don't write in ALL CAPS. Everyone probably knows this by now, but just in case: Text in all caps is interpreted as YELLING in e-mail. Even if you're not yelling, it's more difficult to read text that's in all caps, so do your recipients a favor and use standard capitalization practices. Also, use plain text. I hate HTML e-mail. I tried it for a while, but it's not worth the trouble of sending or receiving it. All those pretty colors and fancy type faces and styles make me want to puke. Finally, say what you have to say in as brief and plain a manner as possible. If you can't say it in plain text, you don't have anything worth saying.

JW: What about the length of an e-mail message?

GK: The ideal length for an e-mail is five sentences. If you're asking something reasonable of a reasonable recipient, simply explain who you are in one or two sentences and get to the ask. If it's not reasonable, don't ask at all.

My theory is that people who tell their life story suspect that their request is on shaky ground, so they try build up a case to soften up the recipient. Another very good reason to keep it short is that you never know where your e-mail will end up—all the way from your minister to the attorney general of New York. There is one exception to this brevity rule: When you really don't want anything from the recipient, and you simply want to heap praise and kindness upon her. Then you can go on as long as you like!

JW: Man, that's a lot of good advice there...

GK: Wait, I'm just getting warmed up. Make sure you "quote back." Even if e-mails are flying back and forth within hours, be sure to quote back the text that you're answering. Assume that the person you're corresponding with has fifty e-mail conversations going at once. If you answer with a simple, "Yes, I agree," most of the time you will force the recipient to dig through his deleted mail folder to figure out what you're agreeing to. However, don't "fisk" either. Fisking is when you quote back the entire message and respond line by line, often in an argumentative way. This is anal if not downright childish, so don't feel like you have to respond to every issue.

And don't FUQ up, that is, fabricate unanswerable questions. Many people send e-mails that are unanswerable. If your question is only appropriate for your psychiatrist, mother, or spouse, then ask them, not your recipient. When I get this type of message I go into a deep funk: (a) Should I just ignore the message? But then the person will think I'm an arrogant schmuck; (b) Should I just give a cursory answer and explain that it's not answerable? (c) Should I carefully craft a heartfelt message probing for more information so that I can get into the deep recesses of the sender's mind and begin a long tail of a message thread that lasts two weeks? Usually, I pick option (b).

There's one more type of unanswerable message: the open-ended question that is so broad it should be used in a job interview at Google. For example, "What do you think of the RIAA lawsuits?" "What kind of person is Steve Jobs?" "Do you think it's a good time to start a company?" My favorite ones begin like this: "I haven't given this much thought, but what do you think about…?" In other words, the sender hasn't done much thinking and wants to shift responsibility to the recipient. Dream on. The purpose of e-mail is to save time, not kill time. You may have infinite time to ask essay questions but don't assume your recipient does.

JW: How do you deal with hostile e-mails?

GK: I try to chill out before I answer. This is a rule that I've broken many times, and each time that I did, I regretted it. When someone writes you a pissy e-mail, the irresistible temptation is to retaliate. (And this is for an inconsequential e-mail message—no wonder countries go to war.) You will almost always make the situation worse.

A good practice is to wait twenty-four hours before you respond. An even better practice is that you never say in e-mail what you wouldn't say in person—this applies to both the sender and recipient, by the way. The best practice is to never answer and let the sender wonder if his e-mail got caught in a spam filter or didn't even matter enough to merit a response. Take my advice and do as I say, not as I have done—or will do.

JW: Something tells me you have a definite opinion about e-mail attachments.

GK: How often do you get an e-mail that says, "Please read the attached letter," then you open the attachment, and it's a dumb-shiitake Word document with a three-paragraph message that could have easily been copied and pasted into the e-mail? Or, even worse, someone believes that his curve-jumping, paradigm-shifting, patent-pending way to sell dog food online means you'll want to receive his ten-megabyte PowerPoint presentation? Now that lots of people are opening messages with smart phones—sending files when you don't have to is a sure sign of bozosity.

JW: Bozosity? Did you coin the term?

GK: Actually, I first heard [Lotus Development founder] Mitch Kapor use it. I stole it from him—actually I made a career out of "outing" the term. Bozosity comes in two flavors: First, there is the loser bozo. This is a person who hasn't done anything but can tell everyone else why they won't succeed. He's a loser. He's easy to ignore. Second, there is the winner bozo. This is the dangerous one because he's rich, famous, powerful, and therefore "smart" (big leap of faith). But successful innovators are sometimes the biggest bozos vis-à-vis the next curve. For example, the minicomputer revolutionaries couldn't understand or embrace the personal computer revolutionaries, but yet they kicked the shiitake out of the mainframe guys.

JW: You've written that you suffer from Ménière's disease, and you have a novel theory on how you got it.

GK: The symptoms of Ménière's include hearing loss, tinnitus [a constant ringing in the ear], and vertigo. There are many medical theories about its cause: too much salt, caffeine, or alcohol in one's diet, too much stress, and allergies. Thus, I've worked to control all these factors. However, I have another theory. As a venture capitalist, I have to listen to hundreds of entrepreneurs pitch their companies. Most of these pitches are crap: sixty slides about a "patent pending," "first mover advantage," "all we have to do is get one percent of the people in China to buy our product" startup. These pitches are so lousy that I'm losing my hearing. There's a constant ringing in my ear, and every once in while the world starts spinning.

JW: What do you think of people who walk around wearing Bluetooth ear pieces?

GK: They flunked out of Secret Service training.

QUOTES ON "S"

SAINT

Saint, n. A dead sinner revised and edited.

AMBROSE BIERCE

Saints should always be judged guilty until they are proved innocent.

GEORGE ORWELL

SAN FRANCISCO

I'd never set foot in San Francisco. Of all the Sodoms and Gomorrahs in our modern world, it is the worst. It needs another quake, another whiff of fire—and—more than all else—a steady trade wind of grapeshot. That moral penal colony of the world.

AMBROSE BIERCE

San Francisco is a self-consciously civilized place, pleased by its reasonable scale and unreasonable hills, proud of the slightly loopy beaux arts buildings and the great swaths of pastel houses, altogether seduced by its own fey charms.

KURT ANDERSEN

In San Francisco there's a sign outside a downtown smut arcade that reads, "Got porn?"

IAN SHOALES

In San Francisco, Halloween is redundant.   WILL DURST

--------------------- SANITY ---------------------

Sanity is a cozy lie.   SUSAN SONTAG

--------------------- SANTA CLAUS ---------------------

Santa Claus has the right idea: visit people once a year.   VICTOR BORGE

--------------------- SATIRE ---------------------

Satire is a sort of glass, wherein beholders do generally discover everybody's face but their own.   JONATHAN SWIFT

Satire is moral outrage transformed into comic art.   PHILIP ROTH

You can't make up anything anymore. The world itself is a satire. All you're doing is recording it.   ART BUCHWALD

--------------------- SALARY ---------------------

The salary of the chief executive of a large corporation is not a market award for achievement. It is frequently in the nature of a warm personal gesture by the individual to himself.   JOHN KENNETH GALBRAITH

--------------------- SCANDAL ---------------------

Scandal is gossip made tedious by morality.   OSCAR WILDE

--------------------- SCIENTIST ---------------------

I believe that a scientist looking at nonscientific problems is just as dumb as the next guy.   RICHARD FEYNMAN

SCHIZOPHRENIA

Schizophrenia is a successful attempt not to adapt to pseudosocial realities.
R. D. LAING

SCHOOL DAYS

School days, I believe, are the unhappiest in the whole span of human existence. They are full of dull, unintelligible tasks, new and unpleasant ordinances, brutal violations of common sense and common decency.
H. L. MENCKEN

Show me a man who has enjoyed his school days and I'll show you a bully and a bore.
ROBERT MORLEY

SCHOOLMASTER

The average schoolmaster is and always must be essentially an ass, for how can one imagine an intelligent man engaging in so puerile an avocation?
H. L. MENCKEN

SCOTT, WILLARD

Willard Scott smiles so much, I don't think he has a central nervous system.
LEWIS BLACK

SCOUT TROOP

A scout troop consists of twelve little kids dressed like schmucks following a big schmuck dressed like a kid.
JACK BENNY

SCREENWRITERS

Schmucks with Underwoods.
JACK WARNER

SCRIPT

There is no such thing as a good script.   JOHN FORD

SELF-CRITICISM

Under a forehead roughly comparable to that of Javanese and Piltdown man
are visible a pair of tiny pig eyes, lit up alternately by greed and concupiscence.
                                                            S. J. PERELMAN

SELF-DENIAL

Self-denial is the shining sore on the leprous body of Christianity.
                                                            OSCAR WILDE

Self-denial is not a virtue; it is only the effect of prudence on rascality.
                                                    GEORGE BERNARD SHAW

Self-denial is indulgence of a propensity to forego.   AMBROSE BIERCE

SELF-HATRED

He who despises himself esteems himself as a self-despiser.
                                            FRIEDRICH WILHELM NIETZSCHE

There is luxury in self-reproach. When we blame ourselves we feel no one
else has a right to blame us.   OSCAR WILDE

SELF-KNOWLEDGE

"Know thyself?" If I knew myself, I'd run away.
                                            JOHANN WOLFGANG VON GOETHE

Know thyself! A maxim as pernicious as it is ugly. Whoever observes himself arrests his own development. A caterpillar who wanted to know itself well would never become a butterfly. ANDRÉ GIDE

I am the only person in the world I should like to know thoroughly.
OSCAR WILDE

───────────────────────── SELF-LOVE ─────────────────────────

To fall in love with yourself is the first secret of happiness. I did so at the age of four and a half. Then if you're not a good mixer you can always fall back on your own company. ROBERT MORLEY

To love oneself is the beginning of a lifelong romance. OSCAR WILDE

He who is in love with himself has at least this advantage—he won't encounter many rivals. G. C. LICHTENBERG

If we were not all so excessively interested in ourselves, life would be so uninteresting that none of us would be able to endure it.
ARTHUR SCHOPENHAUER

I find that when I do not think of myself I do not think at all. JULES RENARD

In an age when the fashion is to be in love with yourself, confessing to being in love with somebody else is an admission of unfaithfulness to one's beloved.
RUSSELL BAKER

───────────────────────── SELF-RESPECT ─────────────────────────

Self-respect: the secure feeling that no one, as yet, is suspicious.
H. L. MENCKEN

—————————— SELF-SACRIFICE ——————————

Self-sacrifice enables us to sacrifice other people without blushing.

GEORGE BERNARD SHAW

—————————— SENATORS ——————————

The founding fathers, in their wisdom, devised a method by which our republic can take one hundred of its most prominent numbskulls and keep them out of the private sector where they might do actual harm.

P. J. O'ROURKE

There ought to be one day—just one—when there is open season on senators.

WILL ROGERS

—————————— SENILITY ——————————

I am in the prime of senility.   JOEL CHANDLER HARRIS

—————————— SENTIMENTALITY ——————————

Sentimentality is a superstructure covering brutality.   C. G. JUNG

Sentimentality is the emotional promiscuity of those who have no sentiment.

NORMAN MAILER

—————————— SEX ——————————

Sex is God's joke on human beings.   BETTE DAVIS

Sexual intercourse is a slight attack of apoplexy.   DEMOCRITUS

Sex: the thing that takes up the least amount of time and causes the most amount of trouble.   JOHN BARRYMORE

Sex is work.   ANDY WARHOL

Sex is one of the most wholesome, beautiful and natural experiences that money can buy.   STEVE MARTIN

The sexual drive is nothing but the motor memory of previously remembered pleasure.   WILHELM REICH

Sex is a pleasurable exercise of plumbing, but be careful or you'll get yeast in your drain tap.   RITA MAE BROWN

The pleasure is momentary, the position ridiculous, and the expense damnable.
                                                    LORD CHESTERFIELD

Nothing in our culture, not even home computers, is more overrated than the epidermal felicity of two featherless bipeds in desperate congress.
                                                    QUENTIN CRISP

Is sex dirty? Only if it's done right.   WOODY ALLEN

In the duel of sex, woman fights from a dreadnaught and man from an open raft.   H. L. MENCKEN

If your sexual fantasies were truly of interest to others, they would no longer be fantasies.   FRAN LEBOWITZ

Men and women, women and men. It will never work.   ERICA JONG

If a man and woman, entering a room together, close the door behind them, the man will come out sadder and the woman wiser.   H. L. MENCKEN

Sexual enlightenment is justified insofar as girls cannot learn too soon how children do not come into the world.   KARL KRAUS

Why should we take advice on sex from the Pope? If he knows anything about it, he shouldn't.   GEORGE BERNARD SHAW

All this fuss about sleeping together. For physical pleasure I'd sooner go to my dentist any day.   EVELYN WAUGH

Sex is the biggest nothing of all time.   ANDY WARHOL

In the case of some women, orgasms take quite a bit of time. Before signing on with such a partner, make sure you are willing to lay aside, say, the month of June, with sandwiches having to be brought in.
                    BRUCE JAY FRIEDMAN

I've tried several varieties of sex. The conventional position makes me claustrophobic. And the others give me either a stiff neck or lockjaw.
                    TALLULAH BANKHEAD

The big difference between sex for money and sex for free is that sex for money usually costs a lot less.   BRENDAN BEHAN

A woman in a hotel bar told the sportswriter Woody Paige that she would do anything he wanted for a hundred dollars. "I'm in Room 825," he replied. "Go up and write a column and a sidebar."

As I grow older and older
And totter towards the tomb,

I find that I care less and less
Who goes to bed with whom.

DOROTHY L. SAYERS

As one gets older, litigation replaces sex.

GORE VIDAL

Sex hasn't been the same since women started enjoying it.

LEWIS GRIZZARD

Sex has become much more competitive, with the girls becoming sort of predators as well. It's ferocious.

MARTIN AMIS

My husband is German. Every night I get dressed up like Poland and he invades me.

BETTE MIDLER

It doesn't matter what you do in the bedroom as long as you don't do it in the street and frighten the horses.

MRS. PATRICK CAMPBELL

For the butterfly, mating and propagation involve the sacrifice of life, for the human being, the sacrifice of beauty.

JOHANN WOLFGANG VON GOETHE

The ability to make love frivolously is the chief characteristic which distinguishes human beings from beasts.

HEYWOOD BROUN

Instruction in sex is as important as instruction in food; yet not only are our adolescents not taught the physiology of sex, but never warned that the strongest sexual attraction may exist between persons so incompatible in tastes and capacities that they could not endure living together for a week, much less a lifetime.

GEORGE BERNARD SHAW

After coitus every animal is sad, except the human female and the rooster.
                                                                    GALEN

One night I was sitting with friends at a table in a crowded Key West bar. At a nearby table, there was a mildly drunk woman with a very drunk husband. Presently, the woman approached us and asked me to sign a paper napkin. All this seemed to anger her husband; he staggered over to the table, and after unzipping his trousers and hauling out his equipment, said: "Since you're autographing things, why don't you autograph this?" The tables surrounding us had grown silent, so a great many people heard my reply, which was: "I don't know if I can autograph it, but perhaps I can *initial* it."
                                                            TRUMAN CAPOTE

I can't understand why more people aren't bisexual. It would double your chances for a date on Saturday night.   WOODY ALLEN

Social confusion has now reached a point at which the pursuit of immorality turns out to be more exhausting than compliance with the old moral codes.
                                                      DENIS DE ROUGEMONT

Hungarian novelist FERENC MOLNÁR, told that his mistress had been unfaithful to him while he was out of town: "She sleeps with others because she loves them, but for *money*, only with me!"

———————————— SEXUAL REVOLUTION ————————————
The sexual revolution went too far, informationwise. When you find phrases like "suck face" as a euphemism for "kiss," it sort of takes the zing out of intimate personal contact.   IAN SHOALES

No one, thank goodness, advocates that people should go about with long strands of green snot hanging from their noses in the name of nasal freedom, yet quite a few people have been converted in recent years to a belief that it is permissible for them to inflict the sights, sounds and smells of their bodies on any innocent bystander in the name of "sexual freedom."

QUENTIN CRISP

SHAW, GEORGE BERNARD

Bernard Shaw is an excellent man; he has not an enemy in the world, and none of his friends like him.   OSCAR WILDE

It is his life work to announce the obvious in terms of the scandalous.

H. L. MENCKEN

He writes his plays for the ages—the ages between five and twelve.

GEORGE JEAN NATHAN

SHIP

Being in a ship is like being in a jail, with the chance of being drowned.

SAMUEL JOHNSON

SHOPPING

I like to walk down Bond Street, thinking of all the things I don't want.

LOGAN PEARSALL SMITH

SILENCE

Silence is the most perfect expression of scorn.

GEORGE BERNARD SHAW

SIN

Sin is geographical.   BERTRAND RUSSELL

Sin is a dangerous toy in the hands of the virtuous. It should be left to the congenitally sinful, who know when to play with it and when to let it alone.
H. L. MENCKEN

The major sin is the sin of being born.   SAMUEL BECKETT

SINCERITY

It is dangerous to be sincere unless you are also stupid.
GEORGE BERNARD SHAW

A little sincerity is a dangerous thing, and a great deal of it is absolutely fatal.
OSCAR WILDE

I don't think you want too much sincerity in society. It would be like an iron girder in a house of cards.   W. SOMERSET MAUGHAM

SKEPTICISM

Skepticism is the first step on the road to philosophy.   DENIS DIDEROT

I respect faith, but doubt is what gets you an education.
WILSON MIZNER

SKIING

I do not participate in any sport with ambulances at the bottom of a hill.
ERMA BOMBECK

The sport of skiing consists of wearing three thousand dollars' worth of clothes and equipment and driving two hundred miles in the snow in order to stand around at a bar and get drunk.   P. J. O'ROURKE

------------------------------ SMOKING ------------------------------

Smoking is, as far as I am concerned, the entire point of being an adult. Many people find smoking objectionable. I myself find many—even more— things objectionable. I do not like aftershave lotion, adults who roller-skate, children who speak French, or anyone who is unduly tan. I do not, however, go around enacting legislation and putting up signs.   FRAN LEBOWITZ

If you're a smoker and you're telling me that you didn't know that cigarettes are bad for you, then you're lying through the hole in your trachea.

DENNIS MILLER

It has always been my rule never to smoke when asleep, and never to refrain when awake.   MARK TWAIN

I never smoked a cigarette until I was nine.   H. L. MENCKEN

------------------------------ SNOW ------------------------------

A lot of people like snow. I find it to be an unnecessary freezing of water.

CARL REINER

------------------------------ SOBRIETY ------------------------------

There is nothing wrong with sobriety in moderation.   JOHN CIARDI

------------------------------ SOCCER MOMS ------------------------------

Fuck soccer moms.   GEORGE CARLIN

---------------------------------- SOCIALISM ----------------------------------

The function of socialism is to raise suffering to a higher level.

NORMAN MAILER

We should have had socialism already, but for the socialists.

GEORGE BERNARD SHAW

Can you imagine lying in bed on a Sunday morning with the love of your life, a cup of tea and a bacon sandwich, and all you had to read was the *Socialist Worker*?

DEREK JAMESON

---------------------------------- SOCIAL PROGRESS ----------------------------------

As it will be in the future, it was at the birth of Man.
There are only four things certain since Social
    Progress began:—
That the Dog returns to his Vomit and the Sow returns
    to her Mire,
And the burnt Fool's bandaged finger goes wabbling
    back to the Fire.

RUDYARD KIPLING

---------------------------------- SOCIAL SECURITY ----------------------------------

The Social Security system is headed for bankruptcy and total collapse unless it is reformed soon. The good news is, the leaders of both major political parties are well aware of this looming disaster and the need for prompt, decisive action. The bad news is, our political leaders could not take prompt, decisive action if their undershorts caught fire. The Democrats and Republicans have been debating what to do about Social Security for decades now without producing anything other than accusations that their opponents are lying vermin scum. This is true as far as it goes, but it doesn't address the underlying problem.   DAVE BARRY

--------------------- SOCIETY ---------------------

Society is a madhouse whose wardens are the officials and police.
AUGUST STRINDBERG

Society attacks early when the individual is helpless.   B. F. SKINNER

Society is always diseased, and the best is most so.
HENRY DAVID THOREAU

--------------------- SOLITUDE ---------------------

Solitude would be ideal if you could pick the people to avoid.   KARL KRAUS

--------------------- SOUTHERN CALIFORNIA ---------------------

In a thousand years or so, when the first archaeologists from beyond the date-line unload their boat on the sands of Southern California, they will find much the same scene as confronted the Franciscan Missionaries. A dry landscape will extend from the ocean to the mountains. Bel Air and Beverly Hills will lie naked save for scrub and cactus, all their flimsy multitude of architectural styles turned long ago to dust, while the horned toad and the turkey buzzard leave their faint imprint on the dunes that will drift on Sunset Boulevard.   EVELYN WAUGH

There's nothing wrong with Southern California that a rise in the ocean level wouldn't cure.   ROSS MACDONALD

Southern California, where the American Dream came too true.
LAWRENCE FERLINGHETTI

SOUTHERNERS

Southerners are probably not more hospitable than New Englanders are; they are simply more willing to remind you of the fact that they are being hospitable.   RAY L. BIRDWHISTELL

SOY MILK

There's no such thing as soy milk. It's soy juice. Know how come I know there's no such thing as soy milk? Because there's no soy titty, is there?

LEWIS BLACK

SPEED READING

I took a speed reading course and read War and Peace in twenty minutes. It involves Russia.   WOODY ALLEN

When the late President Kennedy was revealed as a speed reader, it took me three hours to read the article about it.   OSCAR LEVANT

SPORTS

The balls used in top class games are generally smaller than those used in others.   PAUL FUSSELL

Serious sport has nothing to do with fair play. It is bound up with hatred, jealousy, boastfulness, disregard of all rules and sadistic pleasure in witnessing violence: in other words it is war minus the shooting.

GEORGE ORWELL

The more violent the body contact of the sports you watch, the lower your class.   PAUL FUSSELL

It is a noteworthy fact that kicking and beating have played so considerable a part in the habits which necessity has imposed on mankind in past ages that the only way of preventing civilized men from beating and kicking their wives is to organize games in which they can kick and beat balls.

GEORGE BERNARD SHAW

Baseball is what we were, football is what we have become.

MARY MCGRORY

Rugby is a beastly game played by gentlemen; soccer is a gentleman's game played by beasts; football is a beastly game played by beasts.   HENRY BLAHA

SPRING

Every year, back spring comes, with nasty little birds, yapping their fool heads off, and the ground all mucked up with arbutus.   DOROTHY PARKER

Spring makes everything look filthy.   KATHERINE WHITEHORN

STARBUCKS

Did I miss a fucking meeting with the coffee? You can get every other flavor except COFFEE-FLAVORED COFFEE! They got mochaccino, frapaccino, chococcino, crapaccino, rapaccino, Al Pacino. WHAT THE FUCK! www.whattheFUCK.com!   DENIS LEARY

From the beginning of time, man has looked at the heavens and firmly believed that the end of the universe ends out in space. It's not true. The end of the universe happens to be in the United States. I have seen it. And, oddly enough, it's in Houston, Texas…I know, I was shocked too…I left the comedy club there and walked down the street. On one corner, there was a Starbucks. And across the street from that, Starbucks, in the exact same building as that Starbucks was a Starbucks. At first I thought the sun was playing tricks on my eyes. But, no. There was a Starbucks across from a Starbucks. And that, my friends, is the end of the universe.

LEWIS BLACK

The more complicated the Starbucks order, the bigger the asshole.

BILL MAHER

STARLET

In Hollywood a starlet is the name for any woman under thirty who is not actively employed in a brothel. BEN HECHT

STATESMAN

A statesman is a successful politician who is dead. THOMAS B. REED

STATISTICS

There are three kinds of lies: lies, damned lies, and statistics.

BENJAMIN DISRAELI

In ancient times they had no statistics so they had to fall back on lies.

STEPHEN LEACOCK

He uses statistics as a drunken man uses lampposts…for support rather than illumination. ANDREW LANG

USA Today has come out with a new survey; apparently, three out of every four people make up 75 percent of the population.

DAVID LETTERMAN

STINK

Every stink that fights the ventilator thinks it is Don Quixote.

STANISLAW J. LEC

STOCKHOLDER

An excellent monument might be erected to the unknown stockholder. It might take the form of a solid stone arc of faith apparently floating in a pool of water.

FELIX RIESENBERG

STRESS

The American way of stress is comparable to Freud's "beloved symptom," his name for the cherished neurosis that a patient cultivates like the rarest of orchids and does not want to be cured of. Stress makes Americans feel busy, important, and in demand, and simultaneously deprived, ignored, and victimized. Stress makes them feel interesting and complex instead of boring and simple, and carries an assumption of sensitivity not unlike the Old World assumption that aristocrats were high-strung. In short, stress has become a status symbol.

FLORENCE KING

STUDIO HEADS

Studio heads have foreheads by dint of electrolysis.

S. J. PERELMAN

STUDENT ATHLETES

Can't anything be done about calling these guys "student athletes"? That's like referring to Attila the Hun's cavalry as "weekend warriors."

RUSSELL BAKER

STUPIDITY

Stupidity is an elemental force for which no earthquake is a match.

KARL KRAUS

Some scientists claim that *hydrogen*, because it is so plentiful, *is the basic building block of the universe*. I dispute that. I say there is more *stupidity* than *hydrogen*, and that is the *basic building block of the universe*.

FRANK ZAPPA

If you attack stupidity you attack an entrenched interest with friends in government and every walk of public life, and you will make small progress against it.   SAMUEL MARCHBANKS

Never underestimate the power of very stupid people in large groups.

JOHN KENNETH GALBRAITH

Never attribute to malice that which can be adequately explained by stupidity.

HANLON'S RAZOR

———————————————— SUBURBIA ————————————————

Suburbia is where the developer bulldozes out the trees, then names the streets after them.   BILL VAUGHAN

Slums may well be breeding grounds of crime, but middle-class suburbs are incubators of apathy and delirium.   CYRIL CONNOLLY

———————————————— STYLING MOUSSE ————————————————

Styling mousse, which is gunk that looks like shaving cream…was invented by a French hair professional whom, if you met him, you would want to punch directly in the mouth.   DAVE BARRY

SUBSCRIPTION CARDS

I have…had a disturbing dream in which I break through a cave wall near Nag Hammadi and discover urns full of ancient Coptic scrolls. As I unfurl the first scroll, a subscription card to some Gnostic exercise magazine flutters out.

COLIN MCENROE

SUCCESS

There is an old motto that runs, "If at first you don't succeed, try, try again." This is nonsense. It ought to read "If at first you don't succeed, quit, quit at once."

STEPHEN LEACOCK

Success is the one unpardonable sin against one's fellows.

AMBROSE BIERCE

Moderation is a fatal thing. Nothing succeeds like excess.

OSCAR WILDE

Nothing succeeds like address.

FRAN LEBOWITZ

Nothing succeeds like the appearance of success.

CHRISTOPHER LASCH

The desire for success lubricates secret prostitutions in the soul.

NORMAN MAILER

The penalty for success is to be bored by the people who used to snub you.

NANCY ASTOR

Success is a great deodorant.

ELIZABETH TAYLOR

Nothing fails like success.

LESLIE FIEDLER

SUCCESS AND FAILURE

Success and failure are both difficult to endure. Along with success come drugs, divorce, fornication, bullying, travel, medication, depression, neurosis and suicide. With failure comes failure.   JOSEPH HELLER

Success and failure are equally disastrous.   TENNESSEE WILLIAMS

SUICIDE

Suicide is belated acquiescence in the opinion of one's wife's relatives.
          H. L. MENCKEN

There are many who dare not kill themselves for fear of what the neighbors will say.   CYRIL CONNOLLY

If you are of the opinion that the contemplation of suicide is sufficient evidence of a poetic nature, do not forget that actions speak louder than words.
          FRAN LEBOWITZ

Dear World: I am leaving because I am bored. I am leaving you with your worries in this sweet cesspool.
          GEORGE SANDERS (suicide note, April 25, 1972)

No matter how much a woman loved a man, it would still give her a glow to see him commit suicide for her.   H. L. MENCKEN

I don't think suicide is so terrible. Some rainy winter Sundays when there's a little boredom, you should always carry a gun. Not to shoot yourself, but to know exactly that you're always making a choice.
          LINA WERTMULLER

Razors pain you
Rivers are damp;
Acids stain you;
And drugs cause cramp.
Guns aren't lawful;
Nooses give;
Gas smells awful;
You might as well live.

DOROTHY PARKER

Guns are always the best method for private suicide. Drugs are too chancy. You might just miscalculate the dosage and just have a good time.

P. J. O'ROURKE

The thought of suicide is a great consolation: With the help of it one has got through many a bad night.   FRIEDRICH WILHELM NIETZSCHE

THE SUN

Thank heavens, the sun has gone in, and I don't have to go out and enjoy it.

LOGAN PEARSALL SMITH

SUNDAY

Sunday: a day given over by Americans to wishing they were dead and in heaven, and that their neighbors were dead and in hell.

H. L. MENCKEN

SUNDAY SCHOOL

A Sunday school is a prison in which children do penance for the evil conscience of their parents.   H. L. MENCKEN

———————————— SUPERMARKET TOMATOES ————————————

You've probably noticed that modern supermarket tomatoes are inedible. This is because they're not bred for human consumption. They're bred to be shipped long distances via truck, which requires that they have the same juicy tenderness as croquet balls. Even as you read these words, top vegetable scientists are field-testing the Tomato of Tomorrow, which can withstand direct mortar fire and cannot be penetrated by any known kitchen implement except the Veg-o-Matic Home Laser Slicer (Not Sold in Stores).

DAVE BARRY

———————————————— SURFNTURF ————————————————

The surfnturf, as I have always envisioned it, is a tiny, aquatic hereford that has horns and a shell—a beast that moves through the depths slowly, in herds, and can both moo and draw flies under water.   CALVIN TRILLIN

———————————— SWEETNESS AND LIGHT ————————————

Nobody's interested in sweetness and light.   HEDDA HOPPER

———————————————— SWITZERLAND ————————————————

Switzerland is simply a large, humpy, solid rock, with a thin skin of grass stretched over it.   MARK TWAIN

Switzerland is a curst, selfish, swinish country of brutes, placed in the most romantic region of the world.   LORD BYRON

The only interesting thing that can happen in a Swiss bedroom is suffocation by feather mattress.   DALTON TRUMBO

In Italy, for thirty years under the Borgais, they had warfare, terror, murder and bloodshed, but they produced Michelangelo, Leonardo da Vinci, and the

Renaissance. In Switzerland they had brotherly love, they had five hundred years of democracy and peace, and what did they produce? The cuckoo clock.
ORSON WELLES in *The Third Man* (Screenplay by Graham Greene)

SYMPATHY

I have no need of your God-damned sympathy. I wish only to be entertained by some of your grosser reminiscences.   ALEXANDER WOOLLCOTT

GEOFF SHACKELFORD

Golf Curmudgeon

Geoff Shackelford is a golf course architect and design consultant. A native of Southern California, he attended Pepperdine University in Malibu on a golf scholarship and graduated in 1994 with a BA in communication. He is the author of ten books on golf history and architecture, and is a regular contributor to numerous golf publications as well as his own Web site, www.geoffshackelford.com.

JW: What's wrong with golf?
GS: Lots of things, but two stand out: slow play and "corporatization." Slow

play is the most painful. Let me give you an extreme example: Not long ago, while taking a spin around one of America's great old courses, I came upon a twosome and their caddy. They appeared to be a father and son out for a quick afternoon round. Well, not quick: The father was frozen over his tee ball. When I stopped my golf cart and got out to inspect a nearby bunker, I noticed out of the corner of my eye that the father still had not hit his shot. I couldn't take my eyes off this fiasco. I barely resisted the urge to break into full [*Caddyshack* character] Al Czervik mode and scream, "LET'S GO-O…WHILE WE'RE *YOUNG*!" I guess the son and caddy sensed my interest, because they turned toward me with embarrassed faces. To think they must go through this forty to fifty times a round! At any rate, prior to the sun setting or the son intervening, the old man finally pulled the trigger, a solid forty-five seconds after locking himself into place with nary a flinch nor a waggle to break up the madness. And I know you'll be shocked to learn that he hit a weak push into the right trees.

This excruciating episode reminded me of a story about John Arthur Brown, the legendary president of Pine Valley who ruled over that great club for fifty-two years. America's number-one course has always been run as an autocracy, with the club president calling all the shots. Brown was notoriously impatient with slow players. One day a foursome of guests was taking its sweet time playing their round. The group had been warned to keep up but were either unable or unwilling to comply. So Brown got in his personal golf cart and drove to where the group's caddies were fore caddying on the thirteenth fairway. Upon his arrival, Brown told the caddies, "That's enough. Take the bags in." With that, he drove off. The caddies picked up the clubs. End of round. End of problem. Sometimes there's no other way to deal with an act as selfish as holding up play.

JW: What causes slow play?

GS: Slow play has many causes, including the example of tour players, technology, architecture, course setup, and even poorly spaced tee times. Slow play is endemic to a world where individuals take themselves too seriously. A lot of slow players have a breathtaking sense of entitlement. They think every shot must be treated as their last, and anyone who dares tell them otherwise is either "mean-spirited" or infringing on their inalienable right to take as much time as they want, regardless of the impact on others. Which is why John Arthur Brown's solution is sometimes the only way to deal with them. No debate, no appeal. Some people are just rude and you have to treat them accordingly.

JW: Aside from Mr. Brown's golf equivalent of capital punishment, what else can be done about slow play?

GS: We could make everyone buy a $300 rangefinder, widen and shorten courses, and make an example of PGA Tour players by assessing two-shot penalties for slow play. But it still wouldn't address the number of rounds ruined by selfishness. Maybe contracts need to be signed by golfers requiring them to leave if they don't play nine holes in a certain amount of time. Or end shotgun tournaments after four and a half hours, regardless of how many holes have been played. Sadly, this is what it has come to.

JW: What about the "corporatization" of the game?

GS: Let's be clear: What's wrong with golf is nothing compared to problems with things that really matter, like health care and education. But if you're a golfer, you know that the game has been taken over by a bunch of corporations frantic to meet analysts' earnings expectations by selling everyone the latest equipment on a rapid cycle. And now golf is also too expensive, commercialized beyond belief, because the equipment manufacturers either became publicly traded companies or were gobbled up by them. Before, when they were privately held, they were friends of the game. Now they're essentially unregulated, and they've become too powerful. But there's one bit of good news, at least to those of us who are sick of the corporate control and want to see their beloved profit margins take a hit: Because the corporations are so greedy, gouging people with $500 drivers and $5 golf balls, they're making the game inaccessible to the masses. Unlike education and health care, golf is optional, and plenty of people are choosing the option to take up bird-watching.

JW: But haven't Tiger Woods and Michelle Wie brought more people into golf?

GS: Tiger has delivered more viewers, as has Wie for the women's game, but not new players, because golf takes too long and is more elitist than ever. The sport parades out various social engineering programs to show that it isn't only for the wealthy, but that's just to make people feel less guilty about the high cost.

JW: You've written extensively on golf course architecture and have codesigned an award-winning layout yourself. Is the short-term-obsessed corporate thinking you talk about reflected in golf course design as well?

GS: Golf courses have had to spend millions of dollars on modifications to accommodate golfers hitting longer and longer, high-tech drivers, and they pass this cost along in the form of higher green fees. Golf has traditionally been controlled by people who, though they described themselves as old-fashioned conservatives, seemed to be infatuated with ostentatious maintenance values and over-the-top design. Nothing excited these old-school types as much as a big-name celebrity designer and a swollen construction tab. "They got—fill in a big name architect—and he spent $35 million!" they'd say with a gleam in their eye. But I think that's beginning to change. Ironically, those big spenders are helping spearhead a move back to more sensible values. While an element continues to celebrate the latest, biggest, gaudiest and most expensive course to come down the pike, more and more golfers from all backgrounds are embracing what might be called the "minimalist" design movement.

JW: Minimalist?

GS: Minimalism is the art of maximizing what nature bequeathed to us.

From the tiniest natural bump to the native grasses thriving on the worst soil, the minimalist looks for ways to maximize his canvas to provide a rewarding, sensible golf experience with low-profile, old-style, rugged-looking golf courses. While some golfers still view the minimalists as a bunch of VW van-driving tree huggers, the success of Bandon Dunes and other minimalist designs has convinced even the most materialistic developers that a great golf course isn't necessarily the most expensive to build or the most perfectly manicured. Growing numbers of golfers are learning to love design features that are found and saved during construction, and to appreciate the use of existing plant material to create a natural look that enhances beauty, saves money, and preserves wildlife habitats.

JW: How else has corporate avarice affected golf course design?

GS: I see a golf course as a true work of art where the elements of function, beauty, and playability all come together. Golf has its versions of Monet landscapes, only we actually get to step into those landscapes and interact with them. Then along comes the golf cart, not only a way for older or handicapped players to enjoy the game but also a major source of revenue for golf course operators, so that architecture now serves the needs of the cart first, and the actual playing of the course becomes secondary. Many of these courses are routed so that the ninth hole comes back to the clubhouse to deliver the cart riders to where they can buy stuff, even though the design suffers because of it. And one of the most acclaimed designers in the game openly brags about his ability to disguise cart paths, but not about the placement of bunkers or the design of greens. Which is like a movie director worrying more about the popcorn recipe than what he's putting up on the screen.

JW: In one of your recent columns you criticized what you deemed an egregious locution in the announcement of the PGA Tour's FedEx Cup: "We're leveraging the equity of the brand...." Can you cite other such linguistic travesties, and can you venture some kind of theory as to where this stuff comes from, and, more important, where it's taking us?

GS: That line about "leveraging the equity" of brands coincided with the announcement of an extremely ugly logo! There are so many "egregious locutions," I'm not sure where to begin. But you should smell a rat whenever you hear, "brand," "platform," "branding the platform," "platforming the brand," "repurposing," "monetizing," "incentivizing," "commoditizing." Then there's "tentpole," "pushback," "gaining traction"…I'm getting dizzy. It's all a product of the MBAs of the world trying to justify their degrees. They want to make everyone else feel stupid. What's frightening is that now a lot of this corporate-speak is coming from everyday folks and, worse, athletes. I actually heard a famous jock say, "At the end of the day, the bottom line is, it is what it is." We're doomed!

JW: You've published ten books with five different publishers, but I gather you haven't always been delighted by the process. What's wrong with book publishing in America?

GS: Where to start? How about, the conglomerate publishers are even more resistant to the benefits of technology than the music industry? I published a book [*The Future of Golf*] using a print-on-demand publisher. It was phenomenal. The entire process was conducted over the Internet, and the book was done in three months. Traditional publishers need a year to turn around a manuscript, presumably to help prepare a marketing plan, which in most cases ends up consisting of mailing a press release to reviewers. But back to print-on-demand, where the books are printed…*on demand.* You don't have an inventory in a warehouse, which is one of the biggest costs for traditional publishers.

Then there's the problem of major publishers' reliance on the opinions of the retail chains' book buyers. I'm sure these buyers are quite good at what they do, but the decision to publish most books comes down to their input.

Publishers used to be shy about revealing this, but now they admit it. I might be able understand if that was one part of the process, but the entire decision whether to publish a given manuscript is based on the feedback they get from Barnes & Noble and Borders. Imagine if television producers turned to affiliates…oh wait, that's a bad example.

I'm constantly amazed at how humorless the publishing world is. I don't know whether they're still in a post-9/11 funk or it's just life as part of a corporate conglomerate, but so many of the editors and publishers I've encountered are scared of humor. The fun, lively, quirky books have been relegated to a few niche publishers, who, thankfully, appear to be doing just fine with those books. As the publishing industry implodes, I pity the editors and others who love books, and especially the independent bookstore owners. Like in the music industry, there are too many people in power just milking a big check as long as they can, and leaving their mess to the next guy. The new American Way.

JW: How do you feel about people who walk around wearing Bluetooth ear pieces?

GS: I don't mind Bluetooth ear pieces that much because people actually look less foolish than they did with a cord hanging from their ear, holding the mike about halfway down. In fact, I've thought about getting one…to give me a cover for muttering to myself.

QUOTES ON "T"

TALK

It is a common delusion that you make things better by talking about them.
ROSE MACAULAY

TANNING

I can't take a well-tanned person seriously.   CLEVELAND AMORY

He was *audibly* tan.   FRAN LEBOWITZ

TAXES

The avoidance of taxes is the only intellectual pursuit that carries any reward.
JOHN MAYNARD KEYNES

New rule: If churches don't have to pay taxes, they also can't call the fire department when they catch fire. Sorry, Reverend, that's one of those services that goes along with paying in. I'll use the fire department I pay for. You can pray for rain.   BILL MAHER

In the lexicon of the political class, the word "sacrifice" means that the citizens are supposed to mail even more of their income to Washington so that the political class will not have to sacrifice the pleasure of spending it.
GEORGE WILL

I'm spending a year dead for tax reasons.   DOUGLAS ADAMS

I wish the government would put a tax on pianos for the incompetent.
                                                             EDITH SITWELL

———————————————— TEACHING ————————————————
Everybody who is incapable of learning has taken to teaching.
                                                             OSCAR WILDE

He who can, does. He who cannot, teaches.   GEORGE BERNARD SHAW

If you can't do, teach. If you can't teach, teach phys ed.   ANONYMOUS

———————————————— TECHNOLOGY ————————————————
For a list of all the ways technology has failed to improve the quality of life,
please press three.   ALICE KAHN

Why in this day and age of modern technology do people still insist on yelling
into the drive-thru? I mean, I've got my little headset, "Welcome to Burger
King, may I take your order?" "WHOPPER! WHOPPER, NO ONIONS!" Excuse
me, um, Chewbacca? I'm bleeding from the ears here, Pacino. We're talking
FOOD here, not missiles, governor. Now DRIVE AROUND.   DANE COOK

There is an evil tendency underlying all our technology—the tendency to
do what is reasonable even when it isn't any good.   ROBERT PIRSIG

Sending someone a birthday e-card doesn't count. If you can't get your shit
together enough to go to Sav-On and pick out an actual physical birthday
card, don't bother. I'm not expecting Hallmark. I know you don't care enough

to send the "very best," but just don't send the very worst. Or else, when you die, I'll be forced to deliver an e-eulogy.   BILL MAHER

TEENAGERS

Like its politicians and its war, society has the teenagers it deserves.
                                                                J. B. PRIESTLEY

TELEPHONE

Telephone, *n.* An invention of the devil which abrogates some of the advantages of making a disagreeable person keep his distance.   AMBROSE BIERCE

Today the ringing of the telephone takes precedence over everything. It reaches a point of terrorism, particularly at dinnertime.   NIELS DIFFRIENT

TELETHON

The telethon invokes in me more terror than mirth. The spectacle of all that self-congratulatory yap masquerading as conscience, of all those chairmen of the board passing off public relations as altruism is truly sickening.
                                                                HARRY STEIN

TELEVANGELISTS

Refried Jesus-wheezing TV preachers.   P. J. O'ROURKE

TELEVISION

Television: chewing gum for the eyes.   FRANK LLOYD WRIGHT

Television is a medium of entertainment which permits millions of people to listen to the same joke at the same time, and yet remain lonesome.
                                                                T. S. ELIOT

Television: the bland leading the bland.   ANONYMOUS

Television—a medium. So called because it is neither rare nor well done.
                                                  ERNIE KOVACS

Why should people pay good money to go out and see bad films when they
can stay at home and see bad television for nothing?   SAMUEL GOLDWYN

Television is now so desperately hungry for material that they're scraping the
top of the barrel.   GORE VIDAL

I don't know if you know about pilots. The way in which our country gen-
erates television, they take one episode, one, and then they take that episode,
produce it, and show it to a room filled with monkeys. And if the monkeys
don't shit themselves, you might have a hit!   LEWIS BLACK

TV executives think that the programs with the highest ratings are what TV
viewers want, rather than what they settle for.   PAULINE KAEL

There is an insistent tendency among serious social scientists to think of any
institution which features rhymed and singing commercials, intense and
lachrymose voices urging highly improbable enjoyment, caricatures of the
human esophagus in normal or impaired operation, and which hints implau-
sibly at opportunities for antiseptic seduction as inherently trivial. This is a
great mistake. The industrial system is profoundly dependent on commercial television and could not exist in its present from without it.
                                       JOHN KENNETH GALBRAITH

Television is for appearing on—not for looking at.   NOEL COWARD

Television is a great leveler. You always end up sounding like the people who ask the questions.   GORE VIDAL

Television is a device that permits people who haven't anything to do to watch people who can't do anything.   FRED ALLEN

Television is the first truly democratic culture— the first culture available to everybody and entirely governed by what the people want. The most terrifying thing is what the people want.   CLIVE BARNES

My father hated radio and could not wait for television to be invented so he could hate that too.   PETER DE VRIES

The young watch television twenty-four hours a day, they don't read and they rarely listen. This incessant bombardment of images has developed a hypertrophied eye condition that's turning them into a race of mutants. They should pass a law for a total reeducation of the young, making children visit the Galleria Borgese on a daily basis.   FEDERICO FELLINI

Television is an invention that permits you to be entertained in your living room by people you wouldn't have in your home.   DAVID FROST

Television has lifted the manufacture of banality out of the sphere of handicraft and placed it in that of a major industry.   NATHALIE SARRAUTE

It is difficult to produce a television documentary that is both incisive and probing when every twelve minutes one is interrupted by twelve dancing rabbits singing about toilet paper.   ROD SERLING

I must say I find television very educational. The minute somebody turns it on, I go to the library and read a good book.   GROUCHO MARX

Television is just one more facet of that considerable segment of our society that never had any standard but the soft buck.

RAYMOND CHANDLER

The first TV babies are now writing with a TV mind that has no attention span at all.   GORE VIDAL

Imitation is the sincerest form of television.   FRED ALLEN

One of the few good things about modern times: If you die horribly on television, you will not have died in vain. You will have entertained us.

KURT VONNEGUT

TV is like taking black spray paint to your third eye.   BILL HICKS

Television has done much for psychiatry by spreading information about it, as well as contributing to the need for it.   ALFRED HITCHCOCK

The TV business is uglier than most things. It is normally perceived as some kind of cruel and shallow money trench through the heart of the journalism industry, a long plastic hallway where thieves and pimps run free and good men die like dogs, for no good reason.   HUNTER S. THOMPSON

I have had my television aerials removed. It's the moral equivalent of a prostate operation.   MALCOLM MUGGERIDGE

You have to work years in hit shows to make people sick and tired of you, but you can accomplish this in a few weeks on television.   WALTER SLEZAK

Seeing a murder on television…can help work off one's antagonisms. And if you haven't any antagonisms, the commercials will give you some.
ALFRED HITCHCOCK

All television is children's television.   RICHARD P. ADLER

The one function that TV news performs very well is that when there is no news we give it to you with the same emphasis as if there were.
DAVID BRINKLEY

Television has raised writing to a new low.   SAM GOLDWYN

Art is moral passion married to entertainment. Moral passion without entertainment is propaganda, and entertainment without moral passion is television.
RITA MAE BROWN

The television, that insidious beast, that Medusa which freezes a billion people to stone every night, staring fixedly, that Siren which called and sang and promised so much and gave, after all, so little.   RAY BRADBURY

If vaudeville had died, television was the box they put it in.
LARRY GELBART

Imagine what it would be like if TV actually were good. It would be the end of everything we know.   MARVIN MINSKY

Television is democracy at its ugliest.   PADDY CHAYEFSKY

I think TV remotes should have a button that allows you to kill the person
on the screen.   GEORGE CARLIN

TEMPTATION

Lead me not into temptation; I can find the way myself.

RITA MAE BROWN

TEN COMMANDMENTS

Say what you will about the Ten Commandments, you must always come
back to the pleasant fact that there are only ten of them.

H. L. MENCKEN

TEXAS

If I owned Texas and Hell, I would rent out Texas and live in Hell.

PHILIP SHERIDAN

THANKSGIVING

Most turkeys taste better the day after; my mother's tasted better the day
before.   RITA RUDNER

Thanksgiving is so called because we are all so thankful that it comes only
once a year.   P. J. O'ROURKE

Thanksgiving dinners take eighteen hours to prepare. They are consumed
in twelve minutes. Half times take twelve minutes. This is not coincidence.

ERMA BOMBECK

We're doing something a little different this year for Thanksgiving. Instead of a turkey, we're having a swan. You get more stuffing.   GEORGE CARLIN

------------------ THEATER DIRECTOR ------------------

Theater director: a person engaged by the management to conceal the fact that the players cannot act.   JAMES AGATE

------------------ THEOLOGIAN ------------------

I have only a small flickering light to guide me in the darkness of a thick forest. Up comes a theologian and blows it out.   DENIS DIDEROT

------------------ THEOLOGY ------------------

Theology is the effort to explain the unknowable in terms of the not worth knowing.   H. L. MENCKEN

------------------ THINKING ------------------

Most people would die sooner than think; in fact, they do so.
BERTRAND RUSSELL

Thinking is the most unhealthy thing in the world, and people die of it just as they die of any other disease.   OSCAR WILDE

Few people think more than two or three times a year; I have made an international reputation for myself by thinking once or twice a week.
GEORGE BERNARD SHAW

There is no expedient to which a man will not go to avoid the labor of thinking.   THOMAS EDISON

TIME

Time is a storm in which we are all lost.   WILLIAM CARLOS WILLIAMS

So little time, so little to do.   OSCAR LEVANT

TIPPING

The man who tips a shilling every time he stops for petrol is giving away annually the cost of lubricating his car.   J. PAUL GETTY

TRADITION

The longer I live the more keenly I feel that whatever was good enough for our fathers is not good enough for us.   OSCAR WILDE

TRAVEL

People travel for the same reason as they collect works of art: because the best people do it.   ALDOUS HUXLEY

Travel is only glamorous in retrospect.   PAUL THEROUX

TRAVELING COMPANIONS

The most common of all antagonisms arises from a man's taking a seat beside you on the train, a seat to which he is completely entitled.

ROBERT BENCHLEY

Whenever I travel I like to keep the seat next to me empty. I found a great way to do it. When someone walks down the aisle and says to you, "Is someone sitting there?" just say, "No one—except the Lord."

CAROL LEIFER

TRUST

People who have given us their complete confidence believe that they have a right to ours. The inference is false; a gift confers no rights.

FRIEDRICH WILHELM NIETZSCHE

TRUTH

The pure and simple truth is rarely pure and never simple.

OSCAR WILDE

Ye shall know the truth, and the truth shall make you mad.

ALDOUS HUXLEY

TWENTIETH CENTURY

The second half of the twentieth century is a complete flop.

ISAAC BASHEVIS SINGER

The horror of the twentieth century was the size of each event, and the paucity of its reverberation.

NORMAN MAILER

TYRANNY

There are few minds to which tyranny is not delightful.

SAMUEL JOHNSON

JOEL STEIN

Participatory Narcissist

Joel Stein grew up in Edison, New Jersey, where he attended J. P. Stevens High School. He received a BA and MA from Stanford University in 1993. After stints as a fact checker, reporter, and sports editor, he is currently a columnist for the *Los Angeles Times* and a regular contributor to *Time*. His journalistic method involves inserting himself into various situations and writing about how they affect him.

JW: You wrote a column titled "Why I Hate Dogs"…
JS: First of all, I hate all animals, very logically, in descending order. So, for

example, large swarms of ants gross me out, but a single ant I'm totally cool with. Pet giraffes freak me out. But dogs really creep me out. They're the only animals I know of that are sexually interested in breeds five hundred times smaller than them. They're worse than frat boys. Dogs are way too eager for human approval. They have more interest in us than their own species. What kind of creature gets its joy from a different species? Dogs have decided that we're the best, whereas other animals are totally happy to ignore us.

JW: What about dog owners?

JS: They think it's totally okay to have their dog jump on you and lick you, as if you enjoy it. And why do they get offended when I refer to their dog as "it"? Was I supposed to be checking out its genitals the whole time?

But what can you expect from people who love their dog so much that they're willing to walk behind it and pick up its feces with their own hands? I've yet to meet a woman for whom I'd do that. Dog salons, dog psychologists, dog antidepressants....While the homeless go ignored, thirty million Americans bought their dogs Christmas presents last year. People knit things for their dogs. A woman I know throws her dog a Bar Mitzvah every year. And that leash-on-a-reel thing that takes up forty feet of sidewalk...hey, save yourself some money: Let your dog run free and use a large stick to trip people with instead.

JW: Do you hate children as well?

JS: No, I like children. I just don't want one. They really get in the way of your lifestyle. And let's face it: Children are idiots. If you've ever had a long conversation with a child, it's appalling how much they don't know: "You've never seen *The Jeffersons*? You're four years old—what have you been doing with your time?" The conversation's over. You walk away. That's why we don't let them have jobs. Can you imagine an office full of children? They'd spend all day telling dumb jokes and talking about their poop. It would be like it was before women entered the workplace.

JW: You've been a critic of children's television, particularly Sesame Street.

JS: *Sesame Street* is being destroyed by idiot cuteness. It still has sharp, funny writing, but the show is being taken over by that patronizing, baby-talking Elmo. He's passive and self-obsessed, always referring to himself in the third person.

When I watched *Sesame Street* in the seventies, the human cast and the Muppets didn't talk down to me with baby voices. Now the human cast gets very little airtime, and the show is dominated by Elmo, Baby Bear, and, now, Abby Cadabby—preschoolers enamored of their own adorable stupidity. The lesson they teach—in opposition to Oscar, Big Bird, Grover, or Bert—is that bland neediness gets you stuff more easily than character. We're breeding a nation of Anna Nicole Smiths. I went to the *Sesame Street* set and had lunch with the human cast members and they're not happy with the "Elmo-ization" either.

JW: How would you fix the show?

JS: I'd take Elmo and his buddies and give them their own show for the idiot spawn, and then give Luis, Gordon, and the cool Muppets their own "Classic Sesame" for the kids who will someday actually contribute to society. Whichever of the two shows you watched would serve as a litmus test for the rest of your life. If we can't save all the kids, let's at least save the ones who can master speaking in the first person. The rest we'll use for reality TV stars.

JW: You wrote in a Los Angeles Times *column, "I don't like being touched by strangers. And by 'strangers,' I mean anyone I'm not having sex with." When did you first notice this aversion?*

JS: Some time in the nineties, when women started hugging you and kissing you on the cheek when they met you. Then *guys* started hugging you. I don't even like to high-five! I just don't see the point. I got sent on a story where I had to get massages. Most people I know love massages, but I was very uncomfortable. I mean, here I was paying someone to give me pleasure and she was trying to make me feel good without turning me on, and that just seemed stupid. I'm incapable of separating pleasurable touch—or any touch, from sexuality.

JW: You wrote a column about spicing up your marriage…

JS: Don't try to spice up your marriage. Any concerted effort to fix your marriage is doomed. It's too late. Whatever patterns you've established…just accept them. Whatever you to try to do to spice up your marriage will be depressing. Every way of introducing something new is essentially buying that Valentine's Day teddy that they sell at Target. You know: the see-through one with the red heart on it. If my wife ever walked out in that, I'd know the marriage had hit bottom.

For that column I watched an advanced sexual techniques video. It was porn with average people instead of porn stars. Watching regular people have sex in regular lighting? Not good. Not just not good as in a total turn-off, but not good as in, "Oh my God, that's what *I* look like?" Horrifying! I also went to an all-female party where they were selling sex toys. I learned that women don't like penises, but they do like plastic things shaped like penises. Which made me realize that it's just men they don't like.

JW: What did you take away from your story about political conventions?

JS: In 2000, I went to both the Republican and Democratic conventions, but all I learned was that both parties love education, respect the military, and prefer the middle class to both poor and rich people.

I hate the middle class. Biggest group of whiners ever. They have two shticks: "We're being ignored!" and "We're shrinking!" These are their constant complaints. Out entire tax code is screwed up because of the middle class. They get every break in the world. It's crazy. Our Constitution was designed to prevent the middle class from having too much power! I blame everything on the middle class.

616 ◆ THE BIG CURMUDGEON

Take the mortgage tax break: Why do we bend over backwards to give money back to the middle class for no legitimate reason? Maybe it's because there are so many of them and they vote. Helping people own a home while poor people have to rent them? When did *that* become okay? We give them tax breaks for having kids! I almost wouldn't mind them getting all these breaks if they'd just stop whining about being ignored.

JW: One of your columns was about substituting for a radio talk show host.
JS: Yes, I filled in as the host of the *Mike Gallagher Show*. The conservative listeners didn't like me very much, partly because I was really bad at it, but basically because they thought I was a liberal, even though I didn't say one liberal thing. I had invited a member of People for the Ethical Treatment of Animals (PETA) on to talk about cockfighting, of which I'm an advocate. I guess just having the PETA woman on the show made listeners think I was a liberal. A caller said she was a terrorist, which I agreed with, since the organization totally disrupted last year's Victoria's Secret fashion show. Then he said she was the same as Osama bin Laden. I questioned that, mostly because PETA hasn't killed anyone. He said that all terrorists were equal and that parsing out evil made me a sympathizer. I questioned his epistemology, at which point he called me a "stupid liberal kike," which caused the switchboard guy to hang up on him. That switchboard guy ruined all the fun.

Since that show, I've come to love the PETA people. I completely disagree with their philosophy, but I think everything they do is awesome. They're the pranksters of our time.

JW: Have you no common philosophical ground with PETA?
JS: Well, I'm down on poultry. I haven't completely cut it out, but I've cut way down on poultry consumption. I realized I wasn't enjoying it. It's the white bread of meat. I don't think people enjoy it, except for a nice rotisseried chicken perhaps, or coq au vin, certainly. But when they just put a lump of chicken on their salad, I don't think they're enjoying that. It's

mindless chicken consumption. So I began to ask myself, Should animals really be killed so I cannot enjoy something? I'll just have tofu instead. But I'm not giving up pork.

JW: You've written several columns about television, particularly daytime TV.

JS: I ventured the theory that daytime talk-show hosts follow some reverse Darwinian law whereby they get less and less threatening every generation. Then I realized something: Know what works best on daytime television? Lesbians. The average American woman sitting at home during the day has a lot in common with a Rosie [O'Donnell] or an Ellen [De Generes]. They have the same anger issues.

JW: What about Oprah?

JS: Oprah is the opiate of the female masses. She teaches women to build self-esteem by confronting the past and setting goals instead of feeling good the old-fashioned way, by having casual sex. The whole idea of talking openly and sharing your feelings is antithetical to the old-time values of emotional repression on which this country was founded. Oprah's magazine has articles on coping that suggest that you "make prioritizing a priority." There's also an awful lot of talk about angels. Her solution to everything is telling you to tack a note to your mirror. Tacking a note to your mirror accomplishes nothing but blocking you from seeing your fat self.

Oprah and other women's shows are popular because men don't watch television. Men neither watch TV nor buy anything. (I'd love to see a study of what men do with their time.) Women read books, women read magazines, women watch TV, women do the shopping. What are men doing with their time? Is there that much golf and pornography in the world?

JW: Men have the Spike channel…

JS: How embarrassing is *that*? I'd rather watch a lifetime of Lifetime.

JW: For another column, you voluntarily deprived yourself of television for a whole week.

JS: It wasn't that bad. I've always watched a lot of TV, but I only have it on when I'm watching it. I don't use it as a background the way some people do. It's depressing when the whole family is having dinner and the TV is on in the background, like it's another member of the family.

JW: You've written about some powerful institutions, from Big Oil to Q-Tips to Wal-Mart.

JS: I know it's surprising to see a different gas price every time you stop at Texonobil, but hey, it's a supply-and-demand thing. We seem to accept massive fluctuations in the stock market, real estate, and the popularity of John Travolta, but for some reason we think gas should always cost the same amount, plus 0.99 of a penny. Yes, I feel bad for people who have to drive to work and can't afford higher gas prices, but we have to understand that in a capitalist system, there are times when things get hard and we have to cut back. Remember sugar rations in World War II, or that Christmas when there weren't enough PlayStation2's to go around? We got through that, and we'll get through this.

There is, however, the possibility that my attitude may all have to do with the fact that I don't own a car.

I wrote a column about how evil Q-Tips are and how a huge percentage of ear injuries are due to Q-Tips. The cotton-swab industry is so powerful that no one—not politicians, not journalists, not even rap artists—has had the *cojones* to stand up to it. Countless Americans have suffered serious eardrum injuries as a result of cleaning their ears with Q-Tips, and countless others have come down with tinnitus. We'll never know the real numbers because the FDA doesn't require manufacturers to report swab malfunctions. Where is the outrage? Well, I'm not afraid to speak out. By the way, two months after the column ran I had to go to the doctor with a bloody ear—yes—because of a Q-Tip!

JW: And Wal-Mart?

JS: Wal-Mart tries very hard not to offend its customers, which makes it do stupid things, like pulling Midge, a pregnant, married doll; making Nirvana change the song *Rape Me* to *Waif Me*; and forcing the Goo Goo Dolls to redesign the cover of *A Boy Named Goo* because a Wal-Mart executive thought the boy with blackberries smeared on him looked like a child-abuse victim. But I love Wal-Mart, not only for the prices, cleanliness, and service, but also for employing people who would otherwise be knocking on my door with religious literature.

QUOTES ON "U"

---------------------------- UGLINESS ----------------------------
It was not until I had attended a few postmortems that I realized that even the ugliest human exteriors may contain the most beautiful viscera, and was able to console myself for the facial drabness of my neighbors in omnibuses by dissecting them in my imagination.   J. B. S. HALDANE

---------------------------- UNIVERSE ----------------------------
My theology, briefly, is that the universe was dictated, but not signed.
                                                CHRISTOPHER MORLEY

It is inconceivable that the whole Universe was merely created for us who live in this third-rate planet of a third-rate sun.   ALFRED, LORD TENNYSON

It is impossible to imagine the universe run by a wise, just, and omnipotent God, but it is quite easy to imagine it run by a board of gods. If such a board actually exists it operates precisely like the board of a corporation that is losing money.   H. L. MENCKEN

---------------------------- UPPER CLASS ----------------------------
If you are an author and give one of your books to a member of the upper class, you must never expect him to read it.   PAUL FUSSELL

QUOTES ON "V"

―――――――――― **VAN GOGH, VINCENT** ――――――――――
Vincent Van Gogh's mother painted all of his best things. The famous mailed decapitated ear was a figment of the public relations firm engaged by Van Gogh's dealer.   ROY BLOUNT, JR.

―――――――――――――― **VCR** ――――――――――――――
I suppose I should get a VCR, but the only thing I like about television is its ephemerality.   P. J. O'ROURKE

―――――――――――― **VEGETABLES** ――――――――――――
I have no truck with lettuce, cabbage, and similar chlorophyll. Any dietician will tell you that a running foot of apple strudel contains four times the vitamins of a bushel of beans.   S. J. PERELMAN

Vegetables are interesting but lack a sense of purpose when unaccompanied by a good cut of meat.   FRAN LEBOWITZ

―――――――――――― **VEGETARIANS** ――――――――――――
Most vegetarians look so much like the food they eat that they can be classified as cannibals.   FINLEY PETER DUNNE

VICE

My only aversion to vice, Is the price.   VICTOR BUONO

He hasn't a single redeeming vice.   OSCAR WILDE

VICE PRESIDENCY

Democracy means that anyone can grow up to be president, and anyone who doesn't grow up can be vice president.   JOHNNY CARSON

The man with the best job in the country is the vice president. All he has to do is get up every morning and say, "How is the president?"   WILL ROGERS

The vice presidency isn't worth a pitcher of warm piss.
JOHN NANCE GARNER

VIOLIN VS. VIOLA

The difference between a violin and a viola is that a viola burns longer.
VICTOR BORGE

VIRGINITY

Virginity is the ideal of those who want to deflower.   KARL KRAUS

VIRGIN MARY

If I had been the Virgin Mary, I would have said "No."   STEVIE SMITH

VIRTUE

Virtue is insufficient temptation.   GEORGE BERNARD SHAW

Virtue has never been as respectable as money.   MARK TWAIN

Woman's virtue is man's greatest invention.   CORNELIA OTIS SKINNER

The love of money is the root of all virtue.   GEORGE BERNARD SHAW

Virtue is its own punishment.   ANEURIN BEVAN

What men call social virtues, good fellowship, is commonly but the virtue of pigs in a litter, which lie close together to keep each other warm.
HENRY DAVID THOREAU

What is virtue but the trades unionism of the married?
GEORGE BERNARD SHAW

VOTING

Giving every man a vote has no more made men wise and free than Christianity has made them good.   H. L. MENCKEN

If voting changed anything, they'd make it illegal.   EMMA GOLDMAN

I never vote for anyone. I always vote against.   W. C. FIELDS

VOX POPULI

Vox Populi, vox humbug.   WILLIAM TECUMSEH SHERMAN

THE FRIARS:
THEY KID BECAUSE
THEY LOVE

The Friars Club was founded in 1904 by theatrical press agents tired of being conned out of show tickets by moochers posing as reporters. They organized as the Press Agents Association, to compare notes and, incidentally, "to establish and maintain a fraternity among men engaged in theatrical enterprises." ("Friar" derives from the Latin, *frater*, or "brother," and the club's motto is *Prae omnia fraternitas*—Before all things, brotherhood.) The club was renamed the Friars after the likes of George M. Cohan, Irving Berlin, and Al Jolson began to join. It's been a sanctuary for entertainers, and a bastion of curmudgeonry, ever since.

The Friars Club became a haven for borscht-belt comedians in the 1950s and '60s, though by then overall membership had declined. Milton Berle used his power and influence to revive the club, and he remained a prominent member (as it were—see the sidebar on page 632) until his death in 2002.

In keeping with the ecclesiastical motif, the officers are designated "abbot" (president), "dean" (vice president), "prior" (second vice president), and "scribe" (secretary), and the Friars' six-story townhouse on East Fifty-fifth Street in Manhattan is called the "monastery." It's a functioning clubhouse, with restaurants and bars named in honor of members: the Milton Berle Room, the George Burns Room, the Frank Sinatra Dining Room, the Billy Crystal Bar. There's also a gym, poolroom, barber shop, and steam room.

The Los Angeles Friars Club was founded in 1947 by East Coast expatriates who missed the New York camaraderie. The offshoot club was a separate entity and acted independently, but there was a large overlap of membership. Darren Schaeffer bought it in 2004 and turned into a commercial venture, renaming it the Friars of Beverly Hills, soliciting non–show-business members, and hiring it out for weddings and bar mitzvahs, which prompted New York Friars abbot Freddie Roman to dismiss it as nothing more than a "catering hall." Indeed, the New York Friars Club has over a thousand members, two-thirds of whom work in show business, whereas most of the Friars of Beverly Hills' seven hundred members are civilians. In any case, the two clubs are no longer affiliated: In 2005, the New York Friars sued the Friars of Beverly Hills for trademark infringement.

Women were always welcome at the New York Friars Club, as long as they stayed on the first floor. According to Barry Dougherty, author of several books of Friars lore and editor of the Friars Club magazine, *The Epistle*, when George Burns and Jack Benny were alive, members would often find Gracie Allen and Mary Livingston—stars in their own right—sitting on a bench in the foyer waiting for their husbands to come out. The Friars made an exception for Sophie Tucker because, according to the late Friars abbott Alan King, "she had balls." She was treated to full membership—she drank, ate, and traded raunchy one-liners with the best of the men. Phyllis Diller crashed the Sid Caesar roast in 1983 dressed as a man and, in 1988, California attorney Gloria Allred successfully sued for reciprocal dining privileges at the New York Friars after she'd persuaded the L.A. club to admit her the year before. New York soon resolved to admit women, and Liza Minnelli became their first dues-paying woman member. The female membership now includes Joan Rivers, Susie Essman, Judy Gold, and Joy Behar.

In 1962, it was disclosed that over a five-year period, various West Coast Friars had been cheated out of large sums at gin rummy by professional criminals using a peephole and a shortwave transmitter. The Friars Club made headlines again in 1993, when Ted Danson, serving as Roastmaster at the Whoopi Goldberg roast, came out wearing blackface. Talk show host Montel Williams stormed out of the room, likened the affair to "a KKK rally," and resigned his membership, while New York mayor David Dinkins, making an inadvertent pun, termed Danson's appearance "beyond the pale." After a photo of Danson made the newspapers, the club issued a public apology.

Despite the occasional scandal and the relative lack of publicity for its extensive charitable work, the image of the New York Friars Club as a show business institution is secure, and its future looks bright: The average age was sixty-five in the late 1960s, but is now a sprightly fifty.

Comedian Richard Lewis, himself now a club elder, explained the joys of Friarhood: "I became a member over twenty years ago. I joined mainly because I love the astonishing history behind it, the food is the greatest and the several million anecdotes that one can hear, on a daily basis, remind me that I haven't been the only performer screwed in show business."

The Friars Club is a fraternal order of outsiders who made themselves insiders, of comedians, actors, publicists and other show folk who invented for themselves a century ago just about the only club in that anti-Semitic age they'd ever be invited to join....Still, even after luring some of the bright new lights of comedy to join them in the last few years, the membership has a median age somewhere between "He used to open for Louis Prima at the Sands" and "He's coding!"   JEFF MACGREGOR

The Friars Club has very high standards. In order to become a member, a man must be either a resident or a nonresident of the state of California. He then must be proposed by, and then vouched for, at least two men who are listed in the phone book. HARRY EINSTEIN (aka "Parkyakarkus")

The Friars Club is like trying to play a game of Jeopardy! where the correct response is always "I don't know who he is, Alex, but I wish he'd cover himself with a towel."   JOEL STEIN

They love to touch. It's all they can do at this point, so they hold your hand, and with the other hand they'll stroke the top of your hand. You have to Purell the minute you leave there.   SUSIE ESSMAN

HONOR BY DISHONOR

If you say something nice to somebody, it's not funny.   ALAN KING

The Friars began insulting each other at their first testimonial dinner in 1906. By the 1950s, the black-tie affairs had turned so raunchy that the club had to create a separate, men-only occasion, the "roast." They were strictly private affairs at which aging comics insulted each other with racial and sexual jokes. It is considered a great honor to be roasted. "We only roast the ones we love," the Friars say. Through the years, the greats of showbiz have been so "honored," including Frank Sinatra, Jack Benny, Milton Berle, Bob Hope, Jerry Lewis, and Johnny Carson (a favorite Roastmaster as well). Televised roasts of Chevy Chase, Rob Reiner, Jerry Stiller, Donald Trump, and Hugh Hefner on Comedy Central have introduced the form to a new generation of viewers.

Frank, this isn't your kind of audience—there's a lot of people here with necks.
                                        PAT HENRY, to Frank Sinatra

---

Frank is a great philanthropist. When Eddie Fisher went bankrupt, Frank opened his wallet and showed him a picture of Gloria DeHaven.
                                        MILTON BERLE, on Frank Sinatra

---

Don't just sit there, Frank—enjoy yourself—hit somebody!
                                        DON RICKLES, to Frank Sinatra

Why are you so bloated? You look like you drowned four days ago.
                                            JEFFREY ROSS, to Jerry Lewis

---

Neil [Simon] is a New Yorker. In fact, when he dies he wants to be cremated and thrown in someone's face.   PAT HENRY

All the playwright is required to do is throw an occasional hump into the leading lady. You don't have to marry all of them, you schmuck!
                                            MILTON BERLE, to Neil Simon

---

Laugh it up!—I laugh when you act.   MILTON BERLE, to Bruce Willis

---

Milton [Berle] had a tough childhood. He was abandoned by wolves and raised by his parents.   JAN MURRAY

He can light up a whole room…just by leaving it.
                                            JOE E. LEWIS, on Ed Sullivan

---

Gene Baylos is a real success story. In 1962, he couldn't afford a 1962 car, and now he lives in one.   JAN MURRAY

Buddy Hackett willed his body to science, but science is contesting the will.
                                            RED BUTTONS

Georgie [Jessel] is a very unhappy man. He just got his first anti-Semitic letter and it was in Yiddish.   JACK CARTER

You might be interested in what happened to Joan Rivers last night: a peeping Tom threw up on her window.   BUDDY HACKETT

Last week, Abe Vigoda tried to enlist at Old Navy.   JEFFREY ROSS

Alan, did you ever think you'd live so long that your prostate would be as big as your ego?   SUSIE ESSMAN, to Alan King

---

Donald, you're not my type.…Too egomaniacal and narcissistic. I can't be involved with a man who calls out his own name when he's climaxing.
                    SUSIE ESSMAN, to Donald Trump

Sally Struthers couldn't be here, but she sent three bags of grain.
                    JEFFREY ROSS

I commend you on all you've done for PETA, wrestling the one-eyed trouser snake with your bare hands, gently cuddling it in your arms, and nurturing it back to health.   SARAH SILVERMAN, to Pamela Anderson

---

I'm so glad Courtney Love is here, I left my crack in my other purse.
                    SARAH SILVERMAN

Al [Franken] has been good to me. He gave me a copy of his latest book. And I'm grateful—it gave me something to give my maid's husband for Kwanzaa.
                    JEFFREY ROSS

Can you hear me over the oxygen tanks?   JIMMY KIMMEL, to Jerry Stiller

---

Richard, you're the first person in history to actually look better on *The Simpsons*.   JEFFREY ROSS, to Richard Belzer

---

Hugh Hefner is so old, his first condom was made out of bark.
                    GILBERT GOTTFRIED

I think it's awesome that Hugh Hefner sleeps with seven women, because eight would be ostentatious. But I know why he needs seven: one to put it in and the other six to move him around.   JEFFREY ROSS

How do they know when he comes? Does dust come out?
                                        DREW CAREY, on Hugh Hefner

I've read just about every issue of *Playboy* since I was fifteen years old and not once did I ever see a playmate say one of her turn-ons was fucking a seventy-five-year-old man.   JIMMY KIMMEL

I won't say Kelsey [Grammer's] girlfriend is young, but when he said, "I love you," she said, "Then buy me a pony." Kelsey would have brought her here tonight, but she has detention.   JEFFREY ROSS

Kelsey Grammer has been in and out of Betty Ford more often than Jerry Ford.
                                        JEFFREY ROSS

Did you enjoy your lunch? I heard your hair ordered the salmon.
                                        SUSIE ESSMAN, to Donald Trump

BERLE'S FUNNY BONE

by Barry Dougherty

Milton Berle was the definitive Roastmaster. He commanded Friars Club Roasts as effortlessly as Captain Bligh did the *Bounty*, and yes, there were attempted comic mutinies along the way for him as well. But he was completely in control. Some would owe this to his bombastic presence. Others, perhaps, to his quick wit and sharp tongue. Still others chalked it up to a lifetime of experience. But many would disagree on all counts and suggest a far more obvious reason–well, obvious if he'd stood at the podium naked, because, you see, many owe Berle's comedy prowess to the size of his penis.

Yes, Milton Berle had a huge schlong. Its size is legendary. To quote many who had an opportunity to catch a glimpse, it had its own zip code. It's no wonder then that when Milton would helm a Roast, he often said that the length of time a man could speak would be based on the size of his penis. If he had a four-inch penis, he could speak for four minutes; a five-inch penis, five minutes, and so on. Berle noted, "Many on this dais will only bow." It also might explain why he spoke longer than anyone else. If he hadn't happened to die, he'd still be at a podium, somewhere, still speaking.

Many comedians took great delight in making jokes about Berle's penis at Friars Roasts and Dinners. Here's a sampling of what they said:

I wouldn't say it's big, but it has a beeper.   JEFFREY ROSS

Milton's cock is the only one in the world with its own heart and lungs.
                                                                JACK CARTER

Milton, your member is so large your foreskin was used to cover the infield at Yankee Stadium.   FREDDIE ROMAN

I saw him in the steam room and I thought he had his son with him.
                                                            DAVID STEINBERG

Some of you may be wondering why Milton Berle would be the Roastmaster for Bruce Willis. I didn't think they had anything in common, but I did a lot of research and I found out they do have a lot in common. Milton Berle HAS the biggest prick in show business and Bruce Willis IS the biggest prick in show business.   STEWIE STONE

Two of the biggest and most famous organs in show business are Milton's and the one at Radio City Music Hall, and both haven't been used in years.
                                                                JAN MURRAY

His whole sex life is what's motivated Milton. Even as a child he was always fascinated with his own penis, especially the head. He thought it was the greatest invention he ever saw because it kept his hand from slipping off.
                                                                RICH LITTLE

I saw him on a golf course sink a four-foot putt with it.
                                                            ROBERT MERRILL

I had the pleasure of seeing Milton's penis. People have asked me, What did it look like? I said, "It looked like a baby's arm holding an apple."

DICK CAPRI

Even in death, Berle's jewels continued to mesmerize his fellow Friars. Freddie Roman made the following announcement at his Memorial in 2002: Good evening ladies and gentlemen. We're delighted to welcome you to the Friars tonight for our tribute to our former Abbot Emeritus, who passed away on March twenty-seventh. On May third, his penis will be buried. We will have a viewing here at the Club [on] May first and second, and you'll need both days.

QUOTES ON "W"

WAITERS

When those waiters ask me if I want some fresh ground pepper, I ask if they have any aged pepper. ANDY ROONEY

WAR

War is, at first, the hope that one will be better off; next, the expectation that the other fellow will be worse off; then, the satisfaction that he isn't any better off; and, finally, the surprise at everyone's being worse off.

KARL KRAUS

As long as war is looked upon as wicked, it will always have its fascination. When it is looked upon as vulgar, it will cease to be popular.

OSCAR WILDE

War is like love; it always finds a way. BERTOLT BRECHT

I can understand why mankind hasn't given up war. During a war you get to drive tanks through the sides of buildings and shoot foreigners, two things that are usually frowned on during peacetime. P. J. O'ROURKE

Wars teach us not to love our enemies, but to hate our allies.

W. L. GEORGE

Human war has been the most successful of our cultural traditions.

ROBERT ARDREY

How is the world ruled and how do wars start? Diplomats tell lies to journalists and then believe what they read.

KARL KRAUS

War is capitalism with the gloves off and many who go to war know it but they go to war because they don't want to be a hero. It takes courage to sit down and be counted.

TOM STOPPARD

I have given two cousins to war and I stand ready to sacrifice my wife's brother.

ARTEMUS WARD

War is God's way of teaching Americans geography.

AMBROSE BIERCE

—————————— WAR CRIMES ——————————

Only the winners decide what were war crimes.

GARY WILLS

—————————— WASHINGTON, D.C. ——————————

People come to Washington believing it's the center of power. I know I did. It was only much later that I learned that Washington is a steering wheel that's not connected to the engine.

RICHARD GOODWIN

Washington is...a city of cocker spaniels. It's a city of people who are more interested in being petted and admired, loved, than rendering the exercise of power.

ELLIOT RICHARDSON

Washington is a city of Southern efficiency and Northern charm.

JOHN F. KENNEDY

Washington is an endless series of mock palaces clearly built for clerks.
ADA LOUISE HUXTABLE

Washington is the only place where sound travels faster than light.
C. V. R. THOMPSON

Washington is *Mr. Smith Goes to Washington* without the happy ending.
HOWARD OGDEN

After two years in Washington, I often long for the realism and sincerity of Hollywood.
FRED THOMPSON

The Supreme Court has ruled that they cannot have a nativity scene in Washington, D.C. This wasn't for any religious reasons. They couldn't find three wise men and a virgin.
JAY LENO

Standing, standing, standing—why do I have to stand all the time? That is the main characteristic of social Washington.
DANIEL BOORSTIN

At a Washington party, it is not enough that the guests feel drunk; they must feel drunk and important.
TOM WOLFE

──────────────── WEDDING ────────────────

Wedding, *n*. A ceremony at which two persons undertake to become one, one undertakes to become nothing and nothing undertakes to become supportable.
AMBROSE BIERCE

The music at a wedding procession always reminds me of the music of soldiers going into battle.
HEINRICH HEINE

A wedding is just like a funeral except that you get to smell your own flowers.
GRACE HANSEN

WELFARE

As far as unwed mothers on welfare are concerned, it seems to me they must be capable of some other form of labor.
AL CAPP

A government that robs Peter to pay Paul can always depend upon the support of Paul.
GEORGE BERNARD SHAW

WEST, MAE

A plumber's idea of Cleopatra.
W. C. FIELDS

WESTERN CIVILIZATION

It would be a good idea.
MOHANDAS K. GANDHI

WHITE BARBECUE

Going to a white-run barbecue is, I think, like going to a gentile internist: It might turn out all right, but you haven't made any attempt to take advantage of the percentages.
CALVIN TRILLIN

WHITE RACE

The white race is the cancer of history. It is the white race and it alone—its ideologies and inventions—which eradicates autonomous civilizations wherever it spreads, which has upset the ecological balance of the planet, which now threatens the very existence of life itself.
SUSAN SONTAG

WICKEDNESS

I prefer the wicked rather than the foolish. The wicked sometimes rest.
ALEXANDRE DUMAS *père*

Wickedness is a myth invented by good people to account for the curious attractiveness of others. OSCAR WILDE

—————————————————— WIVES ——————————————————

Wife: a former sweetheart. H. L. MENCKEN

Wives are people who feel they don't dance enough. GROUCHO MARX

Wife: one who is sorry she did it, but would undoubtedly do it again. H. L. MENCKEN

A man likes his wife to be just clever enough to comprehend his cleverness, and just stupid enough to admire it. ISRAEL ZANGWILL

A good wife is good, but the best wife is not so good as no wife at all. THOMAS HARDY

Never feel remorse for what you have thought about your wife. She has thought much worse things about you. JEAN ROSTAND

Men's wives are usually their husbands' mental inferiors and spiritual superiors; this gives them double instruments of torture. DON HEROLD

I am much too interested in other men's wives to think of getting one of my own. GEORGE MOORE

The trouble with my wife is that she's a whore in the kitchen and a cook in bed. GEOFFREY GORER

A man's wife has more power over him than the state has.

RALPH WALDO EMERSON

The only time some fellows are ever seen with their wives is after they've been indicted.
KIN HUBBARD

A loving wife will do anything for her husband except stop criticizing him and trying to improve him.
J. B. PRIESTLEY

A husband should not insult his wife publicly, at parties. He should insult her in the privacy of the home.
JAMES THURBER

A man's mother is his misfortune, but his wife is his fault.

WALTER BAGEHOT

An ideal wife is one who remains faithful to you but tries to be just as charming as if she weren't.
SACHA GUITRY

We have drugs to make women speak, but none to keep them silent.

ANATOLE FRANCE

My wife has a slight impediment in her speech. Every now and then she stops to breathe.
JIMMY DURANTE

My wife's idea of roughing it is staying at a Holiday Inn with single-ply toilet paper.
ABBY DAN

Basically my wife was immature. I'd be at home in the bath and she'd come in and sink my boats. WOODY ALLEN

Each [of my wives] was jealous and resentful of my preoccupation with business. Yet none showed any visible aversion to sharing in the proceeds.
J. PAUL GETTY

The comfortable estate of widowhood is the only hope that keeps up a wife's spirits. JOHN GAY

My wife doesn't care what I do when I'm away, as long as I don't have a good time. LEE TREVINO

—————————————— WOMEN ——————————————

Woman would be more charming if one could fall into her arms without falling into her hands. AMBROSE BIERCE

A woman will always sacrifice herself if you give her the opportunity. It's her favorite form of self-indulgence. W. SOMERSET MAUGHAM

The way to fight a woman is with your hat. Grab it and run.
JOHN BARRYMORE

A woman will flirt with anybody in the world as long as other people are looking on. OSCAR WILDE

A woman occasionally is quite a serviceable substitute for masturbation. It takes an abundance of imagination, to be sure. KARL KRAUS

A woman's place is in the wrong.   JAMES THURBER

Brigands demand your money or your life; women require both.
                                        NICHOLAS MURRAY BUTLER

After years of effort, women have won the right to be taken more seriously
than they deserve.   STANLEY BING

It's not the frivolity of women that makes them so intolerable. It's their ghastly enthusiasm.   HORACE RUMPOLE (JOHN MORTIMER)

No woman has ever stepped on Little America— and we have found it to
be the most silent and peaceful place in the world.   RICHARD E. BYRD

Women are like elephants to me—I like to look at 'em, but I wouldn't want
to own one.   W. C. FIELDS

Never try to impress a woman, because if you do she'll expect you to keep
up to the standard for the rest of your life.   W. C. FIELDS

Woman was God's *second* mistake.   FRIEDRICH WILHELM NIETZSCHE

God created man and, finding him not sufficiently alone, gave him a companion to make him feel his solitude more keenly.   PAUL VALÉRY

God made man, and then said I can do better than that and made woman.
                                        ADELA ROGERS ST. JOHN

Nature has given woman so much power that the law cannot afford to give
her more.   SAMUEL JOHNSON

On one issue, at least, men and women agree: they both distrust women.
H. L. MENCKEN

Women who insist upon having the same options as men would do well to consider the option of being the strong, silent type.   FRAN LEBOWITZ

That woman speaks eighteen languages, and she can't say "No" in any of them.
DOROTHY PARKER

The charms of a passing woman are usually in direct relation to the speed of her passing.   MARCEL PROUST

Friendship among women is only a suspension of hostilities.
ANTOINE DE RIVAROL

When women kiss, it always reminds one of prizefighters shaking hands.
H. L. MENCKEN

Women give us solace, but if it were not for women we should never need solace.   DON HEROLD

There is nothing that binds one to a woman like the benefits one confers on her.   W. SOMERSET MAUGHAM

The prostitute is the only honest woman left in America.
TI-GRACE ATKINSON

Girls who put out are tramps. Girls who don't are ladies. This is, however, a rather archaic use of the word. Should one of you boys happen upon a girl who doesn't put out, do not jump to the conclusion that you have found a lady. What you have probably found is a lesbian.   FRAN LEBOWITZ

I have *nothing* to say about young girls. They're fine to look at, in the way I would look at a case filled with Shang dynasty glazes, but expecting to carry on a conversation with the average teen-aged young lady is akin to reading Voltaire to a cage filled with chimpanzees. I'm certain they would feel the same alienation for me. I can live with that knowledge.

HARLAN ELLISON

What passes for woman's intuition is often nothing more than man's transparency.   GEORGE JEAN NATHAN

There's nothing so similar to one poodle dog as another poodle dog, and that goes for women, too.   PABLO PICASSO

A woman without a man is like a fish without a bicycle.   GLORIA STEINEM

Show me a woman who doesn't feel guilt and I'll show you a man.

ERICA JONG

The history of woman is the history of the worst form of tyranny the world has ever known: the tyranny of the weak over the strong. It is the only tyranny that lasts.   OSCAR WILDE

Why is the word *tongue* feminine in Greek, Latin, Italian, Spanish, French, and German?   AUSTIN O'MALLEY

Women complain about PMS, but I think of it as the only time of the month when I can be myself.   ROSEANNE BARR

To win a woman in the first place one must please her, then undress her, and then somehow get her clothes back on her. Finally, so she will allow you to leave her, you've got to annoy her.   JEAN GIRAUDOUX

The allurement that women hold out to men is precisely the allurement that Cape Hatteras holds out to sailors: They are enormously dangerous and hence enormously fascinating.   H. L. MENCKEN

Whatever women do they must do twice as well as men to be thought half as good. Luckily this is not difficult.   CHARLOTTE WHITTON

Most women are not so young as they are painted.   MAX BEERBOHM

He gets on best with women who knows how to get on without them.
          AMBROSE BIERCE

Women should be obscene and not heard.   GROUCHO MARX

I hate women because they always know where things are.   JAMES THURBER

Wicked women bother one. Good women bore one. That is the only difference between them.   OSCAR WILDE

What do women want?   SIGMUND FREUD

Biologically speaking, if something bites you it's more likely to be female.
          DESMOND MORRIS

Women are an alien race of pagans set down among us. Every seduction is a conversion.   JOHN UPDIKE

Misogynist: a man who hates women as much as women hate one another.
H. L. MENCKEN

Being a woman is a terribly difficult trade, since it consists principally of dealing with men.
JOSEPH CONRAD

Women fail to understand how much men hate them.
GERMAINE GREER

To babble is to make a feminine noise somewhat resembling the sound of a brook, but with less meaning.
OLIVER HERFORD

The man who asks a woman what she wants deserves what's coming to him.
ALEC WAUGH

A woman will buy anything she thinks the store is losing money on.
KIN HUBBARD

To understand one woman is not necessarily to understand any other woman.
JOHN STUART MILL

Women do not like timid men. Cats do not like prudent mice.
H. L. MENCKEN

We have no faith in ourselves. I have never met a woman who, deep down in her core, really believes she has great legs. And if she suspects that she *might* have great legs, then she's convinced that she has a shrill voice and no neck.
CYNTHIA HEIMEL

WOMEN'S STUDIES

Women's studies is a jumble of vulgarians, bunglers, whiners, French faddicts, apparatchiks, doughface party-liners, pie-in-the-sky utopianists, and bullying, sanctimonious sermonizers.   CAMILLE PAGLIA

WORK

I do not like work even when someone else does it.   MARK TWAIN

Work is of two kinds: first, altering the position of matter at or near the earth's surface relatively to other matter; second, telling other people to do so. The first kind is unpleasant and ill-paid; the second is pleasant and highly paid.   BERTRAND RUSSELL

Anyone can do any amount of work, provided it isn't the work he's supposed to be doing at that moment.   ROBERT BENCHLEY

By working faithfully eight hours a day, you may eventually get to be a boss and work twelve hours a day.   ROBERT FROST

Everything considered, work is less boring than amusing oneself.
      CHARLES BAUDELAIRE

Anyone who works is a fool. I don't work—I merely inflict myself on the public.   ROBERT MORLEY

Hard work is damn near as overrated as monogamy.   HUEY P. LONG

———————————— WORLD ————————————

The world is something that had better not have been.

ARTHUR SCHOPENHAUER

The world is a vast temple dedicated to Discord.   VOLTAIRE

In this world, nothing is certain but death and taxes.

BENJAMIN FRANKLIN

We do not have to visit a madhouse to find disordered minds; our planet is the mental institution of the universe.

JOHANN WOLFGANG VON GOETHE

The world is a prison in which solitary confinement is preferable.

KARL KRAUS

The whole world is a scab. The point is to pick it constructively.

PETER BEARD

In the fight between you and the world, back the world.   FRANK ZAPPA

Is not the whole world a vast house of assignation to which the filing system has been lost?   QUENTIN CRISP

The world is a funny paper read backwards—and that way it isn't so funny.

TENNESSEE WILLIAMS

It's a man's world, and you men can have it.   KATHERINE ANNE PORTER

This world is a comedy for those who think and a tragedy for those who feel.
HORACE WALPOLE

If the world were a logical place, men would ride sidesaddle.
RITA MAE BROWN

The world is a spiritual kindergarten where bewildered infants are trying to spell God with the wrong blocks.   EDWIN ARLINGTON ROBINSON

Maybe this world is another planet's hell.   ALDOUS HUXLEY

God created the world, but it is the Devil who keeps it going.
TRISTAN BERNARD

When you leave New York, you are astonished at how clean the rest of the world is. Clean is not enough.   FRAN LEBOWITZ

It is not a fragrant world.   RAYMOND CHANDLER

The world is so dreadfully managed, one hardly knows to whom to complain.
RONALD FIRBANK

The world is divided into people who do things—and people who get the credit.   DWIGHT MORROW

The world is made up for the most part of morons and natural tyrants, sure of themselves, strong in their own opinions, never doubting anything.
CLARENCE DARROW

The trouble with the world is that the stupid are cocksure and the intelligent are full of doubt.   BERTRAND RUSSELL

Everyone thinks of changing the world, but no one thinks of changing himself.   LEO TOLSTOY

This world is gradually becoming a place
Where I do not care to be any more.
                    JOHN BERRYMAN

———————————————— WRITERS ————————————————

One reason the human race has such a low opinion of itself is that it gets so much of its wisdom from writers.   WILFRID SHEED

Writers have no real area of expertise. They are merely generalists with a highly inflamed sense of punctuation.   LORRIE MOORE

The dubious privilege of a freelance writer is he's given the freedom to starve anywhere.   S. J. PERELMAN

There are no dull subjects. There are only dull writers.   H. L. MENCKEN

Next to the defeated politician, the writer is the most vocal and inventive griper on earth. He sees hardship and unfairness wherever he looks. His agent doesn't love him (enough). The blank sheet of paper is an enemy. The publisher is a cheapskate. The critic is a philistine. The public doesn't understand him. His wife doesn't understand him. The bartender doesn't understand him.   PETER MAYLE

―――――――――――― WRITING ――――――――――――

All writing is garbage. People who come out of nowhere to try to put into words any part of what goes on in their minds are pigs.

ANTONIN ARTAUD

If you can't annoy somebody, there's little point in writing. KINGSLEY AMIS

If I didn't have writing, I'd be running down the street hurling grenades in people's faces.   PAUL FUSSELL

One of my greatest pleasures in writing has come from the thought that perhaps my work might annoy someone of comfortably pretentious position. Then comes the saddening realization that such people rarely read.

JOHN KENNETH GALBRAITH

QUOTES ON "Y"

YEAR

Year, *n.* A period of three hundred and sixty-five disappointments.

AMBROSE BIERCE

YOUTH

Youth is a wonderful thing. What a crime to waste it on children.

GEORGE BERNARD SHAW

Youth is a period of missed opportunities.   CYRIL CONNOLLY

It is one of the capital tragedies of youth—and youth is the time of tragedy—that the young are thrown mainly with adults they do not quite respect.

H. L. MENCKEN

The young always have the same problem—how to rebel and conform at the same time. They have now solved this by defying their parents and copying one another.

QUENTIN CRISP

What is youth except a man or a woman before it is ready or fit to be seen?

EVELYN WAUGH

The denunciation of the young is a necessary part of the hygiene of older people, and greatly assists the circulation of the blood.

LOGAN PEARSALL SMITH

I am not young enough to know everything.

JAMES M. BARRIE

INDEX OF
CONTRIBUTORS